FORWARD WITH CLASSICS

Also published by Bloomsbury

STARTING TO TEACH LATIN,
Steven Hunt

CLASSICS TEACHING IN EUROPE,
John Bulwer

FORWARD WITH CLASSICS

CLASSICAL LANGUAGES IN SCHOOLS AND COMMUNITIES

Edited by
Arlene Holmes-Henderson, Steven Hunt and Mai Musié

BLOOMSBURY ACADEMIC

LONDON · NEW YORK · OXFORD · NEW DELHI · SYDNEY

BLOOMSBURY ACADEMIC
Bloomsbury Publishing Plc
50 Bedford Square, London, WC1B 3DP, UK
1385 Broadway, New York, NY 10018, USA

BLOOMSBURY and the Diana logo are trademarks of Bloomsbury Publishing Plc

First published in Great Britain 2018
Reprinted 2018

A catalogue record for this book is available from the British Library.

Library of Congress Cataloging-in-Publication Data
Names: Holmes-Henderson, Arlene, editor. | Hunt, Steven (Classicist), editor. |
Musié, Mai, editor.
Title: Forward with classics : classical languages in schools and communities /
edited by Arlene Holmes-Henderson, Steven Hunt & Mai Musié.
Description: London : Bloomsbury Academic, 2018. | Includes bibliographical
references and index. | Non-Latin script record
Identifiers: LCCN 2017056914 | ISBN 9781474297677 (pbk.) |
ISBN 9781474295956 (hardback)
Subjects: LCSH: Greek language–Study and teaching. |
Latin language–Study and teaching.
Classification: LCC PA74 .F679 2018 | DDC 480.071–dc23
LC record available at https://lccn.loc.gov/2017056914

ISBN: HB: 978-1-4742-9595-6
            PB: 978-1-4742-9767-7
            ePDF: 978-1-4742-9597-0
            eBook: 978-1-4742-9596-3

Typeset by Integra Software Services Pvt. Ltd.

To find out more about our authors and books visit www.bloomsbury.com and sign
up for our newsletters.

CONTENTS

Contents

LIST OF FIGURES

Table

EDITORS AND CONTRIBUTORS

Mary Beard is one of Britain's best-known Classicists – Professor at the University of Cambridge and Fellow of Newnham College. She has written numerous books on the Ancient World, including the Wolfson Prize-winning *Pompei: The Life of a Roman Town;* has presented highly acclaimed TV series, *Meet the Romans* and *Rome – Empire without Limit;* and is a regular broadcaster and media commentator. Mary is also Classics editor of the *Times Literary Supplement* and writes a thought-provoking blog, *A Don's Life.* Made an OBE in 2013 for services to Classical scholarship, her recent books include the critically acclaimed *SPQR – A History of Ancient Rome* and *Women & Power.* Mary is one of the presenters for the BBC's new landmark *Civilisations* series.

Evelien Bracke was Senior Lecturer in Classics at Swansea University. She taught and researched ancient languages and their applications in modern education. She was Chair of the Cymru Wales Classics Hub, which supports and promotes the teaching and learning of Classics in Wales.

John Bulwer has taught Classics in the European Schools in the Netherlands and Belgium and in the UK. He has been active in Euroclassica for many years and is currently its president.

Paula da Cunha Corrêa is Associate Professor of Greek Language and Literature at the University of São Paulo. She is also Research Scholar of the Brazilian National Research Council researching Greek poetry. In addition, Paula has been responsible for '*Projeto Minimus*: Grego e Latim no Ensino Fundamental', an outreach programme of the University of São Paulo in which undergraduates and graduates teach Latin and Greek to approximately 200 students (fourth and seventh graders) at the Desembargador Amorim Lima public school since 2013.

Rowlie Darby is Course Leader of the Classics Postgraduate Certificate of Education (PGCE) at the University of Sussex, the teacher in charge of Classics at Patcham High School and the Classics for All Hub Coordinator for the South-East Hub (Brighton and Hove). Using Classics for All funding, he initiated Latin provision for other comprehensive schools in the Brighton and Hove area. He served the Joint Association of Classical Teachers (JACT) for five years both as a council member and as a member of the Examination Committee. He has been a moderator and examiner for Ancient History and Latin exams.

Emma-Jayne Graham is Senior Lecturer in Classical Studies at the Open University (OU). She is involved in the production and teaching of a range of OU Classical Studies modules at undergraduate and postgraduate levels, and is especially interested in exploring ways to integrate active discovery-led pedagogies into distance learning materials. Her main areas of research concern the archaeology of Roman Italy, the ancient body, mortuary practices and the treatment of the human body in death, anatomical votives and the materiality of religion.

Editors and Contributors

Edith Hall is Professor of Classics at King's College London (KCL). She is co-founder and Consultant Director of the Archive of Performances of Greek & Roman Drama at Oxford and Chairman of the Gilbert Murray Trust.

Arlene Holmes-Henderson leads research for the Classics in Communities project. She taught Classics in UK schools and has trained teachers at home and abroad. She advises qualification bodies on policy, curriculum and assessment in classical and modern languages. She is a board member of the Association for Language Learning (Language Futures) and the British Curriculum Forum. Arlene has conducted comparative educational research in the United States, Australia and New Zealand as a visiting professor. Now an academic at the University of Oxford, she has an extensive list of publications in the fields of language education policy, pedagogies and practice.

Steven Hunt is Senior Teaching Associate at the Faculty of Education, University of Cambridge, where he has been subject lecturer for the Postgraduate Certificate in Education course in Latin and Classics since 2008. He is President of the Association for Latin Teaching and a member of the boards of several classical associations, including the Classical Association Teaching Board, Cambridge School Classics Project Management Committee and LACTORs. He is Editor of the *Journal of Classics Teaching* and his book *Starting to Teach Latin* was published by Bloomsbury Academic in 2016.

Lucy Jackson is Research Fellow at King's College London. (KCL) She has taught at KCL and Oxford University, where she completed her doctorate on the chorus in ancient Greek drama. Her current research focuses on the afterlife of Greek drama in the Renaissance and in the twentieth and twenty-first centuries. Lucy acted as a consultant for the National Theatre's production of *Medea* (2014), the Almeida Theatre's *Iliad* (2015) and the *Oresteia* at Shakespeare's Globe (2015).

Aisha Khan-Evans taught for several years in comprehensive schools in and around London. After an MA in Education at King's College London (KCL), Aisha combined part-time work on the PGCE there with teaching in a sixth-form college, before becoming subject director for the King's College London (KCL) Classics PGCE in 2006.

Jane Maguire studied German and French at university and then taught modern languages in state comprehensive schools in Norfolk (The Hewett School, Norwich, and North Walsham High School) for twenty years. As the Gifted and Talented Strand Co-ordinator for the Great Yarmouth Excellence Cluster (2005 to 2011), she introduced Latin to a number of primary schools in rural Norfolk. She currently trains others how to teach Latin, working with Classics for All and the Primary Latin Project.

Emily Matters has been teaching Classics for nearly fifty years, mainly in secondary schools. She is the current president of the Classical Languages Teachers' Association to which nearly all Australian Latin and Greek teachers belong. Her immediate mission is to promote the teaching of Latin in primary schools and she has completed the first Classical Greek textbook to introduce the language to young beginners in an Australian context.

Xavier Murray-Pollock is Teacher of Classics at Merchant Taylors' School in London.

Mai Musié is co-founder of the Classics in Communities project and Alumni Rela/ Manager at Pembroke College, University of Oxford, UK. She has recently completed her PhD thesis on Representation of Persians in the Ancient Novel. She did her BA in Classical Civilisation and Master's in Ancient History at Swansea University. Mai has years of experience in access and outreach work with Higher Education (HE) institutions and statutory bodies, including running the Outreach Programme for the Faculty of Classics at Oxford, and has organized and coordinated mentoring and literacy programmes, summer schools and employability projects.

Nicola Felton, formerly Neto was Head of Modern Foreign Languages at Sidney Stringer School in Hillfields, Coventry. A chance conversation with the principal at the school led to her developing a full Classics Department at Sidney Stringer from nothing, which fitted well with the school's and her own energetic agenda to raise aspirations among students and to enrich the curriculum for all. Starting with Latin, Nicola forged strong links with Oxford University, the Cambridge School Classics Project, Classics for All and Warwick School to improve her own subject knowledge and to learn the subject pedagogy thoroughly to teach an initially small band of enthusiastic students. Soon she was offering Classical Greek as well and had persuaded her first students to sign up for A level Latin. In a school which had for many years previously been considered 'failing' and which had burnt down and been beautifully rebuilt, the Classics curriculum offer was extraordinary: a non-selective state school, in one of the most deprived wards of Coventry, with a Classics department to rival those of the private sector! Very sadly, Nicola passed away suddenly in the summer term 2017; but she has left behind a legacy of personal ambition and determination to achieve the highest standards for her many young classicists.

Peter Olive is a teacher of all four Classical A levels, as well as teaching Latin language at Royal Holloway, University of London.

Francesca Richards completed her AHRC-funded doctorate 'Dangerous Creatures': Children's Adaptations of the Odyssey in English 1699–2013 at Durham University in 2015. Her interest in how the Homeric poem has been interpreted for young people grew into three years of developing public engagement projects with arts partners and schools in County Durham. She is now Research Impact Officer for the Social Sciences Division at the University of Oxford, advising academics across more than fifteen departments on a wide range of knowledge exchange, public engagement and impact projects, in both the UK and internationally.

Lorna Robinson founded the educational charity The Iris Project and Iris magazine to promote Classics in state schools in 2006, and runs Latin and Greek projects in state schools across the UK. She has taught Latin and Greek at Cheney School, a large comprehensive school in East Oxford, since 2006. In 2013, she set up the Iris Classics Centre at Cheney, a community hub for all ages to engage with Classics. In 2015, she founded the Rumble Museum, which is working towards being the first Arts Council Accredited museum within a state school in the UK. Lorna has also written a Latin course, *Telling Tales in Latin* (2013), *Distant Lands: Telling Tales in Latin Part Two* (2016), and a Classical Greek course, *Telling Tales in Greek* (2017), all published by Souvenir Press.

James Robson is Senior Lecturer in Classical Studies at the Open University, where his teaching specialisms include the literature and social history of Classical Athens and Classical Greek and Latin languages. He is particularly interested in the use of ICT to support Greek and Latin learners, especially at beginner's level. His previous publications include *Aristophanes: An Introduction* (Duckworth/Bloomsbury, 2010) and *Sex and Sexuality in Classical Athens* (Edinburgh University Press, 2013). More recently, he has co-edited *Sex in Antiquity: Reconsidering Gender and Sexuality in the Ancient World* (Routledge, 2015).

Patrick J. Ryan graduated from the National University of Ireland (University College Cork) with a BA in Archaeology and Ancient Classics in 1997 and an MPhil, awarded for his research on Roman reaction to Greek precedent, in 1999. He served as National Chairman of the Classical Association of Ireland from 2004 to 2006 and is currently its general secretary. An archaeologist by profession, he has a particular interest in fostering the revival of Greek and Latin language and drama in community settings.

Olivia Sanchez is Teacher of Latin and Classics at St Paul's Way Trust School in East London.

Corrie Schumann has a Bacalaureus majoring in Afrikaans and Latin and a Secondary Education Diploma from Stellenbosch University. In 1984, Corrie became a legal Latin lecturer at the University of Pretoria and established the 'Academia Latina Centre' a few years later. Corrie has received numerous awards for her teaching and her dedication to outreach work including the Arthur Patch McKinlay from the American Classical League (1999), the Silver Chalice Award from Ablemedia (2000) and the Award for Excellence in Teaching Research from the Classical Association of South Africa (2001).

Michael Scott is Associate Professor of Classics and Ancient History at the University of Warwick. He has written extensively on ancient Greek religion and sanctuaries, as well as on ancient global connectivity. Over the last five years, he has also been his department's Admissions, Outreach and Widening Participation Officer. He is now its Impact Officer. He has had significant experience in the public communication of the ancient world via books, magazines and newspaper, radio and TV.

Emma Searle is a doctoral student at Merton College, Oxford, currently completing her DPhil thesis on the domestic consumption of art in Roman Italy. She did her BA in Classical Archaeology and Ancient History at Wadham College, Oxford, and worked as a field archaeologist specializing in Roman material culture before doing an MSc in Classics at the University of Edinburgh. For her doctorate, Emma returned to Oxford where she also teaches Roman history and material culture as well as Latin language and literature. In addition, Emma has extensive outreach experience, having been involved in various widening participation programmes at both college and university level including the Oxford Latin Teaching Scheme (OxLAT), an outreach programme of the Faculty of Classics at the University of Oxford.

Kathryn Tempest is Senior Lecturer in Roman History and Latin Literature at the University of Roehampton. Her research concentrates on the literature, history and political life of the late Roman republic, with particular interests in oratory and rhetoric, all aspects of Cicero, ancient letters and biography. She is the author of *Cicero: Politics and Persuasion in Ancient Rome* (Continuum, 2011; reprinted by Bloomsbury, 2013); *Hellenistic Oratory: Continuity and Change* (Oxford University Press, 2013), which she co-edited with Christos Kremmydas; and *Brutus: The Noble Conspirator* (Yale University Press, 2017).

Lana Theron has a Bacalaureus Legum Civilium and Honores in Humanities and Classical Languages from the University of Pretoria. From 1984 until 1989, Lana taught law students as a legal Latin lecturer at the University of South Africa. In 2012 Lana became the assistant to Corrie Schumann at the Academia Latina Centre. In 2014 Lana was made the Online Course Coordinator for the Medical Terminology course.

Zanna Wing-Davey read Classics at King's College, Cambridge, but got her taste for Latin while she attended Camden School for Girls. She has been with The Latin Programme from the start as a dynamic teacher and Director of Latin and as Executive Director for the last eight years. She has also taught Latin and Classical Greek at South Hampstead High School in North London.

FOREWORD
Mary Beard

Fightback of Classics

A decade or so ago, I bravely – or foolishly – agreed to appear on a reality TV show to teach elementary Latin to a group of sixteen-year-olds who had failed to achieve what was then the government target of 5 GCSEs (including English and Maths) at grade A to C. Called 'Dream School', it was the brainchild of the well-meaning celebrity chef Jamie Oliver, who hoped to show that if you exposed a clutch of bored and unsuccessful youths to some celebrity teachers – from Cherie Blair to Simon Callow and Robert Winston, plus the obligatory old Latin lady (me) – you might just inspire them to greater things.

The programme had its popular and controversial moments, notably when David Starkey, the history teacher, chose to call one of the kids, to his face, 'fat' (whether Starkey's play to the gallery with a knowing bit of political incorrectness was worse than the cries of outrage from some equally knowing politically correct viewers, I still haven't decided). But the truth was that if the aim had been to educate the pupils, the people who learnt most were those of us hired to be the teachers. True, most teachers don't have to cope with the television cameras on the back row, or with a savvy group of kids well aware that the way to launch a career from reality television is to behave very badly indeed. But most of us untrained enthusiasts soon learned that making a lesson work in the face of juvenile disenchantment, or of the seductions of new technology (to make our job that bit harder the TV company had issued every pupil with an iPad), was almost beyond us. I was only one of these 'pretend' teachers who went away with an intense admiration for the 'real' teachers of the 'real' classroom.

But I learned more than that. I struggled through a couple of hours with modest success on David Beckham's Latin tattoos (I think that most of the kids sensed that the teacher's heart was not quite in it, though the cameras loved it). I secured almost zero attention when I tried to introduce them to some 'real Latin' (most of them, understandably, thought that it was at best quaint, at worst laughable, that we were about to read some of the real words of Martial written 2,000 years ago: so what … ?). I had, however, two surprising and instructive successes that were sadly never shown on television.

The first was when I turned to the names of British towns. Had they noticed, I asked them, how many ended in something like ' … chester' or ' … caster'? Indeed they had, and could reel off the names of Lancaster, Manchester, Doncaster and so forth. Did they know why? Did they know that all these place names came from the Latin *castra* (for 'military camp') and that centuries ago they had all been ancient Roman forts? Of course, they didn't.

I have always been a bit sniffy about the pleasures of etymology. But I couldn't help being just a little moved by the sight of these children having – as the cliché would have it – a 'light-bulb' moment. Something they had vaguely noticed, but never thought actually to ask about, now fell into place. I nerved myself to say that one day they would explain this factoid to their own children, and probably tell them a bit about that quirky old Latin teacher on the television programme they were once on. For the first time, most of them smiled with some degree of warmth.

The second was even more surprising. In some desperation, for one of the last lessons I planned to do Roman numerals, and I had not expected much interest. But, in fact, I presented the intricacies of the Is, the Vs, the Xs, up to the Ls and Cs and Ds, to the closest thing to a wrapt audience that I had seen in the whole series of lessons. When we had finished, and the cameras were off, I said to them words to the effect of: 'You have texted, played on your iPads, chatted and messed around almost every time we have met, and then we do this boring session of Roman numbers and you sit there quietly and write it all down, could you please explain?'. 'That's easy', said one, 'the date of television programmes is written at the end in Roman numbers – if you don't understand them, you don't know when the programme was made'. Simple, eh?

There are any number of reasons for engaging with the ancient world and classicists, as this book demonstrates, are eloquent in arguing the case: ranging from the excitement of getting to grips with the stunning and challenging literature to uncovering the day-to-day eating habits of the inhabitants of the Roman empire (on the basis of their lavatory contents) or the political challenges laid down by Plato or Cicero. But, even if few people would now put the intricacies of Roman numerals high on their list of priorities, what those naughty pupils were expressing so succinctly – half-engaged as they appeared to be – was one basic tenet of the subject: that those who have the opportunity to study the ancient world find themselves not only looking back into a far distant past but also looking at themselves and their own culture in a new way. Of course, the cultural traditions of the West do not owe everything to the Greco-Roman past and its interpretations. Happily we are a much more diverse culture than that, with many more inheritances, both ancient and modern (none of us would want to return to antiquity, thank you very much). But Classics opens up a debate with some of the foundations of our own certainties. What does democracy mean? Why do we represent the human body as we do? Or even what makes us laugh? Knowing about the numerals at the end of a television programme, or the roots of the geopolitics of Britain, is part of that.

That said, classicists have to confront all kinds of misleading myths. One of the most strident is that Classics has always been for 'toffs', a weapon of the elite for keeping the lower orders in their place by excluding them from the study of 'dead' languages. The fact is that Greek language may always have been on the agenda of only a small minority, partly, but not entirely, defined by wealth and status. But (as Edith Hall's essay shows in a slightly different way) Classics has always been a part of popular culture, classical literature has always been read by millions in translation and everyone – yes everyone – still knows more about the ancient world than they often claim. The success of popular ancient movies, stretching back a century or more, shows that ('I don't know anything about Rome', says someone; 'yes you do; you have seen *Gladiator*', we reply). This myth sometimes takes the alternative form that Classics is a difficult subject, and therefore only for the very clever. That is not true either. To be sure, there are some extremely difficult things written in Latin and Greek. Parts of Thucydides are virtually untranslatable, and I have often thought that getting learners to read Tacitus after a couple of years of Latin was the equivalent of making *Finnegans Wake* a set book for beginners' English. But that does not put the more general challenge and pleasure of exploring the ancient world out of the reach of anyone. Classics is no harder, or easier, a subject than any other.

Then there is the politics. Another myth is that the Roman empire underpinned the British empire and that therefore Classics is somehow inseparably linked to imperialism and exploitation, the intellectual arm of a past that we would rather forget. There were, of course, British imperialists who saw a correlation with the Roman version of world power. But many Roman writers themselves were concerned to subvert, not promote, the very idea of empire. Or, to put it another way, the most effective criticisms of Roman imperial power came from Romans ('they make a desert and call it peace', as Tacitus put it in the second century AD, a better summation of 'conquest' than anyone has come up with before or since). The related stereotype is that Classics has always been deeply conservative, a bastion of the Right versus the Left. Again, it is true that the old and new Right have often tried to claim Classics for themselves sometimes powerfully (and they are doing so vociferously now). But the long history of Classics challenges that. For every Goebbels, with his enthusiasm for Greek tragedy, there is a Marx, whose doctoral dissertation was on ancient philosophy. It is important not to forget that many of the biggest social political reforms in the West, from universal suffrage to gay rights, have been launched (for good or, occasionally, bad motives) on classical principles.

And, more than that, Classics as an educational discipline has been one of the best of all at radically reinventing itself with new questions and new audiences. It is true that there is an occasional chorus of gloom that presents the heyday of classical learning as lost in the past, and the subject as in slow but terminal decline. Indeed no one who has classical interests at heart should be remotely complacent about the position of classical subjects in the school curriculum across the world. But anyone who fondly imagines that Classics in (say) the late nineteenth century was in better shape than now would be well advised to go and take a look at some of the exam papers sat by university students at the time, which to be honest often appear easier, less challenging and far less interesting than our own. In some ways, the subject is flourishing as it has never done before. At my own university more students are studying Latin and Greek than ever (to be sure, Classics is studied by a smaller proportion of our undergraduates, but in terms of raw numbers it is at an all-time high – partly thanks to a relatively new pathway open to students who have not had the opportunity to study ancient languages at school). And the contributions to this book offer exciting glimpses into the initiatives that lie behind the subject's success, in many countries of the world, whatever the difficulties it may face: from new methods of teaching at every level and in new media, to a glorious commitment to set no limit on the places and people that the subject can and should reach – far beyond my own efforts, valiant and occasionally enjoyable as they were, with place names and Roman numbers.

ACKNOWLEDGEMENTS

The Classics in Communities project was launched with funding from the University of Oxford Knowledge Exchange Seed Fund and the John Fell Fund. Since 2013 the project has received funding from a number of donors. Thanks are due to the Society for the Promotion of Roman Studies, the Society for the Promotion of Hellenic Studies, the Classical Association, the A. G. Leventis Foundation, the Institute of Classical Studies, the University of Oxford Faculty of Classics, the University of Cambridge Faculty of Classics and Classics for All. In addition, the project would like to thank its associate partners, The Iris Project, The Latin Programme: Via Facilis and *Minimus*, for their invaluable support.

INTRODUCTION

Arlene Holmes-Henderson, Steven Hunt and Mai Musié

What is 'Classics in Communities'?

The Classics in Communities project is a partnership between the University of Oxford, the University of Cambridge and the Iris Project. It was set up in response to the primary curriculum reforms, which were implemented in England from September 2014. In the key stage 2 (KS2) Languages curriculum policy, for the first time, Classical Greek and Latin can be chosen for study by pupils aged six to eleven in place of a modern language. The project particularly targets schools where classical languages have not previously featured on the curriculum. It has twin aims: to equip teachers in primary schools with the skills and knowledge necessary to teach these languages; and to conduct parallel research to determine the impact of classical language learning on children's cognitive development.

Activities of the Classics in Communities project

Website

The Classics in Communities website (classicsincommunities.org) acts as a hub for teachers interested in introducing Latin and Greek in their classrooms. It includes a summary of published resources for classical languages, an overview of the funding available from various sources, details of university departments offering outreach around the UK, as well as resources requested by teachers including skill progression grids for primary Latin, 'how to get started' guides for Latin on the curriculum and as a club, and pedagogical videos to support teachers in their professional practice.

Conferences

The project held a launch conference at Corpus Christi College, Oxford, in November 2013. This event attracted a wide range of participants including primary teachers, secondary teachers (of Classics, Languages, History and English), academics, trainee teachers, outreach officers, subject association representatives, educational policy advisors and school leaders. More than 100 delegates attended, including colleagues from South Africa, the United States and Europe. Keynote speeches were given by Professor Edith Hall (KCL) and Dr Michael Scott (University of Warwick), both of whom are contributors to this volume. In addition to plenary sessions, parallel sessions covered a wide range of Classics education topics, including working with museums, teaching literacy using Greek literature in translation, empowering older students to lead junior Latin clubs, collaboration with Classics teachers across Europe and boosting community cohesion through Greek drama.

A second Classics in Communities conference was hosted by the University of Cambridge's Faculty of Classics in September 2015. Again, more than 100 participants came from a variety of contexts, including adult educators, publishers and charity representatives. Some delegates had travelled from Australia, the United States, Ireland and Sweden to be part of the one-day event. Professor Tim Whitmarsh (University of Cambridge) and Tom Holland (celebrated author and broadcaster) gave the keynote addresses. High on the agenda for this event was the sharing of strategies to widen access to the study of classical languages and civilizations for all learners. In addition to an open roundtable discussion, we heard from teachers setting up new Latin hubs in Tower Hamlets, Hackney and Coventry, as well as representatives from Classics for All and the Kallos Gallery who want to support the learning and teaching of Classics at all levels. Many of the projects discussed at the conference are explained in more detail in this volume.

Celebration of Greek language and culture education

Together with the Greek ambassador to the UK and the High Commissioner of Cyprus to the UK, the Classics in Communities project hosted a 'Celebration of Greek' event in summer 2016 in London. This event raised the profile of teaching Greek in schools with the aim of boosting the number of children with access to the language and its associated rich historical, literary, philosophical and visual culture. The event brought together those people currently teaching some form of Greek in diverse contexts. These included classicists, theologians, philosophers, ancient and medieval historians, modern Greek linguists and members of the Hellenic community in the UK. For more information about the strategies identified to promote and extend the reach of Greek language and culture education, see Mitropoulos and Holmes-Henderson (2016).

Classical languages regional teacher-training workshops

Given that the KS2 Languages curriculum reform expressly named Latin and Greek as languages suitable for study in the primary phase, the Classics in Communities project sought to equip primary teachers, through training events, with the subject knowledge and confidence they needed to teach Latin and Greek in their schools. In 2014–2015, one-day teacher-training workshops were held at KCL, the University of Oxford, the University of Cambridge, Lordswood School Birmingham, the University of Glasgow and Queen's University Belfast. These training days brought together those primary teachers interested in (but hitherto unfamiliar with) teaching Latin and Classical Greek with experienced teachers and academics. This cross-sectoral structure was selected to ensure a degree of self-sustainability in the regions – it was crucial for primary teachers to meet experienced teachers and academics so that they felt supported in their new classical adventure. Equally, secondary teachers and academics in universities enjoyed the opportunity for dialogue and were keen to establish open channels of communication for knowledge exchange across educational phases. The events were publicized to the local educational authorities by the local university, by the University of Oxford outreach team and by the Classics in Communities project (by email and through social media). Full bursaries were available for teachers, thanks to the generosity of the Society for the Promotion of Roman Studies and the Society for the Promotion of Hellenic Studies. Glasgow was the most popular venue, with twenty-two participants. Belfast had the fewest attendees, just ten. The training day was broadly divided into two: Latin in the morning and Greek in the afternoon.

After a welcome from the local host and an introduction from the Classics in Communities team, the benefits of teaching Latin in the primary classroom were discussed, as were some of the challenges of setting up a new language in a school. Participants had the opportunity to try out some Latin learning of their own and asked a number of questions about which pedagogical approaches were suitable for teaching a classical language. One of the sessions included a thirty-minute talk from a local primary teacher who outlined their top tips for introducing Latin at key stage 2. The cascade of this information from a fellow teacher who had actually been through the process was particularly valuable for participants and allowed them to have many practical questions answered.

The afternoon was spent introducing teachers to the Classical Greek alphabet and helping them transliterate accurately. Exercises exploring vocabulary, derivations and present tense verbs gave them a flavour of the content of Classical Greek at key stage 2. Various resources were shared and their suitability for use with children at key stage 2 were discussed.

Feedback from the workshops, together with more information about the subsequent implementation of Latin and Greek in primary schools, can be read in Holmes-Henderson (2016).

Educational research

Alongside its training focus, the Classics in Communities project is conducting an educational research study into the impact of learning Latin on children's cognitive development. It is a longitudinal study in which quantitative attainment data are being collected from a number of schools, in partnership with the Iris Project and the Latin Programme. In order to get a better understanding of the impact of learning Latin beyond baseline and progress measures of cognitive attainment, qualitative research methods are being used in school visits to hear the situated perspectives of key stakeholders including pupils, teachers, school leaders and parents.

Initial analysis of the data reveals positive trends in the development of literacy skills, when a classical language is used as the medium for (or supplement to) literacy learning. The impact of learning Latin on children's development of critical skills and global awareness is also being explored. Data collection and analysis are currently ongoing and detailed results will be published in due course.

Digital resources

In response to requests from teachers, teaching resource videos have been produced to help less experienced teachers of classical languages to see the content and pedagogical elements of a 'model lesson'. These exist for teaching Latin cases, teaching Latin verb tenses, teaching the ablative absolute, teaching the indirect statement, introducing the Greek alphabet and teaching the definite article in Greek. They can be viewed on the Classics in Communities website. Making these freely available online has been beneficial to teachers currently delivering Latin in their schools but has been particularly useful to those without previous experience of teaching Latin and Greek. Teachers have welcomed the opportunity to learn about effective pedagogy from experienced practitioners.

International collaboration

Since 2013, the editors have collaborated with teachers and academics in the United States, New Zealand, Australia, Portugal, Brazil, Canada and South Africa. International visits have been made, conference presentations have been delivered and the chapters contained herein provide a flavour of the collaborations undertaken to date.

Hunt provides an overview of the social justice agenda in UK politics over the last decade and describes its influences on Classics education in policy and practice. Hunt, in a second chapter, investigates the comprehensible input (CI) approach to Latin teaching and considers why it has grown in popularity in the United States yet remains little practiced in the UK.

Searle provides an overview of 'access agreements' between UK higher education institutions and the Office of Fair Access aimed to increase participation from under-represented groups into higher education. Searle offers the Oxford Latin Teaching Scheme as an example of how university Classics departments can engage effectively and successfully with the access and outreach agenda.

Jackson describes a knowledge exchange fellowship in which she provided specialist consultancy to the National Theatre in London for its production of *Medea*.

Scott evaluates the positive influence of the 'impact' policy agenda within UK higher education on public engagement and outreach. He describes various initiatives undertaken by the Faculty of Classics at the University of Warwick to engage local young people in the study of the ancient world.

Matters explains the developments in curriculum policy affecting the uptake of Classics in Australian schools.

Corrêa discusses the establishment and development of a Latin course for young children in São Paulo. She explains how teachers in local schools were supported by students and staff from the University of São Paulo.

Bulwer provides an overview of the teaching and learning of classical subjects in Europe. He identifies countries where Classics is supported by curriculum policy and showcases a range of creative initiatives in those countries where Classics is marginalized by educational policy.

Bell reflects on the impact of the *Minimus* series of books on the learning and teaching of Latin and Classics for young children in the UK and worldwide.

Wing-Davey describes the work of the Latin Programme, which provides Latin teaching for pupils in schools in London.

Maguire summarizes the results of introducing the teaching of Latin to primary schools in Norfolk, England.

Darby provides a personal reflection on the possibilities and pitfalls of teaching Latin as a 'non-specialist' teacher in Brighton and Hove, England.

Robinson charts the creation and development of the Iris Classics Centre at Cheney School and its busy calendar of Classics-related activities.

Olive and Murray-Pollock describe the establishment of the East End Classics Centre at BSix College in Hackney, London. They reflect on the challenges and triumphs of this endeavour and provide advice for others who may wish to pursue similar goals.

Sanchez and Felton highlight the educational benefits of teaching Latin on the curriculum in a socially and ethnically diverse London borough and Coventry.

Schumann and Theron chart the creation and development of the Academia Latina Centre at the University of Pretoria, which aimed to introduce Classics into South African schools and prisons.

Ryan explains how the performance of classical drama can promote community cohesion, with specific reference to the Orchard Yard players in County Tipperary, Ireland.

Richards provides a commentary on a university research project which sought to take Greek literature to the local community in North-East England.

Bracke describes a project to widen access to the study of Classics for children and their parents in Wales.

Khan-Evans researched what factors affect sixteen- to eighteen-year-olds when choosing subjects for study. She shares findings which suggest that Classical Civilisation has a broad appeal in England.

Robson and Graham describe the design and delivery of an open access digital Latin course for learners of all ages as part of the Open University's commitment to widening access to Classics.

Holmes-Henderson and Tempest interrogate the contribution of Classics to the cultivation of twenty-first-century skills. These are the skills required for school pupils and university students to flourish as citizens, employees and lifelong learners.

Hall details the history of Classics education in British schools and comments on the relationship between social class and access to Classics.

References

Holmes-Henderson, A. (2016), 'Teaching Latin and Greek in Primary Classrooms: The Classics in Communities Project', *Journal of Classics Teaching*, 17 (33): 50–53.

Mitropoulos, A. and Holmes-Henderson, A. (2016), 'A Celebration of Greek Language and Culture Education in the UK', *Journal of Classics Teaching*, 17 (34): 55–57.

PART I
EDUCATION POLICY AND THE EFFECT ON THE PROVISION OF CLASSICS IN SCHOOLS

CHAPTER 1

GETTING CLASSICS INTO SCHOOLS? CLASSICS AND THE SOCIAL JUSTICE AGENDA OF THE UK COALITION GOVERNMENT, 2010–2015

Steven Hunt

This chapter details the effects the education policies of the UK Coalition Government of 2010–2015 have had on the teaching of classical subjects in English schools, with particular reference to its social justice agenda. For the members of the government, 'social justice' meant the provision of equal opportunities at schools to students of all backgrounds to attain the sorts of qualifications which led to worthwhile employment or entrance to university: the gap between the educational attainment of poorer and richer students was thereby to be reduced. While changes to Classics education may be only a sideline to the many other much bigger changes which were set in motion, they are perhaps of great significance to a school subject area which had been long neglected, if not maligned, by successive governments since the Minister of Education Kenneth Baker's Education Reform Act (Department of Education 1988). For the purposes of this chapter, Latin, Classical Greek, Ancient History and Classical Civilisation (under the umbrella title 'Classics') mean the teaching of those subject areas in schools.

On 6 May 2010 the UK coalition government came to power. An uneasy yoking together of Conservative and Liberal Democrat politicians, the government settled down rapidly to distinguish itself from the supposed failures of the previous Labour administration. Far quicker than most in the development of policy initiatives was the Department for Education (DfE), under Conservative Secretary of State for Education Michael Gove. Although Gove was relieved of his post in 2014, his legacy continues to the present: unfinished business awaits and the full impact of the reforms has yet to be realized. This chapter intends to show how and why Latin and, to a lesser extent, the other classical subjects taught in English secondary schools were enlisted in the government's intention to advance social justice. I start with an attempt to explain the rationale for the inclusion of classical subjects as part of Gove's education reforms, and then reflect on the three areas of reform themselves: curriculum, pedagogy and assessment. Finally, I examine the impact on teacher training and try to assess the longer term effect of the reforms on the position of Classics in schools and whether they will meet the desired aim of achieving greater social justice. It should be mentioned at the start that Gove's reforms do not reach to Scotland, Northern Ireland or Wales, who have devolved powers over their own school systems.

Gove's team and the neo-traditional reforms

The reform programme had to embrace the interests of both coalition partners, but please especially Gove who had already developed very strong views. In 2009, he had declared 'talking down' (=Hall)

his reverence for the sort of education he himself had received at the private school Robert Gordon's College and at the University of Oxford, where he read English as an undergraduate, in a speech to the Royal Society of Arts:

> Education has an emancipatory, liberating value. I regard education as the means by which individuals can gain access to all the other goods we value – cultural, social and economic – on their terms. I believe education allows individuals to become authors of their own life story. I know from my own experience that the opportunities I have enjoyed are entirely the consequence of the education I have been given. Perhaps I value education so much because it has given me so much – but what it has given me most is the chance to shape my own destiny. Lack of access to the best is a sort of deprivation. (Gove 2009)

When Gove took office, what 'the best' might comprise became highly contested, especially when it transpired that it was Gove himself and his team which defined it. Apart from a very few select individual teachers who worked closely with him (Burn 2015), other teachers who might have been able to give him a set of wider perspectives were barely consulted beforehand, despite the fact that they would shortly be becoming responsible for implementing the new curriculum and being held accountable by it (Lightman 2015). Meanwhile, Gove ignored the university education faculties, whose members he and his friends demonized as 'The Blob' (Young 2014), for supposedly propagating the 'failed orthodoxy of progressive education' and being resistant to change (Peal 2014). Dissenters - some high profile - were publicly derided as 'enemies of promise' (Gove 2013b). Gove saw the restoration of a neo-traditional education as the *only* means to counteract what he and his colleagues saw as years of decline in educational attainment in England and a concomitant increase in social inequality. He later found evidence for this decline and justification for his reforms in the 2012 PISA international league tables (Gove 2013c). But back in 2010, at the start of his ministerial career, the rhetoric of change was needed, favourable newspaper headlines were expected and speed was vital: education ministers notoriously did not last long in post, nor was it clear how long the Coalition Government itself would stay in power. He had no need of experts to get in the way of what seemed almost a personal crusade.

The individual members of the ministerial team had differing priorities: there was a Conservative focus on new types of state-funded school, higher standards, discipline and a Liberal Democrat one on social mobility. All together they made up an 'ideas-rich team, often in conflict with each other' (Seldon and Snowdon 2015). Even among the Conservatives there was potential for confusion between the policies: the Schools' Minister Nick Gibb was especially interested in the neo-traditionalist ideas of the American educational theorist Ed Hirsch (1996) and devoted himself to the minutiae of defining standards and the individual elements of the curriculum. Such an authoritarian approach was not much mirrored by Gove's special advisers Rachel Wolf and Dominic Cummings, who were interested instead in school autonomy and were much more libertarian in views. Gove seemed interested in everything and somehow held it all together. Although his coalition partners Clegg and Laws found him increasingly difficult to work with (Clegg 2016), he was given carte blanche by the prime minister to do whatever was necessary to achieve his reforms. This he did, with little outside scrutiny and with significant impact on the whole profession of education.

Pro-Classics voices

Commentators have described the package of reforms as a 'restoration curriculum' (Ball 2013, p. 107). It is perhaps easy to see, then, how classical subjects might find comfortable homes there. But where did the espousal of the benefits of Classics for all arise from? It is hard to tell, but the combination of ideas and personalities somehow came together to advance the teaching of Latin (at least a particular version of it) in state-funded schools, and the other classical subjects (or most of them) received recognition. One of the most visible contributors to the public discourse was Old Etonian and Oxford classicist Conservative MP, journalist and author Boris Johnson, who had long talked up the value of a classical education, frequently peppering his political speeches and newspaper articles with classical references. Later, as Mayor of London, he wrote to Gove to persuade him to include Latin and Greek in the new curriculum: it was, he said, in danger of becoming the 'fodder of the independent sector' (Johnson 2010). This perhaps chimed with Gove's sense of social mission. In a later speech to the private Brighton College, Gove decried the way in which the private schools seemed to keep hold of the 'glittering prizes' of the most selective universities in their own 'gilded hands' (Gove 2012b), and it was generally felt that university Classics courses were dominated by privately educated students (Peel 2015), despite strenuous efforts by the universities themselves to encourage applications from state schools. Johnson therefore inaugurated the London Schools Excellence Fund to improve the quality of teaching in London state schools across all subjects. From this fund a special grant of £250,000 was awarded to train non-specialist state school teachers in London via the charity Classics for All, which had been set up by the retired university Classics lecturer, author and journalist Peter Jones. Johnson also personally donated to the project and publicly lent support to the charity's fund-raising. Drawing on existing teachers' expertise and supported by the London universities, the project – Capital Classics – was successful in training teachers in a 'network of over 70 London schools' (Classics for All 2015).

There were other strong voices around Gove in support of Classics. Cummings himself had read Ancient and Modern History at Oxford: he was a man of strong views, determination and drive. A small number of Gove's political and personal friends from his journalism days were equally vociferous: Toby Young, author, journalist and founder of the West London Free School – among the first of the new range of state-funded 'independent' free schools (and with a distinctive classical theme to its curriculum) - spoke spiritedly for the inclusion of Latin in all schools (Young 2011); Neville Gwynne, author of the neo-traditionalist Gwynne's Latin textbook and teacher of Latin to Young's own children (Grice 2013); and Harry Mount, journalist and author of a populist Latin textbook, which proved an unlikely best-seller at Christmastime (Mount 2010). It is unclear how much direct influence they had on developing a policy to restore the place of Latin in the new curriculum, or whether they ever met formally or not to agree on the message, but all three regularly used the mouthpieces of the *Daily Telegraph* newspaper and *The Spectator* magazine to make positive comments on the value of Latin and to laud Gove's efforts to bring it to a wider school audience. The apparent alignment of Latin with a right-wing educational agenda did not go unnoticed and not without concern (Beard 2012).

The curriculum

Reforms of the curriculum took place in three main areas: the primary schools, the creation of the English Baccalaureate measure and the abolition of 'non-subjects'. I shall take each in turn.

Primary schools

The Minister for Schools Nick Gibb played a significant role in the introduction of ancient languages in key stage 2 of the new curriculum for primary schools. In some 500 private preparatory schools there was a flourishing environment of Latin and, to a lesser extent, Classical Greek (Bass 2003), feeding in through the Common Entrance Examination to the major private schools, where the ancient languages were still strong. In the state sector, however, Latin was far rarer and Classical Greek almost unknown. In 2010, at a meeting organized by Sheila Lawlor's right-wing think tank *Politeia* on the subject of the possible introduction of Latin in primary schools, Gibb spoke of his indebtedness to Hirsch's ideas about 'cultural literacy and the importance of knowledge building upon knowledge' (Gibb 2010). Going on to describe the prevalence of Latin in modern culture, he mentioned those aspects of teaching it which chimed with the ministerial team's objectives: a focus on the 'mechanics of language' and the support it offered for learning a modern language (Gibb 2010). Referring to the attainment gap between students from wealthier and poorer backgrounds, he claimed,

> The fact that the opportunity to learn Latin is so rare in the state sector is one of a range of factors that has led to the width of that gap. Spreading these opportunities is part and parcel of closing that attainment gap and helping to create a more equal society. (Gibb 2010)

Christopher Pelling, the then Regius Professor of Greek at Oxford, added further benefits for learning Latin, drawing on evidence from the United States which suggested that improvements could be made to poorer students' literacy, oracy and intercultural understanding (Pelling 2010). The meeting achieved its purpose: Latin and Classical Greek were for the first time included in the list of languages approved for teaching in primary schools from 2013 (Department for Education 2013). Research conducted by the author has not been able to reveal from where the impetus for the meeting originated. It is unlikely, however, that *Politeia* would have gone to the trouble of commissioning an expensive event with journalists and such speakers as Gibb present without some initial ministerial or higher level encouragement.

A number of issues immediately arose. The programmes of study for languages in the primary schools instructed that students should make 'substantial progress' in one language between the ages of seven and eleven (Department for Education 2013). Content and realization were left unspecified. Gibb suggested at the time that the new school autonomies afforded to head teachers would 'enable Latin and Ancient Greek to flourish', if they wanted (Gibb 2010). But the old problems of finding age-appropriate resources, the lack of timetable allocation and shortage of trained teachers remained. And what was meant by 'substantial progress' in one language? Most students in the state and private sectors achieved a *whole GCSE* in Latin in four years in secondary schools. A group of teachers and academics from the Classics subject organizations went to the top to ask. Elizabeth Truss, the junior minister for Children and Childcare, allowed herself to be briefly interviewed. She was upbeat: the deputation afterwards less so. The intention, she said, was that one language would be taught in primary schools: the idea that Latin could support a modern foreign language (as was actually stated in the curriculum documents and which we had assumed meant that Latin and a modern language together could be studied at this time) was rebutted. Instead, if Latin was the one language studied, schools would not offer a modern language at all. In answer to a question as to where the Latin teachers would come from, she said she could foresee secondary school teachers visiting feeder primaries on a peripatetic basis (an unlikely scenario, we thought, for Latin, which lacked sufficient teachers in the secondary sector in the first place). Otherwise, she suggested, we could forge links with non-government organizations: for example, she said, the Goethe Institute had offered upskilling courses for teachers of German and the Chinese government was sending Mandarin teachers across from mainland China. While we sat there in bemusement wondering if Caecilius might pop by to help out with some basic Latin lingo, the special adviser sitting next to the minister cut the meeting short when he opined 'It's Year Zero now'. The message was clear: if we really wanted Latin to have a chance, we would have to get creative and do it ourselves – outsourcing was the way forward. The Classics subject organizations themselves would have to take responsibility for training teachers and providing publicity and paying for it all themselves. Truss and the DfE were merely providing the opportunity. This dependency on charitable bodies to achieve government policies was to become a feature of the DfE's practice (Spohrer 2015). The rapidity with which those involved in the subject associations have accomplished so much is a credit to the people who work for them, almost always as volunteers in their spare time, often for no pay, and on a shoestring budget.

Classicists first looked at the resources which they had. One likely way of encouraging take-up of Latin in primary schools was to appeal to the idea that learning Latin helped develop students' English literacy. In fact, the effectiveness of using Latin for this purpose is much contested (Lister 2007). Experiments in economically poor districts in the United States in the 1970s had suggested a generally positive impact on students' literacy rates (Mavrogenes 1981), although the courses consisted of small-scale language awareness courses based around word derivations and storytelling rather than Latin courses per se (Masciantonio 1979). In the UK, Barbara Bell's *Minimus* Latin book had originally been designed to improve students' understanding of English grammar through Latin (Bell 2003), as had Lorna Robinson's *Literacy through Latin Iris Project*. Both could be seen also to fit neatly in with Gibb's social justice agenda. Encouraged by this, Bell herself stepped up training direct to school teachers and to university students across the country (Bell 2015) while *Iris* too extended its reach from Oxford, using Classics undergraduates going out into primary schools near their universities (Robinson 2016). University Classics departments were spurred on to develop more outreach activities into primary schools to help build awareness of Classics and raise aspirations about higher education (Lovatt 2011). Classical charities also made an impact: Classics for All funded low-cost solutions for teacher training in Latin in primary schools for teachers with little or no subject knowledge (Maguire and Hunt 2014) and gained success in promoting Classics hubs nationwide (Hodgson and Murray-Pollock 2016); while Classics in Communities, a partnership project between the Universities of Oxford and Cambridge, ran teacher-training workshops around the UK (Holmes-Henderson 2016), produced resources to support teachers of Latin in primary schools and showcased current practices in two international conferences in 2013 and 2015. By contrast, there has been much less demand for Classical Greek, with the alphabet and lack of suitable resources often cited. For this and Classical Civilisation too, the *Cambridge School Classics Project* started developing web-based materials. The Classical Association's funding of the free online *Journal of Classics Teaching* should be considered part of the increased promotion of Classics to a wider audience and sharing of good practice. One could say that such actions reinvigorated the subject organizations too; but for a minority subject like Classics, with little financial backing of their own, it was a very challenging, if rewarding, time.

There were a number of anomalies too, and it was typical of the nature of Gove's reforms that while there was much speed about the setting out regulations, there was little consideration about implementation or development of practice or monitoring of success except by student examination outcomes. An opportunity was therefore missed to link the ancient languages to the programme of study for history, which included Romans and Greeks, and which might have delivered the sort of intercultural understanding mentioned by Pelling at the *Politeia* meeting (Pelling 2010). Another much bigger curiosity was the absence of any mention of the ancient languages at key stage 3. It might have been assumed that this would be a suitable follow-up for the four years of Truss' substantial study expected of foreign languages at key stage 2. However, the DfE explained that it was always its intention that more students should study *modern foreign languages* at GCSE than before, whose economic value was perhaps more obvious than Latin or Classical Greek. The suspicion has to remain that Latin in the primary school was included by Gibb because of its supposed value in improving students' knowledge and understanding of English grammar and as a means for supporting a US-style 'language-rich curriculum' (Gibb 2012) rather than something which was intrinsically worthwhile and which led to further study in secondary school.

The English Baccalaureate (EBacc)

Nevertheless, Classics had now been given a toehold in the primary schools. But the lack of reference to it in the curriculum at key stage 3 diminished the impact it could have had. It was known to university classicists that outreach should focus on key stage 3 of the secondary school while students were still deciding what subjects to take for GCSE (Sandis 2009). Teachers knew that students who wished to have a good chance at passing a GCSE in Latin needed more than a couple of years' exposure to the subject at key stage 4 alone (Lister 2007). There seemed to have been some half-heartedness about the DfE's initial reforms, therefore: to have gone to the trouble of encouraging primary schools to offer ancient languages and then to set up a barrier to its continuance – depending on where the student lived or what sort of school they went to – abrogated all sense of social justice. A roundabout way to achieve this was found whereby the DfE nudged schools into amenability using the newly invented English Baccalaureate measure (EBacc) – not a measurement of a student's success but of a school's success in five subject areas. Under the EBacc students were strongly recommended to study from a range of so-called 'facilitating' subjects – drawn from a list published by the most research-intensive universities as being of especial value when considering the academic suitability of applicants

(The Russell Group of Universities 2016). Latin, Classical Greek and Ancient History found their places once again in key stage 4 under the aegis of this new measure. Gibb explained the choice of subjects:

> A core academic education remains an aspiration for all and the government is determined to stand with parents and teachers to make it a reality. (Gibb 2015)

Having raised the profile of these classical subjects in this way, the government no doubt hoped that schools would decide for themselves whether they needed to offer them in key stage 3 as foundation for the GCSE years. From that point classical subjects stood among the select band of government-approved subjects at both key stage 2 and key stage 4. But the gap between the two remained glaring.

Non-subjects

With the government having partially secured the position of Latin in the new curriculum, its next education reforms almost scuttled it straight afterwards. Gove wanted to reduce the number of vocational qualifications which he perceived to be of little academic worth. Alison Wolf was appointed to rationalize the huge number of overlapping vocational qualifications (Wolf 2011). These qualifications were assessed by different methods to the traditional GCSEs, including by more practical assessment tasks as suitable for practical qualifications and by assessment by portfolios of evidence. A large number had – for reasons of the length of time taken to fulfil the examination specifications – been deemed to be worth two, three or even four GCSEs. Gove suspected that schools were manipulating their position in the comparative school league tables by putting students into these multiple GCSE equivalent courses rather than the supposedly more academic traditional GCSEs and thereby boosting their league table positions but simultaneously denying their students access to the more academic universities. Among these vocational qualifications were the WJEC Latin Certificates in Latin Language, Roman Civilisation and Latin Literature. They had been first offered in 2010 in response to teachers' anxieties that the pre-existing OCR Latin GCSE had become too difficult to accommodate in the restricted timetable of the average school (Stephenson 2014). The certificates were in fact accredited by the examinations regulator Ofqual as GCSE equivalents, but configured under the vocational qualifications criteria; thus they offered more flexible learning pathways, such as an option of controlled assessment, which was not permitted for a GCSE qualification. Continued validation of the WJEC qualifications by Ofqual was vital: as validated vocational qualifications they counted for school performance points, and as an approved language they also contributed to the EBacc. Both of these aspects acted as major incentives for head teachers to offer them, if they wanted. Their dismissal as 'non-subjects' would be disastrous. With some judicious political lobbying by university academics, WJEC Latin survived Wolf's purge. Indeed, they went from strength to strength and have contributed to a rise of 25 per cent of entries in GCSE-equivalent Latin examinations between 2010 and 2014 (Cambridge School Classics Project 2014). It seems bizarre in hindsight that a qualification which was seen in straightforward numerical terms to be improving the access to Latin which the government desired could so easily have been lost as part of a bigger educational policy drive. This was not an isolated event, as we shall see later.

Other 'non-subjects' fared less well. Although Latin, Classical Greek and Ancient History had been safely admitted to the EBacc measure, the non-linguistic Classics GCSE called Classical Civilisation remained outside. As a recognized GCSE and A level subject of long standing, it had not been swept away with other 'non-subjects', but it appeared undervalued and ignored by ministers. This happened despite valiant efforts by teachers and academics to show it possessed equal weight to Ancient History, whose subject matter, if not its methodological approach, it closely resembled (Liveley and Liddel 2014). Representations were made by members of the examinations teams and the Cambridge School Classics Project direct to Members of Parliament in the tea room of the House of Commons itself, without success. What was most strange, in the interest of ministers in promoting social justice through access to higher education, was that the subject of Classical Civilisation at A level had had a far better track record of bringing students from poorer backgrounds into the study of Classics at leading universities (Hunt 2014) than *any of the other* classical subjects. How many more might take the subject at A level if they knew of its existence at GCSE? All students had prior knowledge of the Greeks and Romans from key stage 2; GCSE Classical Civilisation could be delivered comfortably in the two years of key stage 4; existing staff in every school could teach it without significant training costs, given decent resources (Hunt 2013). But there seemed to be some kind of continuing opposition at the highest ministerial levels to Classical Civilisation, described famously by Boris Johnson as insufficiently 'crunchy' compared with the linguistic classical subjects (Carr 2007). The DfE defended its reasoning by saying that Classical Civilisation did not contain enough history to be counted for the EBacc. It is clear that whichever civil servant made the decision looked no further than the *title* of the course rather than the *content*.

Pedagogy

The ministerial team's enthusiasm for a neo-traditional curriculum now started to extend to recommendations to the way in which subjects were taught. There was no approved pedagogy for Latin as it had escaped the kind of scrutiny that had applied to practices in the 1988 National Curriculum core subjects. Instead, Classics teachers had long been free to employ a number of distinctive approaches which reflected their own circumstances, interests and students. Ultimately, however, all students would study original Roman authors and take the same GCSEs and A levels, which had led to a certain similarity of teaching at the higher levels. While grammar-translation approaches continued in some schools, the reading-comprehension approach was overwhelmingly popular among teachers and students (Tristram 2003): Morwood described the brand leader course book, the Cambridge Latin Course (CLC), as of 'central importance to the survival of Latin' (Morwood 2003, p. xvii). Pat Story explained that the CLC succeeded because it served two student audiences: firstly as a valuable education for those who did not carry on, and secondly as a subject-specific one for those who did (Hales and Paul 2013, p. 358). But despite the CLC's track record, Gove's DfE Latinists seemed to approve of the more traditional methods. In another part of the interview mentioned above, Johnson initially derided the CLC for its focus on the domestic lives of Caecilius and his family (Carr 2007); in public print Gwynne (2014) and Mount (2013) both berated it loudly for its supposed inadequate attention to grammatical detail. Yet if Gibb was really looking for a course which had repeatedly proven itself in delivering students from all backgrounds to read Classics at university, then it already existed in the CLC, as Joanna Paul has noted (2013). Ideology, however, seemed to require something else. In a 2016 address to the *Sutton Trust* Gibb indicated his general thinking, which seemed to adhere towards the more traditional teaching of his own youth:

> Sometimes you have to almost allow teachers to use methods that have been so out of fashion for 20, 30, 40, 50 years, you have to take active measures to enable those teachers to use those methods and they are free to do so. (Barker 2016)

Nothing, of course, was preventing teachers from using any course – traditional or not. Most teachers were probably mixing methods of all sorts – engaged in the simple process of teaching and using whatever worked for them. Gibb's interesting phrase 'have to almost allow them' implied some sort of coercion. And, indeed, in the case of Latin teaching, it could be said that the reforms did just that. The 'active measures' turned out to be forcing changes in teaching methodology to more traditional types by using the leverage of new, supposedly more rigorous formal grammar assessment at GCSE and A level. The impact of these is detailed below.

Assessment

GCSEs

Gove felt that in general students were not being served well by the public examination system. Ever-rising examination grades (a long-held desire of all governments – for who would want to see grades go *down*?) had led him to believe not that his predecessors' education policies had been working, but that instead there was a 'dumbing down' of quality, brought on by competition between examination boards and a proliferation of increasingly easy examinations and assessment routes (Gove 2012a). Mere recommendations for students to take up the EBacc-approved GCSE subjects were insufficient in themselves: in addition Gove sought greater intellectual challenge in GCSE subject content, as well as a change in the grading structures of the new examinations and in the ways in which schools were to be held accountable by the new measurements. For Latin and Classical Greek, this would have to impact upon pedagogy, because essentially the content would have to remain the same – Virgil is Virgil, however you look at it. He therefore enlisted the support of the examination boards (which he had only just identified as the cause of the problem of dumbing down) and of the university academic community (but definitely not members of 'The Blob' from the Faculties of Education) in the design of reformed qualifications, starting with a tranche of core subjects – English, Maths and Science. Latin and Classical Greek were to be reformed in the second tranche, as being on the list of approved foreign language subjects; Ancient History and Classical Civilisation in the third. The A level Consultation and Advisory Board (ALCAB) was instituted by Gove to convene the university academics. Its purpose was to ensure that university academics – not the actual teachers of the A levels – could make recommendations about the subject content of the examinations specifications so that the examinations would be fit for purpose as preparation for university study. The small number of Classics academics who took part wisely consulted the teachers as best they were able (although this was outside their remit) and in due course recommended that the A levels in Latin and Classical Greek were already pretty much fit for purpose and needed no major substantive changes. In 2014, the DfE could do no more than accept their arguments – but only up to a point, as we shall see. In 2015, however, the DfE decided that ALCAB would not need to reconvene for Ancient History and Classical Civilisation after all (whether for lack of finances or because the Classics ALCAB had not deemed that as much had to be changed as the DfE had expected). Instead, consultation was to be arranged by the examination boards themselves (supposedly the root of the problem, as we saw above), with DfE oversight. Debate focused on how the Latin and Classical Greek GCSEs could be made more challenging to fit with Gove's thesis that there had been a dumbing down in standards. Discussions initially took place between Dominic Cummings, Gove's special advisor, and Peter Jones, the university lecturer, about how to make Latin and Classical Greek more 'rigorous' (Cohen and Jones 2014). Gove had already declared his hand in a speech about how the new foreign languages GCSEs should have a 'clear emphasis on the importance of translation – including the study of literature of proven merit' (Gove 2013a), this being what university academics had said was deficient in modern language teaching. For ancient languages, of course, the study of literature in the original had long been the *raison d'être* of the subjects and had formed an increasing proportion of the examinations since the 1980s (Cambridge School Classics Project 2012). Translation and the study of literature had never gone away. What *had* gradually decreased was English to Latin translation: the unreformed GCSEs did not have it, and it only appeared as options at AS and A levels. Amidst the discussion, two more conferences backed by Sheila Lawlor's *Politeia* think tank were suddenly called at which the twin (and some might say oppositional) issues of widening participation while increasing the challenge of Latin GCSEs were discussed. Lawlor reiterated the problems of Latin's missing link at key stage 3 (Lawlor 2013), while Cambridge Classics lecturer David Butterfield suggested that the retention of a short-course (half) GCSE would ease the burden of teaching where the timetable allocation was low (Butterfield 2013). Lawlor's was a point worth making. The DfE ignored it. Butterfield's proposal sadly proved to be impossible as Gove's reconfiguration of papers in the GCSEs meant that short-course GCSEs disappeared altogether. Both might seem to have had possibilities for widening participation and contributing to the aim of improving social mobility. There was more under consideration. To meet the government's requirement that the new GCSEs should provide increased intellectual challenge, Butterfield (2013), supported by three teachers from selective schools, also argued for the translation from English to Latin to be reinstated as an option in the GCSE. Such an option had long been lost from the examinations due to low interest, high costs and problems with comparability. But while the conference had sensibly recommended *optionality* as a compromise and a return to what previous examinations had offered, Gove made translation from English into Latin *compulsory*, giving himself to understand that the supposed extra difficulty of such a task would raise the general academic rigour of the whole examination. The same would apply to Classical Greek. Following an outcry from teachers, for whom teaching yet another element just for the purpose of making an already challenging examination yet harder was a burden too far (especially if he wanted more to study it), Gove offered as an alternative to the option an extra set of grammar questions. By now the minister had somehow created a completely new set of stumbling blocks to widening access to the languages. The move towards an even more traditional examination privileged a particular pedagogical approach. This was one which lacked modern resources, needed specialist teaching (already in short supply) and demanded extra time on top of already curtailed timetables, and one which was historically disliked by most teachers and students (Hunt 2016b).

Up until that point, there had been a lack of interconnectedness between the decisions Gove had made about classical subjects, but over all they had much enhanced the provision of Classics. This moment was the tipping point. From then on there was an obvious contradiction: on the one hand, the trajectory of general education policy was meant to deliver social justice by encouraging more students to take up classical subjects which would in turn have the potential to provide them with greater access to the more academic universities; on the other, the policy demand for greater intellectual challenge was turning out to be hugely detrimental by making the classical subjects harder than ever to achieve success in. *Really?*

Meanwhile, another policy was making things worse: the requirement for parity of difficulty of examinations (in order to use GCSE examination results to measure student attainment fairly and to use the grades for teacher and school accountability and league tables) meant that a number of features of the previous examinations had to be lost. Thus short courses, modularized examinations and controlled assessment were abolished – all of which had been successful in encouraging schools to offer classical subjects off-timetable, for example, or with non-specialist teachers. It is likely, in my opinion, that the abolition of the short course will result in the extinction of Classical Greek in many schools, offered as it is at lunchtimes as an enrichment class and barely able to be completed in such circumstances as a full GCSE. Meanwhile, the WJEC Latin Certificates, which had been successful in attracting some 3,000 extra candidates after only a few years of availability, and which had only recently survived the Wolf Report, and which had been approved for the EBacc and for school performance points, would lose this status in 2018. This would mean schools would be unlikely to offer them after this date if they could not gain credit in league tables for them. While Gove wanted more students to take classical subjects, he simultaneously narrowed the routes by which they might have done so. While the idea of school autonomy and freedom of choice was still propagated, the curriculum was more and more curtailed: Latin and Classical Greek GCSE contained prescribed percentages of language testing by means of written translation, comprehension, English to Latin translation or grammar identification and set numbers of lines of original unadapted literature. In practice, this has meant that each examination would closely resemble each other, with differences of detail only in the types and format of literature which the examinations offered. Credit here should be offered to the WJEC examinations board, which rapidly developed a fresh GCSE in Latin to meet the new criteria and still managed to continue to provide some of the flexibility in assessment which had been such an attractive feature of the old certificates.

Further tinkering with assessment at GCSE might narrow student choices even more, however. The new *Progress 8* measurement of school accountability would measure a student's progress over their choices of eight GCSEs (including the five EBacc subjects) instead of the previous measure of the total number of good pass grades in five GCSEs (including English and Maths). This measure was introduced to combat some of the evidence that schools were focusing too much on students on the Grade C/D borderline, at the expense of students at both ends of the attainment spectrum (Laws 2016). The grading system for the reformed GCSEs would change from A*–G to 9–1. At present some 44 per cent of students – who tend to be from a selective educational background – score a Grade A* (Cambridge School Classics

Project 2014). In the new regime Grade 9s will be allocated only to the top 20 per cent of students achieving grades 8–7 (present grades A* and A). Both of these reforms are likely to depress enrolment: what head teacher will encourage a student to enroll in a subject, already notoriously difficult, without careful thought when the new measures are likely to show negative or at best neutral progress for school accountability purposes? And what student, scanning the subjects which will deliver them most likely the highest grades, will choose the ancient languages which, despite the range of candidates being skewed towards the highest attainers, still only deliver 20 per cent of Grade 9s – and those rarely in their own school?

None of this shall worry the private schools, who do not have to submit to these measurements. Instead, there are reports of a number of private schools developing their own examinations (including one for Classical Civilisation) set, marked and moderated by their own teachers, and a rise in the uptake of International GCSE examinations (Clark 2015). Universities accept the IGCSEs for matriculation. But because none of the International GCSE qualifications are subject to the examinations' inspectorate Ofqual's scrutiny, this liberty is denied to state schools, thereby reinforcing the divide between state and private sectors and tilting the playing field towards the private sector once again.

A levels

While the Ministry concentrated on Latin and Classical Greek, questions arose about Classical Civilisation and Ancient History. At one stage it did not look as if they would be reformed at all: sudden death at GCSE, as head teachers would not put on subjects without school performance points. At A level they were popular: examination entries outstripped Latin and Classical Greek and were predominantly in the state sector, most likely because the linguistic A levels did not attract financially viable classroom groups (Hunt 2014). With some judicious lobbying by the examination boards and university academics, the subjects got their chance, were reformed and received accreditation in 2016. Their long-term survival, however, is questionable. There is evidence that AS level had attracted students who had no previous experience of classical subjects before they came to sixth-form colleges where it was offered; succeeding at AS, they continued to A level and university (as Khan-Evans relates in this book). Gove's requirement that AS level examinations should not count as part of the A level might further reduce the subjects' attractiveness.

The most serious worry, however, is the reduction in funding, which is likely to affect all classical subjects: in the state sector a combination of a rise in school staffing costs and changes to the allocation mechanism has delivered a funding crisis; in the private sector austerity has also impacted hard. A straw poll carried out by the author of thirty-two state and private schools with strong Classics departments showed that twenty-nine out of thirty-two were not going to offer AS levels in any subjects, and only seven would continue to offer four A levels. Twelve thought the impact on Latin would be detrimental; fifteen thought similarly for Classical Civilisation or Ancient History (Hunt 2016a).

The impact of these reforms taken together in the long term is unclear. The effect on student enrolments may make Classics classes economically unviable, especially in the state sector, thereby undoing earlier efforts to improve provision. Of course, schools may choose to accept their freedom to offer whichever qualifications they want to their students and to consider the accountability measures as unnecessarily intrusive. Only a few head teachers are willing to say this in public – primarily those personally lauded by Gove himself and thus protected from censure (Birbalsingh 2015, p. 27). Others may be more risk-averse.

Initial Teacher Training (ITT)

Many head teachers have been prevented from offering classical subjects due to the lack of staff with subject expertise or training. Getting advice was difficult. When I started my career in 1987, there were two of Her Majesty's Inspectors in Classics for the UK and the Local Education Authority provided courses for language teachers in their schools. Now there are none. Gove disbanded virtually all the nationally co-ordinated programmes. In 2010, a number of initiatives had seemed promising for developing Classics in state schools. One of these had been the independent/state school partnerships, in which government money promoted the sharing of expertise and teaching between the sectors (Khan-Evans and Hunt 2010). These were cancelled. Also cancelled was the previous government's aim for all teachers in state schools to be qualified to Master's level. By 2012, Lord Adonis, a previous minister of education under the Blair Labour Government, was lamenting the dearth in the UK of specialist, high-quality teachers trained to Master's level, which were common in other state jurisdictions (Adonis 2012, p. 218). Yet the academies movement itself, Adonis' creation, was part of the problem: competition and claims of intellectual copyright seem to have deterred collaboration between schools (Glatter, quoted in Pring (2013, p. 159)), while Initial Teacher Training (ITT) itself was being taken away from the higher education institutions (HEIs) and either not being replaced or being encouraged to take place elsewhere. DfE policy privileged school-led School Direct (SD) training and Teach First (TF) over the HEI-led PGCE. The SD courses depended on partnerships with the same HEIs that had provided the PGCEs; but Gove was already burning bridges even as he constructed them and there remained doubt that the PGCE would survive (Burn 2015, p. 57). Meanwhile, academies and free schools could use their autonomy to employ unqualified staff, if they wanted. The combination of all these changes suggested that far from creating a new set of opportunities for training teachers, for Classics at least, SD and TF have not been good recruiters (Hunt 2016b, p. 5); meanwhile, focus groups set up by the DfE suggested unqualified teachers were not popular (Laws 2016, p. 458). The policy continued to be promoted, however, despite the evidence. A nadir was reached in 2013 when the number of teacher trainees in Classics reached a perilous low of twenty-nine for the whole of the UK (Hunt 2016b, p. 5). The allocation of places on the PGCEs had been reduced by the DfE by a blanket 25 per cent – a situation the main civil servant *in charge of* teacher recruitment told the author he found (with no sense of irony) 'shocking'. Such small numbers going forward might have made the PGCE courses themselves economically unviable. It is fortunate that since then pragmatism has outweighed ideology and the number allocated for the Classics PGCE has risen to around 50 nationally in three centres – the University of Cambridge, KCL and the University of Sussex – and may rise again. In most other subject areas, SD can work well: schools select 'colleagues' to join them in well-established, often quite large departments (Seldon and Finn 2015, pp. 280–281); but for Classics, tiny or non-existent departments make poor recruiting grounds and schools look to the PGCE courses as a reliable supplier.

The DfE has also shown its intent to continue to support Classics in other formal and occasionally informal ways. In 2014, Gove allocated a significant grant to the University of Oxford Classics Faculty to train more Classics teachers for state schools. Political ideology would not mean turning to the existing HEI-led PGCE courses. Instead, Gove and Cummings wanted a set of alternative intensive courses to fast-track state school teachers of other subjects into Classics teaching (Cohen and Jones 2014). These courses, based at the University of Oxford, were to be promoted under the management of Christopher Pelling, whom Gove dubbed the 'Classics Czar' (Pelling 2014). Pelling sensibly entrusted this training programme to the Cambridge School Classics Project which worked on a number of initiatives involving the Faculties of Education at Cambridge and KCL its own distance learning courses and a number of weekend and day courses across the UK. In total over 450 such teachers were trained over two years (Cambridge School Classics Project 2016). More informal channels of communication have also benefitted Classics. Ministers had taken to reading social media to assess the effectiveness of their policies in practice through the 'voice of the teachers' (Old 2015, p. 57). In 2014, it was through a Twitter storm initiated by Mary Beard, the Cambridge classicist, that Dominic Cummings found out that the training bursary for Classics was zero that year – a sure-fire disincentive to applicants. The £26,000 bursaries which he reinstated are now at their highest ever and signify that Classics remains as much a priority to the government as modern foreign languages, which attract the same amount. Such direct interventions have been rare; but where they have occurred, they have been helpful to Classics. It is a matter for debate whether decision-making for the subjects based on direct ministerial contacts or ministerial ear-bending is a sufficiently reliable one for the future.

Conclusion

In February 2014, Gove lost his post. Just before this happened, he had given a speech at the London Academy of Excellence which still showed his personal belief in the part that Classics might play in improving social mobility:

> Classics is one of those subjects where most university places are taken up by independent school students and I think that's wrong. We should be giving state school pupils the chance to compete on a level playing field. (Gove 2014) *e clues by Cfork*

Few would disagree about the sentiments, although the methods might be contested. However, his poll ratings showed he was a deeply divisive figure (Seldon and Snowdon 2015) and had lost the trust of his coalition partners and of the prime minister himself (Clegg 2016). He was replaced by Nicky Morgan. She lost her post in the government reshuffle of 2016. Her replacement Greening has yet to make any pronouncements about Classics. Gibb remains.

The total effect of Gove's policies is yet unclear – and not just in Classics. The pace of reform has been sometimes giddyingly fast; even his supporters are equivocal, and as his friend Tim Hands noted, he 'failed to achieve certainties in the present and created multiple uncertainties for the future' (Hands 2015, p. 43). The paradoxes between different elements of policy are obvious in Classics and it will take years to find out what the full impact will be. His education policy offered freedom and opportunities, but burdened the schools, without providing support, and adding a raft of other measures to push students into only those subjects it perceived as valuable (Spohrer 2015). Latin, Classical Greek and Ancient History were the lucky recipients of this rhetorical largesse. But the DfE failed to consult widely, missed opportunities, narrowed choices and ignored advice. Under the present government classical subjects continue to be a partner in the mission to improve social mobility, by encouraging greater access to the subjects for students in state schools and encouraging their students to have similar aspirations to attend university as their privately-educated peers. It is a moot point whether classical subjects have achieved any of these in significant numbers as a result of government policy at the time and in the way intended, whether there has been lasting impact or whether the initiatives (some of which are recounted in the pages of this book) would have happened anyway.

What, in the meantime, have the subject organizations learnt from this period?

Classical subjects have seemed to have become rather closely aligned with a right-wing, neo-traditionalist curriculum. Their position within the curriculum is dependent on the personal support of members of the government. Major policy decisions overwhelm the delicate ecology of minority subjects; individual errors are corrected when noticed by individual ministerial decrees. Consultation by the DfE is weak; it is dependent on the examination boards to create a key stage 4 and key stage 5 curriculum, and on the consulting teachers. Classics subject organizations are more organized but disconnected from DfE decision-making. At key stage 2 Latin and Classical Greek are allied to DfE policies to improve English literacy and as a support for modern foreign languages. Modern foreign languages are more important than ancient ones at key stage 3. At key stages 4 and 5 classical subjects are seen as a means of 'levelling of the playing field with private schools' (Gove 2014) for access to university Classics. Latin and Classical Greek are prioritized over Ancient History and Classical Civilisation. ITT seems currently supported through the PGCE, and, although there are still insufficient places made available, the allocations of placements seem more predictable after considerable fluctuation. Charities and university Classics departments have taken responsibility for continuing professional development. Classics still seems to be a priority for this government – at least it has not taken it away and the current bursary awarded for teacher training, at £26,000, continues to be among the highest awarded of all subjects as an incentive for teachers to become trained in order to meet demand (Department for Education 2017). The task is to use this current favouritism to ensure a longer term future for the subjects and to ensure the joined-up thinking, which is currently lacking, is addressed. In the meantime, Classics has been caught in a peculiar bind. On the one hand, it has been embraced by this government as a way of improving social justice at primary and secondary levels: this is perhaps welcome news. But on the other, it has become embroiled in an education policy which renders it even more challenging for students to succeed in, and ties it more closely into a complex and stifling accountability system which only applies to the state sector. The independent schools retain the freedom to choose their own qualifications outside the GCSEs and A levels if they do not like them and they do not have to submit their results to DfE and their pedagogy to Ofsted scrutiny. Whether the policy of getting Classics into schools survives the present government or the next one, there are interesting times ahead for all the classical subjects in state and independent schools.

WHY IS Classix partic-assoc w social justice agenda?

References

Adonis, A. (2012), *Education, Education, Education*, London: Biteback Publishing Ltd.

Ball, S. (2013), *The Education Debate*, 2nd edn, Bristol: The Policy Press.

Barker, I. (9 March 2016), *Schools Minister Nick Gibb: 'Teachers Should Be Free to Use 50-Year-Old Teaching Techniques'*. *Times Educational Supplement*. Available online: https://www.tes.com/news/school-news/breaking-news/schools-minister-nick-gibb-teachers-should-be-free-use-50-year-old. (Accessed 24 March 2018).

Bass, B. (2003), 'Classics in Prep Schools', in J. Morwood (ed.), *The Teaching of Classics*, 67–72, Cambridge: Cambridge University Press.

Beard, M. (22 June 2012), *Saving Latin from the Tory Party*. *Times Literary Supplement*. Available online: http://timesonline.typepad.com/dons_life/2012/06/saving-latin-from-the-tory-party.html. (Accessed 24 March 2018).

Bell, B. (2003), *Minimus*, in J. Morwood (ed.), *The Teaching of Classics*, 61–66, Cambridge: Cambridge University Press.

Bell, B. (2015), 'Report of the Primary Latin Project: February 2015', *Journal of Classics Teaching*, 31: 41–42.

Birbalsingh, K. (2015), 'Free Schools: Making Success Sustainable', in R. Peal (ed.), *Changing Schools. Perspectives on Five Years of Education Reform*, 25–33, Woodbridge: John Catt.

Burn, K. (2015), 'The Gove Legacy in the Curriculum: The Case of History', in M. Finn (ed.), *The Gove Legacy. Education in Britain after the Coalition*, 47–62, London: Palgrave Macmillan.

Butterfield, D. (2013), 'Why Learn Latin?' in *Latin for Language Lovers. Ancient Languages, the New Curriculum and GCSE*, 4–9, London: Politeia.

Cambridge School Classics Project (2012), *Changing Demands in Latin and Ancient Greek Examinations 1918 to 2012*, Cambridge: Cambridge School Classics Project (unpublished report for the DfE).

Cambridge School Classics Project (2014), *Report on the WJEC Latin Qualifications*, Cambridge: Cambridge School Classics Project.

Cambridge School Classics Project (2016), Report on the DfE/CSCP Teacher Training Initiative, *Unpublished presentation at the Cambridge School Classics Project Annual Conference.*

Carr, S. (2007), 'An Interview with Boris Johnson', *Journal of Classics Teaching*, 1: 1–3.

Clark, R. (14 March 2015), *Now More than Ever the 'I' in IGCSE Is for 'independent'*. *The Spectator*. Available online: http://www.spectator.co.uk/2015/03/the-i-in-igcse-is-for-independent/. (Accessed 24 March 2018).

Classics for All (2015), *Capital Classics*. Classics for All. Available online: http://classicsforall.org.uk/regional-hubs/london-capital-classics/. (Accessed 24 March 2018).

Clegg, N. (2016), *Politics. Between the Extremes*, London: Vintage.

Cohen, J. and Jones, P. (2014). 'ex cathedra', *ad familiares*, 47, London: Friends of Classics.

Department of Education (1988), Education Reform Act, London: Her Majesty's Stationery Office.

Department for Education (2013), *Languages Programmes of Study; Key Stage 2*. Department for Education. Available online: https://www.gov.uk/government/uploads/system/uploads/attachment_data/file/239042/PRIMARY_national_curriculum_-_Languages.pdf. (Accessed 24 March 2018).

Department for Education (2017), *Bursaries and Funding*. Get into Teaching. Available online: https://getintoteaching.education.gov.uk/funding-and-salary/overview. (Accessed 24 March 2012).

Gibb, N. (2010), Latin for Language Learners. Opening Opportunity for Primary Pupils. *Speech to Politeia*, London: Politeia.

Gibb, N. (7 February 2012), On Reading: Greater Expectations, *Speech to Stockwell Park High School.*

Gibb, N. (11 June 2015), The Social Justice Case for an Academic Curriculum, *Speech to the Policy Forum.*

Gove, M. (30 June 2009), What Is Education For? *Speech to the Royal Society of Arts.*

Gove, M. (26 March 2012a), The Future of Education. *Speech to the Association of School and College Leaders*. Department of Education. Available online: https://www.gov.uk/government/speeches/education-secretary-michael-goves-speech-to-ascl. (Accessed 24 March 2018).

Gove, M. (10 May 2012b), A Coalition for Good – How We Can All Work Together to Make Opportunity More Equal, *Speech to Brighton College*.

Gove, M. (5 February 2013a), The Progressive Betrayal, *Speech to the Social Market Foundation*.

Gove, M. (23 March 2013b), *I Refuse to Surrender to the Marxist Teachers Hell-Bent on Destroying Our Schools: Education Secretary Berates 'the New Enemies of Promise' for Opposing His Plans*. The Daily Mail. Available online: http://www.dailymail.co.uk/debate/article-2298146/I-refuse-surrender -Marxist-teachers-hell-bent-destroying-schools-Education-Secretary-berates-new-enemies -promise-opposing-plans.html. (Accessed 24 March 2018).

Gove, M. (3 December 2013c), Secretary of State for Education Michael Gove's statement in the House on the OECD's 2012 PISA results. Department for Education. Available online: London: www.gov. uk/government/speeches/2012-oecd-pisa-results. (Accessed 24 March 2018).

Gove, M. (3 February 2014), *Speech to the London Academy of Excellence, London. The Independent*. Available online: http://www.independent.co.uk/news/education/schools/prep-on-school-premises- and-an-increase-to-latin-and-greek-teaching-in-secondary-school-the-gove-9105080.html. (Accessed 24 March 2018).

Grice, E. (13 April 2013), *The Glamour of Grammar. An Object Lesson. The Daily Telegraph*. Available online: http://www.telegraph.co.uk/education/9987974/The-glamour-ofgrammar-an-object-lesson. html. (Accessed 24 March 2018).

Gwynne, N. (2014), *Gwynne's Latin*, London: Ebury Press.

Hales S, and Paul, J. (2013), 'Pompeii and the Cambridge Latin Course', in S. Hales and J. Paul (eds.), *Pompeii in the Popular Imagination. From Its Rediscovery to Today*, 356–366, Oxford: Oxford University Press.

Hands, T. (2015), 'The Gove Legacy in the Independent Schools: The Making and Unmaking of a Supreme Soviet', in M. Finn (ed.), *The Gove Legacy. Education in Britain after the Coalition*, 34–46, London: Palgrave Macmillan.

Hirsch, E. (1996), *The Schools We Need and Why We Don't Have Them*, New York: Doubleday.

Hodgson, H. and Murray-Pollock, X. (2016), 'Classics for All: Establishing the Classics Hub', *Journal of Classics Teaching*, 33: 48–49.

Holmes-Henderson, A. (2016). 'Teaching Latin and Greek in Primary Classrooms: The Classics in Communities Project', *Journal of Classics Teaching*, 33: 50–53.

Hunt, S. (2013), 50 Years of Classical Civilisation, *Fifty Years of the Joint Association of Classical Teachers*, 25–33.

Hunt, S. (2014), 'Statistical Appendix to Championing Classical Civilisation and Ancient History', *Journal of Classics Teaching*, 29: 11–14.

Hunt, S. (2016a), Gove's Classicists, *Unpublished Presentation Given at the Classical Association's Annual Conference*.

Hunt, S. (2016b), *Starting to Teach Latin*, London: Bloomsbury Academic.

Johnson, B. (17 March 2010), *Mayor Urges London State Schools to Teach Latin*. BBC News. Available online: http://news.bbc.co.uk/1/hi/england/london/8571662.stm. (Accessed 24 March 2018).

Khan-Evans, A. and Hunt, S. (2010), '(R)evolution in Classics', *Journal of Classics Teaching*, 20: 4–7.

Lawlor, S. (2013), 'Latin GCSE: Aims and Means', in *Latin for Language Lovers. Ancient Languages, the New Curriculum and GCSE*, 2–3, London: Politeia.

Laws, D. (2016), *Coalition. The Inside Story of the Conservative–Liberal Democrat Coalition Government*, London: Biteback Publishing.

Lightman, B. (2015), 'The Gove Legacy in State Education', in M. Finn (ed.), *The Gove Legacy. Education in Britain after the Coalition*, 14–33, London: Palgrave Macmillan.

Lister, B. (2007), *Changing Classics in Schools*, Cambridge: Cambridge University Press.

Liveley, G. and Liddel, P. (2014), 'Championing Classical Civilisation and Ancient History. An Open Letter to the DfE and Ofqual', *Journal of Classics Teaching*, 29: 11–14.

Lovatt, H. (2011), 'Sitting on the Fence or Breaking through the Hedge? Risk-Taking, Incentives and Institutional Barriers to Outreach Work among Academics and Students', in G. Baker and A. Fisher (eds.), *Arts and Humanities Academics in Schools. Mapping the Pedagogical Interface*, 28–42, London: Continuum.

Maguire, J. and Hunt, S. (2014), 'The North Norfolk Latin Cluster Group: Two Case Studies'. *Journal of Classics Teaching*, 30: 41–44.

Masciantonio, R. (1979), 'A FLES Latin Lesson – Philadelphia Style', *Latin Teaching*, XXXV (6): 29–31.

Mavrogenes, N. (1981), 'Latin in the Elementary School: Help for Reading and Language Arts', *Latin Teaching*, XXXVI (1): 39–46.

Morwood, J. (2003), *The Teaching of Classics*, Cambridge: Cambridge University Press.

Mount, H. (1 December 2010), *Latin Returns – te, Michael Gove, discituri salutamus*. The Daily Telegraph, Available online: http://blogs.telegraph.co.uk/culture/harrymount/100049427/latin-returns-te -michael-gove-discituri-salutamus/. (Accessed 23 April 2018).

Mount, H. (17 September 2013), The Tragic Dumbing Down of Latin in Our Schools, *The Daily Telegraph*.

Old, A. (2015), 'Social Media: Did Blogs Break the Blob?' in R. Peal (ed.), *Changing Schools. Perspectives on Five Years of Educational Reforms*, 55–66, Woodbridge: John Catt Educational Limited.

Paul, J. (2013), 'The Democratic Turn in (and through) Pedagogy. A Case Study of the Cambridge Latin Course', in L. Hardwick and S. Harrison (eds.), *Classics in the Modern World. A 'Democratic Turn'?* 143–156, Oxford: Oxford University Press.

Peal, R. (2014), *Progressively Worse. The Burden of Bad Ideas in British Schools*, London: Civitas.

Peel, M. (2015), *The New Meritocracy. A History of UK Independent Schools, 1979–2015*, London: Elliott and Thompson Limited.

Pelling, C. (2010), *Latin for Language Learners. Opening Opportunity for Primary Pupils*, London: Politeia.

Pelling, C. (9 February 2014), Giving the Gift of Ancient Tongues, *The Sunday Times: Education*.

Pring, R. (2013), *The Life and Death of Secondary Education for All*, London: Routledge.

Robinson, L. (2016), *Latin at Key Stage 2*. The Iris Project. Available online: http://irisproject.org.uk/ index.php/projects/literacy-through-latin/39-latin-at-key-stage-2. (Accessed 23 April 2018).

Sandis, E. (2009), 'The Oxford Perspective on Classics Outreach', *Journal of Classics Teaching*, 16: 3–5.

Seldon, A. and Finn, M. (2015), *The Coalition Effect 2010–2015*, Cambridge: Cambridge University Press.

Seldon, A. and Snowdon, P. (2015), *Cameron at 10. The Inside Story 2010–2015*, London: William Collins.

Spohrer, K. (2015), 'Opening Doors or Narrowing Opportunities? The Coalition's Approach to Widening Participation, Social Mobility and Social Justice', in M. Finn (ed.), *The Gove Legacy. Education in Britain after the Coalition*, 101–115, London: Palgrave Macmillan.

Stephenson, D. (2014), 'WJEC Level 2 Latin: A Teacher's Viewpoint', *Journal of Classics Teaching*, 29: 45–47.

The Russell Group of Universities (2016), *Subject Choices at School and College*. The Russell Group of Universities. Available online: http://russellgroup.ac.uk/for-students/school-and-college-in-the-uk/ subject-choices-at-school-and-college/. (Accessed 23 April 2018).

Tristram, D. (2003), 'Classics in the Curriculum from the 1960s to the 1990s', in J. Morwood (ed.), *The Teaching of Classics*, 6–19, Cambridge: Cambridge University Press.

Wolf, A. (2011), *Review of Vocational Education – The Wolf Report*, London: Department for Education.

Young, T. (3 February 2011), Forget Mandarin. Latin Is the Key to Success. *The Spectator*. Available online: http://blogs.spectator.co.uk/2011/02/forget-mandarin-latin-is-the-key-to-success/. (Accessed 23 April 2018).

Young, T. (2014), *Prisoners of the Blob. Why Education Experts Are Wrong about Nearly Everything*, London: Civitas.

CHAPTER 2
WIDENING ACCESS TO CLASSICS IN THE UK: HOW THE IMPACT, PUBLIC ENGAGEMENT, OUTREACH AND KNOWLEDGE EXCHANGE AGENDA HAVE HELPED

Emma Searle, Lucy Jackson and Michael Scott

Shattering the class ceiling: How the outreach agenda is helping to widen access to Classics

Emma Searle

This chapter provides an overview of the development of university outreach work over the past fifteen years and how the expansion of the higher education agenda to include the provision of outreach as a statutory obligation has increased access to classical subjects, with specific reference to the University of Oxford. Changes in the perceived purpose and value of outreach work catalyzed by the Higher Education Act (2004) and subsequent government policies have effected changes in the types of activities provided by the central university and by individual departments and colleges. These have resulted in the development and introduction of strategic schemes and long-term academic enrichment programmes for school pupils belonging to target demographics. The first section of this chapter discusses several such programmes introduced by the Faculty of Classics and Oxford colleges in recent years with a view to demonstrating some of the ways in which universities can provide sustainable, long-term opportunities to study the ancient world for school pupils who would otherwise be unable to do so.

'Outreach' is used as a general term for all activities targeted at school pupils from 'non-traditional' backgrounds. These include women, people with disabilities or those from socio-economic or ethno-cultural backgrounds that are historically under-represented at university level[1] – with the aim of widening access and increasing participation among those who have previously been largely excluded from higher education in the UK.[2] The Office for Fair Access (OFFA), the independent public body set up under New Labour's Higher Education Act (2004) to monitor and regulate 'fair access' to higher education in England, is tasked with ensuring that universities which charge 'top-up' tuition fees (currently up to a maximum of £9,250 per annum for undergraduate courses) are demonstrably working to increase participation among under-represented groups and are spending a proportion of those fees on initiatives to safeguard and facilitate equitable access to higher education through outreach work and on-course financial support (Department for Education and Skills 2003b, p. 85; Clarke 2004; OFFA 2004).[3] Universities set their own targets in an 'access agreement' but these must be approved by OFFA, and the director of Fair Access to Higher Education has the power to prevent any HE institution charging fees above the basic level (currently £6,165 per annum for full-time undergraduate courses) if it cannot satisfy the regulator that it is making adequate provision.[4]

Over the past fifteen years, the colleges and departments of the University of Oxford have offered numerous different kinds of events and activities, such as subject taster sessions, study days and workshops for school students, other one-off subject-specific events, open days and summer schools (the UNIQ programme has been particularly successful),[5] often developed in response to feedback from secondary schools and sixth-form colleges, in order to support and encourage applications from pupils from the 'non-traditional' backgrounds discussed earlier. This variety and flexibility was, to a certain extent, *a good thing* and was successful in informing these pupils (and their teachers) about Oxford and higher education in general: 'de-mystifying' the admissions process, providing opportunities to visit the university and develop an understanding of what it might be like to study here and encouraging all to consider applying to the university. Our collective efforts have contributed to increasing inclusivity and diversity over the last decade (although there is, of course, more to be done).[6]

Are all outreach activities, in and of themselves, uniformly a good thing? Do they make substantive contributions to achieving the desired outcome of a more inclusive and diverse academic community? Research conducted by the Sutton Trust[7] indicates that no outreach event constitutes a meaningful 'intervention' by itself alone.[8] Universities cannot maintain a 'hit-and-run' approach towards their widening participation aims: focused and sustained long-term, academic enrichment schemes are vital. However, the lack of a nationwide and collaborative framework makes this type of work difficult. England used to have a national framework to monitor and coordinate outreach work: established in 2004 it was called *Aimhigher* and provided outreach activities for young people from disadvantaged backgrounds through partnerships involving around 2,500 schools, 300 sixth-form colleges and 100 universities collaborating on a national, regional and local area basis.[9]

The 2010–2015 Conservative/Liberal Democrat coalition government closed the programme (along with many other nationally coordinated programmes) at the end of the 2010/11 academic year. David Willetts, the then minister of state for Universities and Science, announced that universities were being given 'increased responsibility' for widening participation and would need to show they were attracting poor students to be allowed to charge higher fees (effectively equating the complexities of under-representation with an economic issue). Faced with the removal of a framework which would have assisted in the achievement of this new responsibility, universities in most regions have had to reinvent the wheel and are currently (re-)establishing collaborative networks to replace *Aimhigher*. In the Oxfordshire area we have *IntoUniversity Oxford South East, Study Higher* (a collaborative partnership between the University of Oxford, University of Reading, Bucks New University and Oxford Brookes University), *Oxford for Oxford* and *Target Oxbridge* (both run by the central Widening Access and Participation team) and the 'link colleges' programme in which every school in the country is linked with an Oxford college.[10]

Although OFFA disseminates their view of good practice, the overall situation remains fragmented, with no national strategic overview, and is dependent on the neoliberal vein. The Conservative government has left this crucial aspect to the vagaries of the 'market'. The tripling of tuition fees in 2010, the slashing of education budgets and the removal of the Education Maintenance Allowance[11] from poorer college students, while simultaneously closing down *Aimhigher*, provide greater obstacles to achieving social mobility in our education system.

Providing opportunities

Fortunately, the Faculty of Classics realized the need for specific objectives (and substantive, critical analysis of what the most efficient ways of achieving those outcomes might be) relatively early in the 'outreach-scene' and the Classics outreach programme was established in 2004 (Sandis 2009). From its inception the aim has been less about 'raising aspirations' and much more about breaking the link between educational opportunities and family background, so that all young people are provided with the opportunity to fulfil their potential, regardless of their background, school or where they live.[12] Pupils from poor and black and minority ethnic (BME) backgrounds are typically just as 'aspirational', if not more so, as their more privileged counterparts: they are often simply denied the opportunities (with the right support) to realize their aspirations and so mitigate their aspirations in the face of likely disappointment. It is not enough for outreach teams to arrive in a school, wax lyrical about higher education and not provide any means of achieving that. Effective outreach requires long-term ongoing engagement and support, the resources and opportunities for students to raise their attainment, as well as the reassurance that they are very much welcome and indeed enthusiastically *encouraged* to apply regardless of whether they fit the perceived 'Oxford student' stereotype propagated by the media.

GCSE exam reform and widening participation

The introduction of the National Curriculum in the 1988 Education Reform Act (Department of Education 1988) dramatically reduced the number of school hours available for teaching classical subjects, causing a steady decline in the number of exam entries for Latin at GCSE/ Level 2 and a shortage of Classics-trained teachers. However, starting in 2011 the number of exam entries started to increase and by 2014 were higher than they had been in seventeen years (CSCP 2015, p. 7). There are now more non-selective state schools (553) offering Latin than selective state and independent schools combined (515), based on continuous data gathering by the Cambridge Schools Classics Project (CSCP 2015, p. 3).

This resurgence is largely the result of the actions taken out of concern that the OCR Latin GCSE was only undertaken by a small number of extremely able pupils (typically at selective state and independent schools) as it failed to assess the full ability range, creating a significant barrier to non-selective schools using it to offer Latin to all their students. The high volume of content in the OCR qualification was simply too difficult to accommodate in the restricted timetable of the average school, particularly non-selective state schools, as the average number of teaching hours made available by schools where they were using it was a whopping 342 hours (Stephenson 2014; CSCP 2015, pp. 14–15, 19). Some independent schools were even allocating in excess of 400 hours' teaching time: something very few state schools would be able to do (particularly given the context of education budget cuts). The introduction of the WJEC Level 2 Certificates in Latin Language & Roman Civilisation and Latin Literature in 2011 helped widen access to a broader ability range by offering more flexible learning pathways (such as the option of controlled assessment, which was not permitted for a GCSE qualification), and a more flexible set of options which aimed to suit the needs of *all* schools since they are able to examine and recognize a more comprehensive, broader ability range. In 2014, 2,845 pupils were entered, bringing the total number of Latin exam (both WJEC and OCR) entrants to

11,699 (up from 9,355 in 2010): a 25 per cent growth (CSCP 2015, p. 8). For the schools with fewer teaching hours available, it is clear that the WJEC qualifications presented a more viable option, although the time required to deliver them still exceeds the DfE's guided teaching hours for a GCSE qualification (120–140 hours) (CSCP 2015, p. 17).

This progress was, however, jeopardized by the DfE's desire to make Latin and Greek 'more rigorous' (Cohen and Jones 2014) by reverting to the more 'traditional' GCSE examination, which privileged a pedagogical approach that lacked modern, affordable resources, required specialist teaching (already in critically short supply) and more teaching hours than were available in restricted timetables, and one which was historically disliked by most teachers and students (Hunt 2016). The WJEC Latin Certificates, which had been successful in increasing the number of students with access to Latin by 25 per cent in only a few years of availability, would lose their eligibility for inclusion of the English Baccalaureate (EBacc) and the calculation of school performance points in 2018, likely resulting in schools no longer offering them after this date since they could not gain credit from them in league tables. Fortunately, the WJEC examinations board was able to develop a new Latin GCSE (for teaching from 2016) which satisfies the DfE's new criteria while still providing some of the flexibility in assessment which had been such an attractive feature of the old certificates: hopefully, this means that the increase in exam entries and students with access to Latin continues.[13]

OxLAT Latin Teaching Scheme

As Hunt discusses in the previous chapter, the changes to education and examinations made by Michael Gove, the secretary of state for education under the Conservative/Liberal Democrat coalition government, have made it very difficult for underfunded and under-resourced state schools to actually offer any classical subjects, particularly the language-based ones of Latin and Classical Greek. So, although there has been an increase in the provision of Latin in the state sector, the vast majority of maintained schools are still prevented from offering it due to the severe cuts to their financial resources, resulting in a funding crisis, and a chronic shortage of staff with relevant expertise or training.[14] With only a few notable exceptions, this is unfortunately the case for nearly all state schools in Oxfordshire and its surrounding areas.[15] Therefore, the Classics Faculty decided to provide Latin teaching for selected pupils in Years 9 and 10 (thirteen- to fifteen-year-olds) attending state schools in the Oxfordshire area that have no Latin provision. We offered free tuition in Latin language and literature *ab initio* through to GCSE.

The first scheme started in January 2008, with the first cohort of students taking their Latin GCSE in summer 2010; the second cohort began in January 2010, taking their exams in summer 2012. Results were promising, ranging from a couple of A*s at the high end to a majority of Bs and Cs and several participants have actually gone on to study Classics both here and elsewhere at undergraduate level. Unfortunately, due to a funding shortfall the faculty was not able to run the scheme for a 2012–2014 cohort, but in 2014, thanks to a generous grant from the Stonehouse Educational Foundation, the faculty was able to relaunch the scheme.

Lessons take place on Saturday mornings in the faculty building and are taught by two professional Latin teachers, overseen and assisted by the scheme co-ordinator (Emma Searle). Essentially the scheme replicates the teaching that students would experience were they taking the subject as a GCSE option at school: the lessons (each three hours long and separated by a fifteen-minute break) are scheduled during Oxfordshire schools' term times so we are able to provide students with a routine and learning structure that is similar, albeit more intensive, to that which they experience at school. They are expected to consolidate their learning in class with appropriate study time at home each week, aided by an online learning environment, the OxLAT Online Learning Support Hub, where students are able to access all the resources needed during their course and which helps them to maximize their performance in their final GCSE exams. Homework is roughly the same as one would expect for any late key stage 3 and then GCSE subject.

The most recent cohort (comprising twenty-five students from fifteen schools across Oxfordshire, Berkshire, Buckinghamshire and Northamptonshire) started in January 2015 and sat their GCSE examinations in June 2017 after many months of intensive work. Despite the intensity of the work this cohort achieved absolutely stellar results: fifteen A*s, four As, two Bs and one C. More importantly, the opportunity has allowed our students to realize their personal and academic interest in the ancient world, and to engage with the languages, literature, history and culture which have inspired Classics students at Oxford for generations. In addition, members of the faculty based at Trinity College have very generously organized a continuation programme for students who have completed the OxLAT course. This 'Advanced Programme in Classics and the Ancient World' offers our OxLAT *alumni* the opportunity to extend their Latin language skills post-GCSE and experience more broadly the study of the ancient world: ancient history, archaeology, beginners' Classical Greek and Greek literature.

In the application process we request multiple pieces of information regarding the applicant's background as well as their current academic record, and when selecting students for participation in the scheme we weigh this information judiciously. We request this information in order to ensure that we select students who will benefit most from the scheme: with preference given to those from low-income households (i.e. eligible for free school meals), those with no parental participation in higher education and those from black or other minority ethnic backgrounds. There is, of course, no requirement to meet any of these criteria and all applications are considered in context.

The motivation to establish the scheme was the knowledge that the faculty could not just attempt to stimulate an interest in classical subjects by one-off or intermittent visits to local state schools, but needed also to provide school pupils with the opportunity to realize that interest if we were going to have any long-term success in getting a larger and more diverse number of young people involved in the study of the ancient world. Being an extra-curricular, however, the scheme is not helping to establish and expand Latin provision in schools (this has to remain a long-term aim). The intensity and supra-curricular nature of the scheme also means that it generally only appeals to very able and well-motivated students in the upper ability range (the best-scoring As and A*s in their other GCSEs, and the weakest B and Cs) due to the extra (and *heavy*) workload. This, of course, does not achieve the aim of encouraging the provision of classical subjects in a comprehensive education system. Any potential ways of addressing this to make it more accessible and available to a wider ability range (and on-timetable) have to be considered seriously. There exists a broader tension in priorities and some degree of hypocrisy: we deride the fact that access to Latin is restricted to a narrow, very able group of students, while simultaneously offering Latin to a small group of very able students. Some might argue that something is better than nothing, but ultimately our aim is to 'seed' enthusiasm in the hope that it will generate Latin in schools or in communities which we could then support in other ways. There seems to have been some success in this aim: Wallingford School (secondary) and Aureus School (secondary) in Didcot, as well as several primary schools across Oxfordshire, have introduced Latin to the curriculum and the faculty looks forward to working in close partnership with Classics for All to establish and contribute to the Oxfordshire Classics Hub.

Outreach and impact

The most recent Research Excellence Framework (REF) assessment (2013/14) included several changes in focus, particularly the addition of 'impact beyond academia' as an assessment criterion representing 20 per cent of a department's mark, and, as Michael Scott discusses later in this chapter, many research councils in the UK now require detailed plans of 'impact activities' as part of academic research project proposals. The faculty's outreach programme is an effective means for the departments and individuals to deliver these 'impact' requirements for both research grants and the REF: they are an established and typical method of public engagement that provides the types of events and activities which can be measured in the 'impact' factor. One particular approach which has been popular in recent years is the adaptation of current research to produce teaching materials relating to the ancient world that enrich a variety of subject areas in the primary and secondary school curriculum. 'Classics' is an expansive and diverse subject area, and the investigative approaches encompassed by the term have been dispersed and designed to integrate into existing subject structures, allowing all students to learn about the ancient world. We have produced materials for use in History, English language (and other linguistics-based subjects, such as Modern Foreign Languages), English literature and textual analysis, Drama, Art, Religious Education, Philosophy & Ethics and even Citizenship, which includes the spiritual, moral, social and cultural development of pupils. This 'packaging up' of current research into teachable material not only allows school pupils to experience a 'taster' of Classics but also helps demonstrate the broader social and cultural significance of the various aspects of ancient world studies by relating them contextually to other areas of human knowledge and experience.

Where the faculty does specialize in terms of the production of teaching and learning resources for classical subjects, that is, with a view to those schools which are able to offer Latin, Classical Greek, Ancient History and/or Classical Civilisation, the priority is to support and increase access to classical subjects for state-school students. We are producing a series of short, 'bite-size' mini-lecture videos, designed specifically for the new OCR GCSE and A-level specifications for Latin, Classical Greek, Ancient History and Classical Civilisation and these, which will shortly be available online on our website (www.classics.ox.ac.uk) as part of an increasing range of materials, are intended to help schools introduce one (or more) of the new GCSE and A levels by providing them with relevant free, up-to-date and engaging teaching resources. We are also producing a smaller series aimed at a more general audience with the aim of providing videos which provide an introduction to various subjects (*e.g.* the Roman Republic, Alexander the Great, Egyptian art and architecture) that are accessible to all.

The faculty takes a leading role for Classics education and outreach activities in the UK. This is not only to share its passion and the benefits of its resources widely and beyond the university, but it is also to ensure that primary and secondary school pupils without access to Classics have the opportunity to discover the subjects and explore their interests without barriers to their curiosity. Through running open days, workshops, school visits and long-term academic enrichment programmes, such as the OxLAT Latin Teaching Scheme, the faculty aims to ensure the wide enjoyment of these subjects and the engagement of future generations of undergraduates who will go on to study Classics at Oxford and at other universities. These initiatives have significant value beyond merely the avoidance of penalization by OFFA. In prospective students, we want to see *enthusiasm* and *potential* (not necessarily coupled with extensive previous exposure and experience). We know from experience that applicants who have not studied Classics in depth before arriving here can, and do, become capable and accomplished classicists, of whose achievements we are very proud.

Conclusion

In times of financial, social and educational inequality, it is all the more important that we increase our efforts to help provide students from disadvantaged social, economic and educational backgrounds with equality of opportunity and equity of educational support and enrichment. Despite the challenges presented by educational reforms over the past seven years, there is still cause for optimism if university departments take a lead in offering substantive opportunities for young people to engage meaningfully with Classics and with higher education.

Knowledge Exchange

Lucy Jackson

Knowledge Exchange, an element in the UK 'Impact' agenda much supported and promoted in the past five years, is where an academic and non-academic partner or institution undertake a project or begin a relationship where they exchange expertise and knowledge for their mutual benefit. In this section, I weigh up how Knowledge Exchange in particular can help to widen access to Classics in the UK. Drawing on my own experience during a six-month Knowledge Exchange Fellowship in 2014, I explore how larger non-academic institutions with considerable digital resources and their own cultural reach can be exceptionally helpful for reaching wide and new audiences.

Although 'Knowledge Exchange' is recognized by the higher education funding councils as a separate category under the broader heading of 'Impact', there is a good deal of overlap with public engagement and outreach in terms of its potential and the activities it entails. This was particularly so with the Knowledge Exchange project I took part in during the spring and summer of 2014 at the National Theatre in London. I had pitched the project to The Oxford Research Centre for the Humanities (TORCH) and, over the course of six months I provided the Archive, Learning, and Digital departments of the theatre with academic support in the run-up to and run of their production of Euripides' *Medea* (March to August 2014). In exchange, I was allowed to sit in on the rehearsals for the play and see just how an ancient Greek tragedy is produced for a modern theatre stage. The 'exchange' I was engaged in, then, was with two fairly separate groups within this institution: in basic terms I gained knowledge from the theatre practitioners in the rehearsal room, and 'gave' knowledge to the Archive, Learning, and Digital departments.

In practice, of course, the kinds of exchange of knowledge were more complex than the above outline suggests. As well as learning a huge amount in the rehearsal room (much of which I am still analyzing, writing up and benefiting from), I was sometimes called on to provide contextual information for the theatre-makers, particularly in the earlier part of the process: I provided a fact sheet about the characters and concepts in the script; there were two sessions where actors fired any and all questions they had about classical antiquity (from the brothels of Corinth to the politics of slavery during the rise of Christianity); some actors asked for advice about where to find more information about their characters in other Greek and Roman texts. In all these interactions, I was keen to present the classical world in as accessible a way as possible. Many actors had had absolutely no previous encounters with the classical world before reading the script of *Medea*. Some expressed how daunted they felt because of this. The rehearsal room too, then, was a place where I needed to be ready to provide easy access to the classical world among fiercely intelligent and knowledgeable professionals. This was both access work and access training, albeit on a relatively small and *ad hoc* scale.

The business of interacting with larger audiences came with the public engagement aspects of the Knowledge Exchange project. I wrote seven short articles on various aspects of the ancient Greek world for the educational online resource pack, and over the course of the play's run, I led five public events related to the production (two 'In Context' sessions, a Continuing Professional Development (CPD) teacher-training event and two Archive learning days for seventeen- to eighteen-year-old students). It was in this branch of the fellowship that I felt I could do two main things to widen access to Classics. First, build, together with the National Theatre, a set of resources to foreground Classics as an interdisciplinary, interesting and vital part of our theatre culture, the humanities and our national culture more generally. Second, gain access to the theatre's own existing and developing audiences, and provide ways-in for those audiences to engage with Classics themselves.

A Knowledge Exchange project with a large, established and publicly funded institution like the National Theatre had some significant advantages in terms of reaching new audiences and articulating the qualities and interest of Classics.

Increasing the size and diversity of audiences is not just good business for a large theatre (as it is for more and more Classics and Ancient History departments today), but it is also a requirement for most Arts funding bodies such as the Arts Council, the National Lottery as well as foundations such as the Esmée Fairbairn Foundation or the Peter De Haan Charitable Trust. In many ways, then, those seeking to make a subject like Classics available beyond what individual schools provide have very similar aims to larger theatres. Such consonance of aims makes for both a satisfying and productive partnership. Larger institutions such as the National Theatre will already have contacts, resources and platforms in place that allow a much wider reach than is customary for an individual academic. In addition, I learnt a huge amount about finding and communicating with new audiences from the theatre's Learning department.

That being said, locating partner institutions for Knowledge Exchange where the presence of an academic might be less familiar, or ones that might be only beginning to establish public engagement or outreach programmes, has its own benefits. As it was, my activities at the National Theatre were very much pre-determined and circumscribed by that institution's experience and practice. Furthermore, the size of the National Theatre and the various departments and other activities going on at the same time meant that some resources did not, in fact, make it to their intended audiences; for example, a hitch with other contributors to the education pack meant that it was not available during the run of *Medea* and is still not available on the theatre's website. Work with smaller institutions might give a real opportunity for innovative ways to disseminate new ideas, research areas and attractive aspects of Classics and its study, as well as sometimes being able to react more quickly than was possible at the National.

So how did this Knowledge Exchange project widen access to Classics? The production and the events and resources developed around it had audiences of different sizes. Online, inevitably, is where one can get the greatest numbers of viewers but the levels of audience engagement are relatively difficult to gauge. The short films related to *Medea* and to other recent productions of Greek tragedy at the National, 'Modern Interpretations of the Chorus' and 'Women in Ancient Greek Theatre', are still available on YouTube and have together had over 80,000 views. The online exhibition 'Greek Tragedy at the National Theatre: 1964–2014' that I curated with the guidance of the National Theatre's Digital department can still be accessed and used by schools and individuals.

More immediately rewarding, however, were the public engagement events that took place during the run of the production. During the fellowship I worked with Jane Ball, the Secondary and Further Education Programme Manager, to develop an Ancient Greek Theatre Archive Learning Day that would allow sixth-form students to come to the National Theatre and use archive resources to deepen their understanding of the production of *Medea* and of Greek tragedy more generally. The majority of students at these Archive days were Theatre Studies students from state schools. They had little or no prior knowledge about ancient Greece but, using the archive materials as a starting point, we were able to have discussions that opened up the world of classical Greece, as well as of theatre and theatre archives. A greater range of ages and backgrounds were in the audiences of the two 'In Context' sessions that I gave together with fellow classicist Dr Rosie Wyles, but these were more traditional National Theatre audience members, many of whom had seen other Greek plays and even studied Classics at school and university.

What can be truly potent in Knowledge Exchange projects (and arguably outreach and public engagement work too) is that the relationships forged in an initial project can continue to develop. In my case I have continued to work with members of the Learning department at the National and in 2015 I ran a four-week short course on ancient Greek drama, making use of the digital and physical resources of the theatre's archive. It was a fee-paying course (although bursaries were available) yet it allowed thirty participants from a surprisingly broad range of backgrounds further access to what Classics has to offer. Their professions ranged from theatre designers, lawyers, psychotherapists, translators and students, and they hailed from South Africa, Venezuela, Korea, Egypt, the United States, as well as the UK. This variety not only led to very different kinds of discussion each week but also highlighted how my prior understanding of target audiences for classical outreach were far, far too conservative. It was, without a doubt, the profile and resources of the National Theatre that allowed such a course to happen.

What I hope to have shown here is that Knowledge Exchange can be of significant help in widening access to Classics. The building of strategic relationships with institutions like the National Theatre can bear fruit in the short and long term. I have passed over the manifest personal benefits to be gained as academics from these kinds of projects, in terms of both research and also developing communication skills and becoming more aware of one's own professional qualities and the qualities of one's subject. The primary potential for Knowledge Exchange to make a difference to how Classics is seen and used by a wider community, however, is still to be found in the public engagement and outreach activities that accompany such endeavours. Knowledge Exchange may not be the ideal vehicle for widening access (and nor should be – it was not designed to do so), but it can be a substantial and helpful tool as part of other strategies.

How the impact and public engagement agenda has helped

Michael Scott

Impact and public engagement are now firmly, and without doubt, part of the UK universities agenda. This has, however, not always been the case. Pre-2013/14, while departments and universities to differing extents encouraged and supported their academics to take on (in addition to their normal university duties) public engagement work (above all within schools), and while UK classicists in particular had a strong track record of public engagement as part of the more general push to ensure the continued survival and growth of their subject, there was perceived to be little gain for the university in such efforts beyond brand recognition and a warming sense of giving back. Indeed, in some cases, taking on public engagement projects alongside academic research was counselled against in case it led to a devaluing of academic reputation.

Much of that changed post the decision to include 'impact' as 20 per cent of a department's mark in the Research Excellence Framework (REF) exercise of 2013/14. The REF is a national system to assess the quality of research within the UK's higher education institutions, and the results are linked directly to how much funding each institution subsequently receives from government. In turn 'impact' was defined as 'an effect on, change or benefit to the economy, society, culture, public policy or services, health, the environment or quality of life, beyond academia'.[16] As a result, promoting, supporting and engaging successfully with impact not only had a financial upside for universities as part of their overall REF settlement, but was also a new measure in which universities could compete for rankings and thus overall UK position. Over the same period, many research councils in the UK moved to formally demand detailed plans of impact activities as part of academic research project proposals, and indeed created calls for projects specifically geared towards impact.

It is fair to say that not many academics involved with the impact submission for REF 2013/14 remember the experience fondly. As with the introduction of any new measure, there were substantial difficulties in understanding the meaning of 'impact' as defined by REF, producing case studies that reflected sufficiently that definition, and most crucially, collecting and providing the qualitative and quantitative evidence required to prove effective impact (especially as the impact measure was introduced part way through the REF cycle). While those who undertook public engagement work in direct relation to specific academic research projects and outputs, and who did so in ways that allowed them easily to gather the necessary data (focused on demonstrating how peoples' understanding and knowledge had been changed as a direct result of contact with their specific piece of public engagement), were well versed to create an impact 'case study', those whose public engagement work was more widely spread across their discipline rather than directly related to their own specific research outputs, or who reached out to much less tangible and contactable (but often bigger) audiences, had to work harder to make their public engagement 'fit' a REF impact case study.

The build-up to REF 2013/14, the assessment of the submissions by the different REF panels and specifically the impact element of the REF have also now been studied by Lord Stern, who has produced recommendations for the next REF exercise, scheduled for 2020/21.[17] His recommendations in particular advocated a loosening of the demands for what an impact case study looks like, allowing for the inclusion of wider public engagement initiatives. And while we do not yet know how impact will be officially defined and by what criteria it needs to be measured in 2020/21 (which in itself is a problem for people doing impact/public engagement work since 2014 as they can only guess at the yard stick they will be asked to measure themselves against in 2020/21), it is likely in my view that impact will form an even bigger part of the REF exercise, and so grow further in importance for universities. That is certainly the view being taken by universities, who since 2014 have been spending a lot more time, money and effort in supporting impact projects and impact measuring by their academics in preparation for 2020/21.

How has this reorientation of the university agenda towards officially promoting and supporting impact as part of the 'role' of the university in the twenty-first century helped the provision specifically of Classics in the UK? In relation to my department of Classics at Warwick, I think the answer is a positive one. On the one hand, department members have been very successful in securing large external Arts and Humanities Research Council grants with deeply embedded public engagement and impact agendas (*e.g.* Prof Alison Cooley's Ashmolean Latin Inscriptions Project (AshLI) with its extensive public engagement provision for the public as well as specifically for schools and the recent securing of an AHRC Follow-on Funding for Impact and Engagement award).[18] And at the same time, many members of the department have felt much more supported in giving our time to regularly speak in schools across the country – both those who do not currently offer any classical teaching and those with partial and full classical offerings.

The biggest difference, though, is the way in which we have been encouraged and supported to develop our own major public engagement events and initiatives for schools, and as a result begin to build lasting networks of public engagement and support across schools in our local area. Since 2014, for example, Warwick Classics has significantly expanded its Warwick Classics Drama Festival. Built around the pre-existing tradition of the Warwick Classics undergraduates putting on a Greek tragedy/comedy each year, we have secured sufficient funding from the university in each year since 2014 to move this performance to the main stage of the Warwick Arts Centre with professional backstage support, host a public performance and crucially a schools' day. This full-day event, free to all attendees, includes a series of lectures and seminars from Warwick Classics staff about the play, its themes and the context of dramatic production in ancient Greece, alongside a performance of the play. In 2015 and 2016, this event was filled to capacity with 560+ school children from around the country, both those studying classical subjects and those not, with strong positive feedback. It is now the largest Arts and Humanities public engagement event hosted at Warwick. In 2016, we sought to expand its reach by working with one of Warwick's Outreach Schools programmes (known as IGGY) and other groups to film both the play and short 'bite-size' versions of the lectures, which are now online as part of an increasing range of school teaching resources for Classics.[19]

It is through this flagship event that we have also sought to build more permanent relationships with schools who are seeking to expand their Classics provision. One such example is the Sidney Stringer Academy in Coventry. Sidney Stringer is an inner-city non-selective academy for eleven- to eighteen-year-olds which has a rich cultural diversity; the vast majority of pupils come from a British-Asian Muslim background. The local area has a very high level of unemployment and social and economic disadvantage. A high proportion of students receive free school meals and the 16–19 Bursary Fund. The school first brought students to the Warwick Classics drama festival in 2014. Since then, we have developed the relationship between Warwick Classics and Sidney Stringer with individual talks by Warwick postgraduates and staff at Sidney Stringer alongside continued attendance at the Drama Festival, as well as supporting the Head of Classics in her work to expand the provision of Latin (and Classical Greek) in the school curriculum. I also took on the role of co-director of the Sidney Stringer Classics Hub alongside the Head of Classics at Sidney Stringer and the Head of Classics at Warwick School. This hub was successful in winning a Classics for All project grant in 2014/15 to expand the provision of Latin and Greek across the school.[20] It has also recently been successful in a second Classics for All grant to introduce GCSE Classical Greek onto the curriculum, and the hub is now looking to become a centre for teacher training to help introduce Latin at other schools in the area.

None of this would have been possible without the substantial financial support of Warwick University and its widening range of impact and public engagement funds, as well as support from IATL, the University's Institute for Advanced Teaching and Learning. In the future, we hope to harness the university's increased support for impact, public engagement and widening participation activities to achieve three major goals. The first is to make impact and public engagement (as well as widening participation/outreach), specifically targeted at supporting access to Classics in schools, an activity which undergraduates, postgraduates and staff from the department can work on together as a joint project. In this regard the department supports financially a postgraduate outreach ambassador and a series of undergraduate ambassadors who help at key public engagement events and are encouraged to contribute to wider schools' initiatives (the Warwick Classics postgraduate students, for example, developed and taught the first Warwick Sutton Trust Summer School in Classics in 2016).

The second goal is to continue to grow the range of Classics teaching resources for schools provided by Warwick Classics, not only through future Drama Festivals but also by linking to projects created out of our teaching modules (*e.g.* videos created by students in our Hellenistic world modules published on our Warwick Classics YouTube channel; our regular coin and textual criticism blogs; and the ancient Greek sacred sites database – already being used as a research database by schools – created by the Greek Religion module).[21] In addition, the university has also, thanks to its securing of Higher Education Innovation Funding from HEFCE (Higher Education Funding Council for England), been able to support the department with a major strategic impact grant to develop a new ancient global history web portal (Oiko.world), for use by the public and in schools, to bring different ancient civilizations existing around the globe in antiquity into comparison and connection with one another.

The third goal is to continue to strengthen Warwick Classics' position within the community by developing further our permanent links with local schools and supporting Classics provision in association with our neighbouring universities in the West Midlands. In 2018 and 2019, Warwick Classics will also be a partner university in the AHRC-funded national Advocating

Classics Education (ACE) project. Working with ACE, along with Classics for All, and the Warwick University Widening Participation Development Fund, we hope to be able to expand the number of Classics hubs (copying the model developed with Sidney Stringer Academy) within the West Midlands.

The example of Warwick Classics, I think, shows how much has been achieved following the introduction of the Impact agenda. It has encouraged universities to not only value but support, in terms of both digital and administrative resources and finance, a wide range of public engagement and outreach activities intended for a wider range of audiences, as well as their curation into impact narratives. And while we still do not know what Impact for REF 2020/21 will look like in detail, the spreading of Classics provision in UK schools will, I hope, continue to be well served by this new agenda.

Notes

1 These diverse aspects of 'background' highlight the crucial need to recognize the intersectional nature of an individual's identity and to consider the interaction of related systems of oppression, domination and discrimination and their impact. We can not only address one form of marginalized identity: issues relating to gender, ethnicity, sexual orientation, disability and socio-economic class cannot be observed separately or addressed in isolation but must be considered holistically. See www.ox.ac.uk/about/increasing-access for details. On the importance of intersectional outreach work, see Cullinane and Kirby (2016); Evans (2009); Lehmann (2007); Reay et al. (2005, 2009, 2010).

2 The phrase 'schools liaison' is used by some colleges and departments and at other universities as an umbrella term covering all activities with school pupils, whether from under-represented groups or not. For overviews of widening participation policy and research up to 2007, seeGreenbank (2006), Kettley (2007) and Spohrer (2015); for Classics outreach, see Lovatt (2011).

3 New Labour's Higher Education Bill (2004) sought to introduce variable tuition fees but during the parliamentary debate of the bill (2003 to 2004), there was considerable concern (across all parties and among the wider public) that the amount of debt new graduates would face could dissuade some potential students from entering higher education altogether. See Sanders and Goddard (2003); Callender and Jackson (2005, 2008). In response, New Labour proposed to institute a regulator (OFFA) to ensure that universities and colleges took steps to mitigate such dissuasion. Although some parts of the UK did not implement top-up fees (university funding is a devolved matter for Scotland, Wales and Northern Ireland), most universities and colleges in the UK are located in England and are therefore subject to monitoring and regulation by OFFA. See Department for Education and Skills (2003b, 2004a, b). Further details are available at www.offa .org.uk.

4 A copy of Oxford's own 'access agreement' with OFFA is available at www.ox.ac.uk/about /facts-and-figures/admissions-statistics/undergraduate/additional-info/access-agreement-target -categories. (Accessed 1 April 2018).

5 UNIQ is a programme of free summer schools at Oxford University aimed at students studying their first year of further education and who are based at UK state schools/colleges.

6 We have increased the number of applications from students educated in the UK state sector, and in 2016, 58 per cent of places went to applicants from state-maintained schools, up from 47.8 per cent in 2004 (although school type is a crude and sometimes misleading indicator of disadvantage); one in four UK students admitted in 2016 is from a low-income household and thus receives additional financial support in the form of an Oxford Bursary; and 12 per cent of UK

undergraduates of known ethnicity admitted to Oxford for 2015 entry were BME (not far short of the 15 per cent of UK undergraduates at other Russell Group universities but some way short of the 20 per cent of UK undergraduates across all UK universities). A comprehensive breakdown of Oxford's admissions statistics for the period 2007–2016 is available here: https://public.tableau .com/views/UoO_UG_Admissions2/Summary?%3Aembed=y&%3Adisplay_count=yes&%3Ashow Tabs=y&%3AshowVizHome=no. (Accessed 1 April 2018).

Admissions statistics for previous years are available at: www.ox.ac.uk/gazette/ statisticalinformation/#d.en.6207. (Accessed 1 April 2018).

7 The Sutton Trust was founded by Sir Peter Lampl in 1997 and is a foundation which improves social mobility in the UK through evidence-based programmes, research and policy advocacy.

8 Sutton Trust (2008, 2015).

9 McCaig et al. (2008: 2) and Riddell (2010): 75*ff.* provide a useful account of the development of *Aimhigher*.

10 More information is available at: www.ox.ac.uk/admissions/undergraduate/applying-to-oxford /teachers/link-colleges. (Accessed 1 April 2018).

11 The Education Maintenance Allowance (EMA) is a financial scheme applicable to UK students who are aged between sixteen and nineteen to continue in education. The scheme is no longer available in England (cancelled in 2010) but is still paid in Scotland, Wales and Northern Ireland.

12 The 2011 reforms demonstrate once again the Tory ideology of 'freedom' from centrally co-ordinated and funded initiatives and their policy of moving away from an interventionist, direct model of government towards indirect 'governance' through networks and a combination of public, private and philanthropic agents. See Ball and Junemann (2011); Riddell (2013) and Spohrer (2015).

13 www.wjec.co.uk/qualifications/latin/latin-gcse. (Accessed 1 April 2018).

14 See Hunt, this volume.

15 See, for example, the work of Dr Lorna Robinson, director of the Iris Project and the Iris Classics Centre, hosted at Cheney School in Oxford and supported by the Faculty of Classics to bring Latin to primary schools in the east of the city, including some of the more deprived areas such as Barton and Blackbird Leys. For further details, see http://irisproject.org.uk/index.php/literacy-through -latin. (Accessed 1 April 2018).

16 The meaning of 'impact' and its distinction from public engagement and outreach work has been much debated. Here, impact is understood not as a particular kind of activity, but as a particular which storyline of activities: an academic publication plus resulting public engagement/ outreach work links directly to the publication plus recording and measuring of the changing understanding/outlook of those members of the public who have been engaged through those activities. Taken all together, these elements make up an 'impact case study' for REF.

17 www.gov.uk/government/publications/research-excellence-framework-review. (Accessed 1 April 2018).

18 www2.warwick.ac.uk/fac/arts/classics/research/dept_projects/latininscriptions/. (Accessed 1 April 2018).

19 www2.warwick.ac.uk/fac/arts/classics/research/outreach/. (Accessed 1 April 2018).

20 http://classicsforall.org.uk/case-studies/sidney-stringer-academy-in-coventry. (Accessed 1 April 2018).

This is not the only Classics for All project Warwick Classics has been involved with in the Midlands: Warwick Classics postgraduate students and staff have also contributed to projects teaching teachers how to deliver classical subjects in the classroom in the Birmingham area (Solihull Consortium 2014).

21 www.youtube.com/channel/UCbOUT4_M3WXXKuEeIhYRYRA www2.warwick.ac.uk/fac/arts /classics/students/modules/greekreligion/database/. (Accessed 1 April 2018).

References

Aberdare, A. (2013), 'Promoting the Teaching of Classics in Schools', *Journal of Classics Teaching*, 27: 64–67.

Archer, L. (2007), 'Diversity, Equality and Higher Education: A Critical Reflection on the Ab/uses of Equity Discourse within Widening Participation', *Teaching in Higher Education*, 12 (5): 635–653.

Ball, S. and Junemann, C. (2011), 'Network Governance and Coalition Education Policy', in R. Hatcher and K. Jones (eds.), *No Country for the Young: Education from New Labour to the Coalition*, 51–68, London: Tufnell Press.

Barr, N. (2011), *Assessing the White Paper on Higher Education*, London: London School of Economics.

Beard, M. (2012), 'Saving Latin from the Tory Party', *Times Literary Supplement*, 22 June 2012. Available online: http://timesonline.typepad.com/dons_life/2012/06/saving-latin-from-the-tory -party.html. (Accessed 23 July 2017).

Bostock, J. (2014), *The Meaning of Success: Insights from Women at Cambridge*, Cambridge: CUP.

Bradford, S. and Hey, V. (2007), 'Successful Subjectivities? The Successification of Class, Ethnic and Gender Positions', *Journal of Education Policy*, 22 (6): 595–614.

Brown, P. (2013), 'Education, Opportunity and the Prospects for Social Mobility', *British Journal of Sociology of Education*, 34 (5–6): 678–700.

Brown, R. and Carasso, H. (2013), *Everything for Sale? The Marketisation of UK Higher Education*, London: Routledge.

Burke, P. (2013), 'The Right to Higher Education: Neoliberalism, Gender and Professional Mis/ recognitions', *International Studies in Sociology of Education*, 23 (2): 107–126.

Cabinet Office (2009), *New Opportunities: Fair Chances for the Future* (Policy Paper), London: Her Majesty's Government. Available online: www.gov.uk/government/uploads/system/uploads /attachment_data/file/228532/7533.pdfpdf. (Accessed 23 July 2017).

Cabinet Office (2011), *Opening Doors, Breaking Barriers: A Strategy for Social Mobility* (Policy Paper), London: Her Majesty's Government. Available online: www.gov.uk/government/uploads/system /uploads/attachment_data/file/61964/opening-doors-breaking-barriers.pdf. (Accessed 23 July 2017).

Callender, C. (2011), 'Widening Participation, Social Justice and Injustice: Part-Time Students in Higher Education in England', *International Journal of Lifelong Education*, 30 (4): 469–487.

Callender, C. and Jackson, J. (2005), 'Does the Fear of Debt Deter Students from Higher Education?', *Journal of Social Policy*, 34: 509–540.

Callender, C. and Jackson, J. (2008), 'Does the Fear of Debt Constrain Choice of University and Subject of Study?', *Studies in Higher Education*, 33: 405–429.

Cambridge School Classics Project (2009), *A Survey of Access to Latin in UK Secondary Schools*, Cambridge: CSCP. Available online: www.exams.cambridgescp.com/. (Accessed 23 July 2017).

Cambridge School Classics Project (2009), *A Statistical Report on Latin in UK Secondary Schools*, Cambridge: CSCP. Available online: www.exams.cambridgescp.com/files/. (Accessed 23 July 2017).

Cambridge School Classics Project (2012), *Changing Demands in Latin and Ancient Greek Examinations 1918 to 2012*, Cambridge: Cambridge School Classics Project (unpublished report for the DfE).

Cambridge School Classics Project (2015), *Who Is Latin for? Access to KS4 Latin Qualifications. An Investigation into the Viability of the DfE's Proposed Ancient languages GCSE subject content (April 2014)*, Cambridge: CSCP. Available online: www.exams.cambridgescp.com/files /ks4qualsresearch2015.pdf. (Accessed 23 July 2017).

Cambridge School Classics Project (2016), *Report on the DfE/CSCP Teacher Training Initiative*. Unpublished presentation at the Cambridge School Classics Project Annual Conference.

Cashmore, L. (2013), 'Expanding the Teaching of Latin', *Journal of Classics Teaching*, 28: 56.

Clague, A. (2013), 'WJEC Latin Certificates', *Journal of Classics Teaching*, 28: 72–73.

Clague, A. (2014), 'WJEC Latin Certificates: Summer 2014', *Journal of Classics Teaching*, 30: 52.

Clancy, S. (2011), 'Measuring the Social Impact of Schools Outreach', in G. Baker and A. Fisher (eds.), *Arts and Humanities Academics in Schools. Mapping the Pedagogical Interface*, 43–58. London: Continuum.

Clarke, C. (2004), Letter of instruction to Sir Martin Harris, Director for Fair Access to Higher Education, 25 October 2004. Available online: http://webarchive.nationalarchives.gov .uk/20100210151716/http://www.dcsf.gov.uk/hegateway/uploads/OFFA%20final%20guidance%20 letter%20October%202004.pdf. (Accessed 23 July 2017).

Cohen, J. and Jones, P. (2012), 'Surveying Perceptions of a Classical Education', *Journal of Classics Teaching*, 25: 6–7.

Cohen, J. and Jones, P. (2014), 'Ex Cathedra', *Ad Familiares* (Journal of the Friends of Classics), 47, London, Friends of Classics.

Cullinane, C. and Kirby, P. (2016), *Class Differences: Ethnicity and Disadvantage*, Sutton Trust. Available online: www.suttontrust.com/wp-content/uploads/2016/11/Class-differences-report_References -available-online.pdf. (Accessed 23 July 2017).

Department for Business, Innovation and Skills (2011), *Higher Education: Students at the Heart of the System* (Higher Education White Paper), London: Her Majesty's Stationery Office. Available online: www.gov.uk/government/uploads/system/uploads/attachment_data/file/31384/11-944-higher -education-students-at-heart-of-system.pdf. (Accessed 23 July 2017).

Department for Business, Innovation and Skills (2012), *Widening Participation in Higher Education*, London: Her Majesty's Stationery Office. Available online: www.dfes.gov.uk/hegateway/uploads /FResponsesHEWP.pdf. (Accessed 23 July 2017).

Department of Education and Science (1988), *Education Reform Act* (Act of Parliament), London: Her Majesty's Stationery Office. Available online: www.legislation.gov.uk/ukpga/1988/40/pdfs /ukpga_19880040_en.pdf. (Accessed 23 July 2017).

Department for Education and Skills (DfES) (2003a), *Widening Participation in Higher Education*, London: Department for Education and Skills.

Department for Education and Skills (2003b), *The Future of Higher Education* (Higher Education White Paper), Norwich: Her Majesty's Stationery Office. Available online: http://webarchive .nationalarchives.gov.uk/20040117000548/http://www.dfes.gov.uk/highereducation/hestrategy/pdfs /DfES-HigherEducation.pdf. (Accessed 23 July 2017).

Department for Education and Skills (2004a), *Higher Education Bill* (Parliamentary Bill), London: Her Majesty's Stationery Office. Available online: https://publications.parliament.uk/pa/cm200304 /cmbills/035/2004035.pdf. (Accessed 23 July 2017).

Department for Education and Skills (2004b), *Higher Education Act* (Act of Parliament), London: Her Majesty's Stationery Office. Available online: www.legislation.gov.uk/ukpga/2004/8/pdfs /ukpga_20040008_en.pdf. (Accessed 23 July 2017).

Doyle, M. and Griffin, M. (2012), 'Raised Aspirations and Attainment? A Review of the Impact of Aimhigher (2004–2011) on Widening Participation in Higher Education in England', *London Review of Education*, 10 (1): 75–88.

Evans, S. (2009), 'In a different Place: Working Class Girls and Higher Education', *Sociology*, 43: 340–355.

Finn, M. (2015), *The Gove Legacy. Education in Britain after the Coalition*, London: Palgrave Macmillan.

Francis, B. and Hutchings, M. (2017), *Chain Effects: Annual Report 2017*, Sutton Trust. Available online: www.suttontrust.com/wp-content/uploads/2017/06/Chain-Effects-2017.pdf. (Accessed 10 August 2017).

Francis, B., Hutchings M. and P. Kirby (2016), *Chain Effects: Annual Report 2016*, Sutton Trust. Available online: https://www.suttontrust.com/wp-content/uploads/2016/07/Chain-Effects_08.08.2016_With-front-cover-1.pdf. (Accessed 10 August 2017).

Goddard, C. (2013), 'What Does the Media Think of Us?', *Journal of Classics Teaching*, 28: 54–55.

Gorard, S., Smith, E., May, H., Thomas, L., Adnett, N. and Slack, K. (2010), *Review of Widening Participation Research: Addressing the Barriers to Participation in Higher Education. A report to HEFCE by the University of York*. Available online: www.ulster.ac.uk/star/resources/gorardbarriers .pdf. (Accessed 23 July 2017).

Graham, C. (2013), 'Discourses of Widening Participation in the Prospectus Documents and Websites of Six English Higher Education Institutions', *British Journal of Sociology of Education*, 34 (1): 76–93.

Greenbank, P. (2006), 'The Evolution of Government Policy on Widening Participation', *Higher Education Quarterly*, 60 (2): 141–166.

Harris, M. (2010), *What More Can Be Done to Widen Access to Highly Selective Universities?*, OFFA. Available online: https://www.offa.org.uk/wp-content/uploads/2010/05/Sir-Martin-Harris-Fair-Access-report-web-version.pdf. (Accessed 23 July 2017).

Harrison, N. (2011), 'Have the Changes Introduced by the 2004 Higher Education Act Made Higher Education Admissions in England Wider and Fairer?', *Journal of Education Policy*, 26 (3): 449–468.

Hatcher, R. and Jones, K. (2011), *No Country for the Young: Education from New Labour to the Coalition*, London: Tufnell Press.

Higher Education Funding Council for England (1998), *Widening Participation in Higher Education: Funding Proposals*, Bristol: HEFCE.

Higher Education Funding Council for England (2006), *Widening Participation: A Review*, Bristol: HEFCE. Available online: http://webarchive.nationalarchives.gov.uk/20100303162906/http://www.hefce.ac.uk/widen/aimhigh/WPfinalreviews.pdf. (Accessed 23 March 2018).

Higher Education Funding Council for England (2007), *HEFCE Strategic Plan 2006–2011*, Bristol: HEFCE. Available online: www.hefce.ac.uk/data/year/2008/HEFCE,strategic,plan,2006-11,/. (Accessed 23 March 2018).

Higher Education Funding Council for England (2008), *Guidance for Aimhigher Partnerships: Updated for the 2008–2011 Programme*, Bristol: HEFCE. Available online: www.hefce.ac.uk/pubs/hefce/2008/08_05/. (Accessed 23 March 2018).

Higher Education Funding Council for England (2014), *Outcomes of Access Agreement, Widening Participation Strategic Statement and National Scholarship Programme Monitoring for 2012–13*, Bristol: OFFA/HEFCE.

Hunt, S. (2012), 'Classics Teacher Vacancies 2010–11: Not Meeting the Demand', *Journal of Classics Teaching*, 25: 2–6.

Hunt, S. (2014), 'What Does the Media Think of Us? (part 2)', *Journal of Classics Teaching*, 29: 19–20.

Hunt, S. (2016), *Starting to Teach Latin*, London: Bloomsbury Academic.

Jones, K. (2016), *Education in Britain: 1944 to the Present*, 2nd edn, Cambridge: Polity Press.

Jones, R. and Thomas, L. (2005), 'The 2003 UK Government Higher Education White Paper: A Critical Assessment of Its Implications for the Access and Widening Participation Agenda', *Journal of Education Policy*, 20 (5): 615–630.

Kettley, N. (2007), 'The Past, Present and Future of Widening Participation Research', *British Journal of Sociology of Education*, 28 (3): 333–347.

Khan-Evans, A. and Hunt, S. (2010), '(R)evolution in Classics', *Journal of Classics Teaching*, 20: 4–7.

Kilby, M. (2014), 'Key Stage 4 Latin Initiative', *Journal of Classics Teaching*, 30: 52–63.

Laws, D. (2016), *Coalition. The Inside Story of the Conservative–Liberal Democrat Coalition Government*, London: Biteback Publishing.

Lehmann, W. (2007), '"I Just Feel Like I Don't Fit in": The Role of Habitus in University Drop-out Decisions', *Canadian Journal of Higher Education*, 37: 89–110.

Lockhart, R. (2009), 'Independent Schools and Social Mobility', *Independent Schools Council Bulletin* 25: 10–14.

Lovatt, H. (2011), 'Sitting on the Fence or Breaking Through the Hedge? Risk-Taking, Incentives and Institutional Barriers to Outreach Work Among Academics and Students', in G. Baker and A. Fisher (eds.), *Arts and Humanities Academics in Schools. Mapping the Pedagogical Interface*, 28–42, London: Continuum.

McCaig, C. (2014), 'The Retreat from Widening Participation? The National Scholarship Programme and New Access Agreements in English Higher Education', *Studies in Higher Education*, 9 June 2014. Available online: DOI: 10.1080/03075079.2014.916672. (Accessed 23 March 2018).

McCaig, C. and Adnett, N. (2009), 'English Universities, Additional Fee Income and Access Agreements: Their Impact on Widening Participation and Fair Access', *British Journal of Educational Studies*, 57: 18–36.

McCaig, C. and Bowers-Brown, T. (2007), '*Aimhigher: Achieving Social Justice?*' Paper presented at the British Educational Research Association Annual Conference, Institute of Education, University of London, 5–8 September, London. Available online: www.leeds.ac.uk/educol/documents/168534.htm. (Accessed 23 March 2018).

McCaig, C., Bowers-Brown, T., Stevens. A. and Harvey, L. (2006), *National Evaluation of Aimhigher: Survey of Higher Education Colleges and Work-Based Learning Providers*, Report to the Higher Education Funding Council for England.

McCaig, C., Stevens, A. and Bowers-Brown, T. (2008), *Does Aimhigher Work? Evidence from the National Evaluation*, Sheffield: Centre for Research and Evaluation.

Office for Fair Access (2004), *Producing Access Agreements: OFFA Guidance to Institutions*, Bristol: OFFA.

Office for Fair Access (2010), *Submission by OFFA to the Independent Review of Higher Education Funding and Student Finance*, OFFA. Available online: www.offa.org.uk/wp-content /uploads/2010/02/OFFA-Fees-Review-submission-first-call-for-evidence-January-2010-FINAL.pdf. (Accessed 23 July 2017).

Office for Fair Access (2015), *Strategic Plan 2015–2020*, OFFA. Available online: www.offa.org.uk/wp -content/uploads/2015/03/OFFA-Strategic-Plan-2015-2020.pdf. (Accessed 23 July 2017).

Office for Fair Access (2016), *Closing the Gap: Understanding the Impact of Institutional Financial Support on Student Success*, OFFA. Available online: www.offa.org.uk/wp-content/uploads/2016/11 /Closing-the-gap-understanding-the-impact-of-institutional-financial-support-on-student-success. pdf. (Accessed 23 July 2017).

Office for Fair Access and Higher Education Funding Council for England (2014), *National Strategy for Access and Student Success*, OFFA/HEFCE. Available online: www.gov.uk/government/publications /national-strategy-for-access-and-student-success. (Accessed 23 July 2017).

Passy, R., Morris, M. and Waldman, J. (2009), *Evaluation of the Impact of Aimhigher and Widening Participation Outreach Programmes on Learner Attainment and Progression*, London: NFER.

Partington, R. (2011a), 'Latin Stages a Comeback in the Classroom', *Journal of Classics Teaching*, 23: 11–12.

Partington, R. (2011b), 'The Threat to Latin Posed by Teacher Shortages', *Journal of Classics Teaching*, 23: 12–13.

Pelling, C. (2010), *Latin for Language Learners. Opening Opportunity for Primary Pupils*, London: Politeia.

Pelling, C. (2014), 'Giving the Gift of Ancient Tongues', *The Sunday Times: Education*, 9 February 2014.

Pennell, H., West, A. and Hind, A. (2005), *Evaluation of Aimhigher: Excellence Challenge Survey of Higher Education Providers*, London: DfES.

Pickering, K. (2014), 'The Classics Are on the Rise Again! Or at Least Some of Them Are!', *Journal of Classics Teaching*, 29: 17–18.

Pike, M. (2016), 'Latin in the 21st Century', *Journal of Classics Teaching*, 33: 6–7.

Purchase, G. and Orgee, A. (2014), 'Reform of Latin and Classical Greek GCE and GCSE Qualifications: Latest Information from OCR', *Journal of Classics Teaching*, 30: 51–52.

Reay, D., Crozier, G. and Clayton, J. (2009), 'Strangers in Paradise? Working-class Students in Elite Universities', *Sociology*, 43: 1103–1121.

Reay, D., Crozier, G. and Clayton, J. (2010), '"Fitting in" or "Standing out": Working-class Students in UK Higher Education', *British Educational Research Journal*, 36: 107–124.

Reay, D., David, M. and Ball, S. (2005), *Degrees of Choice. Social Class, Race and Gender in Higher Education*, Stoke-on-Trent: Trentham Books.

Riddell, R. (2010), *Aspiration, Identity and Self-Belief: Snapshots of Social Structure at Work*, Stoke-on-Trent: Trentham.

Riddell, R. (2013), 'Changing Policy Levers under the Neoliberal State: Realising Coalition Policy on Education and Social Mobility', *Journal of Education Policy*, 28 (6): 847–863.

Sanders, C. and Goddard, A. (2003), 'Rebel MPs Steadfast against Variable Fees', *Times Higher Education Supplement*, 19 December 2003.

Sandis, E. (2009), 'The Oxford Perspective on Classics Outreach', *Journal of Classics Teaching*, 16: 3–5.

Schwartz, S. (2004), *Fair Admissions to Higher Education: Recommendations for Good Practice*, Nottingham: Department for Education and Skills.

Seldon, A. and Finn, M. (2015), *The Coalition Effect. 2010–2015*, Cambridge: Cambridge University Press.

Social Mobility and Child Poverty Commission (2013), *State of the Nation 2013: Social Mobility and Child Poverty in Great Britain*, London: Her Majesty's Stationery Office.

Spohrer, K. (2011), '"Deconstructing Aspiration": UK Policy Debates and European Policy Trends', *European Educational Research Journal*, 10 (1): 53–63.

Spohrer, K. (2015), '*Opening Doors or Narrowing Opportunities? The Coalition's Approach to Widening Participation, Social Mobility and Social Justice*', in M. Finn (ed.), *The Gove Legacy. Education in Britain after the Coalition*, 101–115, London: Palgrave Macmillan.

Stephenson, D. (2014), 'WJEC Level 2 Latin: A Teacher's Viewpoint', *Journal of Classics Teaching*, 29: 45–47.

Sutton Trust (2004), *The Missing 3, 000: State School Students Under-represented at Leading Universities*, London: Sutton Trust.

Sutton Trust (2008), *Increasing Higher Education Participation amongst Disadvantaged Young People and Schools in Poor Communities*, London: Sutton Trust.

Sutton Trust (2015), *Evaluating Access*, London: Sutton Trust. Available online: www.suttontrust.com /wp-content/uploads/2015/12/Higher-Education-Access-Report-1.pdf. (Accessed 23 July 2017).

Sutton Trust (2017a), *Class Ceiling*, London: Sutton Trust. Available online: www.suttontrust.com/wp -content/uploads/2017/01/APPG-on-Social-Mobility_Report_FINAL.pdf. (Accessed 10 August 2017).

Sutton Trust (2017b), *Aspirations Polling 2017*, London: Sutton Trust. Available online: www .suttontrust.com/wp-content/uploads/2017/08/Ipsos-MORI-young-people-omnibus-survey-2017 .pdf. (Accessed 10 August 2017).

Thomas, L. (2002), 'Student Retention in Higher Education: The Role of Institutional Habitus', *Journal of Education Policy*, 17: 423–442.

Thomas, L. (2017), *Understanding a Whole Institution Approach to Widening Participation: Final Report*, OFFA. Available online: www.offa.org.uk/wp-content/uploads/2017/10/Understanding-a-whole -institution-approach-to-widening-participation-final-report-September-2017.pdf. (Accessed 14 October 2017).

Thompson, J. and Bekhradnia, B. (2011), *Higher Education: Students at the Heart of the System. An Analysis of the Higher Education White Paper*, Oxford: HEPI.

Universities UK (2005), *From the Margins to the Mainstream: Embedding Widening Participation in Higher Education*, London: Universities UK.

West, A., Hind, A., Pennell, H., Emmerson, C., Frayne, C., McNally, S. and Silva, O. (2006), *Evaluation of Aimhigher: Excellence Challenge Synthesis Report: Surveys of Opportunity Bursary Applicants and Economic Evaluation*, DfES Research Report RR709. Slough: NFER.

Wright, A. (2012), 'Fantasies of Empowerment: Mapping Neoliberal Discourse in the Coalition Government's Schools Policy', *Journal of Education Policy*, 27 (3): 279–294.

Yorke, M. and Thomas, L. (2003), 'Improving the Retention of Students from Lower Socio-economic Groups', *Journal of Higher Education Policy and Management*, 25: 63–74.

Links

'Greek Tragedy at the National Theatre 1964–2014' (online exhibition): www.nationaltheatre.org.uk /backstage/gci/greektragedy.

Modern Interpretations of Greek Chorus (YouTube video): www.youtube.com/watch?v=MlXi8LfKv -0&t=34s.

Women in Greek Theatre (YouTube video): www.youtube.com/watch?v=lM3SxO0Erq8.

CHAPTER 3
CLASSICS IN AUSTRALIA: ON SURER GROUND?
Emily Matters

Access to classical languages is about to become easier for children throughout Australia. Latin and Classical Greek have recently been added to the list of languages approved for inclusion in the national Australian Curriculum. Substantial work has been done on curriculum content for these two languages with the aim that in all parts of the country, schoolchildren and their teachers will be able to study Latin or Classical Greek if they choose to do so. The Australian Curriculum Framework for Classical Languages, with separate content for Latin and Classical Greek, was released in its final form on 19 December 2016 (*Framework for Languages* 2016).

This chapter provides an outline of the position of classical languages in Australian schools, since the federal structure of the nation was established at the beginning of the twentieth century. It describes recent developments regarding the inclusion of Latin and Classical Greek in the new Australian Curriculum, at present at secondary school level only. The possibility of expansion into the primary years is discussed, in connection with the focus on literacy that is one of the key features of the Australian Curriculum. To complete the picture of Classics in Australia as an area of growth and vitality, a description is given of the activities and events for schoolchildren and adults that take place on a regular basis in Sydney and Melbourne.

A brief historical summary

Since 1901 Australia has been governed as a federation of six states and two territories, each with autonomy over its educational structure, curricula and public examinations. The difference between systems has been, in some respects, substantial, affecting such essentials as the starting-age for primary and secondary schooling, required subjects and their content, and final-year assessment and credentials.

The story of classical languages in Australian schools since the beginning of the twentieth century reads very much like the story of Classics in British schools. In 1901, Latin was compulsory for university entrance, but this requirement was gradually dropped, faculty by faculty, until its abolition by the end of the Second World War. The effect on school enrolments was drastic: in New South Wales (NSW) the percentage of candidates presenting Latin for final school examinations dropped from 79.5 per cent in 1901 and 67.4 per cent in 1931 to 18.6 per cent in 1946 (Matters 2005, p. 41). The 1950s and 1960s saw an increased emphasis on science in the school curriculum and a strong move to comprehensive state schooling; both these developments tended to marginalize the teaching of classical languages – and indeed of modern languages too. The dropping of the Latin liturgy in the Roman Catholic Church led to its removal from the curriculum in all but a few Catholic schools by the 1970s. By 1975, Latin candidates were only 1 per cent of the total candidature for the NSW Higher School Certificate (Latin Teachers' Association 1978).

In the early 1970s, then, it looked as though Latin was doomed in Australian schools. It was no longer taught in Western Australia. In the eastern states, however, the importation from Britain of new courses such as *The Cambridge Latin Course, Ecce Romani* and *The Oxford Latin Course* stimulated a revival of Latin in tune with contemporary teaching methods. Classical Studies, as a foundation course, also enjoyed a wave of interest in the late 1970s and early 1980s, and was taken up as promising a student-centred, discovery-based, interdisciplinary course, very much in accordance with the educational trends of the time.

It is safe to say that absolute numbers for Latin stabilized in the late 1970s, in two Australian states at least (although the greatly increased numbers of students completing secondary school made the proportion of Latin students even smaller). The number of final-examination candidates, totalling about 400, has remained fairly constant in the two most populous states, NSW and Victoria, drawn almost entirely from academically selective state schools and traditional-style independent schools (about forty schools in NSW[1] and seventeen in Victoria[2] in 2015). One should add that about twenty to thirty students present Latin for the International Baccalaureate in the same two states. Comprehensive state schools and Catholic systemic schools remain Latin-free zones. In other states, there are now only three Queensland[3] schools offering Latin, three in the Australian Capital Territory[4] and one in Tasmania[5] (in which Latin is part of a pre-tertiary high schools programme offered by the University of Tasmania).

What makes NSW and Victoria different? In the former, there is a strong tradition of academically selective state schools in the greater Sydney area which dominate results in the Higher School Certificate. Despite moves to abolish or limit such schools in the 1970s and 1980s, the most prestigious of them survived and helped to stem the drift of middle-class children to private schools. In recognition of this effect, the NSW government has been increasing the number of selective schools since the 1990s. A number of these schools offer Latin and some even offer Classical Greek. In addition, the majority of traditional-style independent schools teach Latin, with a small number offering Greek as well. In Victoria, not only is the influence of traditional independent schools socially stronger than in other states, but language study for the Victorian Certificate of Education is rewarded by bonus points for university entrance. Both factors encourage the continuation of Latin as a school subject.

Classical Greek in this country has always been a subject with very small enrolments, now taught only in NSW and Victoria in some leading independent schools and a few selective state schools, mainly for boys only. In recent years, some Greek Orthodox schools have added Classical Greek to their curriculum. As the Victorian Certificate of Education does not offer a course in this subject, Victorian students sit the NSW Higher School Certificate examination in Classical Greek. Recent moves by prominent members of the Greek communities in Sydney and Melbourne to support the teaching of Classical Greek have been most welcome.

The uneven availability of Latin and Classical Greek is only one example of the many differences in educational opportunity afforded to children in different parts of Australia. All these significant differences between state systems have also caused disruptions in education for those thousands of children moving interstate each year and created powerful arguments in favour of a national curriculum. Early in the twenty-first century this idea, discussed for decades, finally became reality.

The establishment of the Australian Curriculum and the inclusion of classical languages

The educational philosophy of the Australian Curriculum was inspired by a document entitled 'The Melbourne Declaration on Educational Goals for Young Australians' (2008), the product of a meeting of the education ministers from all the states and territories with Julia Gillard, then deputy prime minister and minister for education in the federal government. The stated goals in this document were:

- Australian schooling promotes equity and excellence.

- All young Australians become successful learners, confident and creative individuals, and active and informed citizens.

Among the more specific recommendations were a strong emphasis on literacy and numeracy, increased engagement with Australian indigenous cultures and a greater awareness of Asian societies. One of the eight specified 'Learning Areas' was 'Languages', again with the qualification 'especially Asian languages'.

A National Forum on Languages was held in Sydney in October 2010, attended by about 150 delegates from all states, representing many language groups. As I was then president of the Classical Languages Teachers Association (CLTA), I attended this meeting, proving to be the only representative of classical languages there. Seated at a table of assorted delegates from different parts of the country, I found myself explaining to incredulous but unexpectedly supportive listeners that, yes, Latin and Classical Greek were still being taught in some Australian schools.

The focus of discussion for the forum was a *Draft Shape Paper: Languages for the Australian Curriculum*, issued in 2009. Largely the work of a team of linguists from South Australia, this paper drew attention to the value of language learning, with emphasis on communication and cultural links. A number of European and Asian languages were mentioned, but nothing about classical languages. Considerable attention was given to indigenous Australian languages and it was proposed that a 'framework' curriculum for indigenous languages should be created, so that any individual Australian language could be slotted in as necessary (Australian Curriculum and Assessment Reporting Authority 2009, pp. 75c and 78).

Shortly afterwards, a small delegation of Classics teachers and supporters from NSW and Victoria went to Parliament House in Canberra to press our case with Peter Garrett, then minister for education. In addition, as president of the Classical Languages Teachers Association, I prepared a submission which included a rationale for classical languages and a table correlating key phrases from the 'Melbourne Declaration' with the contribution of classical languages to these goals. The tangible result of these various approaches was the insertion of a short paragraph about classical languages in the final edition of the *Shape Paper for the Australian Curriculum: Languages* (2011):

25. *Classical languages* The study of classical languages provides learners with a key to the literature, history, thought, and culture of the ancient world. A unique feature of the study of classical languages is the opportunity to engage closely with cultures and societies that are removed in time and place from our own, and is [*sic*] a bridge between the contemporary world and the civilisations of antiquity.

Following the proposed model for indigenous languages (of which about sixty are still spoken), it was decided that there should be a Framework for Classical Languages, allowing a yet unspecified number of ancient languages to be included eventually, such as Classical Hebrew (an established course in NSW alone), Sanskrit, Classical Arabic or Classical Chinese, if demand for any of these should arise in the future.

Work began first on writing curricula for Italian and Chinese, with other modern languages following. These curricula were composed for all years 'Foundation to 10', that is, for ages five to sixteen, encouraging language teaching at all stages of primary and secondary schooling until the two final years. Eventually, in 2015, not without some controversy in Parliament, the federal government approved funding to develop a Classical Languages Framework and specific curricula for two classical languages, Latin and Classical Greek. This funding, however, covered the first four years of secondary school, Years 7 to 10 only, with no provision for primary education.

The first meeting of the 'expert panel' on classical languages was convened in Sydney at the offices of the Australian Curriculum, Assessment and Reporting Authority (ACARA) in April 2015. As well as six teachers of Latin and Greek from NSW and Victoria, the initial meetings included two representatives of Classical Hebrew and one spokesman for Sanskrit, to ensure that these subjects fitted into the definition of 'classical languages' and the broad rationale for learning them, which were the first sections of the curriculum to be composed. (As mentioned above, Classical Hebrew is already an established course in NSW; Sanskrit, though taught in at least two schools, has no official syllabus as yet.) Work then continued over a number of months on the construction of curricula for Latin and Classical Greek. The Draft Classical Languages Framework and the curriculum content in Latin and Classical Greek were released on 19 May 2016 for public consultation. These underwent several processes of review, including comment from practicing teachers, before being launched in final form in December 2016. The full text of the documents can be read on the ACARA website.[6]

Now that the Australian Curriculum for Latin and Classical Greek is finalized and made available, all schools in the country will be able to teach these subjects in Years 7 to 10. Individual schools, teachers and students will have access to a structure and content that will enable them to design a viable programme for learning Latin or Classical Greek to suit their needs, even in states where there is no provision for these subjects at present.

The provision of an Australian Curriculum does not, in itself, mandate its use throughout the country. While several states have adopted the Australian Curriculum as it is, NSW has followed the plan of creating its own syllabuses in all subjects, incorporating features of the Australian Curriculum while upholding the autonomy of the state authority (NSW Education Standards Authority). No doubt a revision of the existing Latin and Classical Greek syllabuses will take place in NSW in due course, now that the Australian Curriculum in these subjects is released. As previously mentioned, the existing NSW syllabuses in Latin and Classical Greek include the primary school years. In this state alone, therefore, there is currently official provision for Latin and Classical Greek to be taught in primary schools.

So far, there have been no moves to create an Australian Curriculum in any language subjects for the final two years of secondary school, but no doubt these will follow in time.

Primary schooling and Latin for Literacy

The Preamble to the 'Melbourne Declaration on Educational Goals for Young Australians' (2008, p. 5) stated:

> Literacy and numeracy and knowledge of key disciplines remain the cornerstone of schooling for young Australians.

The Shape of the Australian Curriculum: Languages (2011) expanded greatly on the theme of literacy acquisition through language study:

> 45. Learning languages develops overall literacy. It is in this sense 'value added', strengthening literacy-related capabilities that are transferable across languages (*e.g.* the language being learnt and the learner's first language), across domains of use (*e.g.* the academic domain and the domains of home language use), and across learning areas.

Further paragraphs (46 and 47) developed this theme in more detail, referring to the cognitive processes required in language learning and the relevance of these processes to the improvement of literacy.

The general references of the above paper can be applied much more specifically to Latin and Classical Greek in an English-speaking country such as Australia. About 60 per cent of English words are derived from Latin and Greek (Ullman 1922, p. 83). In academic or scientific contexts, the proportion of Latin and Greek derivatives is much higher. Even the most elementary lessons in Latin or Classical Greek lead to discussions of words which are usually beyond the everyday vocabulary of young learners. The expansion of English vocabulary is frequently mentioned by Classics students as a benefit they attribute to their learning of Latin or Greek. One can add the long list of Latin phrases used in English (*in memoriam, de facto, ad nauseam*) and the expressions derived from classical mythology (*Oedipus complex, Achilles' heel, Trojan Horse*) to demonstrate that a knowledge of classical languages assists in the comprehension of literary and sophisticated English texts.

It would be advantageous for Australian primary schoolchildren if the successful programmes in Latin for Literacy that have operated in the UK for a decade now, under the auspices of The Iris Project, The Latin Programme and other organizations, could stimulate similar initiatives in Australian education. While there are some primary schools with Latin programmes, these operate in isolation at present, run here and there by an enthusiastic class teacher, a volunteering parent or a university student with an interest in promoting Classics. There is, so far, no concerted approach.

Support, however, can be found. In September 2015, thanks to a grant from the Classical Association of NSW, I visited England to investigate the teaching of Latin in primary schools. I also attended the 'Classics in Communities' conference in Cambridge and heard inspiring accounts from those who were implementing such programmes, often as volunteers, in some of the most needy schools in the country. There certainly seemed to be positive effects on the literacy scores of children who participated in the Latin programmes. I was particularly impressed with the partnerships that had developed between independent schools and state schools in their vicinity, in which teachers and senior students offered lessons in Latin (and other subjects too) to younger children who would not otherwise have such an opportunity. The lessons I observed were well planned and appeared beneficial to both the senior students who had to prepare them and to the children who clearly enjoyed and learned from them.

On my return to Australia I presented a report on my findings to the Classical Association of NSW and also to a meeting of the writing team for classical languages for the Australian Curriculum. In addition, I presented the key aspects of my research at a meeting of the Classical Languages Teachers Association as the first step to convening a gathering of people who are already teaching Latin in some form in primary schools. Recent discussions with senior executive members of the NSW Education Standards Authority have had positive results, in that they were impressed by the good effect of Latin on general literacy, as demonstrated in Britain, and were more than happy to use the existing NSW primary syllabus in Latin to spearhead 'Latin for Literacy' in this state. Steps are now being taken to provide professional learning opportunities for primary school teachers to acquire some basic Latin and to embed this in their classroom practice. If these moves prove successful, I hope they will, in turn, stimulate ACARA to expand the Australian Curriculum for classical languages to include the primary years.

Lively teachers, lively students: Classical events in New South Wales and Victoria

As in many other countries, school curricula in Latin and Greek are supplemented by a range of enrichment activities run by volunteer teachers. The Teachers' Wing of the Classical Association of Victoria organizes an annual teachers' conference and regular study days for senior students (https://classicsvic.wordpress.com).

A wider range of student-centred activities is offered annually by the Classical Languages Teachers Association, based in Sydney. Boys and girls in Year 8 (age 13 – often the first year of Latin study) can attend a weekend Classics camp with a very full and varied programme. There are indoor activities (Bingo with Latin numbers, film snippets, trivia quiz), crafts, outdoor exercise (bushwalk to the 'Underworld', ancient athletics), role-play (gladiatorial school) and drama (mythology plays). This camp, held annually since 1976, is filled to capacity with about 180 children from a dozen or more schools, accompanied by their own teachers who organize and supervise the activities.

Evening functions held every year include an exciting classical quiz for Years 7 to 10 (ages 12–16) and a Latin reading competition for Year 9, with individual and choral sections, interspersed with Latin community singing. Associated with the reading competition is a competition in classically inspired art and design, with entries displayed and judged on the same evening. Senior students are offered a not-so-formal dinner, with prizes for dressing up in classical attire and a challenging group quiz. Some also take part in the international CICERO competition and share experiences with their counterparts in Britain, Europe and now other countries around the world (https://ciceroconcordia.wordpress.com/). More serious academic events sponsored by the CLTA are an all-day Latin Study Seminar for both Higher School Certificate and International Baccalaureate candidates, and an essay competition on the prescribed texts for both Latin and Classical Greek. A new initiative is a *symposion* for Higher School Certificate Classical Greek candidates, held for the first time in 2015 (Greek food, lectures and readings from Homer).

A possibly unique initiative in NSW was the establishment of a combined schools drama festival in 1982, in which schoolchildren perform plays entirely in classical languages. Held every ten years, the four festivals so far have included Greek tragedies, a dramatization of Virgil's *Aeneid* 4 and two musical shows scripted from authentic Latin and Greek texts. These have been ambitious, professionally-directed productions attracting large audiences and considerable media attention.

The Classical Association of NSW sponsors a reading competition in Latin and Greek for Years 10 and 11. To provide a meaningful day out for entrants, a programme of talks and exhibitions is organized at the University of Sydney on the days of the preliminary rounds. The Classical Association also sponsors a very successful Latin Summer School held for a week every January at the University of Sydney. This event offers courses for all levels and age groups, from beginners to advanced readers, as well as an attractive programme of general talks and social activities. All information on classical activities in NSW can be viewed on the website: http://classics.org.au/.

The teaching of classical languages in Australia is now set to move beyond the lively pockets in the most populous states to enable children all over the country to share in this rich and illuminating heritage. As the world community becomes more closely connected, many more young Australians now study and travel abroad and take part in international events and exchange programmes. There have been distinguished Australian classicists on the world scene for a long time now, and perhaps there will be even more in the future. The purpose of a classical education, however, is not primarily to produce classical specialists. My hope is that from this time forward the general population of young Australians will have a deeper appreciation of their cultural and linguistic debt to the Greek and Roman world which, in turn, will enable them to understand, share in and contribute more generously to the global community.

Notes

1   Data from NSW Education Standards Authority (formerly the NSW Board of Studies) http://www .boardofstudies.nsw.edu.au/bos_stats/.

2   Statistics for Victoria are available at file:///C:/Users/Emily/AppData/Local/Microsoft/Windows /INetCache/IE/TJ46BIK0/vce_lote_latin_16.pdf.

3   Brisbane Grammar School, Brisbane Girls' Grammar School and St Philomena School offer Latin in Queensland.

4   Canberra Grammar School, Canberra Girls' Grammar School and Dickson College teach Latin in the Australian Capital Territory.

5   St Michael's Collegiate School is the Tasmanian school.

6   http://www.australiancurriculum.edu.au/languages/framework-for-classical-languages/nature-and -purpose-of-the-framework.

References

Australian Curriculum and Assessment Reporting Authority (2009), *Draft Shape Paper: Languages for the Australian Curriculum*.

Australian Curriculum and Assessment Reporting Authority (2011), *Shape Paper for the Australian Curriculum: Languages*. Available online: https://acaraweb.blob.core.windows.net/resources/Final_-_Languages_Consultation_Report_25_November_2011.pdf. (Accessed 1 April 2018).

Australian Curriculum and Assessment Reporting Authority (2016), *Framework for Languages*. Available online: http://www.australiancurriculum.edu.au/languages/framework-for-classical-languages/nature-and-purpose-of-the-framework. (Accessed 1 April 2018).

Latin Teachers' Association (1978), *Minutes of Inaugural Meeting*, Classical Languages Teachers Association of Australia.

Matters, E. (2005), *Aeneas in the Antipodes – The Teaching of Virgil in NSW Schools from 1900 to the Start of the 21st Century, Unpublished PhD Thesis*, University of Sydney. Available online: http://hdl.handle.net/2123/716. (Accessed 1 April 2018).

Melbourne Declaration on Educational Goals for Young Australians (2008), Available online: http://www.curriculum.edu.au/verve/_resources/National_Declaration_on_the_Educational_Goals_for_Young_Australians.pdf. (Accessed 1 April 2018).

Ullman, B. (1922), 'Our Latin-English Language', *The Classical Journal* (CAMWS), 18 (2): 82–90.

CHAPTER 4

REINTRODUCING CLASSICS IN A BRAZILIAN PUBLIC SCHOOL: PROJECT *MINIMUS* IN SÃO PAULO

Paula da Cunha Corrêa

This chapter describes the background, creation, implementation, shortcomings and achievements of an experimental project called *Projeto Minimus*, developed at the University of São Paulo, Brazil, which has successfully iintroduced Latin and Greek languages, respectively, in the fourth and seventh grade curriculum (for nine- and twelve-year-old students) at a public school in 2013, after Greek and Latin had not been taught in Brazilian schools for more than fifty years.

Background

The instruction of Greek and Latin in Brazil started to decline in the 1960s, when it was declared no longer compulsory in school curricula. Since the 1970s, Greek and Latin were designated as 'dead languages' in school legislature and have gradually become restricted to religious seminaries and universities (Sobrinho 2013, pp. 39–63; Prata and Fortes 2015). In this chapter, I shall describe a programme that reintroduced Greek and Latin in a public school in São Paulo (public schools in Brazil are state or municipal schools, not private schools). It started with a group of Latin and Greek lecturers and undergraduate and postgraduate students from the University of São Paulo at the beginning of 2013, and continues to this date (a more detailed and extensive account of the project may be found in Leme et al. 2013).

In 2011, a conference on Ancient Greek Language and Civilization, held at the European Cultural Centre of Delphi, Greece,[1] and attended by fifty teachers of secondary education and postgraduate students from Brazil and Portugal, found that not a single elementary, middle or even high school in Brazil offered Classical Greek, while Latin was limited to a few religious seminaries. Inspired by the Classics charity 'Classics for All',[2] based in the UK that reintroduced Greek and Latin to state schools, we realized something similar could be done in our public schools, despite all the differences that exist between our countries, cultures and school systems.

This was not the first outreach project in Classics in Brazil, but it was the first to focus on the instruction of classical languages (for other Classics projects in Brazilian schools, see Zanirato and Sousa 2013, pp. 137–152, and Rolim de Moura and Garrafoni 2015). A series of reasons led us to this; although the number of public (state and federal) universities in the country has increased, our public elementary, middle and high school systems have been neglected by all governments for the last sixty years. The fast-growing number of students has not been accompanied by the necessary increase in the budget allocated to public schools. In consequence, the quality of education on offer in public schools has been progressively deteriorating, as the performance in university entry exams attests.

Brazil's illiteracy rate on the whole has greatly decreased in the last fifty years, but it still remains extremely high and has not improved at the expected rate: in 2014 the government estimated that 8.3 per cent of Brazilians (fifteen years old or older) were illiterate, a total of approximately 13.2 million people. According to UNESCO, 38 per cent of the illiterate Latin Americans are Brazilian, and Brazil is the eighth country in the world with the largest number of illiterate people.[3]

It is evident that the disregard concerning lower education affects directly the greater investments made in the higher levels, and our students have been arriving, year after year, less prepared for university. At our Faculty of Letters at the University of São Paulo, a first-year basic curriculum for all students, with classes in Portuguese language, linguistics, literary theory and an introduction to Classical Studies, was created in part to remedy the ever-increasing gaps in our students' high school education.

Classicists have long championed the advantages of teaching Latin and Greek in schools (DeVane 1997). Likewise, we believe that the study of Greek and Latin during the early years may favour the development of our students' native Portuguese linguistic capacities in terms of reading, vocabulary and grammar, besides aiding the acquisition of modern foreign languages and developing logic and critical thinking. In view of all this, and because the reintroduction of Classics in school curricula could also offer new job opportunities for university students, a small group of colleagues and students began a project called *Projeto Minimus* in 2013, inspired by and named after Barbara Bell's *Primary Latin Project* and *Minimus* books (Bell and Forte 1999).

Creating *Projeto Minimus*

The first thing we had to choose was the teaching materials. For Latin, it was quite simple, since Barbara Bell authorized us to translate *Minimus* (Bell and Forte 1999) in order to test the book with a class of fourth grade public school students (children between nine and ten years old). If it worked, we planned to acquire the rights and publish a Brazilian version. Luckily, the editor anticipated us in obtaining the rights and published the translation made by Fábia Alvim, one of the students who participated in the project for over a year (Bell and Forte 2015). For Greek, however, we did not find a suitable beginners' language method for small children, or even for teenagers who had no previous experience in Latin. Therefore, after examining various methods, we decided to translate and adapt the first chapters of *Athenaze* (Balme and Lawall 2011), adding texts and exercises from other ancient Greek language books. This year, since the students who will be taught Greek have already had a year of Latin, we will try to use the Brazilian translation of JACT's *Reading Greek* (*Aprendendo Grego* 2014).

From the start, the greatest difficulty was to find schools that would accept such a project. An elementary and middle public school called Escola Municipal de Ensino Fundamental Desembargador Amorim Lima, which is very close to the University of São Paulo, was suggested. To our surprise, when Latin and Greek extra-curricular classes were offered, Ana Elisa Siqueira, the school principal, asked if the entire fourth and seventh grade classes could be taught throughout the academic year, in both the mornings and afternoons, within the curriculum. Brazilian public schools, as well as most schools in the private sector, have no full-period courses. That is, schools have two shifts: one group of students has classes from 7:00 am to noon, another from 1:00 pm to 6:00 pm. Because of this, extra-curricular classes in public schools are particularly rare due to the restricted space and limited transport (school buses are not offered after regular classes). In the case of the principal's proposal, this was mainly due to the fact that this school favours inclusiveness in all aspects. Therefore, her idea was to introduce Latin in the fourth grade and Greek in the seventh grade as regular and obligatory classes for all.

Whereas the most common response from school principals nowadays is that if they were to add another language to the school curriculum, besides English and Spanish, they would prefer a modern language; the principal at Amorim Lima embraced our project with great enthusiasm. However, we were not expecting to have such a large number of students, and my colleague and I could not teach 250 children, twice a week, in the mornings and afternoons, on top of our regular activities at the university. Therefore, it was only through participation of undergraduate and postgraduate students, who were interested in teaching at school level, that we were able to accept the principal's proposal.

The first Greek and Latin classes at Amorim Lima began effectively in February 2013 (the academic year in Brazil begins in February and ends in December), after *Projeto Minimus* had been formally registered as an outreach project of the University of São Paulo. It is noteworthy that in spite of the serious financial crisis at the university, since the beginning of the project we counted on the assistance of the 'Culture and Outreach Prorectorate', and for the 2013/14 academic year we obtained from the Onassis Foundation USA six scholarships for graduate students who were teaching Greek. The support of the University of São Paulo and the Onassis Foundation USA was fundamental, but the funding has not been constant and at times we have only succeeded due to the volunteering efforts of students and colleagues.

Implementing *Projeto Minimus* at the *Escola Municipal De Ensino Fundamental Desembargador Amorim Lima*

At the beginning of the academic year, we assigned two of our students to teach each class, according to the traditional system of Brazilian elementary schools – a teacher and an assistant are usually assigned to an average class-size of thirty-five to forty children. However, we soon realized that this scheme did not work well at Amorim Lima: our student-teachers were unable to maintain discipline in class, and this affected the delivery of the courses. It was chaotic. In part, this was due to the fact that the great majority of our teachers were undergraduate and postgraduate Classics students who had no experience in teaching and, in particular, no experience in teaching children and teenagers. But the main reason was because we did not take into consideration in our planning of lessons that this was not a conventional school.

In 2003, the present school principal, with the support of the school's council, adapted the experience of 'Escola da Ponte' (Bridge School) and its educational project, created in 1976 by José Pacheco in Portugal, to the particular characteristics of the Amorim Lima school's community. Amorim Lima differs from other schools in that the students are not distributed in classes, but in small tutorial groups of five to nine students, each tutor being responsible on the whole for approximately twenty students. Physically, the school is also unusual, as most of the walls which separated the different classes were pulled down in order to create two enormous common rooms: one for students from first to fourth grade, the other for fifth to ninth graders.

Annual study programmes are organized in 'research plans' created by the school. Based on the specific subjects of regular student handbooks, these research plans present multidisciplinary activities concerning all-embracing themes that relate the different areas of study. Students sit together in their small tutorial groups, although they work on their research plans individually. Whenever the students have questions or difficulties, they first consult the others in their group, to see if anybody can solve their problem and, if not, they then call on one of the tutors that circulate from group to group in the room. Thus, the teachers' main activity is to supervise the groups and to elucidate individual problems nobody in the group is able to solve, although there are a few lecture-style classes for subjects such as Maths, Portuguese, English, and to which we now added Greek and Latin.

Students have the freedom to choose the order in which they wish to work on their study plans. When they are finished with a specific matter or project, they organize a portfolio that is handed to their tutor who then decides whether the student is ready to progress to another study plan, or not. Tutors meet with their groups every week in order to evaluate each student's progress. In this system, in which independence and responsibility are fostered, students do not have tests or exams, but are evaluated by their tutors through the work they have accomplished and are allowed to progress at their own rate.

After a few weeks, we realized we would have to adapt to the school's system in order to guarantee the project's success. At first, we had arranged the desks individually in rows, in the traditional manner, with a teacher lecturing from the front. However, we soon discovered that this did not work, and so we divided the students into their habitual tutorial study groups. In some classes, we had a teacher per tutorial group, sitting at each table with the children; in others, the students worked independently in their groups, attended by two or three teachers who moved from group to group, supervising all. Thus, because of the school's different operational system, instead of having two teachers per class, we required three or four. As a consequence, our teaching staff increased from the initial twelve at the start of 2013 to twenty teachers, in order to be able to teach 250 students twice a week, in both the morning and afternoon classes.

To our surprise and dismay, we also came to discover that even in a school that is not in the city's outskirts but that is located just beside the University of São Paulo, there are fourth and even a few seventh grade students that have difficulties in reading texts in Portuguese. Since these children are in school and have basic reading and writing skills, they are counted as literate both by our national census and by the school system. This shows how our educational deficits are even greater than governmental statistics may indicate. The school also has a larger than average number of students with special needs. This is due to the fact that many private schools do not accept students with special needs (despite the law requiring them to), and because Amorim Lima's unique system in allowing children to progress at their own rate is particularly suited to them. Furthermore, there is an influx of new immigrant students throughout the year, mainly from other bordering countries, that are fluent in Spanish, but not in Portuguese. Despite these difficulties, we obtained bursaries from the University of São Paulo for two undergraduates to develop parallel work with students that require special attention. It was evident that we were not succeeding in teaching this particular group Greek or Latin – and some, due to their greater difficulties, were frequently disruptive in class, hampering the work of other students and making teaching frustrating, even in the new small tutorial groups.

Although maintaining student discipline has always been a challenge, requiring our student-teachers to relate to children and teens necessitated that we adapt our teaching method to reflect the school's system of classes. This facilitated real progress. By the end of the first year, some fourth grade students managed to complete *Minimus* Book I, and some of the seventh grade students could read short, adapted Greek texts.

Although the project's focus has always been on language instruction, the teachers also developed extra materials that introduced the students to various aspects of classical mythology: history, politics, theatre, poetry, music, arts and architecture. Other university faculty members were also involved in the project and delivered 'special talks': narrating and discussing myths, preparing adapted Aristophanic scenes for the students to rehearse and stage, discussing problems of ancient philosophy and democracy, and presenting episodes of the Homeric poems through two Brazilian rappers.[4]

Recognition of the project's success at Amorim Lima – The culture festival on classical antiquity

Every year the school elects a world culture to celebrate during a week of festivities. In these events, under teacher supervision and orientation, students prepare exhibits, projects and plays related to the selected culture that take over the school's three floors. *Projeto Minimus* was so successful that within our first year the school board chose classical antiquity as the theme for its culture festival. Thus, for the 'Classical Antiquity Culture Festival' of 2013, all students at Amorim Lima prepared exhibitions on various aspects of the ancient world. For example, they made demonstrations of Pythagorean theorems and geometric constructions, labyrinths where they played the roles of the Minotaur, an almost life-size papier mâché wooden horse and a comic book *Odyssey*, in which the story was narrated through photos of the children acting out the different characters.

Figure 4.1 Students acting out scenes from the *Odyssey*.

Figure 4.2 Seventh graders acting out a scene from the *Odyssey* in Portuguese.

There were also displays of ancient natural textile dying processes, of a Roman school's writing utensils, of Greek democratic institutions and ancient Olympic sports. The seventh graders produced an *Antigone* in Portuguese with some help from our teachers. The morning Latin teachers organized an entertaining ten-minute 'pocket *Aeneid*' staged by the fourth graders while the afternoon Latin classes prepared a video on the history of Rome.

In addition, we organized a week of evening lectures delivered by the University of São Paulo's Classics department faculty members, and these were attended not only by the Amorim Lima students and staff but also by the students' parents and the local community. Lectures covered a range of ancient topics, from an introduction to the *Aeneid* and the foundation of Rome, Hesiod's *Theogony*,[5] the myth of Prometheus and Pandora, a discussion of these same myths in the context of Plato's *Protagoras*, to an exhibition of scenes of classical mythology in cinema.

By the end of our first year, the degree of proficiency in Latin and Greek in the classes varied from child to child, although this was the case in all other subjects at this school which respects each student's individual pace. While some only learnt a few words and simple sentences, or advanced three or four lessons in *Minimus*, others had completed all twelve chapters in *Minumus* I. Some students mastered only the Greek alphabet and basic transliteration, while others were able to translate the texts in *Athenaze*. The same range of outcomes was visible in the subsequent years of the project.

Figure 4.3 Fourth graders present ten-minute 'pocket *Aeneid*'.

Figure 4.4 A History of Rome video production.

Shortcomings and achievements

It would have been interesting to observe whether the students, after a year of Latin or Greek, revealed a greater advancement in their Portuguese language and Maths skills. Similar programmes delivered in North American schools maintained a control group that did not study Latin, and with which they could compare the students that took Latin and/or Greek classes (DeVane 1997). In the case of Amorim Lima, the principal asked us to teach all the students. Therefore, we chose not to deny lessons to any specific group for the benefit of statistical results and in consequence, we cannot assert by means of numbers that our project did in fact make a difference.

We were, however, able to evaluate the efficiency of the Latin and Greek language teaching methods used in our specific context. In this case, while *Minimus* worked very well and motivated the younger children, the majority of the seventh graders found *Athenaze* difficult and not very enthusing. There are, however, a few considerations to be made in this respect. In the first place, when students study *Athenaze* in other parts of the world, they usually have already studied some Latin, and this obviously facilitates the learning of Greek grammar. Secondly, the initial texts in *Athenaze* that describe Dikaiopolis' hard life in the country were not appealing to our urban teenagers. We have searched for Greek methods for children or teens, equivalent or similar to *Minimus*, but we still have not found anything suitable.

In 2014, Fernando Gorab Leme developed a 'research plan', similar to those used at Amorim Lima for all other subjects, that favoured a more independent study, including supplementary practical exercises for the *Minimus* Student Book (Leme 2015). The Greek teachers prepared different activities to make their lessons more attractive, introducing adapted texts from other books, such as those in JACT'S *Reading Greek* (JACT 2014).

By the end of 2013, Amorim's principal manifested the school's intent in maintaining the Latin and Greek classes as an integral part of the curriculum. In 2014, we managed to introduce elective Latin II and Greek II classes for those who wished to further their studies during regular school hours. Until 2015, we had obtained from the University of São Paulo's 'Culture and Outreach Pro-Rector' a sufficient number of bursaries to fund the teachers working on the project. However, in 2016, we were notified that our project would not be granted a single bursary from the university. For a full year the project persevered due to the relentless enthusiasm of our volunteering students. We are constantly struggling for funds to cover at least our teachers' transportation costs, and our greatest difficulty has been to secure a stable number of student bursaries for the project. Now in 2017 we have finally been granted ten bursaries, although these are only for 12 months and there is no guarantee that next year they will be renewed.

A significant benefit Project *Minimus* has brought to the Classics undergraduate and postgraduate students of the University of São Paulo was the acquisition of teaching practice. It offers our students the opportunity – unique in this country – of teaching school students Greek and Latin, through which they put into practice what they have learnt at the university and develop skills in instructing children and teenagers. When *Projeto Minimus* began in 2013, Francisco Morettin, a cinema professor at the University of São Paulo, supervised four students[6] who were interested in documenting the introduction of Greek and Latin at Amorim Lima. With grants from the University of São Paulo 'Culture and Outreach Pro-Rectorate', these students filmed Greek and Latin classes throughout 2013, including the *Culture Festival*, to produce a delightful short documentary film[7] on the school, the students and *Projeto Minimus'* first year.

Maintaining and expanding *Projeto Minimus* – A challenge

From the beginning, our main struggle has been to obtain sustainable funding for our undergraduate and postgraduate students in order to maintain the project at Amorim Lima, and to expand the project to other public and private schools (in 2017, the project is being implemented at Colégio Equipe, a private school in São Paulo, through extra-curricular Greek classes for the school's students and the local community, and at Colégio Oswald de Andrade as a seventh-grade elective). We have learned that, at least in Brazil, the acceptance of such projects depends very much on the school's principal. The children and teenagers are usually surprised when they come to know that they will study Greek and Latin, but very few have a negative reaction, and after a couple of classes most pupils love it. Before the start of the project the principal of Amorim Lima organized a large meeting with the entire school staff and all the parents for us to explain and to discuss the project and its envisaged benefits. Those were the groups we needed to convince, the parents and the school's teaching staff, as we predicted that they would embody the greatest resistance to the reintroduction of Latin and Greek in schools. Pupils may think it is fun, but teachers and parents want numbers and solid data on how this instruction may benefit children in their future studies and careers.

In 2017, *Projeto Minimus* reached its fifth year at Amorim Lima. In spite of the lack of statistical evidence, the students' continued interest in the Latin and Greek classes and the principal's firm intent on maintaining these as mandatory on the curriculum are the most reliable indications of the project's success.

We may conclude that children and teenagers nowadays, despite all the technology that surrounds their daily lives, remain interested in learning ancient languages such as Latin and Greek. With adequate teaching materials, appropriate teaching methods and the enthusiasm of teachers, one may succeed in reintroducing Classics in public and private schools, as *Projeto Minimus* has shown.

Student and staff feedback

This is the feedback from two students from Amorim Lima (Reinará and Sávio) and two of their teachers (Fernando and Marcus) who were undergraduates in 2013, and who took part of the project since the very beginning:

Reinará Práxides (Fourth-Grade Latin): ... *I found it awesome when we were told we were going to have Latin classes, because I knew that in Rome people spoke Latin ... It also helps a bit with Portuguese, to understand the origin of the words'.*

Sávio Campos (Seventh-Grade Greek): 'Greek was a great stimulus to me – I do not know if it was the same thing for you [to other students]. But for me, now I go to the libraries and look at what seemed to be impossible and what I thought I would never know, and I can say: "I know what it means!"'.

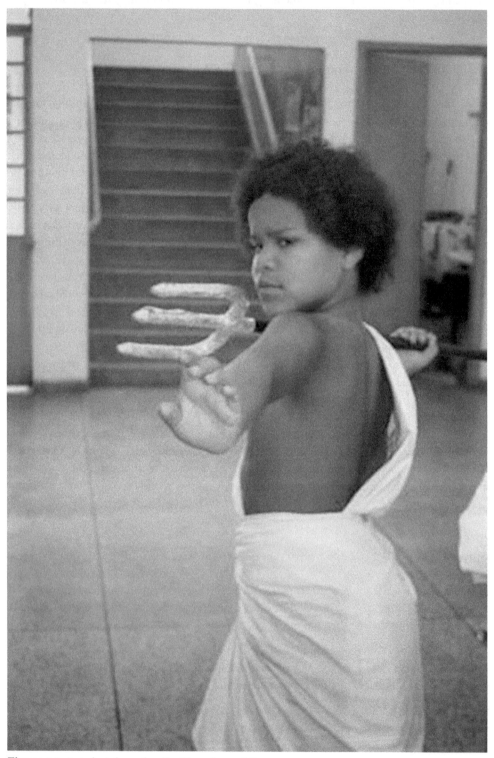

Figure 4.5 A student dressed as the Olympian god Zeus.

Fernando Gorab Leme (Classics undergraduate student, Latin language teacher from 2013 to 2015): '*It was quite difficult for me to build up any expectations regarding this project because it is so different from everything our Brazilian educational context envisages and embraces. Classics were banned from schools quite a long time ago and nowadays people tend to think that Latin and Greek aren't the most useful subjects to teach kids. Our practice, however, has shown much the contrary and it is very rewarding to see a group of children learning languages and about cultures that they would only be able to approach at the University. In my opinion we were able to succeed by presenting Latin and Greek as foreign languages rather than "dead languages", so we can help our students link them to the Portuguese language and see how learning Classics can improve one's understanding of their own tongue. The myths are also a highlight. It is fascinating to see that the kids are so fond of those stories and have modern references to most myths. The response of the students prove we are on the right path and it is very nice to know there is a place for Classics within the school curriculum and that this knowledge can be so fruitful for those who learn, no matter whether they are going to study Latin and Greek in more depth in the future or not.*'

Marcus Vinicius Martins (Classics undergraduate student, Greek language teacher at Amorim from August 2013 to the present): '*In the dialogue I establish with the kids, I think it is important to show them how much Greek we still speak without realising it, from word formation to the most diverse grammatical relations. To discover the origins of words, the manner we use them in our everyday lives, as well as the very conscience of an identity whose linguistic aspect goes back to a culture so distant in time, but that at the same time is so present, with all the cultural heritage, causes a mixture of admiration and interest in their attitudes. That is the moment one has the opportunity to provoke them into thinking about life through language.*'

Notes

1   https://www.eccd.gr/en/events/events-archive/seminars-on-ancient-greek-language-and-civilisation-17th-period/. (Accessed 22 August 2017).

2   http://www.classicsforall.org.uk. (Accessed 22 August 2017).

3   For the Brazilian census, see http://brasilemsintese.ibge.gov.br/educacao/taxa-de-analfabetismo-das-pessoas-de-15-anos-ou-mais.html. (Accessed 22 August 2017).

4   Marcos Martinho dos Santos, Alexandre P. Hasegawa, Adriane da Silva Duarte, Milena Faria, João Angelo Oliva Neto, Roberto Bolzani and André Malta Campos prepared these activities, and for the rappers Max BO and DJ Babão, hear https://soundcloud.com/raphomero. (Accessed 22 August 2017).

5   These lectures were delivered by Alexandre P. Hasegawa, Jaa Torrano, Mary Lafer, Adriano Ribeiro and Elaine Sartorelli.

6   Clara Lazarim, Mariana Moraes, Marília Mencucini and Nayara Xavier.

7   *Doc.Minimus* (2015).

References

Balme, M. and Lawall, G. (2011), *Athenaze: An Introduction to Ancient Greek. Book I*, 2nd edn, Oxford: Oxford University Press.

Bell, B. and Forte, H. (1999), *Minimus: Starting Out in Latin*, Cambridge: Cambridge University Press.

Bell, B. and Forte, H. (2015), *Minimus – Conhecendo o Latim* (livros do aluno e do professor), *trans.* F. Alvim, São Paulo: Filocalia.

DeVane, A. (1997), 'Efficiency of Latin Studies in the Information Age'. Paper submitted for PSY.702: Educational Psychology, Valdosta: Valdosta State University.

Doc.Minimus (2015), [Documentary Film]. Available online: https://youtu.be/3X7nLxpo0ug. (Accessed 22 August 2017).

Duarte, A. (2013), 'Aristófanes vai à escola', *Qorpus*, 9: 1–2. Available Online: http://qorpus.paginas. ufsc.br/como-e/edicao-n-009/aristofanes-vai-a-escola-adriane-da-silva-duarte. (Accessed 22 August 2017).

Joint Association of Classical Teachers (2014), *Aprendendo Grego*, *trans.* L. A. M. Cabral and C. Bartalotti, São Paulo: Odysseus Editora.

Leme, F. (2015), *Latim: Apostila de Exercícios*, São Paulo: Humanitas.

Leme, F., Corrêa, P., Anderson, M. and Oliveira, L. (2013), 'O Projeto *Minimus*: Latim e Grego no Ensino Fundamental', *PhaoS*, 13: 93–117.

Miguel, S. (2013), 'Resurget ex favilla', *Jornal da USP online*, 17 June, no. 1100. Available online: http:// espaber.uspnet.usp.br/jorusp/?p=30292. (Accessed 22 August 2017).

Módolo, M. and Braga, H. (2013), 'O fundamental da lingua clássica', *Língua Portuguesa*, 98: 50–51.

Prata, P. and Fortes, F. (2015), *O Latim hoje: refexões sobre cultura clássica e ensino*, Campinas: Mercado de Letras.

Rolim De Moura, A. and Garrafoni, R. (2015), 'As línguas clássicas no Ensino Fundamental: considerações a partir de uma experiência recente', in P. Prata and F. Fortes (eds.), *O Latim hoje: refexões sobre cultura clássica e ensino*, 167–204, Campinas: Mercado de Letras.

Sobrinho, J. (2013), 'O Latim no Brasil na primeira metade do século XX: entre leis, discursos e disputas, uma disciplina em permanência', *PhaoS*, 13: 39–63.

Sumares, G. (2014), '"Nova Vida para Línguas Mortas', *USP – Revista de Cultura e Extensão*, São Paulo, 11 (suppl.): 12–16.

Universidade de São Paulo (2013), *Escola de Comunicações e Artes*, São Paulo, Brasil.

Zanirato, T. and Sousa, F. (2013), 'Universidade: escola para a sociedade – um relato sobre experiências de pesquisa e extensão', *PhaoS*, 13: 137–152.

CHAPTER 5
CHANGING PRIORITIES IN CLASSICS EDUCATION IN MAINLAND EUROPE
John Bulwer

This chapter outlines the changing ways Classics is regarded across continental European countries today and shows how the subject has a firm place on the curriculum in some but is under pressure in others. In Germany, the Netherlands, Italy and France, Latin and Greek have a substantial presence in schools, although reforms are underway in France. In other countries Classics is a minority subject supported by enthusiastic teachers often in innovative ways. The European federation of Classics teachers' associations, Euroclassica, tries to bring all these countries together and to spread good practice throughout, by introducing a European curriculum and entry-level tests for Latin and Greek on a Europe-wide basis. Classics is taught in most countries as Latin and Greek language, rather than as a separate non-linguistic subject called Classical Civilisation. However, elements of civilization are now regularly included in lessons to broaden out what used to be a more rigorously grammatical pedagogic method. Examples of innovative practice from a number of countries are set out as case studies and the current curricular status of Classics is examined. As is to be expected the main sources of innovation are to be found where the place of Classics in the curriculum is more precarious, but the other countries remain vigilant about their position and consequently are conscious of the need for constant renewal and updating to make sure that pupils are recruited and retained, as Latin and Greek are nearly always optional subjects. Across Europe different attitudes are taken towards the subject but cooperation can help to provide justification for its inclusion in contemporary European education.

Introduction

Classics is *the* European subject. Educated Europeans across the whole region are more likely to have read Ovid or Virgil at school than the canon of accepted authors from another country. Goethe is read in Germany, Racine in France and Dante in Italy, but they are more likely to be read only by specialists in other countries; perhaps only Shakespeare is read in the original language as much as the classic writers of the ancient world. The study of classical civilizations provides common cultural material relevant to the whole of Europe, no matter what their language of instruction. Thus, schoolchildren across Europe are more likely to be familiar in the original with Pyramus and Thisbe than Elizabeth Bennett; with Dido and Aeneas than Jane Eyre. Greek mythology, classical architecture, Roman roads, the burial of Pompeii and Roman foods will all be common currency to young people from Portugal to Greece and from Sweden to Sicily forming part of their common cultural heritage. This can be seen from the set texts for examinations and from the different course books used for beginners' language instruction. In many countries the languages are taught as part of the national curriculum and are regarded as important elements in the education of the country; in others pressure is being put upon Latin and Greek as more demands are made on the time available for instruction. The process is familiar to many already; others are having to face up to this reality for the first time.

What is meant by 'Classics'?

In the programmes of continental European countries, the subject is generally taught as a language course: Latin, with Greek as a later option. Non-linguistic Classical Civilisation does not generally exist as a separate course, with the exception of Denmark. Denmark has had a Classical Studies programme for over a hundred years, dating from a reform which replaced the language teaching with a course for all that included the canonical texts of the Classical world in Danish. The debate in European countries between 'Latin and Greek' and 'Classical Civilisation' centres around the question of whether introducing a non-linguistic course would affect the recruitment to the language courses. It is argued that the 'easier option' in translation would inevitably replace the more difficult one and Latin and Greek as language courses would disappear. The counter-argument is that such courses open up the classical world to more students who would possibly not have encountered anything classical before and who may well be encouraged to learn the languages later as mature beginners (Hall 2015). However, the influence of the idea of Classical Civilisation on the programmes for the languages has been felt and reforms have always been in the direction of adding civilization elements to the language courses. In this chapter 'Classics' or 'Classical Studies' is used as a shorthand term to cover the different names given to the programmes in each country: *Klassieken Talen* (Classical languages), LCA (*langues et cultures de l'Antiquité*, languages and cultures of antiquity) and *Lateinunterricht* (Latin teaching), for example. Ancient History is not usually included under Classics but is a branch of the History department and is taught by historians.

Crisis and stability

It seems that a crisis in Classics teaching can provoke committed teachers into innovation and reform, although a secure place on the timetable does not always mean a lack of reform in teaching materials and methods. Perhaps Germany, Austria and the Netherlands have the highest standards of language learning and the largest proportion of pupils doing Latin and Greek in schools at the present moment, while France, traditionally a leading light in Classical Studies in Europe, is facing a reform of their lower secondary schools which will mean severe cuts to the number of hours per week for Latin and Greek teaching. Italy still teaches Latin in its upper secondary schools in most of its branches of the *liceo* (high school), although the programme remains traditional in the grammar-translation style. Greece also holds Classical Studies dear, with a concentration on ancient Greek language and literature and an emphasis on the place of Greek culture in the broader European culture. Classical Studies in both Spain and Portugal faces pressure on its place in the curriculum, which has caused some innovation and efforts to overcome the cuts. Enthusiasts keep things going in the Scandinavian countries in a limited way, but Latin and Greek can be taught to beginners in the upper secondary in Denmark where Classical Studies is also taught. Belgium, Luxembourg and Switzerland also keep a place for Classics on the timetable and manage to maintain this in the face of reform. Classics also makes an appearance in Russia, Lithuania, Croatia, Macedonia, Poland, Slovenia, the Czech Republic and Malta.

These countries are members of Euroclassica, which is the federation of all associations of teachers of classical subjects in Europe. Mainly centred on countries within the European Union (EU), it also has members beyond its borders in Switzerland, Russia and Macedonia, and in fact included countries such as Croatia and the Czech Republic before they joined the EU. Founded in 1991 it has maintained contact between its member associations for over twenty-five years and has promoted many activities and innovations in Classics which will be examined below.

Teaching methodologies

Hunt (2016: 35f) distinguishes between the different methods of teaching Latin as the grammar-translation approach, the reading approach and the communicative approach. These different approaches can be found represented in the different countries. Many use the grammar-translation approach (Germany, Italy and France for example) but have still taken account of the advantages of the reading method. The Cambridge Latin Course (CLC) is a reading course developed in the UK. It is also well known in other European countries and has been translated and adapted for use in the Netherlands. While its approach still has the power to invoke strong feelings, the style has nevertheless had an effect on many Latin language course books. The more attractive layout and less austere gradient of difficulty of course books in several European countries show the effect the CLC has had. The communicative approach (sometimes referred to as the direct method) is not adopted as a matter of policy by many practitioners in schools, but interest is being shown in it in several different projects and innovations which this chapter will discuss.

Every teacher of Latin and Greek in Europe recognizes the need for more attractive course books and for the use of modern technology in the classroom (just as every other subject taught in schools does) and that more is expected of a pupil in Latin class than some vocabulary and a thorough knowledge of grammatical terminology. In consequence the arguments between making the subject attractive to pupils to recruit and retain them and the maintenance of high linguistic standards are not over and continue to be played out in newspapers and comment columns in the press all over Europe. As Waquet (1998, 2001) shows for France, this argument is not new and while it should be borne in mind that standards were never as high in the past as is often believed, the numbers of those taking Latin or Greek in school are often much lower in most countries than they used to be. On the other hand, when final numbers of Latinists are lower, then it could be argued that overall standards have not dipped, as the quality of the continuing pupils tends to be higher. Comparisons with the past are made more complicated by the fact that many more young people are now in education than when secondary education was not available to all. It is possible that the numbers taking Latin today are actually higher than in the past but drawing from a wider range of social class and ability (this is the case in France). In addition, it is now generally accepted in all countries that Latin and Classics should be offered to all pupils irrespective of background, which was not always the case in the past. In some countries which have a selective education programme based on academic ability, Classics (in the form of Latin and Greek language) tends to stay in the institutions offering university entrance qualifications, but others with a non-selective policy are having to work out a strategy to present Classics in a new way which will appeal to pupils of all abilities, offering them subject matter which is challenging and relevant but accessible. This will inevitably mean changes in the level of difficulty demanded. 'Classics for All' is a positive policy statement but it is a new development and the way to deliver it is still being worked out. The reform in France to include some Classics in cross-curricular project work is a possible way forward but is highly controversial.

Living Latin and other projects

Among other innovations which appear to be emerging is the revival of the communicative approach: the teaching and use of Latin as a living language. Luigi Miraglia's *Accademia Vivarium Novum*[1] has been influential here and it features in the Netherlands, Russia, Spain, Germany and the United States as well as in Italy. The Finnish radio station YLE also broadcasts a weekly news bulletin in Latin: *Nuntii Latini*.[2] Freed from the association with conservative Catholicism, this seems to be a growing movement. To be seen in several countries organized by dynamic local associations of teachers are a number of competitions such as the Classical Olympiad in the Netherlands, the *Certamen Ciceronianum*[3] or the *Certamen Viterbiense della Tuscia*[4] in Italy. In addition many places organize summer schools to bring together interested pupils and to promote in-depth study of the languages at different levels together with enrichment activities such as drama and music, as can be seen in the following case studies.

Promotion of Classics requires an active and committed set of advocates. In many countries schoolteachers and university lecturers cooperate well to set up associations and think tanks to create activities and events to provide outreach to potential new recruits. It is seen as being in the mutual interest of both: the schools provide students for the universities to maintain their courses and the universities support the schools to keep their courses open too. A recent article from America (Cassuto 2016) points out how Classics as a department or as a discipline does better in this regard than some other Humanities faculties. In the following case studies of different countries this kind of cooperation can be seen in action.

Assessment

This has implications for the type of examination that is offered. Some research shows that Latin examinations have been found to be among the most demanding in comparison with other subjects, while results are still good (Coe 2006; Coe et al. 2008; Middleton 2015). This has the effect of making Latin appear to be a subject that can only be taken by those of the highest ability. There exists a real danger that those from a wider ability group are discouraged from continuing to an examination class by the difficulty of the level demanded and, as a result, receive no qualification for their efforts. Similar trends can be seen in other countries (particularly in France, where a drop in numbers between middle and upper secondary schools has been noted). Such trends provide ammunition for those in several European countries who argue that Latin is an elitist subject reserved only for those of the highest ability. However, this situation can easily be remedied by setting tests and examinations of an appropriate level for the ability range. Euroclassica has recognized the need for such an entry-level examination on a Europe-wide basis and since 2011 has been running the ELEX *Vestibulum* (European Latin Examination) for pupils who have had one year of Latin teaching. EGEX, European Greek Examination, also exists for Greek in the same form.

ELEX and EGEX

In common with modern languages, Euroclassica has established a common curriculum for Latin and Greek (The European Common Framework for Classical Languages, ECFRCL) in eight stages. The ELEX is taken after the second level (*Vestibulum*) and is designed to be taken by Latin beginners after one year of teaching. Of course across European countries this means many different things but the intention is that a class that has had the equivalent of four lessons a week of about forty-five minutes for one school year should be able to tackle this test. After a few years' experience teachers have found the best point to offer the test depending on the curriculum constraints of their own particular system. The thought of many young people from diverse backgrounds, languages and cultures all taking the same test paper at roughly the same time and receiving the same certificate for passing the examination is one which appeals to European-minded schools, parents and pupils. From small beginnings in 2011 the numbers for ELEX (Latin) have grown in 2015 to 215 schools taking part in twelve countries. The highest number of certificates awarded to successful pupils was 4,105 in 2014. Over 500 awards were made for EGEX (Greek) in 2015. The test is set in English as a working language and in the language of the country setting the test that year. It is then translated into the language of the country using it, so that it will then be available not only in all the major European languages (English, French, German, Spanish, Italian, Dutch and Swedish) but also in Russian, Macedonian and Croatian and others in future.

There is an example of a test in Appendix 1. Entry-level tests have become recognized as a necessary part of the teaching of Latin and Greek in Europe as otherwise numbers of those taking the languages tend to be underestimated. Numbers taking public examinations are reliable figures, but they can disguise the actual number beginning Latin and Greek. A certificate after one year's Latin or Greek can be a valuable motivation to recruit and retain pupils and the Europe-wide version can instil a sense of commonality between the national groups. As I have argued, Latin and Greek are true European subjects, but as can be seen in France, where figures are regularly gathered, the fall in the numbers (as will be shown below) continuing to take Latin and Greek in the *lycée* (upper secondary school) after leaving the *collège* (lower secondary school) is a cause for concern.

France

France has a long tradition of Classical Studies. The teaching of the languages (Latin and Greek) has always remained in the domain of language and literature and the teacher (*professeur de lettres classiques*) also has a timetable responsibility for the teaching of French (first language). Ancient History and Archaeology have been reserved for the curriculum area of history.

Historically there have been a large number of Latinists and a smaller but substantial number of Hellenists studying Latin and Greek languages in France's state schools. The total number of Latinists in 2016–2017 was 470,697 (Ministry of Education figures from *Coordination nationale des associations régionales des enseignants de langues anciennes* [CNARELA], the national association of Classics teachers), and the total of Hellenists in 2016–2017 was 34,478). Now this position of LCA is under threat. A reform of the curriculum in schools began in 2016. The reform will be introduced first into the *collèges* and is expected to affect the *lycées* later. The reform is seen by the teachers concerned to mean a severe cut to the hours available for Latin; the present regular timetable allocation of a certain number of hours per week will be replaced by the introduction of cross-curricular project work which will cover a number of different topics and areas and will be available for the study of the ancient world. These topics are known as EPI (*l'Enseignement Pratique Interdisciplinaire*, interdisciplinary teaching practice). It is widely felt among teachers who are members of CNARELA that this reform is unwelcome and represents a diminution of the value of the teaching of the LCA. According to Ministry of Education figures made available by CNARELA, figures show that in the first year of the reform (2016–2017) there has been a reduction of 6,000 pupils beginning Latin to just over 150,000. Greek on the other hand has maintained its usual level with over 16,000 beginners in the last year of *collège*. The opposing view of the Ministry of Education is that the subject of LCA is elitist, and as one member of the minister's cabinet puts it 'not very sexy' (he or she had evidently not read Catullus at school). This shows that the languages are regarded, by the government introducing the reform, as difficult and reserved for only the higher ability students and therefore unsuitable to be offered as an option to the whole school. These points are summarized in a debate in the French Senate on 4 May 2016.[5] CNARELA on the other hand argues that exposing pupils from socio-economically disadvantaged areas to Latin and even Greek improves their chances of success in school and therefore in society as a whole. These arguments are familiar and have been debated in many countries in recent times. This is the first time in a generation that French classicists have been faced with this type of threat to the existence of the subject.

A report for the General Inspection for National Education in 2011 gives a thorough account of the position of LCA in France before the present reform was proposed by the Ministry of Education (Klein and Soler 2011). This report highlights a shortage in the number of teachers available to teach LCA as *professeurs de lettres classiques*. The most difficult challenge has been the acknowledged drop in the numbers taking Latin and/or Greek in the *lycées*. French pupils change school at the age of about fifteen, leaving their *collège* to complete their final three years of education at the *lycée*. It is at this point that many pupils abandon Latin and Greek, although there are still nearly 5,000 pupils taking Greek at the final leaving certificate or *baccalauréat*. The teaching of LCA has had a reputation of over-concentrating on the linguistic drills of Latin in an education system which places great store on grammatical and syntactical knowledge. This is no longer a fair accusation – many changes have taken place in methodology including new course books and in the use of new technology in the classroom.

Other problems for LCA in France include the position of Maths as the subject of choice to distinguish between pupils of higher and lower ability. In addition the learning of English in the senate debate mentioned above is described as *le marqueur social*; so Latin has lost its place as being a sign of a higher education. In countries where a second language is seen as a necessary part of a general education, Latin will always be bumped down the list of languages to be learnt. The necessity of English for high-achieving French pupils is a recent phenomenon but is one perceived reason for the downgrading of the importance of LCA. However, Soler points out that there are important differences between the acquisition of a modern language as a means of communication and the teaching of LCA as a linguistic *and* cultural experience for the learner (Klein and Soler 2011). On the other hand, Cibois (2011, p. 233) argues that Latin and Classical Civilisation should be taught separately as distinct subject areas:

> la culture antique doit faire l'objet d'une apprentissage spécifique, non en latin, mais à travers des traductions ; la structure de la langue latine doit être étudiée sur le corpus des expressions latines de la langue française.
>
> (classical civilisation should be the object of a specific area of learning, not in Latin but through translations; the structure of the Latin language should be studied through the range of Latin expressions in the French language.) Author's own translation.

Although there is no separate subject at present which offers the study of ancient texts in translation, classical texts such as Ovid's *Metamorphoses* have sometimes been set as additional reading for the final *baccalauréat* examination in French language taken by all pupils in France.

On the other hand, there is a large number of dedicated and enthusiastic teachers who do a lot to promote the study of Classics in French schools. They are well organized in regional associations which combine into the joint association of French classics teachers. Each year in May and October one of the regional associations presents a short course of a few days. The *voyage scolaire* or school trip is a long-standing tradition in France and destinations in Italy and Greece remain popular. The travel agency Thalassa – Voyages, which has been in business for forty years, specializes in organizing trips for school groups to places of classical interest.

There will certainly have to be a number of changing priorities in teaching Latin and Greek in France over the next few years. It may be that the possibilities offered by the EPI to present them in innovative ways combining the learning of the languages with studies of civilization and other curriculum areas represent an opportunity to change the face of Latin and even widen access to it in relation to pupils and parents. As Klein and Soler (2011, p. 49) point out, '*Les langues et cultures de l'Antiquité sont la plus transversale des disciplines*'. Subjects that are *transversale* or cross-curricular are much in favour in this reform and this is the chance to prove the ability of Latin and Greek and Classical Studies generally to adapt to new situations and to provide relevance and interest to twenty-first-century school pupils.

Spain

Spain has a long tradition of Classics teaching, a language based on Latin and a dedicated teaching force. However, pressure has been placed on the teaching of Classics in schools after the transition to democracy in the 1980s. Teachers have responded with changes to their methods and innovative projects. Some teachers have shown some interest in the idea of spoken Latin, teaching and using Latin as one would a modern foreign language (MFL). As can be seen elsewhere, this trend is finding followers in a number of places. Another project is the *Domus Baebia* in Saguntum (modern Sagunto), near Valencia. Saguntum is famous in Roman history for the siege of Hannibal in 219 BC which triggered the Second Punic war, but it remained a Roman city for centuries and the present city has many traces of its Roman past including the structure of a Roman theatre which has a complex history of destruction and renovation over the centuries. The *Domus Baebia*, named after a local Saguntum Roman family whose members are well documented, is a local institution run by the group *Ludere et Discere* with its own building, two full-time staff and teaching resources which are devoted to the promotion of learning about Roman life. It is fully equipped with all kinds of resources for learning; school groups from both primary and secondary sectors can come and learn through practicing with reproduction didactic materials. There is a section for Roman food, for example, where pupils can prepare food in an authentically Roman way in a Roman kitchen and then eat it at the end of the session. There is even a Roman *latrina* in the kitchen (but it does not function). There are writing materials in a classroom where pupils can practise scratching on a wax tablet or writing on types of paper with pens in Roman cursive script; there is a big military section with a large collection of equipment including an impressive set of shields with which a group can form the *testudo*; there are clothes for dressing up and small groups of school students can often be seen walking around the streets nearby in *stolae* and *tunicae* with evident enjoyment. The vast range of resources has often been hand crafted by local enthusiastic teachers or sourced from various manufacturers. These objects can often be seen in the shops of museums of Roman history for sale, but here there are boxes and boxes of such things for the visiting schoolchildren to handle and to experience. Funding is inevitably precarious but local schools make good use of the facility and the project continues to flourish. International courses have been run here for teachers to train them in the use of the objects and to inspire other similar projects, including for several years the *Academia Saguntina* for pupils and their teachers from an international community, under the auspices of Euroclassica. These often take place in conjunction with the drama festivals and courses which take place regularly in the Roman theatre and the accompanying museum of ancient drama. This is a project which has kept its local funding through a commitment to bringing classical learning to a wide and inclusive public in an innovative and appealing way, and is a model which could be adapted by museums or educational projects in any European country with a Roman background. More information is available on the *Domus Baebia*[6] website.

The Netherlands

Classics, mainly in the form of the Latin and Greek languages, still has a secure place in the Netherlands on the timetable of the *gymnasium* (selective school preparing pupils for university entrance). The *gymnasium* is popular with parents who like the small scale of the schools and the traditional Dutch education it provides. Classics is also available in comprehensive schools which cater for the whole ability range as an optional subject. The secure place it maintains means on the one hand that there is less pressure on the subject from year to year as teacher timetables continue to be filled with lessons and their classrooms with pupils, but on the other hand the usual arguments over the difficulty of the languages and the elitism of the schools continue to rumble on (Crump 2008). There are rumours that reforms are on the way to the curriculum as a whole with Latin and Greek, as in France, characteristically vulnerable and under threat. The fact that classical languages are often taught in selective schools to pupils at the higher end of the ability range does not of itself make them difficult; with suitable adaptation Latin and Greek can be taught at any level but it is difficult to convince administrators and politicians of this fact. Where Latin and Greek are compulsory, problems for Classics teachers are of a different order to those where cuts to the programmes have been made; for the former there are problems of motivation for the whole student body, as some in the class are inevitably going to be more committed to the subject than others, and a continuous need to justify themselves and their place on the curriculum; for the latter there are fewer problems of motivation as the pupils are volunteers who have opted in to the class but there is always the problem of how to get them into the class in the first place. However, at the moment the Netherlands appears to many others to be in an enviable position as regards the number and quality of the candidates they can put forward. In 2016, a total of 10,119 candidates took classical languages in the final university entrance examinations (*Voorbereidend Wetenschappelijk Onderwijs* [VWO], preparatory academic education): 2,824 for Greek and 7,295 for Latin, with a 92 per cent pass rate. The VWO is the final examination for those intending to go on to university study. This figure shows an increase over the last twenty years from just over 6,000 candidates to the present total of around 10,000.[7]

This shows that the extra activities they promote are impressive in quality. The Classical Olympiad (*Klassieke Olympiaden*) takes place every year: an open competition in two categories – one for adults and another for students still at school for translation from Latin and Greek. Candidates go through several rounds before competing in the final. Readers may care to have a go in Appendix 2 at the opening of the set texts for 2016 to get an idea of how challenging the tasks are. Museum tours, drama performances, book launches, quizzes and exhibitions are all grouped together for a regular annual festival, in which the secure place of Classics in Dutch education and in their wider culture is seen.

There are also summer schools: one such school is run by the University of Amsterdam for those approaching the end of their studies in the *gymnasium* and also for university students, teachers and anyone interested in ancient literature. This is a full Classics course covering a wide variety of topics. In addition, there is *Addisco* (www.addisco.nl) which is a kind of support organization for Classics in the Netherlands, supporting former *gymnasium* students in keeping up their Latin and Greek which they may miss in their ordinary life if they do not go on to become professional classicists. Their activities include spoken Latin groups, using the communicative approach seen in other projects. In schools, however, Classics seems to be in a generally healthy state with a workforce of young and enthusiastic teachers who know that they have to motivate their pupils and consequently work hard to make their lessons approachable. As in France, school trips to places of classical interest (Rome, Pompeii, Athens and Delphi) are often organized, continuing the tradition of the Grand Tour of the eighteenth century. They encourage their pupils to make connections between the texts they study and the modern world through the reception of classical themes and myths in European literature and art. By focusing on the material and intellectual culture of Classics, Dutch teachers are exemplifying the valuable role of Classics in preparing young Dutch people for life in the twenty-first century.

Portugal – The PI project

The power of classical drama for difficult pupils in a therapeutic context has been recognized, and this can be seen in Natalie Haynes's *The Amber Fury* as a fictional example of how this can work in a special education unit in Scotland (Haynes 2014). The PI (*Pequena Infância*, Young Childhood) project puts this idea to work in Portugal. PI began as a project of *Thiasos* – the classical theatre group of Coimbra University (Rodrigues and Cação 2011). The group goes to hospitals or social care institutions and presents drama workshops on Greek mythological themes. This is literally a 'Classics in Communities' project. The target group is children and young people aged between four and eighteen years, undergoing medical treatment in hospital or who are fostered in social care away from parental custody. The drama group aims to encourage active participation and to improve human relations and behaviour patterns through drama techniques and performance (including the use of masks and a final show where all the workshops are pulled together). One of their stated aims is to understand and develop ideas of community and self-awareness. Beginning with adaptations of already existing children's texts, they began to write their own versions, going back to the original sources for inspiration and including the narrative cycles of Odysseus and Theseus as well as individual episodes such as Pandora, Midas and Narcissus. Each session is organized into three parts: first a presentation of each character together with a specific personality trait; second a reading of the myth accompanied by the use of stuffed dolls and puppets; and finally the introduction of dramatic techniques of improvisation and mimicry, getting the audience to perform and engage personally with the myth. In hospitals the children generally responded well to the workshops but continuity was a problem as the children moved on fairly rapidly. On the other hand the children and adolescents in the social institutions were present for the sessions more regularly but proved to be more challenging, and their behaviour was more difficult to control without supervision from institution staff. However, by using more drama exercises and concentrating on performance techniques genuine progress could be made, as was shown in one particular case where a boy progressed over several sessions from choosing just to be a stage property to playing the role of Odysseus. At the beginning of the project, the volunteers running the courses were Classics students from Coimbra University but later other members joined the team bringing perspectives and experiences from different departments (Rodrigues and Cação 2011). This is the kind of innovative programme moving in the entirely new direction of drama therapy that can mark out new and less traditional approaches to Classics.

At Colégio São Tomás, a school in Lisbon, a new project has been developed to teach Latin at primary level. This is generally an unusual thing to do in Europe as a whole and the teachers concerned were writing their own material without inspiration from elsewhere. However, reports indicate that, as has been found in other similar projects, younger children respond enthusiastically to something new without the considerable baggage that can accompany Latin learning in later educational contexts.

Germany

Germany continues to have a flourishing and active arrangement for teaching Latin and Greek in schools. The Classics curriculum has not been immune to criticism mounted in a similar way to other countries and German Classics teachers have responded by making the learning process more attractive with more emphasis on learning about the classical world as a whole and not concentrating only on grammatical analysis. Course books have also become more user-friendly for the pupils to learn from. Possession of the *Latinum* certificate of intermediate competence is needed for certain university courses. Language learning is taken seriously in all the German *Länder* which each have individual internal regulations and curricula, and Latin is included in the list of available foreign languages to learn at first, second or third foreign language level; a fourth language is even possible as an option. English is the most popular first foreign language to learn, and Latin comes third after French as the second. The EU recommendation in the Lisbon treaty that all European pupils in schools should learn one plus two languages (first language and two further foreign languages) is thus observed with Latin seen as opening the door to a number of modern languages based on Latin which can be learnt as necessary in later life. The general aims of Latin teaching in Germany are to connect Latin to the pupils' local area, then to Germany and Europe as a whole. The contribution of Latin to precise language competence is regarded as important, including its successful use for pupils with other first languages to learn German (Kipf 2013). With a commitment to multilingualism in Germany, it is clear Latin can play a part in developing the language skills the country needs. With a secure place on the timetable and a motivated and stable teaching force, Germany does not have the same urgent need as other countries for innovative projects and changing priorities. The *Statistisches Bundesamt* (the Federal Statistics Office) gives the figure for 2014 of about 689,000 pupils (8 per cent) who are learning Latin.[8] Teaching in individual schools is often lively and committed and many initiatives are taken up at the local level to engage pupils beyond their classroom learning: museum visits, longer trips to Italy and Greece, local festivals, readings and musical performances. The most interesting curriculum innovation of recent years has been the development of the Biberach Model. This is named after a town in Baden-Württemberg which began teaching Latin and English together at an early age in the primary school. The process of teaching the two languages (ancient and modern) together as a package has proved popular with parents and children and the model has been adopted in a number of schools. A useful summary of Latin teaching in Germany can be found in a Wikipedia article under *Lateinunterricht*.

Northern European countries

In countries further from the Mediterranean, Classics has traditionally enjoyed less of a presence in schools. Small but dedicated groups of teachers in both schools and universities have to rely on individual initiatives to support the teaching of Classics in their countries. **Denmark** was a pioneer in the introduction of classes of Classical Civilisation instead of Latin and Greek languages, but it is possible today to start the classical languages in the upper secondary school (Nedergaard 2006). Classical Studies, however, has been under pressure as a recent campaign to retain Greek at the University of Copenhagen showed; after online petitions and letters to the ministry this campaign had some success. In addition, in recent proposals to change the curriculum, the place of Classics in the state programme has been retained, to the satisfaction of teachers who campaigned effectively to the authorities. The teachers who keep Classics going are dedicated and lively and organize a summer school in Rome at the

Danish Academy for about twenty interested pupils, who study topics from antiquity and the renaissance combined with visits to archaeological sites. Competitions for pupils studying Latin and Greek cultures are also organized within the Danish Gymnasium. The position of Classics within Danish culture may be judged from the fact that the complete works of Plato have only just been translated into Danish for the first time. Having to study Plato in a French, German or English translation only (or the original Greek) would have raised an extra barrier to those wishing to access Classical texts.

Sweden is in a similar position with limits on the ability of schools to offer Latin and Greek although it is possible within the language learning sections of schools (Schough Tarandi 2006). Countries with first languages which are not widely spoken as second or third languages by others have to teach the more common second European languages (French, English, German) as a matter of necessity. Latin and Greek are inevitably going to come further down the list of languages that have to be learnt in schools.

In **Lithuania** Latin is taught in twenty-five schools to over a thousand pupils. The centre of learning is the classical gymnasium in Vilnius, established in 2015 by the initiative and effort of the Lithuanian association of classicists *Societas Classica*. This is the only such school in Lithuania where all pupils study Latin and later Greek but it is hoped that more will open. In other schools in various regions of Lithuania pupils take Latin as an optional subject. There are thirty-two teachers who have no special training but are graduates in Classical Philology from the University of Vilnius with some extra training in pedagogy (figures from *Societas Classica* and the Ministry of Education). Summer schools and competitions are organized, including the Classical Academy, run by *Societas Classica* with the cooperation of the Ministry of Education, for schools each autumn. In addition, there are competitions: one for school children and a national competition in Latin language and culture. An important part of this is a performance of a classical play staged by faculty students of the university; it is the closing event of the national competition and is attended by the participants, students, teachers and the academic community. In February 2016 they put on *Prometheus* by Aeschylus, as a musical. To reach out to the community there is a Classical Club which meets at the café La Bohème in Vilnius every month presenting an open lecture on a variety of topics to a wide general audience. In contrast the situation in **Latvia** and **Estonia** is more restricted and depends on the initiatives of individual teachers.

The same combination of summer school and competition is the basis of the innovative support given to Classical Studies in **Russia**. Each year since 2009 an *Academia Rhutenica* has been organized in Rozhdestvo, a small village between St Petersburg and Moscow. A group of nearly forty pupils from upper secondary schools attend; they are winners of an annual national competition or are already successfully studying Latin and Greek. They are offered lectures and workshops on a wide variety of topics not limited always to the classical texts but including medieval and neo-Latin. University teachers provide lectures on topics ranging from Lucian through Greek history to medieval manuscripts to Erasmus. Instruction for beginners in Greek is also provided. There is a wide range of activities and there are moments of relaxation included in the day which are related to the study of classical themes (Latin Scrabble, quizzes, other games, dancing and songs). Every day there is a session of spoken Latin called *Schola Latina* lasting an hour; this is conducted according to the methodology of the *Accademia Vivarium Novum*, with teachers who have learned through the living Latin method. This is another example of living or spoken Latin where Latin is used as a living language for learning and also as a means of expression. We see other examples of this rising phenomenon in the Netherlands, Spain and Italy. The organizers of this venture are also active in Euroclassica thus continuing the project of bringing Russia back into the fold of European classics after many years of isolation. The difficulties of maintaining Classics in the countries of Eastern Europe under communism are detailed at length in *Classics and Communism* (Karsai et al. 2013).

Central and Southern Europe

In some countries such as **Austria**, Classics continues to have a secure place in the school programme and so the need for innovation is less strong. Projects such as Latin in the primary school or non-linguistic courses in Classical Civilisation do not need to be introduced. There are school trips to Italy (Rome, Venice and Florence) with visits to the classical and renaissance sites to complete an education at the age of seventeen or eighteen. Museums (Kunsthistorisches Museum and Albertina museum in Vienna) and classical sites (Carnuntum, Aguntum, Magdalensberg) are valuable resources for first contact with art and archaeology. Work continues to develop new resources and teaching material including new technologies and a new Latin dictionary for schools. The teachers' association *Sodalitas* arranges courses and updates on innovations in pedagogy through their newsletter *Circulare*. More information can be found on their extensive website.[9]

In **Italy** the position of Latin is established in the programmes of the *liceo classico* (upper secondary with Latin and Greek), *liceo linguistico* (upper secondary with a concentration on modern languages) and *liceo scientifico* (upper secondary with a concentration on sciences). All pupils take Italian language, Maths and other core subjects. This has continued even after the latest reforms to the national educational programme (*Riforma Gelmini* 2010). A recent controversy has surrounded the form of the final examination which has traditionally consisted of an unseen translation from a classical author. Proposals have been to make the final examination (the *Maturità*) less of a purely language test and more of a test of thinking about classical culture (Riva 2016) and this has been the subject of some debate and controversy. The proposal of Maurizio Bettini is to set an examination paper that would ask the candidate to put the text into context and give responses to specific comprehension questions. The arguments, therefore, about the relation between the teaching of the ancient language and the wider non-linguistic aspects of Classical Studies have reached Italy, though without yet going down the full Classical Civilisation route of studying the Greek and Latin texts in translation. There are some signs, however, that teaching methods are being questioned, and that a move towards project work using digital technologies (in some ways similar to Classical Civilisation) is being tried. Traditionally Latin has been regarded as a grammatical study in Italian schools and the *professore di latino* was not concerned with matters that were strictly the preserve of the history or the art department, but with the language. In common with other countries Italy has found that a traditional linguistic approach of pure *grammaticalismo* is not enough to retain the numbers of students opting to take the final exam; 6 per cent of students opt to take the *liceo classico* option, a figure seen as very low in Italy but which other countries might regard differently (Riva 2016). The classical tradition in Italy is, however, so strong that Latin is simply accepted as having a place in the school curriculum, and a controversy over the form of the final examination is not the worst problem to have.

Best known, however, of innovative projects in Italy is the *Accademia Vivarium Novum* run by Luigi Miraglia.[10] Using direct methods of language learning based on Ørberg's *Lingua Latina per se Illustrata*, this organization runs short courses in spoken Latin in Italy. It is influential with other similar projects and appears to be popular with students. There are other pockets of living Latin found in other countries and this phenomenon of acquiring the ability to use Latin as any other modern language, in a humanistic context, is something to be noted.

Switzerland also has a multilingual policy, with the individual cantons having their own structure, with French, German and Italian as national languages, and English as the most used international language. Latin and Greek are difficult to situate in the mainstream curriculum. Countries which by necessity have to use several languages are often open to the prospect of including Latin and Greek in their programmes. It is felt that they offer the possibility of adding more languages as needed based on the foundations that the ancient languages provide. However, the programme of the individual pupil can run the risk of becoming overcrowded. Innovation can be found in the theatrical group GTA (*Groupe de Theatre Antique* [Ancient Theatre Group] at the University of Neuchâtel) which adapts and performs its own versions of ancient drama, both Greek and Latin, and in the archaeological museums which offer educational programmes. The *Antikenmuseum* in Basel offers hands-on workshops on sculpture, Roman life and even one on the influence of the classical world on the Harry Potter books; Lausanne, in the Roman museum at Vidy also offers school workshops on archaeology and inscriptions, including one on how to investigate a Roman crime discovered in an archaeological find; the *Laténium*, the archaeological museum devoted to the Swiss site at La Téne, and the site of *Augusta Raurica* at Augst play their part in establishing the Swiss national story from its earliest ancestors for its young people. An event to promote Latin in today's society takes place every two years at Brugg: the *Lateintag*.[11] This day-long festival consists of dramatic and musical presentations, courses on Latin in films and new technology, historical talks, and topics of local interest. Again an enthusiastic and dedicated team of teachers from school and university are putting on an outreach event to promote Latin and recruit young people to the courses on offer.

Countries which may be overlooked in thinking about Classics are those smaller ones such as **Malta** with a rich classical tradition whose history places it firmly in the ancient Mediterranean world and where interest persists in the teaching of Latin and Greek at school and university level. Malta has three centres of secondary education and a private school, which prepare about eighty pupils in Classical subjects (Latin, Greek and Classical Culture) for final examinations. The University of Malta has some Classics undergraduates and runs teacher training. **Croatia** also has a tradition of local neo-Latin writers and active teachers who promote this in summer schools. Under Euroclassica the *Academia Ragusina* has taken place in 2009 and 2011 at Dubrovnik with a programme for students from all over Europe designed to demonstrate the ways of studying Classics in the region. A small percentage of pupils (around seventy) take a final examination in Latin mainly in the classical gymnasia and another forty take Greek. In **Bosnia and Hercegovina** they have a system with no final state examinations. There is only one Classical Gymnasium in Visoko, near Sarajevo, with up to thirty students per year taking the final examinations and Latin is obligatory for all of them. Greek is optional.

Greece of course has always taught classical subjects in their schools but nearly always in Greek language with scarcely any Latin. In a recent review it was pointed out that the book in question (Cicero's *de Re Publica*) had never before received a complete and fully annotated translation into Greek. Many classic Latin texts still remain untranslated today. The concentration on Greek texts and culture means that the ancient form of the language is still taught in Greek lower and upper secondary schools today to all pupils. Discussion of the form this teaching should take is beginning to emerge with reforms being proposed. There have been calls for the complete abolition of Classical Greek but other proposals put forward the idea of widening the programme to include cultural and contextual questions and the teaching of the ancient texts in modern Greek translation, thus opening up the argument between language and civilization studies we have seen elsewhere. Certainly the programme of Classical Greek language in schools has not changed much recently and some see a degree of curriculum redevelopment as desirable. Others maintain that the programme should not be substantially altered. In addition, problems with teacher recruitment, the prevalence of private lessons given after school and the methodology of the teaching of Modern Greek are mentioned. The relationship between the Modern Greek language and its ancient original form is long and complex and has had political implications in the past. To free up the modern language from its ancient roots is seen by some as a progressive step in the establishment of the modern Greek state. Others see some knowledge of the ancient form of the language essential to an understanding of the modern form. The pride of Greece in its ancestors, however, ensures that the status of the ancient Greeks maintains a position of strength in their consciousness (*Kathimerini* 2016). The readiness of the Greek people to promote their culture is shown by the organization of the summer school *Academia Homerica* which has been run annually on the island of Chios since 1997 for international students to study Homer in an authentic setting. There are also introductory sessions to modern Greek language and culture.

Belgium

Belgium is a country where it is essential for pupils in school to learn languages. Already officially a bilingual country (French/Flemish, with a German-speaking area too) other modern languages are also important, particularly English. Latin and Greek have been seen as a way into promoting language awareness, so that new languages can be added to those learnt at school later if necessary. Teachers believe that a firm base of Latin will mean that Italian, Spanish or Portuguese can be acquired later. Pressure has been put on the ability of some schools to form classes particularly for Greek where numbers are lower and pupils have to combine between schools or groups to keep the classes viable. The disadvantage of a fixed curriculum with Latin and Greek as options is that there may be less room for flexibility to improvise and offer courses off timetable as can happen in other countries, although this is changing with greater autonomy granted to some schools. A project in which Belgium played a leading part is the Classics and ICT Resource Course for Europe (CIRCE) project.[12] This concerned the use of ICT and new technologies in Classics teaching on a European level, and had a valuable input into the training of teachers of Latin and Greek from all European countries running courses at a time when digital technologies were considered innovative. The Flemish Ministry of Education supported the project from the beginning and now hosts the website which provides resources, lesson plans and links; it is available in English, French,

German and Dutch. Both communities of Belgium, together with **Luxembourg**, are strong defenders of the position of classical languages on the curriculum for every school, and show excellent support and cooperation between schools and universities in strong local classical associations.

Erasmus+ projects

A place where Classics can play an innovative role in interschool projects is through the Erasmus+ scheme (formerly Comenius Projects). This EU programme seeks to link schools in different countries to work on a common theme or project. It can involve staff or pupils and can lead to contacts via online methods or visits to different schools in new countries. An Erasmus+ project is a major undertaking and is a lot of work. However, it can involve multiple areas where classicists are strong: languages (ancient and modern), ICT, organizing trips to Europe and the European dimension of education. In addition it is a way of raising the profile of Latin and Classics in a whole school activity. Latin is regarded as a linking topic in many European countries and helps to emphasize the European dimension. Common links can be found in language, literature, history, art and architecture, and many other areas depending on the locality. It is not always necessary to have Latin on curriculum in the partner schools, as the Erasmus+ topic can be promoted as a special project. Such a project could be a motivation to promote the practical use of MFL in schools and to link them to Latin. Examples of the way this has been put into practice are available on the Erasmus+ website.

European course books and resources

Where Latin and Greek are taught as support for the pupils' first language learning it is important that the course book is written in the first language. This is normally the case and where there are a high number of pupils then publishers will be willing to issue a number of different course books. In a small country with small numbers the teachers may look for Latin or Greek resources written in a second language. Euroclassica has issued *European Symbols* (Glatz and Thiel 2015) as an attempt at a European textbook. It consists of a number of chapters from different European countries taking a text in Latin (or Greek) about a foundational or representative aspect of that country (*Magna Carta* for the UK, William Tell for Switzerland, the Lithuanian Parthenon). Lavishly illustrated and with introductions and reading help for the Latin texts in English, this makes a true European resource for intermediate readers and provides fascinating insights into the individual cultures of European countries.

Imperium by Julian Morgan is a Latin course book in three parts based on the life of Hadrian (Morgan 2013).[13] It is fully supported by online and digital resources and can be taught in a paperless classroom. Its European credentials are that it is available in French and German, as well as in English. It is ideal for multilingual schools where Latin classes may take place in different language sections in their own language, but giving the possibility for combining classes at a later stage where all pupils will have covered exactly the same lessons.

Teachers gain enormously from formal and informal links with fellow professionals in different countries, and it is extremely good practice to compare one's own teaching with that of a similar colleague working in another system. The publications of the teachers' associations are a valuable resource here, such as for Germany *Forum Classicum*[14] and for Austria the *Circulare* of *Sodalitas*. The Journal of Classics Teaching, a journal of Classics education pedagogy and practice in English, is freely available through Cambridge University Press.[15]

Conclusion

It is not possible to discern a single trend in European Classics teaching. While it is true to say that all countries recognize the need for new teaching methods and the use of new technology has been embraced everywhere, different challenges and problems arise in different countries. Classics is still strong in many countries but there is always the possibility that a change in politics will begin to question the place of Classics on the timetable, as is the case in France. Others (Germany and the Netherlands) can provide examples of strength and depth and show how to maintain this position; Italy and Greece have the numbers but may look elsewhere for inspiration in innovative teaching. Overall the diverse countries of Europe coming from many linguistic and cultural backgrounds and traditions face many of the same problems (political opposition, accusations of elitism and irrelevance), but they deploy many of the same arguments in response. Cooperation between professionals from different traditions can provide ongoing support and suggestions for innovation. Within Europe the aims and objectives of Classics teaching are similar and ultimately deepen young people's appreciation of the origins of European languages and cultures. Whatever their individual backgrounds and abilities, the classical world is part of their culture. The world they have inherited is fundamentally based on antiquity and they all need to understand where they came from, and what ideas they have grown up with so they can question them, and make their own informed decisions about what they are going to make of their future.

Acknowledgements

I should like to thank all the colleagues in many different countries who provided me with the information on the changing priorities and innovative projects being undertaken by their associations. The continuing tradition of Classical Studies in Europe depends on their dedication. I am grateful to Sofia Carvalho, Elisabete Cação and Ana Seiça Carvalho (Universidade de Coimbra – Centro de Estudos Clássicos e Humanísticos) for information on the PI project. The following colleagues were also very helpful in the preparation of this chapter: Jet van Gelder, Jadranka Bagarić, Horatio Vella, Rasmus Gottschalck, Margarita Kalogridou, Elena Ermolaeva, Nijolė Juchnevičienė, Bärbel Flaig, Hans Joachim Glücklich, Christine Haller and Alfred Reitermayer.

Appendix 1

This test for ELEX consists of a text on a mythological story; questions are selected from the original forty questions. The original was Spanish.

DE IASONE ET MEDEA (Adaptation from Cultura Clásica ed. Editex)

This story tells what happens when love is faced with social prejudices and revenge.

El relato muestra los problemas del amor ante las conveniencias o los prejuicios sociales y verganza.

Medea ex Iasone duos filios procreavit; summa concordia Corinthi vitam agebant. Multi tamen in urbe Medeam non amabant, quod venefica erat. Iasoni Creon, Corinthius rex Creusam, filiam suam minorem, uxorem dedit et exsilium Medeae decrevit. Ea, postquam tantam contumeliam vidit, coronam venenatam auream fecit, Creusaeque donum dedit. Accepit laeta coronam minibus Creusa et subito ardere coepit. Tunc Medea natos suos interfecit et Corintho Athenas venit.

QUESTIONS/CUESTIONES

A. COMPREHENSION A. COMPRENSIÓN

1. Who gave birth to two children of Iason?
1. Quien dió a luz dos hijos de Jasón?

    a. Medea Medea   c. Corinth Corinto
    b. Creusa Creusa   d. Creusa's daughter la hija de Creusa

2. How was Jason´s and Medea´s family life?
2. Cómo era la vida de la familia de Jasón y Medea?

    a. very peaceful muy pacífica   c. not peaceful at all nada pacífica
    b. peaceful pacífica   d. quite peaceful bastante pacífica

B. GRAMMAR B. GRAMÁTICA

13. Which tense is the verb agebant?
13. En qué tiempo está la forma verbal agebant.

    a. Imperfect Pretérito Imperfecto   c. Perfect Perfecto
    b. Future Futuro   d. Present Presente

14. Identify the subject of this sentence.
14. Identifica el Sujeto de la siguiente frase:

Medea ex Iasone duos filios procreavit.

    a. ex   d. procreavit
    b. Medea   e. Iasone
    c. filios   f. duos

C. GENERAL KNOWLEDGE C. CONOCIMIENTOS GENERALES

22. What is urbs? 22. Cual es la el significado de la palabra Latina urbs?

a. people gente

c. queen reina

b. town ciudad

d. sky cielo

24. The triclinium in a Roman house was ….
24. El triclinium de una casa romana era …..

a. the dining room el comedor

c. the bathroom el baño

b. the kitchen la cocina

d. the garden el jardín

The Classical Greek test (EGEX) attracts a smaller number of entries, but follows a similar pattern. Here is a sample test in English and French with some selected questions. Grammatical questions are also included.

The Second Labour of Hercules/Le Deuxième Travail d'Héraclès

Εὐρυσθεὺς ἐκέλευσεν Ἡρακλέα τὴν Λερναίαν ὕδραν φονεῦσαι· αὕτη δὲ τὴν χώραν διέφθειρεν. εἶχε δὲ ἡ ὕδρα κεφαλὰς ἐννέα, τὰς μὲν ὀκτὼ θνητάς, τὴν δὲ μέσην ἀθάνατον. (…) τῷ ῥοπάλῳ δὲ τὰς κεφαλὰς κόπτων οὐδὲν ἀνύειν ἐδύνατο· μιᾶς γὰρ κοπτομένης κεφαλῆς δύο ἀνεφύοντο. συνηγωνίζετο δὲ καρκίνος τῇ ὕδρᾳ δεινός, δάκνων τὸν πόδα. διὸ τοῦτον ἐπεκαλέσατο καὶ αὐτὸς τὸν Ἰόλαον. Εὐρυσθεὺς δὲ οὐ κατερίθμησε τοῦτον τὸν ἄθλον ἐν τοῖς ἄθλοις· οὐ γὰρ μόνος ἀλλὰ καὶ μετὰ Ἰολάου τὴν ὕδραν ἐφόνευσεν.

(Adaptation of Pseud.–Apollod. *Bibl. Myth.* 2.77.1–80.5)

27. How many helpers did the hydra have?
27. Combien d'aides l'hydre eut-elle ?

a. 10

c. 2

b. 8

d. 1

28. Whom did Hercules call in as a helper?
28. Qui Héraclès appela-t-il à l'aide ?

a. the hydra a. l'hydre

c. Iolaos c. Iolaos

b. the crab b. le crabe

d. Eurystheus d. Eurysthée

30. Why did Eurystheus not reckon slaying Lernaean Hydra as the labour of Hercules?
30. Pourquoi Eurysthée n'a-t-il pas compté le meurtre de l'hydre comme un des travaux d'Héraclès ?

a. Because Hercules did not kill the hydra.
a. Parce qu'Héraclès n'a pas tué l'hydre.
b. Because Eurystheus was afraid of Hera.
b. Parce qu'Eurysthée avait peur d'Héra.
c. Because Eurystheus was afraid of Cerberus.
c. Parce qu'Eurysthée avait peur de Cerbère.
d. Because Eurystheus said that Iolaos had helped Hercules.
d. Parce qu'Eurysthée dit qu'Iolaos avait aidé Héraclès.

Appendix 2

Classical Olympiad (the Netherlands)

School Students:

> Sumat igitur ante omnia parentis erga discipulos suos animum, ac succedere se in eorum locum, a quibus sibi liberi tradantur, existimet. Ipse nec habeat vitia nec ferat. Non austeritas eius tristis, non dissoluta sit comitas, ne inde odium, hinc contemptus oriatur. Plurimus ei de honesto ac bono sermo sit: nam quo saepius monuerit, hoc rarius castigabit; minime iracundus, nec tamen eorum quae emendanda erunt dissimulator, simplex in docendo, patiens laboris, assiduus potius quam immodicus.

(Quintilianus, *De Institutione Oratoria* 2.2 1–8)

For adults the text is also challenging:

> Liber itaque Iovis fuit filius, regis scilicet Cretici. Hic cum fuisset adultera matre progenitus, nutriebatur apud patrem studiosius quam decebat. Uxor Iovis, cui Iunoni fuit nomen, novercalis animi furore commota ad necem infantis omnifariam parabat insidias. Proficiscens peregre pater, quia indignationes tacitas sciebat uxoris
>
> ne quid ab irata muliere dolo fieret, idoneis sicut sibi videbatur custodibus tutelam credidit filii.

(Firmicus Maternus, *De errore profanarum religionum* 6.1 1–3)

Both of these unseen texts for translation continue for many more lines.

The final of the Classics Olympiad takes place in a Week of Classics (www.weekvandeklassieken.nl) during which activities take place in different centers in the Netherlands and particularly in Leiden.

Notes

1   vivariumnovum.net/en/summer-school. (Accessed 4 August 2017).

2   areena.yle.fi. (Accessed 4 August 2017).

3   www.certamenciceronianum.it. (Accessed 4 August 2017).

4   www.liceoburatti.gov.it/pg_certamen-viterbiense-_8.htm. (Accessed 4 August 2017).

5   www.senat.fr/compte-rendu-commissions/20160502/cult.html. (Accessed 4 August 2017).

6   www.aytosagunto.es/es-es/ayuntamiento/servicios/CulturaEducacion/educacion/Paginas/domus-baebia.aspx. (Accessed 4 August 2017).

7   www.stilus.nl/index-groot.htm See archief Klassieken (Accessed 4 August 2017).

8   www.destatis.de/DE/Publikationen/Thematisch/BildungForschungKultur/Schulen/BroschuereSchulenBlick0110018149004.pdf?__blob=publicationFile. (see page 21. Accessed 4 August 2017.)

9   www.edugroup.at/praxis/portale/latein.html. (Accessed 4 August 2017).

10   vivariumnovum.net/en/summer-school. (Accessed 4 August 2017).

11   www.lateintag.ch. (Accessed 4 August 2017).

12   www.circe.be. (Accessed 4 August 2017).

13   www.imperiumlatin.com. (Accessed 4 August 2017).

14   www.altphilologenverband.de/. (Accessed 4 August 2017).

15   www.cambridge.org/core/journals/journal-of-classics-teaching. (Accessed 4 August 2017).

Bibliography

Bulwer, J. (ed.) (2006), *Teaching Classics in Europe*, London: Bloomsbury.

Cambridge Schools Classics Project (1988), *Cambridge Latin Course*, 4th edn, Cambridge: Cambridge University Press.

Cassuto, L. (2016), 'What Classics Professors Can Teach the Rest of Us', *The Chronicle of Higher Education*, 17 July 2016.

Cibois, P. (2011), *L'enseignement du latin en France, une socio-histoire*, Québec: Les classiques des sciences sociales. Available online: classiques.uqac.ca/contemporains/cibois_philippe /enseignement_du_latin_france/enseignement_du_latin_france.html. (Accessed 4 August 2017).

Coe, R. (2006), *Relative Difficulties of Examinations at GCSE: An Application of the Rasch Model*, Durham: Curriculum, Evaluation and Management (CEM) Centre, University of Durham.

Coe, R., Searle, J., Barmby, P., Jones, K. and Higgins S. (2008), *Relative Difficulty of Examinations in Different Subjects*, Report for SCORE (Science Community Supporting Education), Durham: Curriculum, Evaluation and Management (CEM) Centre, University of Durham.

Crump L. (2008), 'A Contemporary Subject for a Contemporary Europe', in B. Lister (ed.), *Meeting the Challenge – International Perspectives on the Teaching of Latin*, Cambridge: Cambridge University Press.

Glatz, P. and Thiel, A. (2015), *European Symbols*, Austria: Euroclassica.

Hall, E. (2015), 'Classics for the People: What We Should All Learn from the Ancient Greeks', *The Guardian*, 20 June 2015. Available online: www.theguardian.com/books/2015/jun/20/classics-for -the-people-ancient-greeks. (Accessed 9 August 2017).

Haynes, N. (2014), *The Amber Fury*, London: Corvo.

Hunt, S. (2016), *Starting to Teach Latin*, London: Bloomsbury.

Karsai, G., Klaniczay, G., Movrin, D. and Olechowska E. (2013), *Classics and Communism Greek and Latin behind the Iron Curtain*, Ljubljana: Znanstvena založba Filozofske facultete; Budapest: Collegium Budapest Institute for Advanced Study; Warsaw: Faculty of Artes Liberales.

Kathimerini (2016), 'Minister's Bid to Scrap Ancient Greek in Schools Fuels Debate', *Kathimerini* 7 June 2016. Available online: www.ekathimerini.com/209366/article/ekathimerini/news/ministers-bid-to -scrap-ancient-greek-in-schools-fuels-debate. (Accessed 9 August 2017).

Kipf, S. (2013), 'Ars didactica necesse est colatur. Aufgaben und Perspektiven altsprachlicher Fachdidaktik', in U. Schmitzer (ed.), *Enzyklopädie der Philologie. Themen und Methoden der Klassischen Philologie heute*, 259–275, Göttingen: Edition Ruprecht.

Klein, C. and Soler, P. (2011), 'L'enseignement des langues et cultures de l'antiquité dans le second degré', *Inspection Générale de l'éducation nationale*, 2011–2098.

Lister, B. (ed.) (2008), *Meeting the Challenge – International Perspectives on the Teaching of Latin*, Cambridge: Cambridge University Press.

Middleton, F. (2015), 'Opinion: "Difficult" Latin Risks Remaining a Qualification for Elite Pupils', *Discussion*, 2 November 2015. Available online: www.cam.ac.uk/research/discussion/opinion -difficult-latin-risks-remaining-a-qualification-for-elite-pupils. (Accessed 9 August 2017).

Morgan, J. (2013), *Imperium*, 1–3, York: J-progs.

Nedergaard (2006), 'Denmark', in J. Bulwer (ed.), *Teaching Classics in Europe*, London: Bloomsbury.

Riva, O. (2016), 'Maturità 2016, il futuro del classico e la lite sulle versioni di latino e greco', *Corriere Della Sera*, 29 April 2016.

Rodrigues Á. and Cação E. (2011), 'Projecto Pequena Infância', *Humanitas*, 63: 855–857.

Schough Tarandi (2006), 'Sweden', in J. Bulwer (ed.), *Teaching Classics in Europe*, London: Bloomsbury.

Van Bommel, B. (2016), 'L'enseignement du Grec et du Latin aux Pays-Bas', *La Vie des Classiques*. Available online: *www.laviedesclassiques.fr/article/l'herbe-est-elle-plus-verte-ailleurs-l'enseignement-du-grec-et-du-latin-aux-pays-bas.* (Accessed 9 August 2017).

Vaudano, M. (2015), 'Le latin et le grec vont-ils vraiment disparaître du college?', *Le Monde*, 29 April 2015.

Waquet, F. (1998), *Le latin ou l'empire d'un signe*, Paris: Albin Michel.

Waquet, F. (2001), *Latin or the Empire of a Sign*, London: Verso.

CHAPTER 6

LATIN IS NOT DEAD: THE RISE OF COMMUNICATIVE APPROACHES TO THE TEACHING OF LATIN IN THE UNITED STATES

Steven Hunt

This chapter investigates the increase in the use of communicative approaches to teaching Latin in US schools based on understandings of theories of second language learning. It considers possible reasons for the rise in interest in these approaches and assesses the potential implications for teaching practice more widely there and in other educational jurisdictions. In particular I want to comment on how communicative approaches can be seen to be attempting to broaden the appeal of learning the Latin language to a more diverse school audience than has sometimes been the case before.

Introduction

I will draw primarily on some of my own experiences as a participant observer in demonstration communicative Latin lessons at the *Paideia Living Latin Conference* in New York in 2016, and also from evidence presented at workshops at the Institute of the American Classical League in 2015 and 2017 and from comments on social media sites devoted to communicative practices in Latin teaching in the United States. I suggest that a combination of particular circumstances in the US school system seem to have promoted innovative pedagogical approaches to Latin teaching: these include the drive to improve the study of languages in schools and the impact of the American Standards for Foreign Language Teaching, the need for improvement in student enrolments, the provision of teaching resources and forms of assessment and the desire to appeal to a diverse student population. US Latin teachers know that unless they modify their teaching methodology, in most places Latin will die: funding follows the students. I conclude that, while other countries have their own particular circumstances, the sorts of communicative approaches which are the subject of experiment in the United States have much potential for the enrichment and diversification of teaching practices elsewhere too and can ultimately widen participation among the student population as a whole.

Since the late nineteenth century, Latin teaching has utilized two main methodologies: the grammar-translation approach (in which students are taught to analyse the language) and the reading approach (in which students gain reading proficiency through the reading of graded texts). Both methodologies aim at enabling learners to comprehend original Roman texts; discussion of the language and of the literature typically takes place in the language of the learner. Latin teaching methodologies have tended towards one or other of the two approaches, depending on the teacher's personal choice and use of particular Latin course books. There is no consensus on the approach which a Latin teacher should use, although, broadly speaking, the reading approach seems to have become more widely accepted in the UK, United States and Australia and grammar-translation approaches in the rest of Europe. Readily available reading course books themselves do not tend to follow a completely consistent approach, and Latin teachers are relatively free to use their preferred approach. By contrast, teachers of modern foreign languages (MFL) across the world have adopted communicative approaches: teaching takes place largely in the target language with the aim of providing students with the skills to communicate with native speakers. Among Latin teachers across the world the debate about which of the three approaches are more suitable for use in the classroom is a lively and energetic one. Grammar-translation and reading approaches maintain their popularity by a long way. But in the United States, Latin teachers have been experimenting with communicative approaches for over a decade. In the last few years the internet and social media have enabled teachers to share their experiences, questions and ideas about communicative approaches to teaching Latin and have generated enormous enthusiasm, beyond the United States. A mark of interest is the appointment in 2017 of Daniel Gallagher as associate professor of the Practice of Latin at Cornell University – a 'milestone in the teaching of Latin nationwide', according to the University's Interim President Hunter Rawlings (Delwiche 2017). Does this appointment show recognition of the value of what has been going on in schools for more than ten years?

Plus ça change?

Communicative approaches to Latin teaching are, of course, not new and, indeed, have not been an exclusively US phenomenon. Rouse's 'Direct Method' originated in Edwardian England. In the century before, the teaching of foreign languages had swung back and forth between grammar-translation methods and communicative methods. Rouse, the headmaster of a private boys' school in Cambridge and a classicist, was heavily influenced by German ideas about teaching modern languages through communicative approaches – then called the Direct Method (Stray 1992, 2011). Rouse himself explained the approach in the preface to his book *Latin on the Direct Method*:

> As applied to the teaching of languages, the Direct method means that the sounds of the foreign tongue are associated directly with a thing, an act, or a thought, without the intervention of an English word; and that these associations are grouped by a method, so as to make the learning of the language as easy and as speedy as possible, and are not brought in haphazardly, as are children when they learn their own language in the nursery. It follows that speaking precedes writing, and that the sentence (not the word) is the unit. The method is largely oral, but not wholly so … the idiom, the feeling for a language is easily taught thus, and accuracy can wait. To begin with an attempt at exactitude is to make idiom always difficult, and with mediocre minds, always impossible in the end. It will be seen that the four senses are used to make the impression: hearing first, then speaking, then touch (when the new matter is written) and lastly sight. (Rouse and Appleton 1925, pp. 2–3)

Rouse experimented successfully with the methodology with his Latin classes and was keen to encourage others. Transcripts of lessons suggest a limited vocabulary in the initial stages of instruction and much repetition. *Linguaphone* records of demonstration lessons and his book suggest his methods included speaking, listening and total physical response. A collection of small models, made by Rouse himself, kept in the archive of the Perse School today, suggests that he made use of physical objects in his teaching as well as the written and spoken word. These are all the sort of things we might recognize as components of MFL teaching practices today – even a form of hand-jive to represent the person endings of verbs. But it has to be said that his methods did not only encompass communicative ones: he is reported to have followed them up with explicit grammar explanation and translation into and out of the sort of written Latin exercises which were common features of study at that time (and still often are). After all, he had to hedge his bets: the measure of success of the practice was in getting students from his school into the universities. Without paying heed to the matriculation requirement of translation into and out of Latin, he would have been in serious trouble with his school governing board, the members of which were keenly aware of the importance of the continued success of the students at examinations in attracting parents and their children and thereby ensuring the financial viability of the school. Yet, as headmaster, he was able to put these considerations aside. With his own staff Jones and Appleton able to demonstrate the method as well as he could, Rouse demonstrated that the Direct Method was practicable and effective. The more dynamic and appealing way of teaching and learning Latin spread widely and rapidly, with the practice attracting and impressing visitors from across Britain and continental Europe. To reach an even wider audience he put on demonstration classes at the annual summer schools of the Association for the Reform of Latin Teaching – an organization he founded in 1913 and which is still going strong. He and his followers published frequently in the newly formed Journal of Latin Teaching, set up as a counter-balance to the publications of the Classical Association, much to the chagrin of some of its more traditionally minded members who stuck by the grammar-translation method (Stray 2011).

Rouse met with great success in his day. In the 1954 book *The Teaching of Classics* the authors reported that his Direct Method had been 'enthusiastically adopted by a number of public schools and a large number of grammar schools, both boys' and girls" (The Incorporated Association of Assistant Masters in Secondary Schools 1954, p. 71). There are two points worth noting here: first that the movement attained widespread popularity across all types of school and for all students, and secondly that the public schools (in modern parlance the private schools of ancient foundation) were at that time in the forefront in developing and disseminating innovative practice. The oddity was that despite its apparent attractiveness in time the Direct Method did not enter mainstream teaching methodology after all. Morris (1966), in an otherwise even-handed description, notes that:

This willing participation and interest [of the students] may well be the results of a very able, dedicated teacher rather than of the method; that although the oral method lesson is, in outward appearance, a complete experience of Latin, the inner thoughts of the pupils during the lesson may be very English indeed. Further the sort of Latin used and the situations employed are often quite un-classical, the vocabulary being full of non-classical words, the classroom and things in it having no real parallels in Roman times. Again, a good deal of time can be wasted in explaining in Latin points that could be more swiftly explained in English. Finally, if the aim of oral method is to promote the ability to comprehend written Latin, is it established that the oral method is the best and most economical way of achieving this aim? (Morris 1966, p.13)

Moreover, the Direct Method seemed to require great physical energy, creativity, responsiveness to the demands and interests of the students. Most importantly, it seemed to need a more solid grasp of the Latin language than many teachers thought they themselves possessed. These factors resonate with the situation today: teacher exhaustion was one of the items under discussion at the 2017 American Classical League conference, especially in regard to the use of communicative methods, and threads on social media such as the Facebook site *Teaching Latin for Acquisition* (https://www.facebook.com/groups/AcquireLatin) reiterate similar feelings. Other teachers at the time found difficulty in designing assessments which were based around students' listening and speaking activities rather than around traditional forms of written assessment. Again this remains significant today: the measurable outcomes that are demanded by school managers are far easier to show by vocabulary tests and quizzes, written exercises, essays and project-based learning activities. There have been attempts to remedy this not all that long ago: in the UK the now-defunct School Classics Project GCSE examination for sixteen-year-olds used to allow an oral recitation element to be submitted for coursework. This, however, was lost in the examination reforms of 2000 after concerns were expressed about its comparability with other options. All was not lost: in time some elements of the Direct Method found their way into the reading courses such as *ecce Romani* – with its *responde latine* questions – and the *Cambridge Latin Course*, with its tape recordings, CD ROMs and later DVD recordings. Ørberg too was much influenced by what he read about Rouse and devised his book *Lingua Latina per se llustrata* along Direct Method principles, declaring that:

> There is no need to translate or explain grammatical points in the students' own language; they are enabled to discover for themselves directly the meaning of the words and sentences and the functioning of the grammatical rules. (Quoted in Carter 2011)

Lister's audio versions of the *Iliad* and the *Odyssey* and *Ovid's Metamorphoses* rely on the spoken rather than the written word as ways of making the relatively complex mythological stories accessible to children of all abilities (Lister 2017), and some UK Classical Association events still feature reading competitions – an opportunity on a small scale to remind students that Latin is an intelligible spoken language.

But what other reasons caused the Direct Method not to flourish? Perhaps it also concerned a clash of personalities. Rouse himself was sometimes a less than diplomatic public advocate and found it difficult to win over the School Board which set the national examinations and the more traditionally minded Classical Association which represented teachers and university academics (Stray 1992). Communication of his ideas was slow and cumbersome, entailing a physical visit to his classroom or the annual summer school. Access was clearly limited. What undermined the methodology most substantially, however, was the stranglehold of external examinations. These continued to privilege translation into and out of the classical languages, and while Rouse clearly intended the Direct Method to achieve the same thing merely by a different methodology to the traditional grammar-translation approach, it could easily be misunderstood as, at best, a time-consuming exercise and, at worst, a pointless one. Teachers taught to the test. Listening to or speaking or freely writing in Latin was not assessed and so there was no perceived need to practise them in the classroom. Similar problems seem to bedevil proponents of communicative approaches today both in the UK with the demands of GCSE and A level examinations (Hunt 2016) and in the United States with those of the Advanced Placement examinations (Kitchell 2015). Listening to or speaking Latin is firmly not a requirement. While Rouse's work had demonstrated the efficacy of the Direct Method, the dead hand of centrally set traditional examinations and teachers' tendency for pedagogical conservatism meant that the approach did not catch on as quickly or as widely to survive beyond a few dedicated proponents. Essentially the reason for the failure of the Direct Method to catch on was that there was no urgency to *make* the change. That would have to wait until the 1960s with the growth of egalitarian ideas about education on both sides of the Atlantic and the correlating toppling of Latin from its position at the head of the high table of curricular subjects. It was only then, in the face of possible extinction, or at best relegation, that methodology had to change.

When the change did happen it was necessitated by slightly different concerns. In the UK the demand for change was a sudden one, almost a rupture, pinpointed to the very year. In 1962 Latin in schools faced a simple crisis of survival after the universities of Oxford and Cambridge withdrew Latin as a matriculation requirement within days of each other. Another factor was the increasing pressure to fit Latin into a new curriculum for a changed educational landscape of all-ability comprehensive schools which were being developed in the 1970s (Forrest 1996; Lister 2007; Hunt 2016). Latin, previously kept alive by the universities and a selective education system, needed to seek more attractive teaching approaches for the new era. Despite public cries against change from the Classical Association (Stray 2003), there was no choice. Traditional grammar-translation was out. Reading-based courses such as the *Cambridge Latin Course* (1970) and *ecce Romani* (1971) were developed to take account of modern theories of language learning (Gay 2003b) and the opportunities afforded in a completely new design of the Latin course book (Story 2003). They have been successful in at least stemming the decline in enrolments and popularizing Latin and Classical Studies ever since.

Change was slower in the United States. Indeed, grammar-translation approaches to teaching Latin are still common, both at school and college level. *Wheelock's Latin* (LaFleur 2011), first published in 1956, and *Jenney's First Year Latin* (Jenney 1954), are still widely used. In this, the United States perhaps displays a thinking that is more characteristic of the teaching practices of mainland Europe but under practical circumstances which are more closely aligned with the UK. In the United States the removal of Latin as one of the matriculation requirements for the college system might, one would have expected, have led to a similar diminution in enthusiasm for the grammar-translation approach as had occurred in the UK under similar circumstances. But it continues to be popular among US teachers, just as it does in many of the countries in Continental Europe, where grammar-translation remains the norm. In these countries Latin still provides the key for entry to certain universities or university courses (see Bulwer's chapter in this book), and there seems to be little appetite among teachers for a change of methods (although see van Bommel [2016] for changes anticipated in Holland, for example, in the face of educational reforms and the reduction of teaching time for classical languages in the *gymnasia* academically streamed schools). Latin courses are therefore compulsory and enrolments are high and maintained because of the school–university system. One might suggest that addressing the needs of a diverse student body is not considered important when Latin classes are composed primarily of students selected by prior attainment and intent on university application. In the United States, however, this is not the case. Why then does grammar-translation remain popular? Evidence suggests that students often enroll in Latin courses in the belief that it will help them improve their vocabulary and gain higher grades in the Scholastic Aptitude Test, set by the College Board and widely used for college admission (LaFleur 1981; Craib 1992; Bolchazy-Carducci 2017). I suspect that this idea survives from the programmes in the late twentieth century on the positive impact of Latin-rich language-awareness courses on students' vocabulary in inner cities (Masciantonio 1979; Mavrogenes 1981; Masciantonio 1984; Polsky 1986, 1987, 1998). The grammar-translation approach, with its emphasis on the memorization of lists of Latin vocabulary, drilling of paradigms and charts has been said by some to be helpful in this regard (Singh 1998). Some believe that the grammar-translation approach provides a better understanding of the requirements of the language components of the Advanced Placement Latin examination (Carlon 2011). Grammar-translation has been said to be the fastest method to get students up to reading the sorts of original Latin authors set by this examination in the time available (May 1998). But while these methods worked for some, there has been continued clamour that alternatives needed to be found: the grammar-translation method did not develop the reading skills which it purported to develop among the majority of participating students, and enrolments were falling – students who started Latin soon gave up.

The desire for change was, in fact, not a recent one. As early as 1856 a rise in enrolments in MFL spread alarm among Latin teachers, who saw enrolments in their own discipline begin to fall. Such a situation even then generated calls for the modification of the classical curriculum (Kitchell 1998). In the twentieth century the secure position of Latin in the curriculum continued to be eroded. By the 1920s the traditional teaching methods employed in Latin were not meeting the needs of the students in a mass education programme: an excessive focus on grammar learning was leaving insufficient time to engage students in reading original authors; students who never progressed beyond the elementary stages – that is, most of them – never reached the stage of reading original Roman literature, and so they gained little from the experience which they did have of learning Latin that was valuable for their everyday lives (Kitchell 1998). While the educationalists argued about what should be done, the students themselves voted with their feet. Students could see the point of studying MFL, and studying them was an engaging activity. Latin, by contrast, was less engaging, less purposeful and consequently enrolments declined catastrophically from a high point of 49 per cent of all high school students in 1910, to just 2 per cent in 1985 (Kitchell 2015). By the 1960s, however, all foreign language requirements were gone: Latin was fighting for recognition in the clamour for 'relevant, practical curricula and for electives rather than requirements' (Kitchell 2015, p. 179). If Latin were to survive at all, it would have to exist as one of a number of foreign language electives rather than as a curriculum requirement and it would have to bear scrutiny among what were now its equals.

In the 1970s Latin teachers finally began to take on board teaching approaches which seemed to work for modern languages. Reading approaches began to be embraced with the introduction of North American editions of books like the *Cambridge Latin Course* (1970), *Oxford Latin Course* (1987) and *ecce Romani* (1971) (Sebesta 1998). While the focus of teaching Latin was still to enable students to read the language, US Latin teachers began to realize that the other skills of listening, speaking and writing could also be employed to help and would benefit students in the same class who had different learning styles (Abbott 1998). Some schools and colleges used Ørberg's *Lingua Latina per se Illustrata* (1990) which had originally been published in 1955 and had never caught on in the UK. This book exemplified a fully communicative approach: a Latin narrative, carefully graded in difficulty, for reading and discussion in class, with notes and instructions entirely written in Latin.

In 1994 the United States had its own Latin 'crisis' moment. National anxiety about the small number of students undertaking foreign language learning and the impact this might have on business opportunities in an increasingly global economy led to the 'Goals 2000: Educate America' legislation (Abbott 1998). The legislation strongly encouraged students to take a foreign language in school and resulted in nationally agreed Standards for Foreign Language Learning. The American Classical League, working with the American Philological Association (now the Society for Classical Studies), recognizing the importance of keeping abreast of developments in modern languages teaching, developed its own complementing Standards for Classical Languages Learning (American Classical League and American Philological Association 1997). Both of these documents were updated in 2017. The American Council on the Teaching of Foreign Languages (ACTFL), which now represents modern and classical languages teachers, strongly endorses communicative approaches. In the most recent 2017 'World-Readiness Standards for Learning Languages' one-page summary, the words 'use' and 'using' are mentioned seven times, while there is only one occurrence of the word 'analyze' (American Council on the Teaching of Foreign Languages 2017). Its five goal areas (commonly called the Five C's of Communication, Cultures, Connections, Comparisons and Communities) have a significant impact on teaching practices in foreign languages because they set the criteria for language learning for some forty states (American Council on the Teaching of Foreign Languages 2017). Teachers of classical languages have been proactive in drawing up their own Classical Standards, based on the ACTFL ones, in order to provide further guidance for the particular needs of teaching students to read classical texts. A set of guidelines 'Standards for Classical Language Learning' is in preparation. The document takes as its starting point the student in the classroom and addresses head-on the importance of recognizing student diversity: 'Twenty-first-century language learners come from a variety of cultural backgrounds and possess a wide variety of learning styles' (American Classical League and Society for Classical Studies 2017, p. 2). The document does not stipulate a particular teaching approach, stating '[t]he approach to teaching and learning might emphasize active use of Latin or Greek, a traditional grammar-based approach, a reading-based approach, or a hybrid of all of these' (American Classical League and Society for Classical Studies 2017, p. 2). Grammar-translation does, however, get short shrift. While the document acknowledges that there are 'philosophical differences that govern the various approaches to using interpersonal communications in the Latin classroom', it does go on to suggest that '[t]here is growing evidence that the use of spoken Latin in the classroom facilitates student comprehension of the language, which facilitates reading it' (American Classical League and Society for Classical Studies 2017, p. 15). The reading courses already mentioned offer teachers opportunities for richly communicative practices, but they are essentially hybrid courses. Some offer more explicit instructions to recommend communicative practices (other than reading comprehension) than others, and all contain elements of grammar-translation too. Ørberg's *Lingua Latina per se Illustrata* (1990) and its more modern relative Minkova and Tunberg's *Latin for the New Millennium* (2008) remain popular among teachers looking for materials which are designed to provide students with opportunities to maximize their comprehension of Latin by conducting the lesson as much as possible in Latin. However, some teachers now seek to reject the Latin course book entirely and are working on its replacement with more personalized, interactional and creative forms of communicative teaching and learning basing their ideas on the Second Language Acquisition theories of language input posited by Krashen (1981) and VanPatten (2003). For details of the discussions about these and other practices, see the individual websites of Patrick, Piazza and Maust (2017), Slocum Bailey (2017), Toda (2017) and Schwamm (2017) and the lively discussions on the Facebook site *Teaching Latin for Acquisition* (https://www .facebook.com/groups/AcquireLatin).

Reaching out to new audiences with Latin

From where, then, is the new impetus, some hundred years on, that is once again bringing communicative practices into the forefront of the classics classroom? There are perhaps two main strands to the argument: one is about social equity and the other concerns developments in Second Language Acquisition theories.

The first point is that Latin teachers have found different ways of teaching Latin in order to make it accessible to a wider range of students than before. I have already mentioned above the reported successes of the Latin-based language awareness programmes in the US inner cities in the late twentieth century. Similar 'Latin for Literacy' projects have resurfaced in the UK recently (see, for example, the projects discussed by Bell, Bracke, Robinson and Wing-Davey in this book) and in the United States with the Paideia Institute's '*Aequora*' programme (Butterworth 2016, 2017). These programmes seem to show that Latin does not have to be the preserve of a social or intellectual elite: Latin can be for everyone. For reasons of social justice, the teaching of Latin can take into account students from diverse backgrounds (Sawyer 2016) and with different learning styles (Deagon 2006). Latin can be taught to everybody *provided that teachers make it so.* Communicative approaches offer a richer diversity of activities than the grammar-translation methods can allow. Communicative approaches are intrinsically appealing to students of all types and can be noted to offer learning gains that are not restricted to the purely scholarly pursuit of Classical Studies. Students who never progress beyond the elementary level can receive an educational experience which is worthwhile in itself, involving the development of interpersonal, presentational, creative and linguistic skills and which fit them for their everyday lives (Pike 2016).

The second point is that research into second language learning has developed significantly. Inspired by their colleagues in MFL, some US Latin teachers posit that learners can gain proficiency even in Latin through acquiring it almost unconsciously through listening and speaking activities. Rasmussen (2015) suggests five reasons for using a wider range of communicative approaches in Latin teaching:

1. Students will only gain a full mastery of a language if they practise all four aspects of communication: listening, speaking, reading and writing;
2. Students develop greater fluency in reading if they listen to spoken Latin: the speed of spoken Latin delivers an increased number of words compared with that delivered by a reading method, and the teacher is able to modify the input according to the student's level of comprehension;
3. Students of different ages and learning styles are able to access Latin more easily, and teachers may add more variety to lessons;

4. Spoken Latin as a way of learning Latin has successful historical precedent;

5. Students enjoy learning Latin through listening, speaking and conversation.

Among other US Latin teachers is Bob Patrick, a tireless promoter of the idea of Krashen's theory of Comprehensible Input (1981). In his many writings and public presentations, he notes that traditional Latin classes are appealing only to a minority of learners (Patrick 2011). These students – which he refers to as 'The Four Percenters' – are successful with learning charts and tables, memorizing vocabulary and translating into English random Latin stories drawn from across the world, distant in time and space. They enjoy it and some of them, eventually, become Latin teachers themselves, in turn perpetuating the teaching approaches which they themselves found comfortable. What of the other 96 per cent? Patrick suggests that for too long these have been ignored and even discarded by teachers – collateral damage in the search for traditional Latinists in schools and colleges who can cope with traditional Latin teaching. Declaring that he is motivated by 'the belief that every student in our schools, public or private, has a right to access Latin and its connections' and 'the desire to create Latin programs that are strong and sustainable' (Patrick 2015, p. 109), he strongly argues the case that the use of Comprehensible Input teaching approaches ought to deliver the social fairness and higher student enrolments that have eluded other teachers so far. Among US Latin school teachers, the idea of teaching Latin using Comprehensible Input (Krashen 1981, VanPatten 2003) has now become of sufficient interest that one can describe it as a serious movement within Latin pedagogy today. The movement is fuelled by extensive contributions by teachers of all kinds to social media such as Facebook's *Teaching Latin for Acquisition* (https://www .facebook.com/groups/AcquireLatin) and through well-attended teacher conferences, such as the American Classical League, and teacher-training events. It might be said that social media have circumvented the sorts of difficulties Rouse faced in promoting the Direct Method almost a century ago: now anyone with internet access can join a debate or present his or her experiences across the world.

There is not space here to give more than a cursory look at examples of Comprehensible Input (for published examples of lesson plans, see Patrick 2015, and Slocum Bailey 2016). In general, advocates for Comprehensible Input in Latin teaching argue that students should acquire Latin through frequent, small-scale listening and speaking activities in much the same way as students gain understanding of a MFL through exposure to it through whatever sort of immersion is possible within the confines of the classroom. They suggest that new vocabulary should be strictly limited to ensure that sufficient repetition is achieved. Accordingly a teacher may focus on no more than ten words per lesson, using them again and again in different forms and order within a sentence until the students are able to process the meaning without having to translate into their own language. Various oral and aural techniques are used: the most common are circling, personal questions and answers, story listening, and movie-talks. In these examples, questioning tends to focus on the assumed interests of the students, their personalities, likes and dislikes. The teacher's intention is to include as much compelling and engaging subject matter for every student in the class as possible. Mistakes in students' responses are not corrected: the correct forms are acquired by the teacher remodelling them. Thus, in the early stages teaching reflects the everyday life and experiences as lived by the students, with a focus on the repetition of a small number of items of Latin vocabulary. Teachers tell *ex tempore* stories from their imagination, based on current affairs, using puppets or create them together with their class, again with an emphasis on a small number of repeated words. A short video might provide material for a Latin voiceover, pre-recorded or *ex tempore*, with which students might practise listening to questions and giving answers. Eventually topics are introduced which are more relevant to the ancient Romans and culminate in the reading of original authors. The field of practices seems to be constantly expanding, but in all cases the teacher aims to use as much spoken Latin as possible with the intention that students' exposure to multiple examples of a small, sheltered vocabulary will enable them to acquire the language without formal analysis. Ideally explanation of vocabulary, even grammar, is in Latin. Students themselves are encouraged to speak Latin in response to questions, to contribute to class activities such as plays and stories, through speech and eventually writing.

Krashen has also suggested that students should receive language input through free voluntary reading (2011). The Latin Comprehensible Input movement advocates extensive voluntary, unassessed reading, especially of short stories or novellas written specifically for learners with compelling and often contemporary narratives. Novellas might contain only 100 or 80 or even only 40 distinct items of vocabulary – nearly all of which, at the time of first reading, a student will be expected to have previously acquired. In preparation for the sorts of advanced readings which students might be expected to undertake at the end of a typical four-year Latin course (such as those, for example, for the Advanced Placement exam), teachers try to ensure that the vocabulary is trimmed to those commonly used by the authors to be studied – Caesar and Virgil – which form the bulk of reading. Words not used by these authors and which appear in Latin course books (if use is still made of them) are ruthlessly weeded out.

Others consider input not to be enough. Following more recent theories of language acquisition, which is built around the idea of language output, they advocate free written composition and more sophisticated interactional conversations, discussions and debates with the teacher or each other (VanPatten 2003; Lloyd 2016a). These pedagogical practices seem to be less common at the school level but are popular at the university level and in summer schools such as summer retreats or *conventicula*. Here teachers gather to improve their Latin by immersion for a week or more in convivial surroundings (Tunberg 2011). Some have scoffed at these efforts and characterized them as a vain attempt to restore Latin as a spoken language (Ball and Ellsworth 1996). Others have pointed out that the purpose is simpler and more compelling: participants are not so much learning to speak Latin, but speaking to learn it (Lindzey 2015; Lloyd 2016b).

The living Latin experience

I now describe my own experience as a participant in communicative Latin practices. Several organizations in the United States promote communicative Latin teaching events. Immersive language learning meetings – *conventicula* – are designed both for beginners and also for more experienced language speakers (see Bishop [2017] for a recent list and Coffee [2012] for an account of their development in the United States). They range from one-off conferences and workshops through to well-established summer camps. One of these is the Paideia Institute, which provides Latin for literacy courses for younger students and to encourage teachers to try communicative practices in the classroom. The Paideia Institute invited me to take part in its Living Latin meetings at Fordham University in New York over a weekend in February 2016.

This section of the chapter details some of the experiences which I had over the weekend and my reflections about them.

My first impressions of the event were that the other delegates were much younger and more diverse than I had seen at previous US conferences for Latin teachers, such as those of the American Classical League. Many seemed fresh out of college or in their final college years – new teachers. The delegates filled a large hall – some two hundred or more. There was a particular sense of purpose and excitement. There were a number of newbies (like myself) who made the effort initially to converse in Latin after a fashion and then gave up; others, more experienced, seemed to be interacting much more fluently. Terence Tunberg asked, in Latin, if I wanted a coffee (I think) – at least he pointed to the machine and a cup. I nodded acceptance and tried to recall what he had just said. The Latinist inside me wanted to identify the gender and case of the word – what declension was coffee? What derivation of the word could I think of to help me remember it? Would I be tested on my knowledge of different strengths of coffee – the comparative 'more smooth' or the superlative 'very roasted'? Immediately I had put myself under pressure. But no one else put me under pressure and I quickly relaxed. People of a similar proficiency had been allocated to groups of similarly equipped students. Although I felt my Latin and Greek were good (I have studied them for nearly 40 years pretty continuously, 30 years as a teacher and at that time seven years as a university lecturer in Classics Education, teaching teachers to teach school-age students Latin and Classical Greek), my confidence in Latin as a spoken language was almost zero. Having been the beneficiary of MFL and ancient language teaching in the old style, I knew my charts and tables and I could translate most Latin at sight; but while I could recall a great deal of Latin vocabulary for reading the canonical Roman authors, I was not able to think sufficiently quickly on my feet to find the words for the social situations in which I found myself. *mehercle!* I was put in the beginners' set.

Delegates had been provided in advance with a booklet of Latin and Greek texts which we had been informed we were going to use in the teaching sessions. Inevitably I had tried to translate as many of them in advance as possible on the plane (*frustra!*). I need not have worried. Different presenters used the texts in different ways; none of them seemed to have expected us to have gone to that much trouble, and I realized that 'translation' in the old sense was not what these texts had been given to us for. What intrigued me was the variety of texts, running from Plautus to medieval and even the modern world. There was a description of the discovery of the New World and the extract by Reginald Foster seemed to be about the Apollo moon landings.

I shall try to describe what each of the sessions seemed to achieve – at least from my point of view, as a learner. I have tried hard to be as reflective a participant as I can and hope that the following is useful as an account of what might be possible in a more communicative classroom.

Greek origami

First up was a session in which the tutor taught participants to make a paper boat with instructions entirely in Classical Greek. I have to report that at the time I felt that this was a somewhat ineffective example of the communicative method and I was highly dubious about the activity itself – but read on! At the end of the session I had made a small model of a paper boat which looked pretty much the same as the one that the tutor and my fellow participants had made. But had I understood how to make a paper boat by listening to the Classical Greek? Barely – and I *know* Classical Greek! Or at least I thought I did. All I seemed actually to have done was to have copied the tutor's actions and not followed his words at all. He had told us to fold down the middle of the paper – and I folded down the middle of the paper because I could see him doing it; he told us to smooth the piece of paper *this way* and I followed his actions to the letter. I knew that the task had been completed satisfactorily because I basically knew how to make a paper boat anyway and because when I had finished I had a paper boat in my hands just like the tutor's and everyone else's.

I have to admit that I felt very disgruntled by this at the time.

But on reflection, I came to realize that the practice served a purpose after all – it was teaching a wider point. Let's take the things one at a time. First, I suspect that if I had come to the tutor's lessons week in, week out, I would have picked up a small amount of vocabulary pertaining to boats and origami folding, simply by dint of hearing the same words again and again. I did find myself repeating some of the phrases used by the tutor at the time or mouthing them to myself and feeling the unusual words roll around my tongue: there was a use and a pleasure in that. I enjoyed hearing them repeated by my fellow students in varying degrees of success. The small number of descriptive and instructional words for making a paper boat and the frequency of their utterance would, I feel, have made their acquisition relatively easy. And while I might not have known whether the word for a sail or a hull or a keel was first, second or third declension or whether it was masculine, feminine or neuter, it did not matter *at this beginning stage* in my learning: I was learning to communicate ideas and actions without the slow process of translating into English and certainly without becoming anxious about language terminology. I might only have been exposed to a small number of words, but the repetitions of these words in the classroom and the frequent opportunities to use them meant that I would quickly acquire a decent working vocabulary. This was a task which had a purpose – a simple one, agreed – but one that was concrete and a little bit fun. I had been showing my gradual development of understanding Classical Greek through the making of an object. The sense of achievement when that small paper boat had been made was far more engaging and joyful a way of learning a language than any amount of linguistic analysis could ever be.

Secondly, we knew what the outcome was: to make a paper boat – in terms of both how to make it and what it ought to look like when it was finished. Thus, our motivation was gained because we understood what the purpose of the activity was. Thirdly, the combination of working with the presenter and with each other led to collaboration and the valuing of colleagues' attempts of their own. There was even some humour as individuals tried hard to listen, to pick out words, and then folded the paper in entirely the wrong way only to be helped by their peers. Thus, the feeling of the class was one of mutual endeavor, comfort and success – even if we did not get everything right first, second or even third time. Finally, the repetition of small commands performed in the original language, combined with a kinaesthetic activity – the making of the boat – delivered a strong sense of purpose and reduced or removed the high cognitive demand of merely listening to and interpreting the words, or seeing the words written down (in Greek an even bigger challenge).

These three ideas – the importance of something which is compelling, the positive enjoyment of the classroom interaction, and the repetition of words and actions – all fit into some of the main ideas of Comprehensible Input in the communicative classroom. I felt that I had achieved a positive outcome, using, however simply, the target language. I was not being tested on my language and found wanting. I was using it and believed I could do more.

A tapestry of words

Next came a session in which the tutor – and there were only two students this time – engaged us in Latin conversation. The topic was some of the scenes depicted in a section of the Bayeaux tapestry, a medieval tapestry depicting the events of the invasion of Britain by the Normans in 1066, which contains a running Latin commentary. Given a photocopy of some of the tapestry, the teacher asked questions. What was on the left of the picture? How many men are there on the right? Where are the men? Why are they in the boats? What is the man in the middle of the picture doing? How many trees has he cut down? Often we were able to turn around the questions into the answers. Sometimes we had to recall the words for the objects in the picture. Sometimes we did not know, and there was a crib sheet of extra vocabulary to help. More often the teacher explained what it was in Latin, using synonyms or simple phrases. Bit by bit we had a good, close look at the richly detailed but not overly challenging image, suited to our abilities. The tutor guided the development of our spoken Latin with carefully graded sets of questions: from the factual to the inferential and from mere repetition of vocabulary to the tutor to substitution of noun and verb terminations. What typified the session was the number and types of tutor–student interactions. Incidentally, we would probably not have been able to do this in so much detail in a large class (though a series of questions might have been available) or without some understanding of lexis and morphology first. Tunberg has suggested that communicative Latin teaching is something to improve one's Latin and that it is not necessarily a way of learning it (personal communication, 2016). To my mind, the small scale of the activity, the enthralling subject matter, and the comfortable aspect of working with each other and with the tutor were all rewards in themselves. With practice and consolidation, I could see it working well.

A bit of a wind-up around Virgil

In the third session we investigated an extract from Virgil's *Aeneid* Book 1, 81–87 – the lines where Aeneas is caught in the storm. Again, this seemed to be more the sort of lesson in which students were expected to present their understanding of a passage of Virgil having studied the Latin already. Participants were asked to draw the scene depicted in the lines. The image could next be annotated with individual words and phrases, drawn from the original text by the participant. Once the students had drawn their versions of the events, the teacher asked in Latin a series of questions about the image to which the student responded in kind – this owed much to what had been done in the Bayeux tapestry lesson where student and teacher used interactional communication. A brief transcription is given below:

Tutor	You don't have to make the Latin up on your own; just tell us what [gesturing to the whiteboard drawing] is there.
Student	So; *ignem Iovis … rapidum decidit … e nubibus.*
Tutor	Ah. So. *quis* – who – *quis deiecit … rapidum Iovis ignem?*
Student	[Pointing to the drawing] *ipsa?*
Tutor	*ipsa.* And *quis est ipsa?*
Student	*ipsa est Minerva.*
Tutor	Ah! *ipsa est Minerva. et … Iuno an Minerva disiecit ignem?*
Student	*Iuno non disiecit ignem -*

Tutor	- Ah! -
Student	- *sed … Pallas disiecit ignem.*
Tutor	- Ah! *Pallas deiecit ignem Iovis. estne ignem rapidum an lentum?*
Student	*ignis est rapidum* [gesturing with arm]. Swoosh swoosh swoosh!
Tutor	Ha! *bene bene.* Now, *anglice,* in English, *quid significat rapidum* or *rapidus ignis?* [gesturing to the drawing on the whiteboard]
Student	It's rapid fire, she's throwing a lot of fire in a short period of time.
Tutor	What are we trying to say in English – it's not rapid fire, rapid fire?
Student	It's lightning. It's lightning – so it's in itself quick, but she's also throwing it wicked-quick.
Tutor	Wicked-quick! Ha ha! Okay, so *rapidum ignis Iovis,* so *unde?* – from where – *unde?*
Student	*e nubibus et in caelo* [gesturing above the head].
Tutor	*e caelo. estne nubes est in caelo* [gesturing above the head] *an* – or – *an in terra?* [gesturing to the floor].
Student	*nubes in caelo sunt.*
Tutor	*in caelo sunt.*
Student	[Joking] *in terra est fog.*

Again, I had to wonder if this was a successful ploy or not – how you got to the stage of studying Latin in order to comprehend Virgil without translating was a point of discussion by the students after the lesson ended. Nevertheless the features that I drew from the experience were as follows: through the repetitive nature of the questioning and answering strategy they became increasingly familiar with elements of the story; they chose their own sentences, words or phrases from the original lines and responded with sentences of their own, manipulating the words as far as they were able; the teacher asked many of the same things in different ways (the idea of 'circling' gives the repetition of vocabulary that Comprehensible Input advocates think are important); the small scale of the task (a mere six lines) meant that many repetitions of vocabulary and phrase structures occurred; the enjoyment of the activity was high as the students had been deeply engaged in their own drawn version of the story and wanted to talk about it; the teacher did not perform error correction or even make corrections of his occasional Latin lapses: students believed they could be successful, even if they lapsed. Two years later I can still see the picture one of my colleague participants drew in my mind's eye and recall some of the vocabulary and certainly the events from memory. That must be a good indication that something is working.

Lessons overall so far

A number of issues arise from the experiences of teachers using communicative approaches to teach Latin. I have drawn on evidence from some of the threads on the Facebook site Learning Latin for Acquisition (https://www.facebook.com/groups/AcquireLatin) and from conversations with teachers in the United States and UK.

There is some debate about whether Comprehensible Input is a type of teaching which is broadly part of the communicative approach or a method on all its own. It is generally agreed even by its proponents that Comprehensible Input does not have to consist only of oral/aural exchanges (VanPatten 2003; Krashen 2011). Therefore, Comprehensible Input could fit into any method: reading, communicative and theoretically even grammar-translation approaches.

How much will external examinations and assessment affect the distribution of communicative approaches in the United States and further abroad? In order to fulfil the minimum language requirement, US students only need to enroll in Latin for two years. Apart from internal assessment by their teachers, held accountable to the senior leadership of the school and state requirements, they may never take an externally assessed examination in the subject. Even those who stay for a full four-year programme might never take the College Board's Advanced Placement examination but will only be assessed by their own teachers. Therefore, US teachers have an almost unique opportunity to develop courses which are highly personalized and fit their own and their students' needs and interests. The comparison with other educational jurisdictions is stark. In the UK, for example, it may be difficult to challenge the prevailing assessment orthodoxies: high-stakes examinations of translation, comprehension, composition and literature analysis and the accountability to their schools of teachers for their students' examination results. When every examination mark holds the student, teacher and school to account, innovation and risk-taking are replaced by predictability and examination coaching.

Some advocates of Comprehensible Input posit that the traditional Latin course book is too prescriptive, claiming it prevents teachers from exploring their own subject interests and from offering compelling and engaging materials which are personalized to their students' own interests. How much are teachers prepared, however, to meet the challenge of creating fresh, personalized instruction for every day of their programme? How confident are they in being able to source materials which provide the right sort of stepping stones towards reading original authors? Can shared resources on social media help? To what resources do students refer when they wish to revise? What evidence is there that learning has taken place, so as to be accountable to parents and senior leadership?

A large number of short, simple Latin reading texts have been written by practicing teachers to provide students with free voluntary reading material. The authors claim that the highly restricted vocabulary contained within them provides maximum exposure to language and promotes comprehensible input. The storylines, often based on folk tales or cartoons, are age-appropriate and engaging for the readers. Does the restricted vocabulary make the novella superficial or patronizing? Is it teaching the student how to read Latin – to give them strategies on reading less familiar Latin – or is it giving just the pretence of reading? How is grammar incorporated in novellas which only have 100 unique words?

To what extent is it appropriate for teachers to apply MFL teaching methodologies to Latin? Subject-specific terminology would seem to be one of the more useful tools teachers need to use in Latin teaching – not conversational gambits about beach volleyball. The aim is still to encourage students to be able to read original authors. What is the right balance between communicative and more traditional methodologies? The relatively centralized system of teacher training for Latin in the UK means that there is some coherence about methods and means. In the United States, teacher training is dispersed and many would-be Latin teachers gain teacher qualifications via other disciplines. Do teachers who are trained in MFL have a greater propensity to innovate than traditionally trained Latin teachers?

Does the use of communicative approaches at the school level adequately prepare students for future study? Will an increase in communicative approaches widen yet further the gap between school and university practice? Carlon wondered whether universities were themselves ready to embrace communicative approaches in their own teaching and suggested that academics were needing to be convinced (Carlon 2011). A recent survey of UK university *ab initio* Latin courses indicated that they were overwhelmingly wedded to grammar-translation approaches (Lloyd, 2016a). However, a number of recent events suggest that university academics are beginning to take a serious interest in the movement, of which the appointment of Daniel Gallagher as professor of the Practice in Latin at Cornell is perhaps the most striking. There are others: teachers at KCL and the University of Warwick are experimenting with communicative approaches with their students and calls for papers on communicative approaches to Latin teaching have gone out for both the Classical Association Annual Conference of 2018 in the UK and for the Society for Classical Studies Annual Conference of 2019 in the United States.

Conclusion

At the 2016 ACTFL conference, Bill VanPatten (2017) made three recommendations for incorporating Second Language Acquisition theory in classroom practice:

1. To stop thinking about textbooks and syllabuses and think about language use going on in class;

2. To stop talking at students, but to talk with students;

3. To let purposes and tasks drive what teachers do and inform them how to design units and lessons.

None of the above recommendations seem to be at all contentious. The impetus for pedagogical innovation in Latin teaching is to improve the quality and variety of the teaching and to increase enrolments, especially among the sorts of students which traditional methods of instruction have found hard to reach. The development of communicative practices described in this chapter might meet these challenges in the way that the development of reading course methodology did in the 1970s – but with the additional insight of what teachers know about Second Language Acquisition theories. The communicative Latin movement has grown out of a set of circumstances that seem specific to teachers in the United States. Readers might reasonably be cautious of the gains in learning that are being suggested. Nevertheless, the main features of the pedagogical practices themselves seem to me to be well worth investigating as methods by which all teachers might broaden their repertoire of teaching techniques at the very least, wherever they are and with whomever they teach. There is benefit to be had for all. Latin is not dead.

References

Abbott, M. (1998), 'Trends in Language Education: Latin in the Mainstream', in R. LaFleur (ed.), *Latin for the 21st Century*, 36–43, Glenview: Scott Foresman: Addison Wesley.

American Classical League and American Philological Association (1997), *Standards for Classical Language Learning*, Oxford, OH: American Classical League.

American Classical League and Society for Classical Studies (2017), *Standards for Classical Language Learning commentary*. American Classical League. Available online: https://aclclassics.org/uploads/assets/files/Standards/Standards_for_Classical_Language_Learning_2016.pdf. (Accessed 23 April 2018).

American Council on the Teaching of Foreign Languages (2017), *ACTFL Standards Summary*. American Council on the Teaching of Foreign Languages. Available online: https://www.actfl.org/sites/default/files/publications/standards/World-ReadinessStandardsforLearningLanguages.pdf. (Accessed 24 March 2018).

Ball, R. and Ellsworth, J. (1996), 'The Emperor's New Clothes: Hyperreality and the Study of Latin', *Modern Languages Journal*, 80: 77–84.

Balme, M. and Morwood, J. (1987), *Oxford Latin Course*, 1st edn, Oxford: Oxford University Press.

Bishop, B. (2017), 'A Guide to Conventicula around the World', *Journal of Classics Teaching*, 36: 35–36.

Bolchazy-Carducci (2017), *The Latin Advantage*. Bolchazy-Carducci. Available online: https://www.bolchazy.com/Assets/Bolchazy/extras/LatinAdvantageandSATscores.pdf. (Accessed 24 March 2018).

Butterworth, E. (16 May 2016), *Aequora. Teaching Literacy with Latin*. The Paideia Institute. Available online: https://eidolon.pub/aequora-8accc39de16c. (Accessed 24 March 2018).

Butterworth, E. (2017), 'Latin in the Community: The Paideia Institute's Aequora Programe', *The Classical Outlook*, 2–8.

Cambridge School Classics Project (1970), *Cambridge Latin Course*, 1st edn, Cambridge: Cambridge University Press.

Carlon, J. (2011), 'Educating the Educators', *Journal of Classics Teaching*, 22: 13–14.

Carter, D. (2011), 'Hans Oerberg and his Contribution to Latin Pedagogy', *Journal of Classics Teaching*, 22: 21–22.

Coffee, N. (2012), 'Active Latin: Quo Tendimus?' *Classical World*, 105 (2): 255–269.

Craib, C. (1992), 'Putting the Reading Method into Practice', *The Classical Outlook*, 69 (4): 117–119.

Deagon, A. (2006), 'Cognitive Style and Learning Strategies in Latin Instruction', in J. Gruber-Miller (ed.), *When Dead Tongues Speak. Teaching Beginning Greek and Latin*, 27–49, New York: Oxford University Press.

Delwiche, A. (2017), *Cornell Classics Appointment Marks 'Tectonic Shift' for the Study of Classics*. The Cornell Daily Sun. Available online: http://cornellsun.com/2017/01/30/cornell-classics-appointment-marks-tectonic-shift-for-the-study-of-classics/. (Accessed 24 March 2018).

Forrest, M. (1996), *Modernising the Classics. A Study in Curriculum Development*, Exeter: University of Exeter Press.

Gay, B. (2003a), 'Classics Teaching and the National Curriculum', in J. Morwood (ed.), *The Teaching of Classics*, 20–35, Cambridge: Cambridge University Press.

Gay, B. (2003b), 'The Theoretical Underpinning of the Main Latin Courses', in J. Morwood (ed.), *The Teaching of Classics*, 73–84. Cambridge: Cambridge University Press.

Hunt, S. (2016), *Starting to Teach Latin*, London: Bloomsbury Academic.

Jenney, C. (1954), *Jenney's First Year Latin*, Upper Saddle River, NJ: Prentice Hall.

Kitchell, K. (1998), 'The Great Latin Debate: The Futility of Utility?', in R. LaFleur (ed.), *Latin for the 21st Century*, 1–14, Glenview: Scott Foresman-Addison Wesley.

Kitchell, K. (2015), 'Solitary Perfection? The Past, Present, and Future of Elitism in Latin Education', in E. Archibald, W. Brockliss and J. Gnoza (eds.), *Learning Latin and Greek from the Antiquity to the Present*, 166–183, Cambridge: Cambridge University Press.

Krashen, S. (1981), *Second Language Acquisition and Second Language Learning*, Oxford: Pergamum Press.

Krashen, S. (2011), *Free Voluntary Reading*, Santa Barbara: Libraries Unlimited.

LaFleur, R. (1981), 'Latin Students Score High on SAT and Achievement Tests', *The Classical Journal*, 77: 254.

LaFleur, R. (2011), *Wheelock's Latin*, 11th edn, New York: Collins Educational.

Lindzey, G. (2015), 'The Biduum Experience: Speaking Latin to Learn', *Teaching Classical Languages*, 6 (1): 72–107.

Lister, B. (2007), *Changing Classics in Schools*, Cambridge: Cambridge University Press.

Lister, B. (2017), *Classical Tales*. Classical Tales. Available online: http://classictales.educ.cam.ac.uk/. (Accessed 24 March 2018).

Lloyd, M. (2016a), *Living Latin. Exploring a Communicative Approach to Latin Teaching through a Sociocultural Perspective on Language Learning. Unpublished Thesis*. The Open University.

Lloyd, M. (2016b), 'Living Latin. An Interview with Professor Terence Tunberg', *Journal of Classics Teaching*, 34: 44–48.

Masciantonio, R. (1979), 'A FLES Latin Lesson – Philadelphia Style', *Latin Teaching*, XXXV (6): 29–31.

Masciantonio, R. (1984), 'A Means for Expanding the Teaching of Latin at the School Level', *The Classical World*, 77 (3): 167–170.

Mavrogenes, N. (1981), 'Latin in the Elementary School: Help for Reading and Language Arts', *Latin Teaching*, XXXVI (1): 39–46.

May, J. (1998), 'The Grammar-Translation Approach to College Latin', in R. A. LaFleur (ed.), *Latin for the 21st Century. From Concept to Classroom*, 148–161, Glenview: Scott Foresman: Addison Wesley.

Minkova, M. and Tunberg, T. (2008), *Latin for the New Millennium*, Mundeleion, IL: Bolchazy Carducci Publishers, Inc.

Morris, S. (1966), *Viae Novae: New Techniques in Latin Teaching*, London: Hulton Educational Publications.

Ørberg, H. (1990), *Lingua Latina per se Illustrata*, Unknown: Focus Publishing.

Patrick, R. (2011), 'TPRS and Latin in the Classroom. Experiences of a US Latin Teacher', *Journal of Classics Teaching*, 22: 10–11.

Patrick, R. (2015), 'Making Sense of Comprehensible Input in the Latin Classroom', *Teaching Classical Languages*, 6 (1): 108–136.

Patrick, R., Piazza, J. and Maust, D. (2017), *Comprehensible Input Resources*. Latin Best Practices. Available online: https://latinbestpracticescir.wordpress.com/. (Accessed 24 March 2018).

Piazza, J. (25–27 April 2006), *Observations of Bob Patrick's Classroom*. John Piazza MA. Available online: http://johnpiazza.net/patrickobservation/. (Accessed 24 March 2018).

Pike, M. (2016), 'Latin in the 21st Century', *Journal of Classics Teaching*, 33: 6–7.

Polsky, M. (1986), 'The NEH/Brooklyn College Latin Cornerstone Project, 1982–1984: Genesis, Implementation, Evaluation', *The Classical Outlook*, 63 (3): 77–83.

Polsky, M. (1987), 'The New First Latin Programme', in M. Santirocco (ed.), *Latinitas: The Tradition and Teaching of Latin*, 147–153, Helios, Lubbock: Texas Tech University Press.

Polsky, M. (1998), 'Latin in the Elementary Schools', in R. LaFleur (ed.), *Latin in the 21st Century*, 59–69, Glenview: Scott Foresman-Addison Wesley.

Rasmussen, S. (2015), 'Why Oral Latin?', *Teaching Classical Languages*, 6 (1): 37–45.

Rouse, W. and Appleton, R. (1925), *Latin on the Direct Method*, London: University of London Press.

Sawyer, B. (2016), 'Latin for All Identities', *Journal of Classics Teaching*, 33: 35–39.

Schwamm, J. (2017), The Tres Columnae Project. Available online: http://www.trescolumnae.com/. (Accessed 24 March 2018).

Scottish Classics Group (1971), *ecce Romani*, Edinburgh: Oliver and Boyd.

Sebesta, J. (1998), 'ALIQUID SEMPER NOVI: New Challenges, New Approaches', in R. LaFleur (ed.), *Latin for the 21st Century*, 15–24, Glenview: Scott Foresman-Addison Wesley.

Singh, K. L. (1998), 'Grammar-Translation and High School Latin', in R. A. LaFleur (ed.), *Latin for the 21st Century. From Concept to Classroom*, 90–104, Glenview: Scott Foresman-Addison Wesley.

Slocum Bailey, J. (2016), 'The ARS of Latin Questioning: Circling, Personalization, and Beyond', *The Classical Outlook*, 91 (1): 1–6.

Slocum Bailey, J. (2017), *LIMEN: A Latin Teaching Portal*. Indwelling Language. Available online: http://indwellinglanguage.com/. (Accessed 24 March 2018).

Story, P. (2003), 'The Development of the Cambridge Latin Course', in J. Morwood (ed.), *The Teaching of Classics*, 85–91, Cambridge: Cambridge University Press.

Stray, C. (1992), *The Living Word. W. H. D. Rouse and the Crisis of Classics in Edwardian England*, Bristol: Bristol Classical Press.

Stray, C. (2003), 'Classics in the Curriculum up to the 1960s', in J. Morwood (ed.), *The Teaching of Classics*, 1–5, Cambridge: Cambridge University Press.

Stray, C. (2011), 'Success and Failure: W. H. D. Rouse and Direct-Method Classics Teaching in Edwardian England', *Journal of Classics Teaching*, 22: 5–7.

The Incorporated Association of Assistant Masters in Secondary Schools (1954), *The Teaching of Classics*, Cambridge: Cambridge University Press.

Toda, K. (2017), *CI Reading Strategies*. Todally Comprehensible Latin. Available online: http://todallycomprehensiblelatin.blogspot.co.uk/p/ci-reading-strategies.html.

Tunberg, T. (2011), 'De Instituto Studiis Latinis Provehendis, Quod Annum Iam Decimum In Academia Kentukiana Floret', *Journal of Classics Teaching*, 22: 16–18.

Van Bommel, B. (3 May 2016), *Classics between Prosperity and Crisis*. Addisco. Available online: http://www.addisco.nl/blog/classics-between-prosperity-and-crisis-bas-van-bommel.htm. (Accessed 1 April 2018).

VanPatten, B. (2003), *From Input to Output. A Teacher's Guide to Second Language Acquisition*, Maidenhead: McGraw-Hill.

VanPatten, B. (2017), Interview with Dr. Bill VanPatten at the American Council on the Teaching of Foreign Languages, Boston, November 2016 (K. Rowan, Interviewer).

PART II
CARPE DIEM: FINDING AND TAKING OPPORTUNITIES TO DELIVER CLASSICS FOR ALL

CHAPTER 7
DELIVERING LATIN IN PRIMARY SCHOOLS
Barbara Bell and Zanna Wing-Davey

Minimus – The mouse that made Latin cool

Barbara Bell

In the first part of this chapter, Barbara Bell, the author of the best-selling *Minimus* series of Latin course books for primary schools in the UK and internationally, explains the rationale for the creation of the series, describes some of the latest resources and makes observations about the uses of Latin with younger pupils.

Why Latin at seven?

Throughout my time (from 1994 to 1998) as executive secretary of the Joint Association of Classical Teachers (JACT), I became increasingly convinced of the need for a simple introductory guide to Latin for young children. Most friends and family reacted with surprise,

Figure 7.1 *Minimus* Mouse by Helen Forte.

and sometimes horror, at the news that I was having a sabbatical term to write a Latin course for seven-year-olds. Memories of unhappy Latin lessons with too much emphasis on rote learning and grammar meant that they viewed this as some form of torture that I was imposing on young children.

For me, however, there were several reasons for embarking on this unexpected project. Firstly, I had received a number of letters from parents and teachers asking for an introductory Latin course for primary children. Secondly, the government, concerned about British children's poor standards of literacy and our national ineptitude for learning modern foreign languages (MFL), had decided that language learning should begin at primary school. Dr Nick Tate, chief executive of the Schools Curriculum and Assessment Authority, was quoted on the front page of *The Times Educational Supplement* saying 'Primary language learning is a good idea, but why should it necessarily be French? Why not Latin?' (Times Educational Supplement, 1995). Thirdly, the crunch came when I was teaching the *Cambridge Latin Course* to a Year 7 class and stressed the importance of looking for the verb in a Latin sentence. I said, 'You do all know what a verb is?' and I looked up to a sea of glazed expressions. Further enquiries – adjectives, adverbs, conjunctions – were met with the same blank stares. This was a generation without grammar and it worried me. How could we expect children to start at secondary school and embark on French, German or Spanish when they had no idea how their own language worked? I decided to attempt to write a simple, fun introduction to Latin for young children. The core would be to teach English grammar, including the main parts of speech and to build their English vocabulary through derivation exercises.

Where to set it?

As a secondary teacher of Classics throughout my career, I knew I would need guidance from teachers whose expertise was in the primary sector. Our first crucial discussion was where to set the book. I was keen to set the book in Herculaneum (think of all those essential research trips) but my advisory panel was firm with me: if this book was going to stand a chance of finding a place in state primary schools, it had to fit with what the children were already learning about Roman Britain. As soon as someone mentioned Hadrian's Wall we all agreed that Vindolanda was the ideal setting. Because of its rare anaerobic soil conditions, the artefacts left by Flavius and the family are preserved as if in a sort of time capsule. We also have the famous Vindolanda writing tablets, an extremely important source of information about life in Roman Britain at the beginning of the second century AD. Every chapter in *Minimus* is either based on one of those artefacts or on information from the collection of writing tablets. When journalists ask me why I think the book has been so popular, I have two answers: Helen Forte's wonderful illustrations, which are both historically accurate but also full of fun. Thanks to the illustrations the children quickly identify with the characters in the family and are eager to follow their fortunes. Also the whole book is based on primary source material. The children are fascinated by the story of Vindolanda and its excavations because it is real.

Minimus becoming Maximus

Minimus was published by Cambridge University Press (CUP) in August 1999. Seven thousand copies were printed, which were the anticipated sales in the first year. By Christmas 5,000 copies had been sold and within six months of publication *Minimus* was an international project. I received emails from children all over the world urging me to write more. 'We want to know more about this family. Please, please write more stories.' By the end of the first year 14,000 copies had been sold. In 2004 *Minimus Secundus – Moving on in Latin* was published. This is aimed at slightly older children (aged 10–14) and is more demanding in terms of grammar and vocabulary. In 2007 an Italian version of *Minimus* was published by Loescher. The author, Elisabetta Valfre, combined the content of both *Minimus* books and added a lot more grammar. In 2012 *Minimus* was translated into Slovenian. In 2016 the Portuguese version was published in Brazil. At the time of writing (June 2017), there was serious interest in creating a French version of the book. Currently *Minimus* is being used in Argentina, Australia, Brazil, Canada, Cayman Islands, Denmark, Dubai, France, Germany, Guernsey, Hong Kong, India, Ireland, the Isle of Canna, Italy, Jersey, Kenya, Macedonia, the Netherlands, New Zealand, Portugal, Serbia and Montenegro, South Africa, Spain, Sri Lanka and the United States. It is thrilling to think of primary-aged children in these countries reading and being excited by the stories of the Vindolanda family. Since publication, the first *Minimus* book has sold 10,000 copies a year; almost half of these sales are in the United States. It has been a privilege to visit the United States on seven occasions to speak at the American Classical League (ACL) conferences. Some years ago we appointed two experienced *Minimus* teachers, Ruth Ann Besse and Zee Ann Poerio, to join the Primary Latin Project Committee. They continue to promote *Minimus* in the United States, to answer queries from American teachers and to give them teaching support. I have also paid four *Minimus* visits to Germany and very much enjoyed meeting children in Copenhagen. The Danish children's English was so good that they were learning their Latin through my English textbook.

How is Minimus used?

There have been four clear stages in the way *Minimus* has been used since publication:

Minimus clubs Initially, head teachers offered *Minimus* as an after-school or lunchtime club. There was little time for written work, but the children clearly enjoyed learning about the family at Vindolanda, reading the stories and taking part in various related activities – singing, making Latin birthday cards and word derivations. The *Minimus* clubs became very popular; in fact, we heard of extraordinary stories – a waiting list for children to join the Latin club and one school held a lottery and the children who obtained the lucky numbers were allowed to join the Latin club! As *Minimus* gained momentum, it became clear that we had a serious problem on our hands: there were simply not enough teachers to cope with the huge interest in learning Latin from young children. A brilliant suggestion from a granny, who attended one of my training days, was the creation of what came to be known as the 'Granny Latin' scheme. She suggested there might be volunteers like herself who would willingly go into schools to run some of these Latin clubs, after some training.

We launched the scheme via a press release on 2 May 2000. On 3 May *Minimus* hit the front page of *The Daily Telegraph* (2000), and the interest in this country then spread like wildfire and my life has never been the same again. In six weeks I received 1,200 letters, 500 telephone calls and 600 emails, all from people eager to take part and to share their love of Latin. The volunteer teachers – grannies, grandpas, young mums at home with children, postgraduates and undergraduates – were passionate and committed. Some of those grannies, who began teaching in 2000, are still running *Minimus* clubs! One gentleman ran four voluntary clubs per week. The social benefits were something I had not anticipated. I received some very moving messages: 'My wife died last year and I have felt so lonely and useless. I needed a project – *Minimus* is it'. 'It is fantastic to feel useful again, I love working with young children.' Latin clubs were also run by sixth-form students (aged 17–18) as part of their community service for the Duke of Edinburgh's scheme or the International Baccalaureate examination.

Gifted and talented schemes Head teachers were increasingly required to provide extension material for 'Gifted and Talented' children and again *Minimus* fitted the bill for stretching these most able pupils. The cross-curricular nature of the book made it possible for teachers and children to explore in greater depth aspects of language and civilization which arose from these clubs. Not infrequently a teacher would set up a Latin club for Gifted and Talented children, and when it was so popular and he could see the benefits of Latin, he decided to put *Minimus* on the timetable for a whole year-group.

Preparatory schools I had not anticipated that *Minimus* would be of much interest to British preparatory schools. *Minimus* is a simple Latin book and preparatory schools are required to prepare children for the Latin Common Entrance exam, which has considerable linguistic demands. To my delight I discovered that many preparatory schools were using it and continue to do so. As one teacher said to me 'Common Entrance takes all the fun out of Latin. *Minimus* puts it back.'

Primary language learning The year 2014 was a significant year in the development of *Minimus* in British primary schools. Once again the government has become increasingly concerned about our children's poor ability to learn foreign languages and our low standards of literacy. Much greater emphasis is now placed on the teaching of spelling, punctuation and grammar, and literacy seems to be one of the main concerns of every head teacher that I meet. Just as when I had the original idea for the book in 1995, things have come full circle and in 2014 it was decreed by the then Education Secretary, Michael Gove, that foreign-language learning must begin at primary level. Moreover, children need not learn a MFL – Latin and Greek were among the seven languages offered. This has been a great opportunity for the Primary Latin Project team to show the benefits of learning Latin for all children using *Minimus*, and I am frequently contacted by head teachers wishing to make Latin their designated language.

People sometimes ask why *Minimus* is proving attractive in so many state primaries. Latin can be taught by non-specialists, given sufficient support and training. Many primary teachers, who themselves may not have studied a MFL in any depth, are struggling to deliver them and particularly to speak them with a good accent. Latin does not require the same sort of language knowledge as do MFL. Since *Minimus* can be taught by all class teachers, this makes the timetabling of Latin much easier. Grants are available to help with the start-up costs from the Primary Latin Project. Some of our sponsors, and in particular the Classical Association, have given us money for many years to help schools buy pupils' books, the teacher's handbook, and CDs. The grants are administered by a small committee and reach a school within a month of the school's application. Training is available, and such is the demand that I have now trained a group of a dozen experienced *Minimus* teachers to train others. Thanks to the generous support of Classics for All, we are able to offer training in individual schools, even to small numbers.

Support for teachers

At a conference some years ago, someone said to me, 'Ah, *Minimus*! That's a book for the leafy suburbs in the South of England.' I was horrified; nothing could be further from the truth. There are many excellent examples of *Minimus* being taught in Scotland, Wales, many parts of Ireland and certainly in the north of England. After all, the book is set in Vindolanda; how lucky are the schools that are using *Minimus* along Hadrian's Wall and can take their children relatively easily to see the artefacts! In addition, I have now travelled throughout Britain and have visited many schools which have surprised and delighted me by their choice of adopting Latin – either as a club or more recently as their designated language on the timetable for all children in the school, regardless of ability. I think of a school in the east end of London that was threatened with closure. The head teacher invited me to train her staff as she saw Latin as one of the ways of improving standards. When I thanked her for choosing *Minimus* and asked her why she had done so, she said 'I looked at the choice of languages available. I have nothing against modern foreign languages being taught to young children. However, many of my children are of afro-caribbean origin and they are really struggling with English. Latin will help them to improve their literacy skills much more than a foreign language.'

So how can teachers who know no Latin themselves teach *Minimus* successfully to their young charges? When I run a training event, teachers normally express three main anxieties: their lack of subject knowledge of Vindolanda and Roman Britain, their worries about pronunciation, and their concerns over teaching Latin grammar and explaining clearly when they may have a hazy knowledge of grammar themselves.

My general experience is that young teachers are eager to give it a try and even sometimes feel aggrieved that they have never had the chance to learn Latin themselves. Older teachers are sometimes very concerned that something they remember as a dreary, boring, irrelevant, useless subject is being foisted on young children. I am pleased to report that by the end of the day they have normally been won over by the change in modern Latin text books.

The primary Latin project can offer the following means of support

The **Teacher's Resource Book** is the *sine qua non* of the whole course. All the Latin is translated in the book; it contains historical information about Flavius and his family who lived at Vindolanda; answers to all quizzes and exercises are given; there are many cross-curricular teaching suggestions, and there are thirty-five photocopiable worksheets which are ideal reinforcement of the grammar points and the cultural background to the book. They can be used in lessons or for homework.

For both *Minimus* books there is a CD available on which we recorded all the picture stories, which contain the main points of grammar. The recorders were Classics teachers in Bristol and beyond, who played the parts of the adults, teenage pupils of mine who played the older children in the family, and young children who played Rufus aged three, the cat and the mouse. Again, the CD is extremely useful in the classroom as it makes a welcome change from the teacher's voice, and we tried to make it sound like a family.

The ***Minimus* Website** (www.minimus.com) was created and is maintained by Helen Forte, the *Minimus* illustrator. Along with a great deal of information for teachers and details of forthcoming events, the website contains activities for the children, such as a drag-and-drop activity to dress Flavius in his armour and a garden game to practise matching adjectives and nouns. *Minimus* is also on Twitter: @minimus_latin.

The **Vindolanda Website** (www.vindolanda.com) is a useful website containing information about the archaeological finds from each season. Vindolanda also sells goods which are of use to *Minimus* teachers.

The **Primary Latin Project** awards small grants for teachers in Britain to help with start-up costs of the materials. Throughout the seventeen years since publication we have created over forty teaching support sheets which are available free on the website. Occasionally we have run special *Minimus* events, such as two days at the British Museum and another at the York Museum, as *Minimus Secundus* is based in York. We also hosted two *minidorms* at Wells Cathedral School and Bilton Grange Prep School, where youngsters enjoyed a range of Latin-related activities throughout a long weekend. My team of twelve *Minimus* trainers provide training but also give informal support to teachers in their area, either face to face or over the telephone. Increasingly primary schools delivering *Minimus* are also supported by a local secondary Classics teacher.

Helen and I have written three sets of *Minibooks*, short stories which provide extra reading material for bright children who move through the *Minimus* material quickly. They do not advance the grammar but a set of these is useful in any *Minimus* classroom. They can be given out to children who have finished a task, used for drama or given as prizes in competitions. *Minimus in Practice* is a cross-curricular book, which explores how *Minimus* can enhance all other areas of the primary curriculum, and which contains several quizzes, games and suggestions throughout the academic year. It is a useful addition for those with the time to explore cross-curricular possibilities. We have free *Minimus* publicity leaflets and bookmarks which we will happily send all over the world, and these can be used to promote the books. Our business *Minimus et cetera* sells pencils, stickers, rulers and key rings. The recently published *Pupil Workbooks* are proving to be popular grammar books, both with pupils and teachers. They look extremely lively, thanks to Helen's superb illustrations and there is plenty of space for extra colouring and drawing by pupils when they have completed the grammatical tasks. With two pages of grammar per chapter, they provide a record of what the children have covered throughout the first *Minimus* book, and this can be used as evidence of progress for Ofsted and other inspections. Although *Minimus* was designed for children aged seven to ten, I have been surprised and delighted to hear that it is popular with much younger children. Hence, Helen and I decided to write some material specifically with these young learners in mind. Our newest book, *Minimusculus* (a very little mouse) was published in 2016. Written mostly in English, it introduces the characters in the family and the site of Vindolanda. In response to requests from teachers, it includes Latin numbers (as well as Roman numerals) and Latin greetings.

Conclusion

Minimus has developed way beyond my wildest dreams. To date (June 2017), worldwide sales of the first books have reached 162,000 copies. It has taken forms that I could not possibly have envisaged. The mouse continues to scuttle in all sorts of directions and we strive to keep up.

The story of the Latin Programme – *Via Facilis*

Zanna Wing-Davey

The second part of this chapter provides an overview of a not-for-profit organization which widens access to the study of Latin in London schools. The Latin Programme was established in 2007 to find innovative ways to help state primary school children attain higher literacy levels and thereby improve their life chances. We concentrate on the link between literacy levels and future prospects because, according to the National Literacy Trust (NLT), individuals with good literacy skills are more likely to have higher self-esteem, better health, better jobs and higher wages than those with poor literacy skills.[1]

We work in inner-city London schools teaching literacy through Latin. We use Latin to improve literacy because it is the most orderly, logical, disciplined, structured, systematic, consistent grammar in existence. Latin is also the base of half of the English language. Thus, learning Latin dramatically broadens students' vocabulary while deepening their understanding of English grammar. Our fun yet rigorous approach combines classical Latin with modern English for primary school students.

Background

Ten years ago, in 2007, the Latin Programme – *Via Facilis* (hereafter referred to as the Latin Programme) first began its mission with a pilot project in London. Dr Richard Gilder III, a Classics teacher of many years and a philanthropist, had run successful workshops in Spanish Harlem (an inner-city neighbourhood in New York City) using his innovative method of teaching Latin. Together with a team of thirteen teachers and directors, of whom I was one, we thought we could use this method to improve English literacy in state primary schools in London. At the time, this idea was both radical and a somewhat difficult sell. Indeed, although the Latin Programme – which teaches grammatical concepts in English first, before repeating the lessons in relation to Latin – was free, it was a difficult sell. Perhaps this was because head teachers themselves had never experienced Latin, or because they felt the primary curriculum was already crowded. Days and weeks were spent cold-calling schools by telephone and emailing entire school boroughs, but still only a small number of schools were prepared to take the risk. And we were a risk: we did not use trained teachers (many of the people delivering the Latin Programme were students from University College London) and we had no curriculum and no real strategic plan.

The foundation of the programme was and remains Gilder's method of teaching Latin. He had written a textbook (*Via Facilis*) to aid his teaching in independent secondary schools in the United States, but in its existing form it was not suitable for a primary context. The book's philosophy, that everything in Latin should first be looked at and compared to English, is very different from the pedagogical approach familiar to English classicists. For the students it was at first unfamiliar, unconventional and challenging because they often had no prior formal knowledge of grammatical terms, accidence or syntax. The method of Latin teaching in schools familiar to most classicists is that of the Cambridge Latin Course (CLC). The CLC is designed using an inductive language-acquisition model traditionally used in the teaching of modern languages (Morgan 1968), whereby students are immersed in a narrative, which should be read at a swift pace. Within this model there is little explicit emphasis on grammar – students should come to 'gradually acquire a personal competence in grammar' (Rickets 1972) through repeated exposure. Some teachers supplement the CLC with additional Latin grammar resources in order to achieve the requirements of GCSE and A-Level. The focus is on reading comprehension (Hunt 2016) of Latin with no translation into Latin.

In contrast, the Latin Programme explicitly focuses on translating English into Latin and Latin into English in equal measure, once the understanding of the English grammar has been established. Some might argue that the usefulness of studying English grammar in comparison with Latin grammar is pointless given that Latin is an inflected language and English is not. However, what our programme is keen to impart to students is a mechanism for investigating and understanding grammatical structures, for getting used to analysing and questioning how language works, how and why linguistic patterns matter, and to get students used to the idea that there are patterns in their own language, even if they are not directly relatable to Latin grammar.

In the last ten years, the teaching landscape in London has changed significantly.

Anecdotally, classicists know that Latin and Classical Greek help them with their understanding of English grammar – indeed my only knowledge of grammar was garnered in these lessons as English grammar was not formally taught when I was at my London comprehensive school from the mid-1990s to the early 2000s. We surmised that Latin would work well with students from economically disadvantaged backgrounds who spoke English as a second language, because when Gilder had carried out workshops on Latin in Spanish Harlem in New York City, he had had very positive responses. But this did not constitute any kind of proof, and head teachers (very few of whom had any experience of Latin themselves) were resistant to the transferability of the approach to Latin in London classrooms. However, in 2007/08 the UK was in the midst of a literacy crisis and London schools were under great pressure to improve. In 2006 levels of reading were significantly below those of other European countries, particularly for boys, whose attitudes towards reading and literacy had become increasingly negative (Twist et al. 2007). In 2007, only 67 per cent of students at the end of primary school were achieving expected levels of writing (National Literacy Trust 2008). Nevertheless, we were determined and enthusiastic from the start that the programme would be effective. One way we ensured this was to hold collaborative discussions with head teachers about classroom practice and educational outcomes so that we had a clear understanding of what they hoped we would achieve. During these meetings, we outlined our educational philosophy: we have always taught mixed-ability, whole-class groups. We have not been prepared to offer sessions exclusively for 'high-achieving' students because we believe that Latin is for all and should not be a privilege reserved for the social and intellectual elite. These were the terms that we offered to schools and we have not shifted from them since. So although the schools that implemented the Latin Programme at the beginning knew they were taking a risk, we were completely confident in our arguments that it would make a difference to all the students – not just a few. We just needed a chance to show them.

The pilot began in October 2007 with an intensive period of training with Gilder. In this period he explained the philosophy behind the programme and the finer points of Latin grammar that many of us (thirteen untrained, trained and student teachers with a range of experience) had never come to terms with. Latin Programme teachers then went into schools, taught lessons and, afterwards, met formally every week to share our experiences from the classroom and to plan the next week's lessons. Some ideas were fixed from the outset. For instance, we would ask the children to answer plenary-style questions each week on slips of paper which would be typed up by teachers as blog posts and put on the website (examples can be viewed at www.thelatinprogramme.co.uk/what-students-say-about-the-latin-programme/). Storytelling workshops were used effectively as a way of introducing the programme to schools and thereafter as a regular feature throughout the year. These workshops proved an especially useful way to convey complex ideas in an engaging and immersive way. But as our experience grew, we realized that we would need a range of ways to engage students in this challenging curriculum. Students would be expected to know and understand the present indicative active verb system and endings, the case system and all first declension noun endings and be able to translate from English into Latin and vice versa in their first year (see Appendices 1 and 2 for example exercises and Appendix 3 for the curriculum flowchart). This is where the weekly teacher meetings were key. In these meetings we were able to share our experiences of what was and was not working. Overwhelmingly we found that the songs and games and other kinaesthetic methods we trialled (both the then executive director Annette Kramer and I had backgrounds in drama) were the most effective methods and the key to engaging our students in this somewhat tricky material. As a result, each week each teacher had to prepare a new song or game that they felt would work to explain the particular grammar point we were covering. We used our experiences both inside and outside of the classroom to make the lessons as lively and original as possible. Since one of our new teachers was an amateur rapper, we asked him to create raps about Latin and English literacy that we could add to the collection of resources. The noun song is an example and can be viewed here: www.thelatinprogramme. co.uk/latin-programme/songs-raps/. When children became more confident with technology, they designed their own apps, made their own videos and the blog posts of the initial years were phased out.

In 2009 the NLT reported that teaching of literacy was not engaging students 'in a way which is relevant to the twenty-first century lived experience', and urged teachers to 'tap into the interests and passions of their pupils' and stated that 'the curriculum must evolve in order to embrace non-traditional forms of literacy' (National Literacy Trust 2009).[2] However, in 2009, in five primary schools in London, we *were* engaging students. We *were* enacting the advice from the NLT quoted above – every week from Brent to Lambeth, from Islington to Tower Hamlets. And it worked – results will be discussed later in this chapter. We developed a new curriculum in which these songs, games and raps became an integral part of the teaching and learning experience and which were modes that we used to encourage students to understand seemingly complex grammatical material in both Latin and English.

Grammar had been the dirty secret of Latin teaching for many years. The received wisdom, from my experience teaching Latin and Classical Greek at secondary school level, is that students would be overwhelmed by too much grammar and so one should introduce grammar points slowly and in a piecemeal fashion. But somewhat counter-intuitively, we found as we developed the programme that even the youngest of students responded to a more grammar-focused model of Latin. Using music, games and kinaesthetic methods is essential given the limited time (one hour per week) that we have with students. This seemed to resonate with Ofsted, the national inspection service for state schools in England which, in one report, noted the challenge presented by the Latin Programme with approval:

When pupils are offered good opportunities to contribute, their behaviour improves as they become engrossed in their tasks, and they then make faster progress in their learning. For example, pupils learn Latin with a real sense of excitement, because tasks are challenging and the teacher engages all pupils, ensuring that they are alert and responsive throughout the lesson. In such lessons, pupils make faster progress. (Ofsted 2009, Report for St. Mary's Church of England Primary School)[3]

At present we have no more than one hour a week throughout the academic year. Crucially too, there is no homework because in a primary school context this is impossible to implement consistently across all schools. We must teach the 'meat and potatoes' of Latin in class time alone with no threats of tests. For our students, the only reason for learning is because it is fun and getting it right means that they can understand more. Two teachers from one participating primary school noted the enthusiasm of students for Latin: 'Brilliant — the children loved it and looked forward to it each week'. 'The games enable the children to learn in a non-threatening way. Well done! I really enjoyed the Latin lessons and brushed up on my Latin!' (Class teachers at St Joseph's Roman Catholic Primary School).

Thus after one, two or three years (depending on school curriculum choices), students ultimately find themselves possessing an armoury of Latin and English knowledge which they have little consciousness of having acquired.

In 2011 the Latin Programme received significant financial support from Shine, a charity that improves children's life chances through the funding of educational projects. The grant was over three years and our remit was to expand significantly and to show (by quantitative data collection and analysis) that our programme really does make a difference to children's lives. In this funded period we quadrupled the number of participating students, from eight classes at four schools to thirty-nine classes at nine schools and we have continued to expand yearly even after the grant from Shine ended. Until we received this grant, we had had very positive feedback from head teachers, class teachers and parents but had no concrete, measurable results showing that the programme was working. This changed with Shine. We collected literacy data from our schools, and by examining it Shine was able to reveal that the Latin Programme seemed to be making a real difference to students' literacy results, which are summarized below. Overall the children in our classes are considered underachieving according to the usual criteria: a high number of children whom we teach receive free school meals, have English as a second (or third) language, are from ethnic-minority backgrounds and/or have special educational needs. Therefore our targets were realistic. We wanted to bring at least 50–60 per cent of classes up to a pass in literacy based on the English National Curriculum for key stage 2, and to bring the class average up to or beyond the national average in literacy after two years of Latin instruction. But the results far surpassed our target and by the end of the 2013/14 school year, 92 per cent of our students (those who had studied for three years) were at the expected level for reading, and 83 per cent were at the expected level for writing. And we also saw that the greater the number of years of the programme, the better the results. Students who had learned Latin for one year did well, but results for students who had experienced three years of the programme showed a 10 per cent overall improvement (see Table 7.1).

Table 7.1 Percentage of students at expected level for reading and writing following Latin instruction

Percentage of Students at Expected Level for Reading and Writing		
	Reading	Writing
Students at expected level after one year of Latin	90%	80%
Students at expected level after two years of Latin	92%	85%
Students at expected level after three years of Latin	98%	91%

Students for whom English is an additional language (EAL) are generally regarded as disadvantaged because their level of understanding of English is, on the whole, less advanced than that of native speakers. And given that many of our students speak non Indo-European languages at home, one might question the usefulness of learning Latin. However, we have found, time and time again, that these students truly excel in our classes. Latin acts as a *tabula rasa* for all: the ultimate, yet healthy, leveller. EAL students gain great confidence from the fact that they are so good at this particular subject while they may be marked out as 'behind' in English lessons. And the fact that Latin is a 'new' subject for all at key stage 2 makes it an excellent choice as a primary foreign language. As a student at St Joseph's Roman Catholic Primary School said, 'I like learning phrases and words in Latin than in English. Also, I like finding the clue in the Latin words and what that word is related to.' 'It is fun to learn other languages, in lessons we have lots to do. It is exciting to learn more about English and French through Latin. Latin challenges me, which is great', said another student at St Peter's Primary School.

For impact we have always worked within the curriculum rather than in after-school clubs, break-out groups etc. and, since the government's inclusion (in 2014) of Latin as a foreign language at key stage 2, we provide the foreign-language provision for many of our schools. Before this, the primary-school foreign-language provision teaching had often been somewhat *ad hoc*, with the majority of schools depending on a teacher on the school staff knowing and teaching a chosen language (Driscoll et al. 2004). Our schools have found that they can get far more consistent results by choosing the Latin Programme, as both their literacy and their foreign-language provision will be taken in hand (Department of Education 2013), and that their students will be prepared with a foundation of language learning for secondary school.

We used a variety of different techniques for recruiting schools: workshops in different London boroughs, sessions in public libraries, conferences, contacting schools individually and sending out emails to head teachers. Later, as we garnered evidence for improvement in literacy results, we targeted schools that were in need of support with literacy because of the greater probability that they would be open to new initiatives. This seemed to chime with head teachers' needs, as the head teacher of St Mary's Church of England Primary School reported: 'We have seen a sharp increase in our literacy results as a result. Our ethnic minority children who have English as an additional language are now taking pride in their mother tongue.' The comments of the head teacher of another primary school noted:

> 'We need to continually raise standards in literacy and we hoped that the *Latin Programme* would improve staff and pupil understanding of grammar whilst also covering the need for Modern Foreign Languages. For years we had struggled with French provision and had seen very little progress or achievement. With the Latin Programme we can teach progress and achievement in Latin and SPAG [Spelling, Punctuation and Grammar].'

Once schools began to take on Latin as a foreign language and see for themselves the improvement of their literacy results, the need to cold-call schools diminished and ultimately became redundant. The programme spoke for itself and was its own advertisement.

> 'The *Latin Programme* covers [the] Modern Foreign Language requirement. [It] provides challenging, motivating and thought-provoking lessons. [It] provides an understanding of the structure of languages which should very much support future learning' (Head teacher of a London primary school).

Such word of mouth feedback among school leaders became our most effective means of marketing. One hundred per cent of head teachers surveyed from 2014 to 2016 reported that they would recommend the Latin Programme to other schools.

We had found creative and innovative ways of relaying Latin and language learning to children and we now began to apply this same approach to spreading the word about the relevance of Latin and its impact on children's literacy. With a very small staff, all working part-time from home, our resources were and have always been slim and so we employed a strategist over a period of eight weeks and thought through the most effective and cheapest way to reach more children. We decided on a multi-pronged approach that could be undertaken by our small team: we would look to make connections with other organizations on projects, speak about the programme at every opportunity to any audience, work to engage the media and raise our profile using social media. As a result we formed relationships with Classics in Communities, Classics for All, Cambridge University, University College London and Oxford University. We wrote an article for *Primary Teacher's Update* and I spoke at a number of university conferences. Kimcha Rajkumar, our programme director, engaged with the media and managed to get us featured in *The Independent* on Sunday, BBC World Service and France's answer to CNN, itélé. She also maximized our use of social media, designing twitter and facebook campaigns around #WhyLatin?, #I♥Latin, #LatinResources and #teachLatin, launched our first online fundraising platform and redesigned our website. Thus, we were able to develop the profile of the Latin Programme with virtually no professional marketing. Our growth, however, is restricted by our supply of teachers. Teacher recruitment is still one of our most challenging tasks. When we started we tried using a range of teachers with a variety of training backgrounds, from trained educators to students at University College London with little or no teaching experience. They were thrown into schools and it was hoped that, with the support of weekly meetings, that would be enough. But as the programme developed it became clear that the type of person required to carry out the Latin Programme's unique blend of academic rigour, discipline, creative engagement and commitment had to be both an experienced teacher and a maverick. Every one of our teachers is expected to embody the ethos of the programme, to be confident in handling a class of mixed-ability pupils and to be comfortable using and enacting their own creative resources. As one parent from St Monica's Primary School noted:

'I can say without a doubt that my son has found this class to be one of the most enjoyable classes taught at the school. He has told me that everyone in the class is engaged irrespective of their abilities which shows what an excellent teacher can be like and do. [The *Latin Programme*] is an excellent addition to the curriculum which has helped enormously with his grammar and understanding of language.'

In fact, all of our teachers are actively engaged in professions other than teaching. These range from music and theatre to photography and even marketing. Their work straddles more than one world, each feeding into the other. The classroom becomes a richer environment for learning.

We have a successful teaching-assistant scheme whereby we offer volunteers the opportunity to work with our teachers in schools, and we have also run a teacher-training project, which was funded by the charity Classics for All. Both these schemes have given participants valuable experience in the classroom and of teaching Classics, many of whom have gone on to gain places on PGCE courses or to teach in independent schools and other educational establishments.

As the Latin Programme has grown, so too has the fight to put Classics back on the educational agenda. In the last ten years, we have helped to dismantle the fallacy that Latin and Classics are subjects only suitable for higher-level ability groups and the privileged elite. Our mission is to deconstruct the imposing and daunting grandeur of Classics; we are liberating it from its ivory tower and breaking down prejudices before they have had a chance to fester or even occur. Although the monolithic nature of Classics is often denigrated, for us this has been its strength. Like Shakespeare, it withstands a myriad of approaches, from the reverent to the iconoclastic, yet cannot but retain its essential worth. In our case we have been able to build on an unconventional, boisterous yet sturdy approach to the monolith that surprises and engages the students, to their benefit and to the benefit of the wider community.

We have now created a four-year course or an accelerated two-year course and are in the process of creating an interactive textbook, which we will be able to scale across to schools that do not have the full programme. Demand for our resources is incredibly high and it is very important to us that we are able to affect the wider teaching of Classics and pass on our experiences to other Classics teachers and, in fact, to teachers in general. As a result of this burgeoning demand there are now a number of state primary schools in London where students are on their fourth year of curricular Latin:

'I look forward to it because it is actually exciting to learn more about the ancient world and languages' (Student, St Peter's, Year 6).

It seems like, for the meantime, we are here to stay ...

Appendix 1: A Point of Similarity: The English Verb and The Latin Verb

Example: vocāmus:
  voc/ā/mus
    base: voc- = 'call'
        thematic vowel: – ā-, indicates 1st conjugation
            active personal ending: -mus = 'we' act on 'x'

1. laudō

    ___/___/___

    base: _____ = _____

      thematic vowel: _____, indicates _____ conjugation

        active personal ending: _____ = _____

2. laudās

    ___/___/___

    base: _____ = _____

      thematic vowel: _____, indicates _____ conjugation

        active personal ending: _____ = _____

3. laudat

    ___/___/___

    base: _____ = _____

      thematic vowel: _____, indicates _____ conjugation

        active personal ending: _____ = _____

4. moneō

    ___/___/___

    base: _____ = _____

      thematic vowel: _____, indicates _____ conjugation

        active personal ending: _____ = _____

5. monēs

    ___/___/___

    base: _____ = _____

      thematic vowel: _____, indicates _____ conjugation

        active personal ending: _____ = _____

6. monet

    ___/___/___

    base: _____ = _____

      thematic vowel: _____, indicates _____ conjugation

        active personal ending: _____ = _____

Appendix 2: The English Noun vs. The Latin Noun: Similar … ?

We like **life**. English Case: Objective
Latin Case: Accusative
Latin form: vītam

1. The people of our **homeland**.

   English Case: _____

   Latin Case: _____

   Latin form: _____

2. He buys a rose for a **woman**.

   English Case: _____

   Latin Case: _____

   Latin form: _____

3. He buys a **rose**.

   English Case: _____

   Latin Case: _____

   Latin form: _____

4. They go by **road**.

   English Case: _____

   Latin Case: _____

   Latin form: _____

5. They open the **gates**.

   English Case: _____

   Latin Case: _____

   Latin form: _____

6. A **queen** rules the city.

   English Case: _____

   Latin Case: _____

   Latin form: _____

7. She decorates the poet with a **crown**.

   English Case: _____

   Latin Case: _____

   Latin form: _____

Appendix 3: Curriculum Flowchart

Level 1

Term 1: The Latin Verb
A Introduction to Latin
Identifying parts of speech (concentrating on nouns and verbs)
Tense, person and number
Recognition of and formation of 1st conjugation present indicative active

———

B Principal parts of the verb (English & Latin)
Understanding of the terms present/indicative/active
Identifying person and number

Term 2: The Latin Noun
A 1st declension all cases introduced but Nominative and Accusative in detail
Identify and explore role of the noun in English (pronouns etc)
1st declension Latin noun endings for Nom + Acc learnt through games
Translation of nominative, accusative singular with plural as extension

———

B Genitive, Dative and Ablative cases and case endings
Translation of all cases

Term 3: Translating Nouns and Verbs together
A Revision of present indicative active and full range of knowledge about verbs
Combination with nouns to make simple clauses
Subject/verb agreement with plurals as extension
Syntax (overview: English/Latin/Yoda)

———

B Combination of nouns and verbs to make more complex sentences
2nd conjugation verbs and thematic vowels
English into Latin for nominative and accusative with other cases as extension
Syntax to include placing of other cases

Level 1 is broken into A and B to allow for children in Years 3 and 4 to progress to the more complex concepts of the Level (material B) in their second year. Where significant progress is made in these year groups, advancement to Level 2 will be considered in the third term.

Notes

1   www.literacytrust.org.uk/about/faqs/283_why_is_literacy_important. (Accessed 1 April 2018).

2   www.literacytrust.org.uk/assets/0000/3816/FINAL_Literacy_State_of_the_Nation_-_30 _March_2010.pdf. (Accessed 1 April 2018).

3   https://reports.ofsted.gov.uk/provider/files/946637/urn/101537.pdf. (Accessed 1 April 2018).

References

DfE (2013), *Consultation Report Foreign Languages at Key Stage 2* (February 2013), Department for Education. Available online: www.education.gov.uk/consultations/downloadableDocs/ks2_choice_ of_languages_consultation_ report_final_published%20(2).pdf. (Accessed 24 March 2018).

Driscoll, P., Jones, J. and Macrory, G. (2004), *The Provision of Foreign Language Learning for Pupils at Key Stage 2*, Department for Education and Skills Research Report 572, Canterbury Christchurch University College.

Gilder III, R. (2006), *Via Facilis: Mastering Latin and Understanding Language*, Self-published: Authorhouse.

Hunt, S. (2016), *Starting to Teach Latin*, London: Bloomsbury.

Morgan, G. (1968), *Textbook Analysis: A Refresher Course*, Texas Classical Association. Available online: http://www.txclassics.org/old/exrpts2.htm. (Accessed 24 March 2018).

National Literacy Trust (2008), *Literacy: State of the Nation*. Available online: www.literacytrust.org. uk/assets/0000/3816/FINAL_Literacy_State_of_the_Nation_-_30_March_2010.pdf. (Accessed 24 March 2018).

National Literacy Trust (2009), *Manifesto for Literacy*.

Ofsted (2009), *Report for St. Mary' s Church of England Primary School*. Available online: https:// reports.ofsted.gov.uk/provider/files/946637/urn/101537.pdf. (Accessed 1 April 2018).

Rickets, M. (1972), 'The Cambridge Latin Course: An Appraisal', *Didaskalos*, 4 (3): 165–173.

The Daily Telegraph (2000), There is no better way to learn all about language. Available online: https// www.telegraph.co.uk/education/4791662/There-is-no-better-way-to-learn-all-about-langauage. html. (Accessed 1 April 2018).

Times Educational Supplement (1995), Newspaper article by Nick Tate on 14 July, no longer available.

Twist, L., Schagen, I. and Hodgson, C. (2007), *Readers and Reading: The National Report for England 2006,* PIRLS (Progress in International Reading Literacy Study), Slough: NFER.

CHAPTER 8
LATIN IN NORFOLK: JOINING UP THE DOTS
Jane Maguire

I first considered the idea of Latin for primary children when working with Gifted and Talented children in a somewhat unlikely area of rural and coastal Norfolk where there was significant economic, social and cultural deprivation. Gifted students are those whose potential is distinctly above average in one or more of the following domains of human ability: intellectual, creative, social and physical. Talented students are those whose skills are distinctly above average in one or more areas of human performance. UK government education policy directives between 2002 and 2010 required specialist provision to be made for students so identified in every school (Hunt 2016, pp. 26–27). Latin had very largely died out in the county's state secondary schools and had always been extremely rare in its state primary schools. The Excellence Cluster initiative was part of the government drive to raise standards in schools in areas of disadvantage. Cluster schools were located in areas facing many and varied socio-economic problems. A pilot scheme was introduced using *Minimus* (Bell 1999) in one school in the Norfolk Excellence Cluster, with a group of ten academically able Year 3 children (aged 7). It was envisaged as an enrichment activity designed to challenge them and extend their horizons. For me this proved to be one of the highlights of a long teaching career. It not only confirmed my belief in the intrinsic value of Latin, but it also revealed how successful it could be with young children and the extent of its potential in cross-curricular learning. We sat around a table and learned together, the ten children, their teacher, an interested governor and myself; it proved to be a fascinating and stimulating learning experience for us all.

It became clear from the outset that it was perfectly possible to train non-specialist teachers to deliver Latin in primary schools and that they relished the opportunity to teach something new and unrestricted in terms of the National Curriculum. The Excellence Cluster was able to fund further training and resources and Latin became a valued enrichment activity in many schools in the group, delivered mostly by a team of young Gifted and Talented mentors. It even attracted praise from one inspector from the state schools' inspection organization Ofsted.

This experience demonstrated that Latin was a highly successful activity for able children, but I have since become convinced that it is potentially of huge benefit to all children regardless of ability and there has been a significant development in Norfolk schools, where Latin teaching has grown from small, selected groups to mixed-ability, whole-class teaching.

Introducing Latin to more Norfolk schools

The further extension of Latin in Norfolk came about as the result of the Primary Latin Project successfully applying for one of the first grants awarded by the newly established national charity Classics for All. There were two separate projects involving two distinct groups of schools into which Latin was introduced between 2011 and 2013.

The first cluster comprised a high school and seven of its feeder primary schools. The grant covered a two-year period and the schools were identified on the basis of personal knowledge and geographic suitability.

The first move was to speak to head teachers at one of their regular cluster meetings. When offered a proposal for anything new and before even beginning to consider it, head teachers needed to be immediately convinced that:

1. it will benefit their students

2. it will be feasible in financial, staffing and other practical terms.

The initial reaction from the first group of head teachers was polite curiosity (as no one had ever thought of introducing Latin before). They were persuaded to support the project by the offer of free training, support and funding, along with the acknowledgement that this would support their drive for ever higher standards in literacy as well as supporting many other areas of the curriculum. The inclusion of ancient languages in the list of key stage 2 languages was very helpful (the government had made it a requirement that all pupils at this stage would learn a language from an approved list). Along with French, Spanish, Italian, German and Mandarin, the ancient languages Latin and Classical Greek were also allowed for the first time. Further influencing factors were the fact that the school did not need to find a Classics teacher or even a specialist languages teacher (a relief for some small schools) and that teaching assistants, particularly higher level ones (who were permitted to take charge of classes while the regular teacher was, for example, absent or undertaking lesson planning and preparation), could be trained to support and even deliver Latin themselves. Secondary head teachers were encouraged to see Latin as a subject which offers extra academic challenge, enhances CVs and university applications and which can be a welcome alternative language for those students not attracted by modern foreign languages (MFL).

A model was developed for each of the seven primary schools to have 'project teachers' working in their schools, teaching *Minimus* once a week to small groups of children (average group size of ten to twelve children). These teachers were myself (a MFL teacher with experience of Gifted and Talented provision and, way back, an O level in Latin), a retired local primary head teacher (with a degree in MFL) and a part-time, experienced Classics teacher. Schools selected children as they saw fit using different criteria (but mostly choosing the more able) and identified a member of staff (teacher or teaching assistant), who observed and supported lessons for the first year, working closely with the project teacher. This person then took on his/her own group during the second year, while the project teacher continued with the original children but remained available for discussion and support. The aim was that, at the end of the two years, Latin would be embedded, head teachers would be convinced and teachers would be confident to continue.

At the secondary school a voluntary, after-school GCSE group was established, using the *Cambridge Latin Course* (1998), taught by our Classics colleague. Participation was voluntary and the course attracted over twenty students aged thirteen and fourteen from Years 9 and 10. The ambitious aim was to reach GCSE in two years, with one weekly session – less than half the GCSE recommended allocation. Interest grew in the school and a second grant was awarded to train two of the school's MFL teachers to start teaching Latin to students in top-attaining language sets in Years 7 and 8 (students aged 11 and 12).

The second project centred around two other local secondary schools and their feeder primaries. Again funded by Classics for All, the format was very different, with training given at the outset to enable teachers to deliver Latin independently in their schools. Secondary teachers received three days of training. One secondary school sent two of their MFL teachers and the other a mixture of four teachers and learning support assistants from a range of different subject areas. A two-day primary training course was delivered by Barbara Bell and myself to two primary head teachers, teachers and teaching assistants from eight different schools. Contact was maintained with these schools throughout the following year and pupil progress was monitored.

Conclusions from these two projects

1. The initial approach to schools needed to be professional, informed and enthusiastic. The idea needed to be sold to them. Their two criteria (see above) needed to be addressed quickly and concisely.

2. The active support of head teachers and senior leaders in schools was crucial.

3. Schools working together in clusters of primary and secondary schools benefitted from close cooperation and sharing of experiences. Secondary schools were likely to offer a continuation of Latin to students coming from primary schools where it was already established and primary schools were encouraged by the knowledge that their pupils would have the opportunity to continue their Latin studies, possibly to GCSE. In some cases teachers were shared between schools in the cluster.

4. Training needed to be high quality and sympathetic to the fact that most teachers needed to be given much reassurance and encouragement in order to build up the self-confidence they needed to embark upon this new subject.

5. It was important to explain to children and their parents why they are studying Latin. This was through sending a simple information sheet home and by inviting parents to observe lessons.

6. The model established for the first project (i.e. with specialist teachers working alongside staff in schools for two years) was the best possible and quickly won the enthusiasm of schools, children and parents. It was, however, a very expensive model and the second project (based on simply providing initial training) was also successful, even if it could not establish such close cooperation. The latter model lacked the impact that the first one had on raising the profile of Latin throughout the school and depended more often on the one teacher being able to continue it, sustainability being thus less assured.

7. The two secondary schools who sent MFL staff to be trained had significantly more success in establishing and sustaining Latin. However, initial training proved to be insufficient to prepare non-specialist teachers to teach to GCSE, a much more challenging prospect than teaching to key stage 3, and most teachers needed further

extension training. Both of the more successful schools introduced Latin into Years 7 and 8 as well as trying to sustain GCSE groups.

8. Teaching Latin in curriculum time provides greater status and sustainability than in a club, but some Latin is better than no Latin.

9. It was very rewarding to see how successful some teaching assistants were. Teaching Latin increased both their personal confidence and their perceived status in the school.

10. Without the initial approach, followed by the funding and ongoing support, it is highly unlikely that any of these sixteen schools would have introduced Latin.

11. Feedback from head teachers, teachers, teaching assistants, parents and children was overwhelmingly positive.

12. In order to ensure sustainability and to embed Latin securely into the curriculum there needs to be continued support and monitoring.

Keeping the momentum going

Once established, it was clear that in both groups there needed to be strategies to maintain the momentum. An obvious weakness can be that often everything depends on one teacher, who might subsequently leave the school. Although in some cases this proved to be positive (insofar as that teacher went on to introduce Latin into a new school), in other cases schools needed to be offered fresh training for a new teacher. Other barriers turned out to be Ofsted reports that necessitated a school concentrating all its efforts on improving in key areas, to the exclusion of Latin. It was, however, encouraging that these schools, who reluctantly stopped Latin, said that they saw it as a temporary measure and planned to resume at some point in the future. Also very clear was the need for projects such as these to be monitored and for schools to feel that there was still support available.

During the projects, support for teachers included setting up networks for email exchanges and occasional meetings where experiences and resources could be shared and discussed and new training sessions offered. As project leader I stressed that I would be happy to answer all queries and to visit schools at their request. Teachers were regularly updated through the *Minimus* newsletter and reminders about new publications, events and opportunities. Beyond the book itself, most of the many extra resources were discussed and tried out at meetings. The numerous opportunities for language-based games, songs and drama were also popular. All of this was valuable in boosting the confidence of the teachers and extending their own knowledge of the subject as well as offering opportunities to showcase Latin to parents and governors.

Within schools, particularly the primaries, general interest was generated by an emphasis on the cross-curricular potential of Latin. Children learn about the Romans in key stage 2 History and about Roman numerals in Maths. The most obvious benefits are seen in literacy, as Latin clearly provides such a wonderful insight into the construction of languages and their relation to each other. Grammar, punctuation and spelling are obvious beneficiaries as well as vocabulary building through word derivations. In addition, Latin lays a foundation for modern language learning, as it introduces children to concepts such as the gender of nouns, adjectival agreement and word order. Whole-school Roman projects include cooking Roman food, burying and excavating time boxes, singing, dancing and drama.

Celebration has played an important part. In some individual schools, parents have been invited to watch Latin assemblies or to observe lessons. Sometimes guests were invited in. As a cluster of schools there were larger events hosted by the secondary school with guest speakers and performances by children. One major celebratory event was held at Norwich Castle for parents, teachers, governors and representatives from local government. Our local MPs were kept informed and were supportive.

Publicity was welcomed and regular interest was shown by the local press, radio and television, all of whom wrote or broadcast positive reports and, in a couple of cases, very supportive editorials. These Norfolk schools featured in promotional films professionally shot for Classics for All.

A major partner has been Norwich Castle Museum. There had long been a Roman Day on offer for primary schools, with the emphasis on the Iceni, Boudicca and the Romans. The learning manager was very open to the idea of building in some Latin for schools studying it. The current programme was developed with four activities in which all the children participate. A guided visit to the Roman Gallery now includes identifying objects mentioned in *Minimus*, commenting on the gallery trail produced for children and labelling showcases with simple Latin adjectives. Artefact handling is presented by a costumed character (a retired Roman gentleman) and again highlights objects from *Minimus*, discussing them and naming them in Latin. A costumed Roman soldier leads an active session, demonstrating and naming in Latin his armour and equipment before marching his troops around the castle to orders given in Latin. The fourth session challenges children to perform a short play in Latin. Simple dressing-up clothes, props and masks add to the excitement of this activity.

Although they have neither Classics department nor Classics PGCE course for initial teacher training, the University of East Anglia in Norwich expressed interest and lectures and seminars were delivered to their primary PGCE students. This is clearly fertile ground with students out on placements in different schools before taking up their permanent positions. Feedback from these MFL students indicated not only how useful they felt some knowledge of Latin would be to children prior to learning a modern language but also how teaching it would improve their own command of grammar in particular.

Just a few years ago it would have been a very surprising suggestion that Latin might be back in Norfolk schools. The fact that over the last decade it has seen a revival in over thirty of our schools is due largely to three factors:

1. The quality of the primary Latin course *Minimus*

2. Funding for training and resources from Classics for All

3. Persistence in approaching schools, offering ongoing support and monitoring progress.

The evidence for the success of these projects comes in the words of those involved. The appendix reports many of the positive comments made by students, parents, head teachers and staff about the two projects. If readers would like to set up a similar project, they should get in contact with the charity Classics for All to investigate funding.

Appendix

Feedback from the Latin in Norfolk Project

From primary head teachers:

- *'progress of the Latin children against pre-set targets in Reading and Writing has been outstanding'*
- *'definitely something we want to continue'*
- *'children regard Latin as something special'*
- *'it has exceeded my expectations'*
- *'a breath of fresh air for our children'*
- *'fantastic professional development for the teacher involved'*
- *'Latin has contributed significantly to enriching our curriculum'*
- *'it has had a profound impact on the children'*

From teachers and teaching assistants:

- *'it's really useful for literacy, extending vocabulary and grammar and the derivation of words'*
- *'I have learnt alongside the children – a good confidence builder. The children know I am not an expert so we are all on a level playing field and this gives them confidence'*
- *'I feel as if I have achieved something new and it is something which I really enjoy and love learning about'*
- *'It has given me an insight into how Latin benefits children with their literacy'*
- *'It has introduced me to a language which I had never considered it possible to get even a simple grasp of'*
- *'I am really enjoying it; it has refreshed what I'd forgotten'*
- *'I was surprised that it could appeal so strongly to children'*
- *'This has been a fantastic opportunity both on a personal level and for the children'*

From pupils:

- *'I like History; Latin is really fun and it has helped me with my English and understanding other languages'*
- *'Learning Latin means I've learnt a lot of longer words and what they mean, so I can use them more and know what they mean'*
- *'Latin has helped me read and made me more confident in myself'*
- *'It has helped me with my spelling and understanding longer more complicated words'*
- *'It's helped me so much with confidence and with other subjects'*
- *'I usually find learning new languages quite hard but with Latin I understood everything'*

- *'Minimus books have been a great way of learning Latin'*
- *'It has taught me to write and speak English better'*
- *'Latin is a good language to learn and it will help your learning skills'*
- *'I loved the Norwich Castle day'*
- *'I wish lessons were longer'*
- *'We learn something new every day'*
- *'I didn't want to do modern languages until now'*
- *'When I'm reading, if I find a Latin word I think about it more than I used to'*
- *'It has helped me with my English and I like the help it gives me'*
- *'I love Latin!'*
- *'It's just brilliant'*
- *'It stretched my mind to a different level of learning'*

From parents:

- *'A really great experience. Children are loving it'*
- *'Fantastic project'*
- *'Delighted that my daughter has been selected. She is extremely enthusiastic about her Latin lessons'*
- *'I wanted to say a very big thank you for the wonderful Latin lessons my son has loved so much. I think his passion for this subject will long continue. Thank you for inspiring him'*

References

Bell, B. (1999), *Minimus: Starting Out in Latin*, Cambridge: Cambridge University Press.

Cambridge School Classics Project (1998), *Cambridge Latin Course*, Cambridge: Cambridge University Press.

Hunt, S. (2016), *Starting to Teach Latin*, London: Bloomsbury Academic.

CHAPTER 9
INTRODUCING LATIN IN A STATE-MAINTAINED SECONDARY SCHOOL IN ENGLAND: LESSONS LEARNED

Rowlie Darby

This chapter looks at the journey of one teacher setting up Latin provision in an English state-maintained school and the subsequent expansion to other state-maintained schools in Brighton and Hove and the surrounding area. It looks at considerations when setting up a Latin club, the lessons learned and areas to avoid. This chapter also examines what it means to be a 'non-specialist' Latin teacher and considers whether this terminology is problematic for teachers in delivering a subject that is often perceived as being 'elitist'. Finally, the chapter will conclude with a table of recommendations on replicating this approach elsewhere in the UK and abroad.

The 'non-specialist' label

Firstly, I feel that it is important to clarify the type of teacher that this chapter is addressing – the 'non-specialist' Latin teacher. What is a 'non-specialist' teacher? How 'non-specialist' is a 'non-specialist'? For some intending to tackle their first Latin class this may mean they need to brush up and refresh their 'rusty' GCSE/A level Latin. Some may have studied a classical subject at university. Some, like myself, may never have studied Latin prior to delivering it.

I once joked to a colleague of mine about an upcoming residential Classics trip that I was taking abroad with our school. Accompanying me on the trip were two other members of staff – both teachers in the Modern Foreign Language department and one was a talented jazz musician. I quipped that Jess was the linguist, I was the classicist and that Nick was the pianist. This received the laugh that I wanted. Unfortunately, the laugh was not for the 'clever' word play but for the presumption of calling myself a 'classicist'. In the eyes of the other teachers I was an English specialist who also taught a bit of an ancient language after school. This anecdote possibly highlights a problem with nomenclature when describing a teacher who is teaching beyond their specialism. 'Non-specialist' as a label could suggest a negative connotation and is probably an unsuitable and outdated one with many secondary school teachers increasingly facing fragmented timetables due to staffing issues such as part-time contracts.

Is being a 'non-specialist' of Latin so very different from a teacher being a 'non-specialist' of any other discipline? I don't think so. Hunt (2016), too, thinks that the term 'non-specialist' is wrong and a 'misnomer'. Hunt points out that although many teachers have not taken a PGCE in Classics, they may have experience of classical subjects from GCSE or A level or even degree level. These teachers are well trained and experienced in their subject areas and are more than capable to deliver an additional subject. In fact, teachers in the state and independent sectors often have to deliver more than just the subject in which they were trained. Perhaps another term could be selected that is less negative? One colleague suggested 'para-specialist' which would be in line with 'paramedic', 'paraglider', etc. A definition of a teacher's ability could also reflect poorly on the perceived difficulty or 'rigour' of a subject. The juxtaposition of 'non-specialist' and Latin could send out dangerous mixed messages to students, staff and parents alike.

Griffiths (2010) suggests that the term 'non-specialist' is ambiguous as if a significant majority of those providing a classical subject have some level of qualification in what they are teaching, then they cannot be considered 'non-specialist'. Information provided in a survey of 'non-specialist' Latin teachers showed that 81 per cent had some form of previous Latin qualification ranging from just over a quarter having a GCSE/O Level, a third had gained an A level and 15 per cent held a university qualification (Griffiths 2010). In a sample of 144 teachers, only 27 (19 per cent) had no formal qualification in Latin. Based on these findings, true 'non-specialist' teachers with no qualification in Latin are a small minority of providers (Darby 2010). That small percentage included me. Was being a 'non-specialist' with no formal qualification in Latin a drawback? With reflection, I would say not. What it can mean is the truly 'non-specialist' Latin teacher (with no previous experience at all of teaching the language) will bring few preconceived ideas to the classroom about 'the right way' to learn it – because they are learners too. I found it was a good idea to be completely transparent in communicating with the students and parents that I too was a learner of Latin. This shifts the usual dynamics of the lesson. I found that the students sometimes corrected me – which was fine! – we were all enjoying learning Latin.

Griffiths (2009a, p. 10) also suggests the need to be cautious in giving out labels such as 'non-specialist' as no teachers remain static in their subject knowledge and are constantly moving through different stages of their development. This thought resonates greatly with me as I went from being an English teacher with no Latin subject knowledge to now teaching around a hundred Latin students each year. Again, no one questions my credentials and I still let the students know that I learnt the language not that long ago. It sets a good example of lifelong learning.

It is telling that the teachers who labelled themselves as 'non-specialists' in the Cambridge School Classics Project (CSCP) survey (2008) are actually trained in subjects that have a great deal in common with the teaching of Latin. The 'non-specialist' tag becomes relevant and more significant within secondary education: at primary education there seems to be more acceptance of teaching a wider range of subjects without applying the 'non-specialist' tag (Darby 2008). Those who identified themselves as secondary modern foreign languages (MFL), History and English teachers have obvious and direct ways into teaching particular elements of the subject: the MFL teachers have a wealth of experience to deliver languages (whether ancient or modern) in up-to-date interactive ways which draw upon excellent practice in Assessment for Learning (AfL) techniques. They also usually have proficiency in at least two languages. These often have similarities to Latin in vocabulary or language construction. History teachers are used to delivering strong enquiry-based sessions and can use these skills when investigating Roman Civilisation topics and interrogating cultural contexts. They may also have taught the subject content of the Romans in key stage 2 or 3 History. The English teachers have particular skills in teaching both language and literature to their students. Perhaps it is self-deception, modesty or self-deprecation – or a combination of all three – that leads a teacher to label themselves a 'non-specialist'.

There seems to be a lack of uniformity, too, in how middle managers and senior leaders consider what level of qualification is appropriate for a Latin teacher to have obtained prior to teaching students: 'Secondary Heads and curriculum leaders say that they would expect at least an A level in Latin or Greek to be able to teach these adequately at GCSE Level but one Head did say that enthusiasm and interest by a member of staff would be acceptable' (Soden 2010).

Why introduce Latin?

Latin can be introduced for a number of reasons. It may be that Latin provision needs only to be re-established in some schools. There are many schools where Latin was allowed to die out when the sole Latin teacher left or retired. In this case, it can be reintroduced as an entirely 'new' subject. It could be that the subject is seen as an ideal platform or extension for the more academically able students. It could also be that Latin is used to support Special Educational Needs and Disability (SEND) students who might not be able to access a modern language – avoiding the speaking and listening challenges that are part of the courses. Latin might be rolled out as it is perceived (rightly or wrongly) to be a 'rigorous' subject that carries a great deal of kudos with parents and the community. It could be suggested that Latin is useful if students are thinking about taking up medicine, law and languages. There is a caveat, though – Hunt (2016) warns that in certain quarters Latin is still used to enable students to access certain universities and certain professions.

On school open-evenings, students and parents often question the use and relevance of Latin. In an attempt to dispel myths, the following text appears on the school website:

> possibly the best reason for studying Latin is because it is a fascinating and enjoyable subject in its own right. Students not only learn the language that the Romans spoke but also (and just as importantly) learn about the people using this language – their lifestyles, entertainment and daily routines. (Patcham High School 2017)

From small beginnings ... some key achievements

In 2003, I set up a small after-school Latin club at a non-selective state secondary school on the outskirts of Brighton and Hove. The school had never previously offered Latin. I had never taught Latin before – in fact I had never had a Latin lesson, either. In retrospect, this seems like madness. So why did this happen? Why was Latin chosen over a number of other subjects that could have, quite as easily, been selected as extra-curricular?

2003 was also the year in which *The Teaching of Classics* (Morwood 2003) was published. This collection of articles was groundbreaking in presenting an outline from twenty teachers from different educational backgrounds of the historical development of classical subjects up to the turn of the century. In addition, they looked beyond to the challenges that classical subjects may face in the future.

Two essays seemed immediately relevant to me for guidance in setting up a beginners' Latin club in a comprehensive school. Wilkinson (2003) and Affleck (2003) both drew upon their experience of establishing Latin into their schools both on- and off-curriculum. These essays in particular gave our school the support and confidence to introduce Latin. They enabled us to see how it had been done and what it could look like. What is of great interest, looking back at these essays fifteen years later, is how Latin provision at secondary state schools has improved since the writing of these articles. Students taking GCSE and equivalent exams have increased by about a third from the GCSE entries in 2001 and the data that Wilkinson (2003) presents. Hunt (2016) attributes this to the gradual rolling out of the new Latin WJEC Level 2 Certificates which challenged OCR's monopoly of Latin GCSE.

In 2003, a shortage of teachers coming into the profession to replace those leaving was highlighted as a major issue in the provision of Latin (Affleck 2003). Affleck tells us that the places available for teacher training in Classics had been cut to just three institutions – 'Cambridge University, KCL, and Strathclyde University' (Affleck 2003) with just over thirty trainees able to follow the PGCE courses. By 2016, the numbers had risen to almost fifty when including school-centred initial teacher training programmes (SCITTs) and school direct (SD) teachers. Currently, three higher education institutions provide the majority of the PGCE Classics (with qualified teacher status) placements – the University of Cambridge, KCL and the University of Sussex (Hunt 2016). Although this is an increase from thirteen years ago it is still not enough to 'fill the 150–180 advertised vacancies for Classics posts each year' (Hunt 2016). This may be why 'non-specialists' such as myself have plugged the gaps and launched their own Latin provision.

Over time, the Latin club at my school grew and by 2009 we had had thirty-six students pass through the classroom at Patcham High School. The plan from the outset was always to work towards the Latin GCSE exam and gain recognition for the students who had taken the subject. Unfortunately, this was not possible for some of the older students who had started the club at the beginning. This was one of the main limitations in learning alongside the students – it took us all longer to get to the GCSE than I had previously predicted.

I am often asked what the best way of structuring an after-school Latin club is. I am not sure that there is a definitive answer. Should the club be open to just one year group? Should it be open to all year groups? Should it be invitation only? Should it be open to anyone with an interest in the subject? I have tried a variety of different combinations at different schools (as part of our Classics for All funded outreach), and they all have their pros and cons. What follows is a range of possible models which may prove instructive for others.

The basic model starts with a single, after-school club in one school. Through formal and informal links with other schools in the surrounding area, teachers form a network of mutual support and they offer Latin lessons on-timetable and off-timetable.

Case study 1 – Patcham High School, Brighton

When I first started teaching Latin, the club at my school was open to students of any age and ability who wanted to learn Latin. On one hand, this was good as it meant that the club always had a healthy number of students rather than just two or three from one particular year. On the other hand, due to the different ages, there were sometimes issues such as pacing the work at the right level for everyone and only the students who were in key stage 3 when we started the club would attend the school long enough to complete the course and take the Latin GCSE. However, implementing a vertical group meant that the older students were able to guide and help the younger students. Clearly, there are social and intellectual benefits of this approach: students get to work outside of their peer group. As they move beyond their social comfort zones, students find themselves learning more as they take on the role of teacher, while younger students are stretched and challenged to keep up with the older students.

Initially, the Latin club was run for an hour after school each week and open to whomever wished to attend. It was interesting to see who did attend. Regardless of their abilities, all the students had one thing in common – they were interested enough in the ancient world to give up their time to learn more about it. Some were curious about languages, some were fascinated by ancient history and others were captivated by how the Romans were portrayed in recent films, books and television shows. After ten years of running Latin as an after-school club, it was moved onto the curriculum and now sits alongside the other curricular option subjects in key stage 4.

Wishing to build upon the success of Latin at Patcham, a plan was developed to offer the subject to other local schools in the form of 'hubs' as part of the school partnership programme in Brighton and Hove. Funding was sought and gained from Classics for All to enable this to happen in three further schools.

Case study 2 – Blatchington Mill School, Hove

This was the first Latin hub set up as a partnership initiative with Patcham High School. It was operated in the same way as the original Latin club with one hour a week allocated after school. This hub ran in parallel with the Patcham's Twilight Latin enabling resources to be shared and the opportunity to run joint workshops nearer the exams and even join up to go on a residential trip to Rome. The majority of the students were from one year group; however, there were a small number from other years. Interestingly, one of the Year 8s and two of the Year 9s gained A grades in their WJEC Level 2 certificate. The success of these particular students reaching typical Year 11 GCSE target grades could strongly indicate that the availability of accelerated courses and the implementation of personalization and choice was right for them as they were ready to take their exams up to three years earlier than is customary.

We also trialled inviting students from other secondary schools and one of the local sixth forms to participate. This was partially successful. Although the students from the sixth form were very keen to engage with the course, they found that the pace of the lessons was too slow – especially since they were more used to working as independent learners. These students were able to be accommodated at their college in a one-year fast-track course. Having students from other nearby comprehensives was positive in making tentative links with other schools, but it did not facilitate any sort of solid Latin provision in those schools. Once the students had completed the course and taken their exams, there was still no Latin in their particular school. As this was our first hub, we ran the clubs for longer than we anticipated, taking two groups through their examinations. Since then, the school has put Latin onto the curriculum and has enabled two English teachers to complete Latin Continuing Professional Development (CPD). The first independent Latin group successfully took their WJEC Level 2 Latin exams in 2016.

Case study 3 – Cardinal Newman Catholic School, Hove

At the second hub Latin was again offered for one hour a week. However, the school made the decision to target Year 9 students. This was a practical move as all of the students in this year had been learning Spanish from Year 7 so they picked up how the Latin language worked and made connections with the vocabulary very quickly. The new club generated such interest that around seventy students attended the first lesson. Two separate groups were taught in adjacent classrooms. Four teachers (Humanities and MFL) were following the course and teaching the students alongside me with the intention that they would carry on providing the Latin after the first full cycle of exams thereby providing a working model for sustainability after I left. Eventually, however, the teachers who were going to take charge of the Latin group gained additional responsibilities and promotions within the school and did not have the capacity to fit in extra lessons after school. Running an extra-curricular subject is hugely time demanding – and attempting to do this in alongside other responsibilities can be problematic. Fortunately, staffing for teaching the Latin has now been addressed and the school has relaunched the Latin club. The first cohort sat exams was in 2016. The students achieved a batch of stunning results.

Sustainability can be a real issue. For this reason, it is a good idea to train a group of teachers in any one school, to ensure that there is some continuity when staff members assume additional responsibilities or move schools.

Case study 4 – Varndean School, Brighton

The newest Latin hub in Brighton and Hove is at Varndean School. Like in the other hubs Latin is delivered for an hour each week after school. It is offered as a two-year course for students in Years 7–10 and is run as an extension of the Modern Foreign Languages department. Progress is being made by staff and students. A second cohort of pupils has now begun learning Latin.

Making choices

Textbook

I chose the Cambridge Latin Course (CLC) textbooks as it is a reading course as opposed to the more traditional grammar-translation courses – still predominately the image presented by the media of what Latin teaching and learning looks like. While a grammar-translation course is heavy on the understanding of grammar and vocabulary prior to the translation of Latin, a reading course is designed 'to promote reading comprehension of Latin' (Hunt 2016) through a series of illustrated linked stories and model sentences in Latin which 'drip feed' language features and new vocabulary in each chapter. This I found was manageable for the students on only one hour a week, off-timetable and treated as a Latin 'club'. I am not sure that the students would have persevered with a Latin club that followed a grammar-translation course approach. I am sure, however, that I too at the time did not have the experience to deliver a grammar-translation course when I was learning alongside them.

The final exam results of the students would suggest that the CLC works. However, there has been some criticism of reading courses in their staggered approach to introducing new language features – for instance, the ablative case is not discussed until towards the end of Book III of the CLC – although students have met it without realizing it prior to this. While this might prove annoying to a specialist Latin teacher, it is easy to forget that the students are coming to the language new just as they did when they learnt to read English as small children. Just like then, pictures are used to help their understanding and illustrate the text that they are being introduced to – especially the language features. Would you stop reading the 'The Gruffalo' to a toddler to explain the mouse is using a simple form of the future tense when informing the fox that he is 'going to have lunch with a gruffalo' (Donaldson 1999, p. 2)? I would suggest not. I was in a fairly unique position insomuch as I was learning alongside the students and had no previous knowledge about any Latin beyond the stage that we were working on. Occasionally, there were a few places where unfamiliar vocabulary was used that would not be explained until later in the course. If queried, this could be briefly explained before continuing with the text.

A real benefit with choosing the CLC as our course is the smoother transition to the Latin exams provided by WJEC/Eduqas, as the Cambridge School Classics Project provides additional teachers' resources for this exam specification.

Exam board

The first student ever to sit the GCSE Latin exam in 2007 at Patcham High School had only one exam board to choose from – OCR. It is comprised of four exam papers. This was particularly demanding for students who had received only one hour a week of teaching. The GCSE equivalent WJEC Level 1 and 2 Latin Certificates (introduced from 2010) seemed more suitable for our time-restricted learning context as there was the option to take either the Latin Language Certificate or the Latin Literature papers.

Our students also take the OCR Entry Level Certificates, which can be seen as a stepping stone between the CLC Certificates (basic proficiency certificates offered by CSCP) and the GCSE/Level 2 Certificates.

A new suite of GCSE (9–1) Latin exams is being rolled out for first teaching from September 2016 and first assessment in 2018. Both OCR and WJEC Eduqas now offer exams that seem more comparable in terms of number of papers and content.

Keeping a record of your Latin club's achievements

It is important for the school to keep a record of the Latin club's progress and achievements. I have a number of display books with clear plastic pockets in which I keep press cuttings, certificates, letters about trips and testimonials from parents. As well as being an excellent *aide de memoir* it can be brought out at option evenings, and can inspire teachers from other schools to provide their own Latin courses. Press coverage also positively raises the profile of the subject and the school in the local community.

The transition from extra-curricular to on-curriculum

Once Latin has become established as an after-school subject, there is a very strong argument that it can be embedded within the curriculum of the school. As mentioned earlier, at my school key stage 4 Latin made the transition from a twilight subject to being placed on the school timetable – with a compromise that part of the lessons would be after school as a compulsory activity. This one lesson was a 'twilight' lesson with attendance being recorded as it would be for any other timetabled lesson. Having time after school is useful to augment and support the periods on the timetable but the students have to be reminded that it is not a 'club' and their behaviour and attitude needs to reflect this. Providing students with refreshments and snacks is positive in ensuring that they attend but also provides tired and weary students with a bit of a boost after a long school day.

Teachers may wish to keep Latin as an after-school club, especially if they have other responsibilities or if teaching Latin for one hour a week works within their educational context. There is less pressure if Latin is viewed as extra-curricular. Greater flexibility means wider attendance. In an extra-curricular setting, results are viewed as a bonus rather than as an expectation.

A supportive head teacher will agree to the setting up of a Latin club at lunchtime or after school. Not all head teachers might be so accommodating – especially if they remain adamant that potential Latin teachers are not qualified enough. I was fortunate as all three head teachers of my school have been supportive of the subject and did not mind that I was initially learning alongside the students.

Just as important as getting the rubber stamp of approval from the head of the school is the support of a key member of the senior leader team (SLT) who will drive the initiative from the top. For me, this derived from a feeling that they wanted to support my enthusiasm and preparedness to undertake this enterprise which would in turn support the wider aims of the school to provide enrichment for languages and literacy. It is their enthusiasm and championing of Latin that can enable the subject to move from an after-school slot to being incorporated into the KS4 curriculum; to make the transition from being a small group of usually academically able and curious individuals to a whole class of more mixed ability students; to make contact with other local schools and other enthusiastic members of SLT to champion Latin in their institutions.

Trips and events

Although exhausting to plan and run, trips and events are incredibly important in helping students to escape the confines of the classroom and experience what they have been learning about. Visits to the Colosseum, the Roman Forum, the Pantheon and the Circus Maximus create magical memories while serving as revision for students about to sit exams. A trip to Fishbourne Roman Palace can put King Cogidubnus' residence into perspective for those studying Roman Britain. The British Museum, Museum of London and the National Gallery can offer educational visits for school students tailored to their needs. My students have recently enjoyed visiting the Kallos Gallery in Mayfair. In this small private gallery school groups can get closer to ancient artefacts than they can in most museums as the objects are not surrounded entirely by glass. The impact that this has on students' engagement can be significant as they are dealing with ancient primary source material at first hand. When students can touch and pass round a coin, a lamp or a statuette, the ancient world suddenly comes to life.

Visitors to your school can be really beneficial, too. Over the years, we have invited Caroline Lawrence to talk about her Roman Mysteries series of books, a Roman Centurion from the Ermine Street Guards and handling artefact sessions from local museums. The students have also been involved in mosaic making workshops, playing ancient Roman sport via the PE department and being involved in filming a Greek tragedy. These were set up as either additional extra sessions with the Latin cohort or during subject-specific curriculum days. Other staff perhaps were a little bemused as a Roman soldier walked through the school in full battle gear – but it got everyone talking. PE staff were curious to see whether Roman ball games could enthuse their students just as much as current ones (they did!). These initiatives have raised the profile of Latin and Classics within the school and have helped break down unhelpful perceptions of Latin.

School partnerships

In 2003, there were no state secondary schools in Brighton and Hove offering Latin. At the time of writing (2017) five of the nine schools offer Latin to GCSE level for their students. In addition, one of the local sixth-form colleges also offers Latin as a GCSE equivalent – a real success story in the area. So, how did this happen? Through making close links with Latin teachers in other schools in Brighton and Hove and being supported by a range of organizations such as Classics for All, CSCP, universities, JACT, The Roman Society and others.

Opening strange doors

When I initially set up a Latin club with a small group of interested students, I had no idea where this decision would lead to in five years' time – little did I consider the potential curricular ramifications it might precipitate in ten or fifteen years' time. The initial plan was that we should be working towards our Latin GCSE. There were no grand plans beyond this. Yet, sometimes small ideas have a habit of spiralling and taking on a life of their own. As a result of the decision to start learning Latin with my students, the following things have happened: gaining funding from Classics for All to establish Latin provision in other schools in Brighton and Hove; participation in conferences at Liverpool, Cardiff, Cambridge and Oxford Universities; co-leading the British School at Rome teacher trips; running the PGCE Classics course at the University of Sussex; and completing an MA in Education Studies at Sussex University looking at Latin provision and impact in the local area. To paraphrase Terry Pratchett (1989), *the world is your mollusc …*

Conclusion: What next?

This chapter has presented some aspects of setting up Latin provision in schools as a 'non-specialist' Latin teacher. Some approaches have worked better than others. There are also other strategies that can be used to introduce Latin into schools: using virtual teachers (Skype lessons); university outreach (classicists coming into school or students going into universities); state partnerships with the independent sector and other permutations.

Perhaps one answer for maximum impact in the classroom lies in Latin occupying a more secure position on the school curriculum. The focus could then shift from setting up Latin clubs in individual schools – which takes a minimum of two years per school and does not necessarily guarantee sustainability in that institution. Hunt (2016) says that there needs to be a realistic meeting of expectations from the Department for Education and an honest and reflective approach from the providers:

> governments need to be reminded that they cannot merely wish it [Latin] into existence or provide the opportunity for it to develop as it were from thin air. The subject associations, teachers and universities need to make the case for the continued political and financial support of Latin in state-maintained schools with regular, hard, concrete evidence where success occurs and challenges are identified, and make suggestions about how these might be overcome. (Hunt 2016, p. 173)

Review

Lessons learned on introducing Latin into your school

Communication Communication is key. When communicating about setting up and running your Latin club at your school, be honest – say it like it is! Do not feel you have to be a bona fide 'classicist' to do this. Do not become too worried with the 'non-specialist' tag. First and foremost you are a teacher with experience in planning and delivery of learning. Let students and parents know that you are learning alongside the class, if this is the case. Rather than a sign of weakness this can be very empowering as everyone is pretty much in the same boat with their learning. Keep all parties informed how you are progressing. Do not be afraid to be flexible and change your plans if you need to. If there is a change of plan and you are going to need to take more time to cover the course or the road to the GCSE is going to take longer than anticipated then communicate this. The idea of keeping everyone informed means that there will not too many embarrassing moments.

Collaboration For your Latin provision to work you need allies to collaborate with – both internal and external. Firstly, gain the support and, more importantly, the enthusiasm of a dynamic member of senior leadership team. In addition, are there any other teachers in your school who want to commit and join you on your journey? Recruit! (This will make sustainability more achievable at a later date.) Next, look towards external organizations to support you. Apply for funding and/or support from organizations such as Classics for All or The Society for the Promotion of Roman Studies to enable to launch your Latin provision. Once you have established your Latin provision at your school then you could build beyond the school and work with other organizations to establish a Latin teaching network locally. This could include Classics PGCE providers if they are nearby. Finally, if you feel that you need to improve your subject knowledge then attend one of the many summer schools or CPD events that are offered throughout the year by different providers. Join online communities such as the Classics Library for support and resources and organizations such as the Classical Association.

Sustainability This is the big one. Sustainability of Latin provision should be a priority right from the very beginning. Make a point to consider who will carry on running the Latin club after the partnership/funding has stopped. Also, what would happen if you left? Would the subject leave too? After all the personal effort and support from internal and external agencies, it would be a blow to lose the subject from your school. If you already have a Latin club successfully running see if you can make the transition from extra-curricular to on the timetable. There is a better chance of a subject's survival if it is cemented into the school's curriculum. Build up a department by targeting teachers at your school who share a similar passion for classical subjects and who may have qualifications in the subject. Think about introducing GCSE Classical Civilisation or Ancient History. Become a mentor for PGCE Classics trainees from the institutions which offer these courses. In this way you are not only helping to train the Classics teachers of the future, but you are also showing another important reason for the subject to be a sustainable one in your school. It is more fun having another person to bounce ideas off if you are in a department of one.

References

Affleck, J. (2003), 'Twilight Classics', in J. Morwood (ed.), *The Teaching of Classics*, 159–169, Cambridge: Cambridge University Press.

Cambridge School Classics Project (2008), *A Survey of Access to Latin in UK Secondary Schools*, Cambridge: Cambridge School Classics Project.

Darby, R. (2008), *Why does Latin provision often stop at KS3?*, unpublished MA paper, University of Sussex.

Darby, R. (2010), *Evaluation of the impact of the new KS4 Latin qualifications on schools in and around the Brighton and Hove area*, unpublished MA dissertation, University of Sussex.

Donaldson, J. and Scheffler, A. (1999), *The Gruffalo*, London: Macmillan Children's Books.

Griffiths, W. (2009a), 'Latin in Secondary Schools', *The Journal of Classics Teaching*, 17 (3): 2.

Griffiths, W. (2009b), Personal communication by e-mail, 5 February 2010.

Griffiths, W. (2010), 'Latin Levels among "Non-Specialist" Latin Teachers', *The Journal of Classics Teaching*, 20 (3): 3–4.

Hunt, S. (2016), *Starting to Teach Latin*, London: Bloomsbury.

Morwood, J. (ed.) (2003), *The Teaching of Classics*, Cambridge: Cambridge University Press.

OCR (2010), *New Entry Level Latin – A Practical, Flexible Qualification*, Cambridge: OCR.

Patcham High School (2017), *Latin*. Available online: http://www.patchamhigh.brighton-hove.sch.uk/learning/subject-information/latin/. (Accessed 25 February 2017).

Pratchett, P. (1990), *Pyramids*, London: Victor Gollancz Ltd.

Soden, I. (2010), *Barriers to the Development of Classics Teaching in State Schools*, paper presented at a conference for Classics for All, London, 3 March 2010.

Wilkinson, J. (2003), 'Working at the Chalk Face', in J. Morwood (ed.), *The Teaching of Classics*, 106–116, Cambridge: Cambridge University Press.

CHAPTER 10

CREATION AND IMPACT OF REGIONAL CENTRES OF EXCELLENCE FOR CLASSICS: THE IRIS CLASSICS CENTRE AT CHENEY AND THE EAST END CLASSICS CENTRE

Lorna Robinson, Peter Olive and Xavier Murray-Pollock

Iris Classics Centre at Cheney: The first three years

Lorna Robinson

The Iris Classics Centre at Cheney was officially opened to the public on 14 October 2013, and in that time has evolved in its scope in both expected and unexpected ways from the initial idea that popped into my mind some time during December 2012. This chapter will explore how it began, developed and what it has become today, as well as the plans we have for it in the future.

In 2013, I had set up the Iris Project, a charity intended to promote access to classical subjects in state schools. Cheney School is a large and very diverse comprehensive school, serving the east of the city of Oxford. I contacted David Gimson, the head of History, with whom I had worked when I ran a GCSE Greek club at the school in 2006. He offered his classroom to be the space we used. And so it all began. I contacted Mai Musié, the Classics outreach officer at the Faculty of Classics, University of Oxford, who generously helped to organize the faculty's support for the centre's establishment and some vital early funding. We were all set to go.

The purpose of the centre at its inception – and still today – was to provide a permanent presence within Cheney School for all its pupils to engage with the Classics in a range of ways, and also to provide a place for visitors of all ages from the local community to experience Classics by offering lessons, workshops, storytelling sessions and other events. Activities were to be provided at no charge.

After a year of preparation involving extensively redecorating the space with murals, new furniture and the creation of a classics library and miniature museum of original artefacts, the centre was officially opened with a large community festival on 14 October 2013. Hundreds of local school children, families and visitors attended to take part in Classics-themed activities and stalls. Professor Mary Beard and Dr Armand D'Angour gave opening talks. Throughout its first three years, the centre has offered hundreds of events.

Weekly workshops, talks and classes

Throughout each school term, we have run workshops and courses delivered by a range of volunteers from Oxford University's Faculty of Classics as well as various other institutions such as University College London, The Open University and Oxford Brookes University. University students greatly enjoy and benefit from involvement in the local community – it enables them to learn more about their city, and for many it gives the opportunity to develop their teaching skills and use their subject knowledge in a new setting. We find that their expertise, enthusiasm and commitment are invaluable in inspiring and connecting with the public.

Weekly evening classes have included beginners' Latin, Sanskrit, Classical Greek and Palaeography. Workshops have included drama and the *Odyssey*, artefacts imaging and classical myths. We have also welcomed visiting primary school groups on Wednesday mornings, and the pupils have enjoyed workshops on artefact handling, Roman medicine, Classical Greek and ancient democracy. The talks have attracted a very broad range of community visitors, ranging from parents, staff and students from Cheney School itself, local pensioners and even doctors from the nearby John Radcliffe Hospital dropping in at the end of their shifts. It is no exaggeration to say that all walks of life have been represented, and everyone has enjoyed the highly accessible talks provided by academics and enthusiasts.

Cheney School projects

Every term, we have run projects specifically for Cheney School students across a range of subject areas. Some projects have targeted higher attainers, whereas others have targeted students who struggle with school. Higher attaining students are defined differently by different schools, but in Cheney School it is done by collecting attainment data from their subject teachers. Many have simply been open to any who want to take part. We have delivered a workshop series on Classics and Positive Psychology for Cheney students and others throughout the summer term. The workshops were trialled in the Easter term 2014, and their success led to the project being run for *Cheney Plus* pupils as part of a curriculum project. *Cheney Plus* is a unit within Cheney School where pupils with special needs or those struggling with mainstream school get a personalized curriculum in a dedicated area of the school. These workshops are the first of their kind, and we are making the resources we have prepared available for others to use.

In 2014, Year 8 and 9 Design & Technology students (used twelve-thirteen) began a Roman mosaics project. The project began and with a talk by Dr Will Wootton and an introduction to Roman mosaics. The students then visited Chedworth Roman Villa to see the Roman mosaics there and received a guided tour by a local expert. The team of Cheney students, led by mosaics expert Clare Goodall, had the task of designing and constructing the mosaic. We held two sessions exploring ideas for what might appear in the mosaic, and pupils all gave their views on what they would like to appear on the mosaic. Clare then drew up a design image for the four panels which incorporated the students' ideas, including a backdrop of Oxford city, the Headington shark (a local landmark), a Mini-Cooper car and a bicycle (local manufacturing), the River Thames flowing through all the panels, open books as a pattern at the base of the panels and, of course, the goddess Iris.

In addition to these projects, we have run a Roman sundial project, two ancient cookery projects and ongoing artefact projects. These projects are a vital part of our work in engaging a wide range of students and staff from the school and showing them the breadth of the classical world and its influence. They continue to bring in students who might not otherwise consider learning about Classics, and to engage them in the ancient world, often without them realizing that they have done a Classics project.

Themed days

Every year we have also run several themed days which take over the whole school and fill it with decorations, stalls, workshops and talks. In January 2014, we put on the first themed day event: the Roman Medicine Day. Professor Helen King from the Open University spent the day with us and delivered a series of talks on topics ranging from Galen to the Roman army. Artefact experts Towse and Graham Harrison brought their wide range of original and replica Roman surgical instruments. Pupils got to see some of the grisly equipment used to operate on and treat Romans two thousand years ago, including bone drills and blood-letting cups. The buildings were decorated with graffiti walls, facts about Roman medicine, an apothecary store and a wide range of posters. At lunch time there was Roman food, a healing and poison stall, the opportunity to have fresh wounds painted onto arms and faces, as well as a team of Roman doctors to diagnose and treat the wounded. After school there was a community artefacts workshop followed by an evening talk from Professor King.

Other themed days have included three Classical Myth Days, aimed at pupils in Years 7 and 8, as well as a community after-school workshop. The storytelling workshops were run by the UNMYTHABLE team, who have created a highly acclaimed show based on classical myths which they tour internationally. There was a school-wide competition on one of the days involving the devising of a summary of a classical myth in thirty words: entries were tweeted and put up around school on the day.

We have also created overarching themed days for Year 6 Transfer Days, so incoming students could learn all about the ancient world while attending for the first time. The re-enactment organization Comitatus has come to camp on site at the school overnight for two nights each year, bringing with them eight re-enactors, two horses and their grooms, and an array of armour and equipment. They held six shows on the athletics field for Cheney students and Transfer Day students and they also held community shows for local primary school groups and visitors. Their shows involved displays of their weapons including archery and javelins, live wrestling and bare-back horse riding. Students were able to try the helmets and shields for themselves, as well as meet the horses and re-enactors. Alongside the shows were themed stalls, including face-painting, Parthenon-building, an ancient Greek lucky dip, Greek bracelet-making and mask-making, as well as a display of some of the artefacts the Cheney Classics Centre owns.

This year, the Transition Days were themed on the *Odyssey*. Therefore from start to finish every aspect of the Year 6 (aged ten) visits were filled with activities connected to the story, including a walk-through activity exhibition designed by Year 8 Latinists. Involving our students in the creation of activities at these events has been something that has been especially successful. The students look forward to these events, and their creativity and hard work getting the activities ready is exceptional. Festivals and other large events usually take at least seven or eight months of preparation. Funding is sourced through applying to grant-giving bodies, such as the Oxfordshire Community Fund. Students do not pay, as we want to keep it open to all, but we do encourage donations from those parents who can afford it.

Trips

We have now run two residential trips to Hadrian's Wall as well as many smaller trips – to Bath, Chedworth Roman Villa, the Ashmolean Museum in Oxford and the Kallos Gallery in London. The Hadrian's Wall trips have involved taking almost all the Cheney students studying Classics and have been a wonderful way to build a sense of a cohesive Classics department. We visited Durham Cathedral and the University of Durham for a lecture on Hadrian's Wall on our way north. While there, we visited Arbeia Roman Fort, Bede's World, Housesteads, Vindolanda and the Roman Army Museum. On our way home, we visited Chester's Roman Amphitheatre. Visiting sites enables the students to get a clearer picture of what Roman life might have been like and engages them in a very different way from the engagement they get from classroom learning. It helps them conceptualize and contextualize the learning they have already done. It inspires them by bringing it to life in a very solid and all-encompassing way, when they are confronted with the reality of actually standing in a Roman villa or fort.

Summer schools

Thanks to the generous funding from the charity Classics for All (CfA) and the volunteer time and energy of local independent school teachers, we have been able to offer summer schools in Latin and Classical Greek for children aged seven to fourteen, free of charge, two summers in a row. These have been over-subscribed each year and have been a fun and educational community experience for everyone involved. Each year, a couple of mums have joined their children to learn, in one case with a very young baby. Being able to welcome the whole community and create a sense of vibrant, relaxed but very engaging learning has been central to the ethos of the summer schools, reflecting the broader vision of a centre for everyone.

Growing Classics in the curriculum

When the Classics centre was first set up, the school already offered beginners' Latin and an after-school GCSE class. This is one reason that setting up the centre at the school made so much sense as a small seed from which to grow the Classics centre and a Classics department within the school. Since then, we have worked with the school to offer Latin A level, AS Classical Civilisation and soon GCSE Classical Civilisation, with 40 Year 9s signed up to start. I offer a GCSE Greek lunchtime club, and hope eventually for this to become part of the official offering as well. GCSE and A level Classical Civilisation are offered as curriculum subjects – they are timetabled and funded by the school like any other subject. Latin is offered after school, but is a curriculum choice and counts as one of the students' A levels. Greek is a club, so not funded, and takes place at lunchtimes and during tutor registration time.

The presence of the centre and the constant stream of Classics activities and events have created a sense of status and buzz among students and parents. This has produced challenges in itself – finding space in the curriculum, negotiating space and time with different departments, some of whom have sometimes been a little unsure of the way in which Classics has expanded so quickly and dramatically at the school. My experience has been that it depends largely on how supportive the school leadership team are at any given point when asking for space on the curriculum. We have had some success, but there are still battles to be fought and dilemmas we face. Every school is of course different, but one of the dilemmas here is if, for example, we were to bring Latin GCSE onto the school day, rather than having it as an extra-curricular after-school lesson, it might enhance or might actually reduce attendance – since it would then be timetabled against other GCSE choices rather than available to everyone as an extra. However, as an extra it has its own disadvantages. Being quietly and politely persistent has tended to be my approach – it may be that being more aggressive would be more beneficial, but equally that may have backfired. Having supportive leaders is the most important thing, and winning them over to the value of Classics, through showing that it is in demand by everyone and is not just for a particular sort of student. A generous grant from Classics for All has enabled us to focus on developing Cheney as a hub for students from local schools to take courses with us, and we work with a number of local state schools to provide places for local students to attend our classes.

Rumble Museum

The Classics centre at Cheney School is home to a large and expanding collection of original artefacts, covering a broad range of periods and regions – from ten-thousand-year-old Mesolithic stone tools, ancient Greek and Roman pottery, coins and glass items to medieval and post-medieval pottery fragments, merely a few hundred years old. The collection has grown gradually out of donations from the public. We realized that in order to best preserve, care for, collect and display these items, we needed to seek professional advice and guidance. This triggered a series of projects, which have all become part of a wider vision to establish the first accredited museum within a school.

During this process, we have been immensely fortunate that a sponsor has come forward to back the museum financially, in memory of Jamie Rumble, a young man who dedicated his life to the service of young people. I applied for Working towards Accreditation status from the Arts Council in 2015, and I presented to the Cheney School governors and the senior leadership team, explaining that the museum would benefit the school through a range of ways – incorporating artefacts into lessons, enhancing the learning environment with stimulating displays and involving students in curatorship and display design. I pitched for a large empty space and was granted this. I have since completed a large display area, and through our partnership with the Oxfordshire Museum Services sourced a wide range of artefacts, ranging from First and Second World War items to history of medicine artefacts and more. The full database is on the website at www.rumblemuseum.org.uk. The museum therefore grew out of the original Greek and Roman collections owned by the Iris Project, but now covers all eras.

The future of the centre

The Classics Centre at Cheney has grown beyond anyone's expectations. At its core, however, it is still focused on fulfilling its original intentions: to create an exciting and creative space for Cheney students and the wider community to engage with the Classics. The expansion of Classics into the curriculum and the museum at the school together has been the result of the successful promotion of Classics in the school and local community. The centre has been a strong example of how different organizations can come together to strengthen and develop projects and initiatives. The support we have had from the University of Oxford's Faculty of Classics, the Oxfordshire Museum Services and other institutions has created the opportunity to run events and projects which would never have come to fruition otherwise. So many people have willingly given their time and support to bring Classics to thousands of local people – as well as those from further afield. Sustainability has been achieved through the paid roles created by the school – who have created a brand new *Classics Lead* role specifically for running the centre – as well as the paid teaching for the classes which have grown on the curriculum. There will remain in the near future, at least, a challenge of maintaining the status and presence of Classics at the school. Some of our offerings remain unfunded and/or outside of the main school day; at the moment, it feels that the initiative still relies quite heavily on one person pushing it forward – and this makes it vulnerable for obvious reasons. There is also always a battle to convince everyone that the subject should be integral and not a nice extra for a small number of students. We have made a great deal of headway, but it feels that there is still a long way to go. But three years in, the signs are very good that Classics is something that will grow and grow at Cheney for its students and the whole community: from babies to pensioners and everyone in between.

Links

Arbeia Roman Fort: www.arbeiaromanfort.org.uk
Ashmolean Museum, Oxford
Bede's World: www.bedesworld.co.uk
Chedworth Roman Villa: www.nationaltrust.org.uk/chedworth-roman-villa
Classics Centre at Cheney: www.eoccc.org.uk
Classics for All: www.classicsforall.org.uk
Comitatus: www.comitatus.net
Faculty of Classics, University of Oxford: www.classics.ox.ac.uk
Housesteads Roman Fort: www.english-heritage.org.uk/visit/places/housesteads-roman-fort
Iris Project: www.irisproject.org.uk
Oxford Community Fund: www.oxfordshire.org
Oxfordshire Museums Service: https://m.oxfordshire.gov.uk/cmc/public-site/museums
Roman Army Museum: www.vindolanda.com/roman-army-museum
Rumble Museum: www.rumblemuseum.org.uk
Unmythable: www.out-of.chaos.co.uk
Vindolanda: www.vindolanda.com

Developing Classics teaching in London – Capital Classics: A case study
Peter Olive and Xavier Murray-Pollock

Over the last thirty years, owing partly to the introduction of a National Curriculum for state schools that did not include Latin, there has been a gradual decrease in the teaching of Classics in state schools across the UK. Classics for All was founded in 2010 with the ultimate aim of reversing this decline, largely through offering continuing professional development (CPD) training and mentoring for teachers new to Classics. Since its launch, it has supported over 500 schools, bringing Latin, Greek and Classical Civilisation to 10,000 pupils in schools across the UK. This section examines the efforts of Classics for All (CfA) in reviving the study of Classics in London schools.

The East End Classics Centre – the background

Attempts to revive classical subjects in state schools encounter several obstacles, including the common perception that they are difficult and irrelevant. Where schools do introduce Classics, the journey is not always easy. In the academic year 2014–2015, fewer than fifty Classics teachers graduated from Classics PGCE courses in England, making PGCE-qualified classicists hard to find. Once employed, Classics teachers often find themselves in single-person departments and on fractional timetables. These challenges, combined with the pressures of a crowded curriculum and continuing budget constraints, make fledgling Classics departments with low initial pupil numbers hard to justify. It is, therefore, not surprising that Classics is often overlooked in state schools or taught only in twilight sessions by individual enthusiasts, leaving it vulnerable and unsustainable.

Recently, in an effort to scale up the introduction of Classics in schools, CfA has started to invest in regional Classics hubs. Led by schools or universities with a track record in Classics, these offer CPD and mentoring to support the introduction or development of classical subjects in state schools.

In 2010, a survey privately undertaken by Pembroke College, Oxford, noted the absence of Classics in many state schools in London. In 2012, Classics teaching in London reflected the national picture, with pockets of activity concentrated largely in private schools, or in a few state schools in affluent boroughs, such as Henrietta Barnet School in Hampstead and Camden School for Girls. In autumn 2013, in response to this, a partnership led by BSix Sixth Form College in Hackney, CfA, the Iris Project and the Universities of London and Oxford won support from the London Schools Excellence Fund to address this gap through a programme called Capital Classics. Its aim was to establish two hubs for Classics development in North and East London.

In 2014, the East End Classics Centre at BSix Sixth Form College in Hackney became the first London hub. The college already ran Classical Civilisation at A level and after-school Latin and Greek classes, open to pupils from other local schools. It also boasted designated college space for Classics funded by Pembroke College, Oxford. From its base at BSix, Capital Classics ran CPD for seventy teachers in Latin, Greek, Classical Civilisation or Ancient History in primary and secondary schools. The programme also included an extensive range of enrichment events including lectures and seminars for pupils and teachers.

In primary schools, teachers were trained to introduce Latin at key stage 2, through the Iris Project's publication *Telling Tales in Latin* (Robinson 2013) or the popular course *Minimus* (Bell 1999). In secondary schools, the goal was to introduce Latin or Classical Civilisation at key stage 3 or 4 on the school curriculum.

Work was led by a full-time coordinator employed by BSix College and two part-time coordinators employed by CfA, overseen by a steering committee.

The programme of activities, 2014–2015

Following the set-up and recruitment phase, teachers from primary and secondary schools from the nine north-eastern London boroughs identified by the Pembroke College study were offered support to develop Classics on the curriculum. This was done in a variety of ways. Firstly, Latin language evening classes for teachers at beginner and intermediate level (up to

GCSE) were made available free of charge at Birkbeck College, University of London. Training was given to primary school teachers so that they could learn the basics of Latin grammar and Roman culture with a view to teaching *Minimus* in their primary classrooms. Training in pedagogy was made available to secondary school teachers to help them teach Latin most effectively. In schools without a Latin teacher, postgraduate students from London universities taught Latin on a weekly basis as part of the Iris Project which focuses on Latin for literacy. Finally, enrichment events were run for GCSE and A level pupils and teachers on topics such as Greek Theatre and the *Odyssey*, led by Hackney University Extension Programme.

Emerging lessons

The programme offered useful insights into the challenges of developing Classics in urban settings. Four key categories of lessons emerge from the evaluation and help to plan for the future to create lasting impact.

Recruiting and engaging schools *Word-of-Mouth Works:* The Capital Classics project found that Classics is not an 'easy-sell' and the recruitment of schools is particularly challenging. Blanket e-mails or letters rarely make it beyond the in-tray of busy school offices. Coordinators had most success recruiting schools through word of mouth, named contacts and the use of existing Classics converts to attract new recruits.

The Need for Advocacy: Many teachers new to Classics have negative preconceptions about the subject. Explaining the benefits of Classics to school senior leadership teams and governors with the power to determine the curriculum is vital. Using evidence of the impact of learning Latin on literacy is a particularly useful strategy for persuading primary schools to take it up.

Establishing effective partnerships The Capital Classics programme involved a complex partnership of universities, schools, charities and funders, with priorities which were not always aligned. In the first year of the programme, there was a major focus on lectures and seminars for GCSE and A level students. While enrichment activities supported an important widening participation agenda by encouraging students to apply for Russell Group universities, they did less to develop the capacity of teachers in schools to teach Classics themselves.

Successful continuing professional development The first year of the programme gave coordinators useful insights into some 'dos and don'ts' of running effective CPD for non-specialist classicists, namely:

There Is Strength in Numbers: Training multiple teachers from one school is a useful strategy for ensuring that Classics is embedded in a school. In Kelmscott School, Walthamstow, seven teachers with no Latin attended training at Birkbeck College and the subject is now taught at the school to GCSE level. Training in numbers has encouraged mutual support networks between teachers, has raised the profile of Classics in the school and made lessons easier to timetable. The presence of a number of part-time Classics teachers also means that there is little danger that Latin will disappear if a key member of staff moves on.

Tailor the Training: Although it is possible to train teachers to teach primary school Latin in a few days, ongoing mentoring is crucial for teachers' confidence. Training secondary teachers with no Latin to teach to GCSE level is even more of a challenge. Many of the secondary teachers who attended the Latin course at Birkbeck hoping to teach it the following year needed ongoing local support. Effective training needs to be incremental and underpinned with mentoring and online support; it should also include intensive input on pedagogy as well as subject knowledge.

Use Appropriate Expertise: It is important to ensure that school-based training is led by classicists with classroom experience. While using postgraduate students to strengthen teachers' subject knowledge is useful, most students have little teaching experience and are not well equipped to offer advice on pedagogy. Use of graduate students in classrooms can also create a dependency culture with little quality assurance, where teachers are not given the opportunity to lead classes themselves. Such arrangements leave no measures in place when the graduate student moves on and do not address the staffing shortage in the longer term.

Practical Considerations: Running teacher training and pupils' enrichment events at the same time is a useful way of avoiding expensive cover costs.

Creating flexible and cost-effective hubs At the start of the programme, there were plans to create a second hub in North West London. However, by early 2015 plans were reviewed in response to increasing requests for support from schools across the capital and a concern to make training responsive to local needs. Although BSix still employs a member of staff to supervise its Library of the Ancient World and organize enrichment lectures, Capital Classics coordinators now operate from a central London office enabling the programme to offer more flexible support to smaller hubs across the capital, led by schools including Greig City Academy in Haringey, St Marylebone School in Westminster and Kelmscott School in Walthamstow.

Ensuring a long-term impact

To date the project has, on many levels, been a success. It has exceeded its targets, reaching at least 7,000 pupils and providing training to more than 100 teachers in 87 schools.

Feedback from schools has been largely very positive, and some have already introduced Classics onto the school timetable. However, for many the engagement with Classics is still piecemeal and *ad hoc.* For Capital Classics the real measure of impact will be the number of schools that continue to teach Classics over the next ten years.

With this goal in mind, Capital Classics is now offering more flexible peripatetic support to local 'mini hubs' across London. These are led by schools with the confidence and expertise to support work in neighbouring schools, including feeder primary schools. There is no strict formula for hub development but many capitalize effectively on existing networks between schools.

One strategy is to work with Teaching Schools. These schools, classified by Ofsted as Good or Outstanding, already share their expertise with others through training and CPD and are therefore ideally placed to lead and mentor. One such school, St Marylebone School in Westminster, has been sharing its experience with other schools, offering training to support and mentor Classics teachers in other west London schools.

Working with academy chains and school alliances is also proving fruitful. Brixton Learning Collaborative and Lambeth Catholic Cluster are ready-made networks that meet regularly to discuss policy and practice. Working with such partnerships gives Capital Classics easy access to influential senior school leadership teams and the ability to engage a number of schools at once. This makes more efficient use of CfA staff time and has the potential to extend the reach of Capital Classics more quickly.

In light of teacher shortages, collaboration with school-led Initial Teacher Training providers is also a useful approach. The Harris Multi-Academy Trust, with forty-four schools across the country, has set up a central training base in London to offer its teachers high-quality Initial Teacher Training and CPD. Working in partnership, Capital Classics is now supporting the development of a new training route that will equip teachers to teach Latin or Classical Civilisation alongside another subject. Producing teachers with this versatility will make them more employable and begin to increase the number of qualified Classics teachers entering schools. Work will result in the introduction and strengthening of Classics in several of the trust's schools over the next few years with longer term ambitions to benefit schools across the country.

Although collaborating with existing networks is an efficient strategy, Capital Classics has also supported some enthusiastic stand-alone schools that have created hubs with other schools from scratch. Despite starting a Classics department only a few years ago through the training of non-specialist teachers, Kelmscott School in Walthamstow now runs GCSE Latin and hosts regular Latin CPD for four local schools. In a similar vein, Greig City Academy in Haringey is now piloting a new Classics course at key stage 2 in three local primary schools with a view to sharing it more widely.

Underpinning all of Capital Classics' work is a commitment to fostering Classics in primary schools. The ancient Greeks and the Roman invasions of Britain are required components of the primary history curriculum for key stage 2, and primary school Latin offers an excellent grammatical and etymological platform for studying English and Modern Foreign Languages.

Both Camden School for Girls and the Jewish Community Secondary School in North London are working with feeder primary schools to encourage the take-up of Classics, confident that this will increase the demand for classical subjects in secondary schools in the longer term, making them a regular feature on the mainstream curriculum.

Conclusion

Capital Classics is still evolving and learning; following the start-up phase at the East End Classics Centre, there has been a shift in focus from outreach work and centralized training to investment in smaller school-led hubs led by practicing teachers able to share their subject knowledge and teaching experience with others. Such peer-led training is flexible, draws on classroom practice and offers less-experienced teachers the opportunity to reflect honestly on the strengths and weaknesses of their own classroom practice. With Capital Classics underpinning this local work with training, mentoring and platforms for sharing effective practice, we hope that such school hubs will in time become a largely self-supporting network led by teachers for teachers.

Overall, the biggest challenge remains finding teachers able to teach Classics, or willing to be trained to teach it. Even for those who already teach Romance languages, learning Latin is of course a steep learning curve, and although Classical Civilisation provides an enjoyable and rigorous alternative, its associations with languages perceived as being esoteric can still be off-putting. Feedback from the London Schools Excellence Fund has, however, been extremely positive about our focus on the sustainability; feedback from teachers about training provided by Capital Classics has been similarly positive, and the impact of training seems to represent good value for money. Most importantly, 81 per cent of pupils questioned in our evaluation reported that they had enjoyed their study of Classics.

The revival of Classics in state schools is a long-term project which requires the support of key partners including teacher trainers, universities, schools, volunteers and funders. Evidence suggests that there is scope for a Classics renaissance in London and the replication of successful approaches in other cities across the UK.

References

Bell, B. (1999), *Minimus: Starting Out in Latin*, Cambridge: Cambridge University Press.
Robinson, L. (2013), *Telling Tales in Latin*, London: Souvenir Press Ltd.

CHAPTER 11

DEVELOPING A CLASSICS DEPARTMENT FROM SCRATCH: TWO CASE STUDIES

Olivia Sanchez and Nicola Felton

St Paul's Way Trust, Tower Hamlets

Olivia Sanchez

This section is an account of my experience developing a new Classics department in a comprehensive secondary school in the inner-east London borough of Tower Hamlets. It offers an honest reflection on the challenges of persuading young people to value the study of Classics and how these might be overcome.

Tower Hamlets: London borough of diversity and change

Since the fourteenth century, Tower Hamlets has been shaped by immigration: Flemish, Huguenot, Irish, Jewish and most currently, Bangladeshi, an ethnic group forming 32 per cent of the borough's population (compared with 3 per cent across London), according to the most recent census in 2011 (London Borough of Tower Hamlets 2013). Including other Asian ethnic groups the Asian population is 41 per cent, 31 per cent of the population is white British, 12 per cent is 'Other white' and 7 per cent is black. The borough's Muslim population is 34.5 per cent, making it the borough with the highest percentage of Muslims in England, and the East London Mosque in the borough is one of the biggest in Europe.

The borough is a place of divergence and gentrification, like many inner-city areas across the world. It accommodates the world headquarters of global financial businesses such as J.P. Morgan and KPMG, employing some of the highest paid workers in London, accommodating them in luxurious riverside apartments. It is home to the Cereal Killer Café – a gimmicky eatery which in 2015 somehow became symbolic in the British media of a divided London, where some pay £3.20 for a bowl of cereal, while others can't afford a box of cereal (Butter 2015). It also has the highest proportion of children in poverty of any local authority in the UK at 49 per cent, a waiting list of over twenty thousand for scant social housing, high rates of long-term illness and premature death, and the second highest unemployment rate in London. The borough certainly encapsulates the rapid increase in UK income inequality and the resultant decline in social mobility. Education must play an essential role in mitigating the latter.

Education in Tower Hamlets: Opportunity and transformation

The story of education in Tower Hamlets is more positive. It tells a story of transformation, from the worst in the country to leaders in education, proof that poverty is no excuse for substandard education. Significant funding has facilitated this shift: all of the borough's secondary schools have benefitted from rebuilding or refurbishing from 'Building Schools for the Future', the British government's investment programme in secondary school buildings in England in the 2000s (Building Schools for the Future, Department for Education and Skills 2003). On account of its percentage of students eligible for free school meals (an indicator of economic disadvantage) and its inner-London location, Tower Hamlets receives one of the highest allocations of funding per pupil in the country: £7,007 per pupil in 2015/16, the average in England being £4,612. But this funding was in place before the borough's turnaround in education success, and research by University College London's Institute of Education identifies seven key success factors which drove the borough-wide transformation: ambitious leadership at all levels; high quality teaching and learning; very effective school improvement; effective spending; external, integrated services; community development and partnerships; and a resilient approach to external government policies and pressure (Husbands 2014).

Success of the borough's educational reform began to attract wider attention in the media in 2013, the year in which St Paul's Way Trust, a mixed comprehensive secondary school which epitomizes the success story of Tower Hamlets, achieved its first 'Outstanding' grade from the government's school inspector Ofsted. The school's new building, including for the first time a sixth form for post-sixteen teaching, had opened two years previously, all amidst a sustained, focused and continuing effort towards educational excellence. One way that the latter manifested itself was to offer students opportunities traditionally associated with a private education: tennis coaching, music lessons, internships at multinational companies and Classics. The Classics curriculum at the school, introduced in 2013, consists of compulsory Latin for key stage 3 students (ages 11–14) in the top language sets. Students from that cohort can then opt to study Latin in key stage 4 (ages 15–16) for a GCSE in Latin, a national qualification. Classical Civilisation is taught at A level (pupils aged 17–19).

Classics: The importance of justification on a crowded curriculum

A compelling vision and rationale for Classics is essential when education plays such a high-stake role in a student's future. It is proper that subjects defend their place on a competitive curriculum: a school's principal job is to prepare students for life in our society, and what this entails is continually evolving. They could be learning skills to prepare them in the modern world for well-paid shortage jobs: more science and maths; computer coding; engineering; languages spoken in the emerging economies.

Added to the economic pressure is the ideological threat: the majority of adults have not studied Classics, so they associate it with privilege (Hunt 2016, pp. 16–17). In popular culture Latin is often used as shorthand for other things: 'the lexical equivalent of a barrister's wig – both fuddy-duddy and exotic, eccentric and archaic' (Nunn 2016). Parents and staff might have experienced Classics in some form and been inspired (or traumatized) by it. An influential visitor to the school once told me across a classroom of students that he hated Latin at school. They might be (rightly) ambivalent about the political implications of privilege and class which are antithetical to the ethos of a comprehensive school and seemingly impossible to disentangle from the subject. In order to convince students, parents and staff of the importance of what students are studying, it is important to develop a rationale which not only champions the advantages of Classics but is also pertinent to the specific school context and takes into account the economic and ideological arguments against Latin.

The school's vision for Classics

A vision of Classics by the school's leadership team which counteracted these concerns was necessary: schools have ample excuses to dispense with a Classics department, let alone start one. The school's executive head teacher gives his rationale for introducing the subject:

> Some might ask 'Why waste valuable curriculum time on a dead language or long gone cultures?' My response would be 'Classics provides the learner with an understanding of how the world they inhabit is underpinned by the classical world. The study of Classics fosters understanding, tolerance and empathy, providing students with a broader view of society and the history of ideas. There is strong evidence that students of Classics feel comfortable with computation, concepts and problem solving – you can't get much more relevant than that!'
>
> (Personal communication by the executive head teacher, 10 November 2016)

Focusing on the practical application of Classics and positing that the subject promotes tolerance and empathy help to counteract both the practical and ideological arguments against the subject. My motives for teaching the subject traverse the same territory: I teach Classics to initiate a dialogue with the ancient world on which we have based our society. We can explore a shared heritage through which we might address and learn from about the challenging issues facing our own world, and a key to the development of humanistic thought. I teach Latin to develop skills to deconstruct and improve our understanding and use of English and the Romance languages, as a key to a rich cannon of text and history that continues to be discovered. Classics is the original interdisciplinary subject, encompassing language, literature and history. Students use all these skills in other subjects, but in Classics they learn that they do not have to exist separately, that education is not made up of compartmentalized information. Embedding the study of a new discipline in a school naturally takes time, and teachers of all disciplines experience their own challenges. The challenges I have encountered in encouraging students to study Classics mirror the arguments against the teaching of the subject: economic and ideological. In the following paragraphs I will dissect these issues and discuss how they might be overcome. Schools, universities and associations such as Classics for All do great work to ensure that more young people experience Classics (of which more can be seen at http://classicsforall.org.uk/our-grants/case-studies/), and many of the solutions proposed here are already happening in some form or place. By highlighting these issues and problems, I hope it might help new Classics departments avoid some of the challenges which have beset me over the years, or it might provide some ideas for existing departments wanting to improve their recruitment of students.

The economic argument

Students often make curricular choices based on the promise of financial gain. Classics can seem economically irrelevant: we are living in an era of huge technological advancement with a predicted shortage of graduates in STEM (science, technology, engineering and maths) industries. Classics is the study of societies around two thousand years old. Students will be thinking about the average of £44,000 of debt they might start their working life with in England if they go to university (BBC News 2016). With university fees higher than ever, pathways into further education and employment are serious considerations for young people today, where risks cannot be afforded. Students are encouraged to think of their career paths from the age of 13 when they choose their GCSE options: the subjects they will study along with Maths, English, Science and Religious Education. At age 16, if they choose to stay at school, their A level course choices narrow this down further, with three or four subjects studied, which two years later becomes furthermore specialized at university. Based on my experience in my own school, I would suggest that teachers of Classics therefore must stress the practical applications of Classics from the start of students' study of the subject: how English words are made up of Latin ones, how understanding of this holds the key to decoding unseen English vocabulary, how classical references litter popular and high culture, and how knowledge of them enriches our understanding and enjoyment of these. For how the skills learned from studying Classics can lead to employment, Classics teachers should not struggle alone but can profitably team up with the English and Humanities departments, where students interested in these subjects may have the same concerns about future employment. A helpful resource would be a bank of examples of a diverse range of Classics graduates from a range of universities, to show what students could do if they chose to study Classics, and statistics of pathways which Classics graduates take after their studies. This would help teachers to show students how Classics, a seemingly impractical subject, has practical application and can lead to a successful career.

Challenging the academic stereotype: Classics for all

Classical qualifications encompass a range of curriculum subjects: linguistic and non-linguistic. Universities are impressed by qualifications in all classical subjects, and the fact that it makes a student stand out when applying for higher education is an argument I often use. At our school students are streamed according to ability in languages, and the top two classes study Latin. Latin is therefore perceived as something for the most academically able students, a perception which is then transferred by students to Classical Civilisation at A level. The argument that Classics is an impressive qualification is therefore a double-edged sword: a much-needed weapon in the race to recruit students for further study, potentially a motivator for students considering the subject, but also with the potential to demotivate. However, if students have not been chosen to study Latin, they are deemed not able enough for the subject, which can then extend to them potentially not studying Classical Civilisation, perceiving Classics as not for them. Short-term solutions might be organizing trips to university Classics departments for students interested in studying the Humanities further, speaking in assemblies or at open evenings on Classical Civilisation and getting current enthusiastic students of the subject to spread the word. Ideally, all students would study some aspect of Classics, or have the opportunity to, whether it be Classical Civilisation or Latin. Giving all students the opportunity to study the Trojan War, myth, democracy, the history of the language they speak is not only fairer and beneficial to all but also helps to normalize and embed the subject into a school. There are many routes for this, such as through the Humanities, English or Languages curriculum, after school or voluntary sessions, and there is no one-size-fits-all model. Studying Classics is not for everyone, but schools wanting to create a Classics department with healthy student numbers should think through carefully how they can give all students the chance to experience some Classics in the context of their school and the realit of the curriculum, to avoid transferring and perpetuating the ideology that Classics is only for the few.

Embracing diversity

The elitist reputation of Classics is hard to counter: one of the country's most high-profile classicists is Boris Johnson, the quintessential face of white male privilege: a British politician, author and journalist, whose persona of a semi-shambolic, humorous politician of great intellect is instantly recognizable across Britain. 'Classics people aren't my kind of people, Miss'. 'We're going to be the only people who aren't white, aren't we?' The first quotation is from an A level student, who loved Classics, on why she applied to study Geography at university. The second is a question from A level students about to go on a Classics summer school. Such concerns seem to become more pronounced in older students, those more likely to venture out to universities and meet their fellow classicists. This is not an attack on the privileged or a call for collective guilt, but a recognition of reality: there is space for a wide and diverse Classics community. To end the self-perpetuating myth that Classics is not for everyone, a bank of examples of a diverse range of Classics students and graduates would be a first step to help teachers make this argument. It is also key that students visiting universities meet a diverse range of students studying the subject. Schools teaching Classics can also network with each other to help normalize and own the subject, especially if the subject is studied in small numbers in their own school. By helping students to see how they fit in with the wider Classics community, we can encourage more students to take their study of Classics to higher education.

Ancient world, modern values

More subtly, the study of Classics has traditionally focused on the elite of the powerful, militaristic states of Greece and Rome, but universities have long moved on to exploring more diverse aspects of these societies, such as race, disability and gender. There are resources and much work done on making Classics more diverse and inclusive, including from national exam boards which design GCSE and A level courses, but not always in places on teachers' radars (greater discussion of which can be found in Deacy's guide to embedding equality and diversity in Classics, [Deacy 2015]). Teaching Classics at secondary school level to students between the ages of 11 and 18, it is easy to unthinkingly transmit imperial, militaristic values. For example, the Cambridge Latin Course (Cambridge School Classics Project 2013) provides rich material in the form of stories and characters for challenging the *status quo* and making a comparison with contemporary society. A teacher who fails to make the most of this resource misses the chance to provide students with a more nuanced understanding of Romans and their own society. For example, Bregans the native (Briton) slave is thought by his master and other slaves to be lazy and stupid, possibly because he is a native Briton. This interpretation can be accepted, or challenged, researching what his background and previous life might have been and imagining his current life, discussing how students would act if they were in his situation. More discussion and cooperative work for creating resources by teachers and the Cambridge School Classics Project for Classical Civilisation learning from within the Cambridge Latin Course would be welcome to help Classics teachers reflect upon the values attached to what they teach, to ensure that they are aware of the ambiguities and diversity of the ancient world, to mirror the advancements made in higher education and research and to give students the chance to study and ask important questions about their own society through the prism of the classical world.

Primary school Latin

From 2014 to 2015, St Paul's Way Trust School ran a Latin project funded by the London Schools Excellence Fund (LSEF), a fund established by the (above mentioned) London Mayor of the time, Boris Johnson, to improve the quality of teaching in the capital. The school proposed projects with local primary schools in English, Maths and Latin, and for the Latin strand, we organized a Latin Summer School for students transitioning from primary to secondary school, and trained primary school teachers to deliver the primary Latin course '*Minimus*' (Bell 1999). The project was a unique opportunity to engage the wider community in Classics and raise awareness of the subject. Eight local primary schools were involved in the primary school teacher training, and eighty students attended each of the summer schools, hosted at St Paul's Way Trust School. The summer school gave us the freedom to engage students with Classics in creative ways, with activities such as Roman cookery and building functioning aqueducts at the summer school, and using Classics undergraduates to teach at the summer school brought new energy and ideas to the department while hopefully inspiring a new generation of potential Classics teachers. The next step is to find a way to engage local primary schools in Classics without the generous funding of the LSEF: this might mean a more personalized approach with fewer schools. As local schools seek to equal each other in academic choice and excellence, at least four secondary schools in the borough now employ full-time Classics teachers, and other primary and secondary schools find more flexible ways of offering the subject as part of their curriculum. Pleasingly, Tower Hamlets students now have ever-increasing opportunities to engage with Classics.

Conclusion

Teaching Classics, it is easy to feel victimized or fatalistic about its future – even with its recent popularity and growth, the danger is that it will go out of fashion again, or that as it has been used as a proxy for educational excellence by politicians of the right, so in the future politicians of the left might disregard it as a proxy for elitism and privilege. Hundreds of students at St Paul's Way Trust School have studied Classics, with our first student off to study Classics at university, three years after the department began. Classics teachers are lucky to have so many supporters and resources in the form of universities, charities and museums, little of which has been mentioned in a chapter focusing on overcoming challenges, but which enrich our students' experiences of Classics immeasurably. To paraphrase Wiliam (2017), the influential British educational researcher, every teacher, department and school can improve, not because we are not doing enough, but because we can do even better. Great work has been done in the Classics community, but there is lots more to do.

All of the advantages, none of the cost: Sidney Stringer Academy, Coventry

Nicola Felton

This section charts the introduction of Latin and Classical Greek in a state-maintained school in the West Midlands. The school is in an area of high socio-economic disadvantage and the majority of pupils come from a British-Asian ethnic background. Latin and Greek were introduced to raise aspirations and results have been superb. The benefits of working in partnership with a local independent school and a local university are explained.

Sidney Stringer Academy

Sidney Stringer Academy is an inner-city, non-selective state-maintained academy for eleven- to eighteen-year-olds situated in the inner-city district of Hillfields in Coventry, a large industrial city in the West Midlands. The academy has what is described as a 'rich cultural diversity': the proportion of students from minority ethnic backgrounds is four times the national average and almost all of the students speak English as an additional language. In reality, the overwhelming majority of students come from a British-Asian Muslim background, a fact which makes the academy almost homogenous in its intake. The local area has a very high level of unemployment and socio-economic disadvantage. The percentage of students known to be eligible for free school meals is twice the national average and the percentage of students with a statement of special needs is four times the national average (Ofsted 2013).

The academy opened in 2010 following the closure of its predecessor school. The school then became a sponsored academy. But in 2014, following an Ofsted inspection which judged the academy to be outstanding in all four categories (Ofsted 2013), Sidney Stringer became a sponsor in its own right. Sidney Stringer is now the lead school in the Sidney Stringer Multi-Academy Trust. There are currently five schools in the trust: Ernesford Grange Community Academy, Radford Primary Academy, Riverbank Academy (Special School) and Sidney Stringer Primary. The academy is in the top 8 per cent of schools in the country for student progress and the Maths department is in the top 5 per cent. It is currently oversubscribed and is an extremely popular local school.

The change from school to academy did not impact on student intake. Most students continued to enter the academy with low reading, writing and maths skills. However, with an increased emphasis on academic achievement and excellence as part of the general push towards an outstanding Ofsted grade, the time seemed right to propose that an education in the Classics should become an important part of the academy provision. The reality that the opportunity to study the Classics is increasingly restricted to a privileged few – the study of Latin and Classical Greek is still often used to signify an expensive education – was unashamedly embraced and it was considered that if there is something ostentatiously elitist about restricting Classics to those who can afford to pay for it, then it was all for the better that Sidney Stringer Academy was offering it for free.

Introducing Classics

It was in this favourable climate that I was given the chance to build a Classics department which would offer lessons within the school curriculum. I believe that there are two imperatives for starting any new venture: the backing of the senior leadership team and an enthusiastic client base. There was support from school leaders and I knew from experience of teaching both English and Modern Foreign Languages (MFL) that interest in the classical world could be aroused among my students – beyond my resources to satisfy it. The younger students had been fed a diet of ancient myths, legends and history both in their primary schools and on the Disney channel, while the older ones had enjoyed the rigour and discipline of grammar in English and MFL and their interest was primarily linguistic.

Nevertheless, the question as to why students from a predominantly British-Asian Muslim background would be interested in studying Western ancient civilizations was still an interesting one. There are many different influences woven into our cultural fabric – of which Christianity and Islam are the most obvious in the academy – and *Classics* introduces students to the foundational concepts of *Western culture* with which our students can engage. The exposure to ancient literature and history which the students experience in Sidney Stringer Primary School and our other feeder primary schools has undoubtedly given the students the opportunity, at a very young age, to see a different world through different eyes. It has enabled them to enjoy trying to understand (and perhaps even find some sympathy with) the mentalities of people who thought in completely different ways to us today, and who experienced life in a different global context.

On a more prosaic level, students at the academy are aware of the instrumentality of ancient languages in social exclusion. Qualitative and quantitative data collated from student questionnaires cross-matched with student achievement across the academic spectrum at key stages 2 to 5 showed that not only did 89% of the 250 students questioned consider that a GCSE in either Latin or Classical Greek would be more interesting and enjoyable than a modern foreign language, but they also believed that GCSEs (and eventually A levels) in these subjects would improve their chances of entry to the elite professions. In Coventry there are two private, academically selective, fee-paying schools whose performance data at key stages 3 to 5 consistently outranks all the state-maintained schools. The students (and perhaps more importantly their parents) know this and they also know that Classics is on the core curriculum in both of these schools. Parents and students were not slow to recognize that the addition of Classics to our curriculum would bring all of the advantages of a fee-paying school and none of the cost.

The Classics department opened in June 2013. I was the sole teacher and my only qualifications in Classics consisted of an A level in Latin and the study of Tacitus and Cicero as part of my master's degree in Portuguese at Coimbra University, Portugal. As with the introduction of any new initiative in a school, there were substantial difficulties in understanding the meaning of the term 'Classics' and its definition in relation to the academy. In UK schools Classics usually refers to the study of the Romans and, in a few cases the ancient Greeks, through their language and literature. For some schools I believe that the term 'Classics' is used to include history, philosophy, art and archaeology. Classics can therefore be an umbrella term to cover all four of the examined subjects of Latin, Classical Greek, Classical Civilisation and Ancient History. My long-term plan for the Classics department at Sidney Stringer is to eventually become a faculty which will offer all four subjects; but in 2013, given that I was the sole teacher with limited qualifications, I decided to settle for Latin with a view to gaining such excellent examination results that the case for expansion and inclusion of Classical Greek in 2016 would be won.

I believe it is fair to say that as teachers we believe that examination results are not the only goal, and that enjoyment of a subject is equally (if not more) important. I do not believe that the two are mutually exclusive. Neither do I believe that because a subject is associated with privilege that it should be against the ethos of a non-elective academy. My vision for the department was and is one which is at the heart of academic life in the academy and in which enthusiasm for Classics is high. Students at the academy were therefore selected to study Latin on the basis that the subject would not be too difficult to be of value for them, and that they had a genuine interest in the subject. This was particularly important for the first cohort which was to sit the GCSE with only two years' preparation and upon whose results the future of the department was likely to rest.

The first two cohorts of students began preparing for GCSE Latin in 2013. The first cohort consisted of fifteen Year 10 students who were to begin their *ab initio* course with a view to sitting the GCSE in 2015 and the second cohort of twenty Year 9 students – who were therefore more fortunate in terms of time allocation – sat the exam in 2016. All the students have gained the highest A* grade (with the exception of one who gained an A). Seven students from the 2013 cohort have continued Latin to A level with results ranging from A to C. We now begin teaching Latin in Year 7 in order to ensure that all students who have chosen to study Latin at A level gain a grade A through sufficient exposure to Latin at a younger age. On the back of these results, the case for Classical Greek has been won and twelve students from our current Year 10 began studying for their GCSE in June 2016.

The importance of seeking support

Three factors have enabled the Classics department to thrive. First, none of this would have been possible without sufficient support from a number of individuals and organizations. As I have mentioned, first and foremost, there has been support from senior management which has meant in real terms that I have not had to defend the place of Classics on the curriculum. It has also meant that I have been able to offer the students a whole range of extra-curricular opportunities. These have included an annual trip to either Rome or Athens, study visits to Chester and Cirencester and full funding for places for some of our students at the JACT Latin Summer School in Wells during the summer. Partial financing was also available for A level students at the JACT Greek and Latin summer school at Durham University. I have also had financial support from the charity Classics for All which has enabled the academy to become a Classics hub with support from Warwick School and Warwick University. With this financial support we were also able to pay for a retired teacher from the independent sector to deliver part of the A level Latin course and to employ a teacher to deliver the Classical Greek GCSE. Training was also given to two teaching assistants who helped deliver literacy through Latin in Year 8 to a group of mixed-ability students in the English department.

Second, I have been fortunate in being able to call upon the help of some brilliant teachers. The academy has hosted guest speakers from Warwick, Birmingham and Oxford universities to deliver lectures to the students. These lectures gave the students the opportunity to complement their academic programme and encouragement for further exploration of the classical world. Dr Michael Scott of Warwick University and some of his doctoral students have talked to the students on subjects ranging from medicine in the ancient world to an exploration of original footage from the television documentary 'Rome's Invisible City' (BBC 2015). Year 8 students attended a series of weekend workshops at Birmingham University in 2015 where they experimented with Roman cookery and wrote raps related to aspects of life in ancient Rome. Christopher Pelling of Oxford University delighted the students with his lecture on Cleopatra and other Oxford academics lectured on subjects as diverse as Cicero's *de Imperio* and Roman portraiture. I am also particularly grateful to Will Griffiths of the Cambridge School Classics Project and Steven Hunt of Cambridge University who both visited the academy and gave classes on the ablative absolute to my students.

Third, a dynamic relationship has been fostered between Warwick School's Classics department and Sidney Stringer Academy. We have been able to take advantage of the independent sector's years of expertise and were offered free teaching from one of its highly qualified members of staff. I sometimes think that the maintained sector is reluctant to ask for help from the independent sector, more from a misplaced sense of moral superiority than for any other reason. I looked at the situation quite simply. Who gets the best results? Warwick School had a track record of A* results and I was determined to see how that worked in practice and achieve the same. Close collaboration between Warwick School Classics Department and Sidney Stringer Classics Department has also resulted in a broadened world view for both sets of students. We have experienced shared educational visits to Bath and the British Museum which have enabled the students to spend time getting to know others they might not normally gravitate towards.

Looking to the future I hope to create more exciting opportunities for an increasing number of diverse and enthusiastic pupils who will derive rewarding and life-enhancing possibilities from their experience of their classical studies.

References

BBC (2015), *Rome's Invisible City*, Producer: Harvey Lilley, Presenters: Alexander Armstrong and Michael Scott.

BBC (2016), 'English degree debt "highest in English-speaking World"', *BBC News*, 28 April 2016. Available online: www.bbc.co.uk/news/education-36150276. (Accessed 17 February 2017).

Bell, B. (1999), *Minimus Pupil's Book: Starting Out in Latin*, Cambridge: Cambridge University Press.

Butter, S. (2015), 'Cereal Killer Cafe owners: What it's like to be the most hated men in London', *Evening Standard*, 1 October. Available online: www.standard.co.uk/lifestyle/london-life/cereal-killer-cafe-owners-what-its-like-to-be-the-most-hated-men-in-london-a2970776.html. (Accessed 10 August 2017).

Cambridge School Classics Project (2013), *Cambridge Latin Course Book 2*, Cambridge: Cambridge University Press.

Deacy, S. (2015), *Embedding diversity and quality in the curriculum: A classics practitioner's guide*, The Higher Education Academy. Available online: www.heacademy.ac.uk/system/files/resources/EEDC%20Classics%20Online.pdf. (Accessed 17 February 2017).

Department for Education and Skills (2003), *Building Schools for the Future*. Available online: http://webarchive.nationalarchives.gov.uk/20130323070818/https://www.education.gov.uk/publications/eOrderingDownload/DfES%200134%20200MIG469.pdf. (Accessed 11 September 2016).

Hunt, S. (2016), *Starting to Teach Latin*. Cambridge: Cambridge University Press.

Husbands, C. (2014), 'The transformation of Tower Hamlets: How they did it', *Institute of Education Blog*, 15 January. Available online: https://ioelondonblog.wordpress.com/2014/01/15/the-transformation-of-tower-hamlets-how-they-did-it/. (Accessed 14 September 2016).

London Borough of Tower Hamlets (2013), *Ethnicity in Tower Hamlets: Analysis of 2011 Census data*, February. Available online: www.towerhamlets.gov.uk/Documents/Borough_statistics/Ward_profiles/Census-2011/RB-Census2011-Ethnicity-2013-01.pdf. (Accessed 17 February 2017).

Nunn, G. (2016), 'Right to Rome? The debate over Latin on the curriculum', *The Guardian*, 19 August. Available online: https://www.theguardian.com/media/mind-your-language/2016/aug/19/right-to-rome-the-debate-over-latin-on-the-curriculum. (Accessed 17 February 2017).

Ofsted (2013), *Sidney Stringer Academy*, London: Ofsted.

Russell Group (2016), *Informed Choices: A Russell Group guide to making decisions about post-16 education*. Available online: http://russellgroup.ac.uk/media/5457/informed-choices-2016.pdf. (Accessed 10 August 2017).

Wiliam, D. (2017), *Embedded Formative Assessment*, Bloomington: Solution Tree Press.

CHAPTER 12

ACADEMIA LATINA: WORKING IN SOUTH AFRICAN SCHOOLS AND PRISONS

Corrie Schumann and Lana Theron

Introduction

During the 1980s, when the United States of America was a vanguard in Latin studies, Corrie Schumann, at the time a Latin lecturer from Pretoria, the administrative city of South Africa, visited the country on an international research initiative (Academia Latina 1989). Contemporaneously, Schumann enrolled for a course in Medical Terminology at Georgia University. On her return, Schumann was determined to promote the Latin language and the Classics in South Africa. As a result of her interminable effort and tenacity, the Academia Latina centre was founded at the University of Pretoria (UP) in 1989 with the idealistic motto: *Vivit Lingua Latina*.

Initially, the centre formed part of the Latin department, a division of the Faculty of Humanities at UP; however, ultimately it developed into an autonomous centre headed by Schumann within the Department of Classics. Schumann pursued a rigorous campaign to encourage a new appreciation of the Latin language and the Classics in general, by focusing on several different projects, including community projects and programmes aimed at primary and secondary levels of education.

'The Academia cannot build real houses for less privileged people,' said Schumann at the time; however, we agree with Joégil Lundquist who said the following (Lundquist 1989),

> I make a motion that we build a new schoolhouse out of the
> bricks of the old schoolhouse – and that we don't tear down the
> old schoolhouse, 'til the new one is built!

Schumann said,

> We picked up the old bricks laying around and started building a new schoolhouse, not of brick and mortar, but an intellectual one that enabled us to teach pupils from every community. We tried teaching school children a hundred Latin root words, because learning even a few Latin root words gets you hooked and before you know it, you're a self-learner, an autonomous scholar! The centre is a matchless stronghold of Latin in a country where there are eleven official languages and where the different languages have to compete with one another for recognition.

Educational authorities in South Africa have been striving to provide quality and satisfactory education to all learners. Poverty, for instance, is one of the many challenges

The authors would like to thank Dr Carina van der Westhuizen for her contribution to this chapter

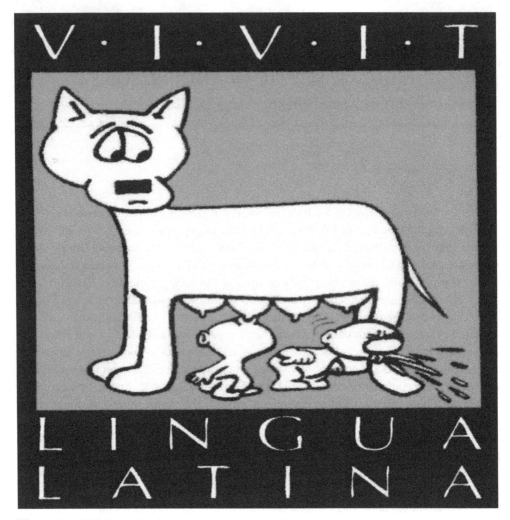

Figure 12.1 *Vivit Lingua Latina.*

that educational institutions are currently struggling to overcome. According to a report by UNICEF (United Nations International Children's Emergency Fund) on Children's Rights to an Adequate Standard of Living, '11.9 million children (64 per cent of all children) live in income poverty' in South Africa (UNICEF n.d.). Taking the context into consideration, it is conceivable that limited resources are available to aid in the development of studying ancient European languages within South Africa.

The ancient language has been in decline throughout South African schools for the latter part of the twentieth century. Furthermore, Latin as a subject is now scarcely available to study at secondary level. Presently, only a small number of secondary schools in South Africa offer Latin studies to their learners. Latin as a school subject is taught from Grade 8 (age 14) to Grade 12 (age 18) as a second additional language at St Mary's School for girls and St John's College for boys situated in Johannesburg. According to the Annual School Survey of South Africa, conducted in 2011, 'the majority of learners in ordinary schools in South Africa were taught in English (approximately 67%), followed by Afrikaans (approximately 10%) and isiZulu (approximately 7%) and isiXhosa (approximately 6%)' (Department of Basic Education 2012). According to the National Education Policy Act of Section 4, students are currently allowed 'to be instructed in the language of his or her choice, where this is reasonably practicable' as long as it is one of the eleven official languages of South Africa (Veriava et al. 2017). The Academia Latina believed that teaching non-English-speaking pupils Latin root words and English words derived from Latin could only enhance their English language skills and vocabulary contributing to a brighter future for the youth of South Africa. Following the centre's commencement, the Academia Latina extended its programmes to the following groups of persons: primary and secondary school pupils, university students, adults, pensioners, friends of the Classics and lastly, the individuals who participated in the community engagement projects. Unfortunately, accurate data on the number of pupils, students, pensioners and so forth is not available, because over the years the archives were lost.

The various programmes previously offered by the Academia Latina are outlined below.

Programmes offered by the Academia Latina

Schola Latina

In 1989, Schola Latina classes were made available at the UP campus. The purpose of the Schola Latina project was to encourage pupils ranging from ages 10 to 12, specifically Grades six and seven, to take Latin as a formal subject at a secondary educational level. Approximately 300 primary school pupils from 72 primary schools in South Africa were invited to attend Latin lessons once a week on the main campus, which granted them the rare opportunity to gain insight into the many facets of functioning like an authentic UP student.

Lecturers from UP, University of South Africa (UNISA) and school teachers offered honorary services to assist in the campaign with a single agenda, which was to enable Latin to thrive. They enthusiastically taught their learners basic Latin words and furthermore explained the introduction and relevance of these words in the English language. The frequent, yet inadvertent, use of Latin in everyday life was emphasized during lessons to establish a connection between the learners and their current worlds. The children were taught derivatives from basic Latin words, listened to classical mythological tales and started each lesson by singing a song called *Floreat Roma* in unison.

The fascinating and informative project remained active for many years and was an enriching and efficacious experience for both the learners and the *magistrae* involved. This eventually came to an end, because it coincided with learners' extramural activities and was then absorbed by the Schola Scripta course.

Schola Fles

SCHOLA FLES (a programme for **F**oreign **L**anguage in **E**lementary **S**chools) was launched in the United States by Dr Rudolph Masciantonio as a bridging programme to assist children in augmenting their English-language skills. The programme was aimed at assisting elementary school learners with the development of basic skills in the following categories: reading, writing, speaking and listening. Cross-cultural and linguistic studies based on the ancient Roman world were used to progress the learners' understanding of their intricate selves in their current circumstances. The FLES programmes included lessons regarding the following topics: *Familia Romana*, *Numeri Romani*, *Corpus Meum* and *Pompeii*.

South Africa has eleven official languages, namely Sepedi, Sesotho, Setswana, siSwati, Tshivenda, Xitsonga, Afrikaans, English, isiNdebele, isiXhosa and isiZulu. According to the South African Census conducted in 2011, only 9.6 per cent of the population's first language was English (Statistics South Africa 2012). Even though English is rarely the mother tongue of most South African learners, as mentioned in the introduction of this chapter, most ordinary school learners' language of teaching and learning (LOLT) in the country is English (Department of Basic Education 2012). Accordingly, there is the need to promote the English language among South African pupils whose mother tongue forms part of the other ten official languages of South Africa. The centre was enthusiastic to expand this programme according to the necessities of the above-mentioned learners. In 1991, four pilot FLES groups in three different provinces were selected and monitored by the Academia Latina, in cooperation with the Department of Basic Education. The various groups were situated at Glenmore Primary School in KwaZulu-Natal, Cornerstone College in Gauteng, the Lowveld Christian School in Mpumalanga and at the University of the Orange Free State in Bloemfontein. On commencement of the course, pupils were required to provide their arithmetic and English grades to the Academia Latina. On completion of the course, it became apparent that their arithmetic and English grades improved. The learners' communication skills were thoroughly evaluated after they completed the pilot FLES course. The evaluations revealed improvements in the learners' reading, listening, speaking and writing abilities. The learners' abilities within the scope of comprehension and memory of the English language and their analytical skills also improved. Mrs Zenia Barnard from Cornerstone College said:

> This Latin course has without a doubt extended their vocabulary. Not just by introducing new words to them, but also by showing them the roots and derivatives of words. One highly delighted student remarked that she knows what the 'aqueous' in the aqueous cream that she has been using implies. They now have the confidence to analyze a word to find the meaning.

As English is not the most spoken language in South Africa, many students experienced immense difficulties in grasping the language. This course, however, successfully addressed most of the learners' relevant concerns. Mrs Hurlin, the principal of Cornerstone College, said, 'The knowledge that our students have obtained through the Cross-Cultural Language Enrichment (CCLE) has made a world of difference to their understanding and use of English. Not only has their vocabulary expanded through the study of the Latin roots but they have also acquired the ability and confidence to understand the meanings of unknown words derived from Latin'.

The following comments on the FLES course were received from learners speaking isiZulu, SiSwati and SeSotho:

> 'I love Latin. Just like soccer!'
> 'I have learned new English words which come from Latin words,
> which I can use when speaking or writing English!'

Primary and secondary school pupils were given a taste of the Trojan War when FLES tutors escorted them, after school, to the sports centre of UP, where they were given the opportunity to release margarine containers, representing the Greek fleet, onto the water of a large pond. Imagine the risk of falling in the water with your Roman cloak, the excitement of seeing the ducks fleeing from the Greeks and your triumphant whoops of joy when your margarine boat reaches the Trojan coast! At the same time, the pupils were hardly able to contain their excitement for their next outing, building their first Trojan horse!

Schola Scripta

South Africa's vastness (size) gives rise to a set of problems, including a lack of resources and remote living conditions resulting in long distances to be travelled to urban areas. A correspondence course, called SCHOLA SCRIPTA, was developed in 1990 to provide pupils in all nine provinces with a unique opportunity to access and discover Latin, including the riches of the classical world. Schola FLES eventually came to an end when it clashed with many extramural activities. For this reason, Schola Scripta replaced Schola FLES. The Academia Latina needed financial support to implement the correspondence course. Therefore, students were charged a set fee per module within a specified period. The Schola Scripta course curriculum was designed to be appropriate for pupils of all ages. The youngest learner who completed the course was twelve years of age. Mrs Helen Weich, formerly a scientist, enroled

Figure 12.2 School pupil releasing the Greek fleet for the Trojan War.

for the correspondence course at ninety-three years of age and even though she was the oldest learner to have completed it, she did so with admirable enthusiasm and excitement. Almost 2,000 students, children and adults successfully completed the correspondence course and received a certificate from UP. The course comprised of four modules. During the school holiday in July, the Academia Latina took the liberty of offering a winter school opportunity for all Schola Scripta learners. The benefit of winter school was a chance for each student to concentrate on his or her own assignment under the supervision of a tutor allocated specifically to his or her module.

Students were granted examination opportunities in either June or November. They were therefore permitted to study at their own pace and allowed to complete one course annually or one per semester. After completing Schola Scripta IV, students were authorized to follow the first *Oxford Latin Course* as a correspondence course at North-West University. North-West University is situated in Potchefstroom, which is in the North-West Province of South Africa. Students who enrolled for this course had to submit written assignments to qualify for admission to the final examination. The assignments were reviewed by the course lecturers and once completed, returned to the students.

SCHOLA SCRIPTA consisted of four modules:

1. An introduction to the Latin language.

   This module consisted of basic language structures and vocabulary for the enrichment of English and Afrikaans vocabulary based on Latin root words. It also aimed at improving the understanding of scientific terms directly derived from Latin for professions such as medicine, law, botany and zoology. This course served as a foundation for learning new languages related to Latin namely, French, Spanish, Italian, Portuguese and Romanian (all of which are known as the Romance languages). As mentioned in the Government Gazette of the Republic of South Africa, 'historical practices of the past gave prominence to English and Afrikaans' (Department of Basic Education 2015); for this reason Latin mottos, abbreviations and expressions used daily in both English and Afrikaans were also included in the curriculum of this course. UP was a double medium university, teaching in English and Afrikaans. The Latin derivations, for instance, were only taught in English, because most learners understood English, therefore ensuring that students were not excluded. In 2015, however, a new language policy was proposed by the Department of Education which aimed to 'promote multilingualism and respect for all languages in the country'.

2. A treasure box of classical mythology.

   Stories about Greek and Roman gods and the adventures of legendary heroes such as Hercules, Jason and Ulysses were taught to expand the learners' knowledge of classical mythology.

3. The richness of classical culture.

   In this module students were taught about the Roman family, how Roman names worked, their religion, war and other aspects of a family's daily life. Students were encouraged to compare the Roman way of life with their own lives. Through the in-depth study of Pompeii they discovered the influence the Romans had on various present-day customs.

4. An overview of Roman history.

In this module students learned about the discovery of the city of Rome, where the Romans came from and major events in Roman history up to the formation of the Roman Republic, the life of Julius Caesar, the emperors and the fall of the Western Roman Empire. The history allowed students to develop a better understanding of how the Romans played an imperative role in Europe and the reasons why their influence could still be felt.

On the successful completion of the Schola Scripta course, students received a certificate issued by the Academia Latina, University of Pretoria.

SPQR days

Pupils from the Gauteng and North-West provinces of South Africa, who took Latin as a secondary school subject, were invited to attend the annual SPQR days offered by the Academia Latina at UP. Gauteng is one of the nine provinces in South Africa and geographically the smallest province; however, it is the economic hub of South Africa, as both Johannesburg and Pretoria are situated within the province. The drive behind the SPQR event was to connect Latin learners from various schools with one another and to give them an opportunity to experience the energy associated with the subject, ensuring their continuous interest in classical studies. The schools that participated in this event were Afrikaans Hoër Meisieskool, Afrikaans Hoër Seunskool, Benoni High School, Hoërskool Die Wilgers, Hoërskool Waterkloof, Hoërskool Randburg, Hoërskool Menlopark and many more. The number of schools that participated eventually increased to forty schools when all the pupils who took a foreign language were invited. The first SPQR day was hosted in 1990. It turned out to be a terrific day comprising of captivating songs, exhibitions and dramatized readings. Each year a new theme was chosen for the day and all activities revolved around the chosen theme. Essentially, all the Latin lecturers from UP and UNISA assisted in planning and coordinating the activities for the day. The Drama Department of UP also collaborated with the above-mentioned staff to ensure a dynamic day of learning. Friendships among both the students and the lecturers involved in the Classics formed on those days. The SPQR days were popular for connecting the Latin language with both joyful and gratifying moments, which created an awareness among the students that Latin was not only vibrant but also contemporary. Some of the themes included *Varia*, *Musica*, *Theatrum*, *Ludi Romani*, the *Aeneid*, *Hereditas Nostra*, *Hannibal* and *Mons Olympus*.

When the *Aeneid* was the theme of the day, pupils travelled to the UP amphitheatre pretending to be Trojan refugees on what was dubbed 'the Romulus train'. Performances by pupils from the various schools depicted the competition among the following; the goddesses, the abduction of Helen, the *Donum Graecum*, the fall of Troy, Dido's conflict between duty, love and finally her suicide.

The most spectacular SPQR day was undoubtedly the one celebrating the *Vita Hannibalis*. While numerous Latin pupils arrived at the UP sporting SPQR banners, four elephants entered through the gates of the university, causing a traffic jam of note: *Hannibal ad portas!* The elephants were on their way to the amphitheatre, each wearing a cloak displaying the letters SPQR: *Senatus Populusque Romanus*. The pupils portrayed Hannibal's route across the Alps by means of plays and reading competitions. At the end Mr Hannibal and Miss Carthage were crowned and lifted onto an elephant amid thunderous applause! The four elephants on campus proved a disaster for the Campus Control Unit, as they found it challenging to protect the storm water drainage system from being trampled by the elephants' feet! Hannibal's elephants truly conquered the UP campus, just like Hannibal's elephants did with Rome in *c.* 218 BCE. On average 200 Latin high school learners and teachers attended the SPQR days yearly. All SPQR days were held on a Friday for nine consecutive years and permission was given by the Department of Basic Education for learners to attend during school hours. Unfortunately, the SPQR days were discontinued in 1998 after the Department of Basic Education withdrew their permission and pupils were no longer permitted to attend the event during official school hours.

Schola Scripta Law (SSLAW)

In 1994, Latin was no longer a requirement for advocates in South Africa as specified in the Admission of Advocates Act of 1994 and in 1995 all Latin language requirements for advocates were abolished. Consequently, there was a significant decline in enthusiasm to study Latin, as it was no longer required for completion of a law degree at most universities and would merely be for individual enrichment (General Council of the Bar of South Africa 1994). Since that time universities have had a choice in 'determining their degree requirements', for instance

Figure 12.3 Elephants at the University of Pretoria's amphitheatre wearing cloaks displaying the letters SPQR – tracing Hannibal's route with elephants.

abolishing Latin as a prerequisite for medicine or law degrees (Brohy 2012). In 1996, 800 law students enrolled for Latin at UP. Devastatingly, after this watershed decision that it was no longer a prerequisite, only 12 Latin students remained in the department at the beginning of 1997. The Schola Scripta Law (SSLAW) was introduced to fill this gap and was offered since 2002 following requests by a few law students, who realized the importance and relevance of the Latin language pertaining to their studies and their future careers as legal practitioners. Schumann and others attended law lectures at the beginning of each year to recruit students for this course. Many people who attended the lectures presented by the Law Society of South Africa were also recruited for the SSLAW. The Latin department sponsored two tutors, who lectured two SSLAW classes per week, to assist students registered for this course. The Academia Latina unfortunately lacked the financial resources to provide a tutoring service independently; however, they did provide three hours of extra tutor time per week to students who required it. The Academia Latina found that community projects enabled students to master the legal language skills needed in their future legal careers. Even though it was a short correspondence course in formal legal Latin, it nevertheless taught students to read passages from Justinian and Gaius in the original Latin form. Students received a study guide which included applicable excerpts from the original Latin legal texts, including the necessary vocabulary and comprehensive notes to aid their understanding of the course material. The course consisted of four modules. The students were given a choice to write their formal examination in either March, June, August or November. Students were permitted to write the examination on the completion of a module; therefore, a student could complete the SSLAW course in a period of one year. Students were also given the freedom to work according to their own pace.

Once a student successfully accomplished the course, the student received a certificate from the Pretoria Society of Advocates. The certificate issued by the Pretoria Society of Advocates was considered very prestigious within the legal realm of South African law. The sought-after SSLAW qualification opened doors for many students seeking career opportunities in South Africa. For Whezi Phiri, an outstanding student, the qualification enabled him to proceed with his studies in his home country Malawi, which would otherwise not have been possible. While he studied in Malawi, he was unable to take the full-time Latin course offered by his local university. When he learned of the SSLAW correspondence course, he was overjoyed with the knowledge that he could continue his passion, with the required Latin foundation that he needed to excel.

Schola Scripta Theology

SCHOLA SCRIPTA THEOL was a short correspondence course that focused on improving the student's understanding of the *Novum Testamentum*. This course was developed after a request was issued by students who belonged to the Theology department at UP. The course, however, was not compulsory, but was made available to students interested in the original Latin texts. The students received a study guide including the following: *Biblia Sacra Vulgatae Editionis* comprising passages, vocabulary, notes and translations from the Vulgate. The first passage, for example, was titled 'Sanctum Jesu Christi Evangelium Secundum Lucam caput 11'. SCHOLA SCRIPTA THEOL was discontinued, because there was a lack of interest from theology students at UP. As a result of the disinterest in the course, the content remained limited in comparison to other courses offered by the Academia Latina.

Medical TerminoLogy (MTL)

Following Schumann's visit to the University of Georgia, the Academia Latina established a project focused on terminating the 'parrot learning' method regularly used for memorizing Medical TerminoLogy (MTL). MTL is no longer offered by the Academia Latina centre; however, the Latin department still offers the course to UP students. In 1998 there were only nineteen students registered for MTL; however, by 2007 as many as 1,050 students registered for the module. Currently, about 1,200 students from medical and medical-related fields annually enroll for the module. MTL is currently a first-year semester module at UP and consists of Latin and Greek-derived basic structures of medical terms. It is a compulsory module for all students registered at the medical faculty and other medical-related fields, including both veterinary sciences and biological sciences. Students registered for the MTL course are taught basic Latin and Greek roots, enabling them to understand the basic principles of term usage. Classical mythology is also taught to medical students, helping them to memorize various diseases, for instance, as explained in a textbook for medical assistants. 'The Roman goddess of love, Venus, is associated with lustful desires. A portion of the female anatomy, the *mons veneris* (*mons pubis*), and venereal diseases were named after her' (Proctor and Young-Adams 2011). The content of this course makes it manageable for students to master the difficult terms that they encounter during their studies. MTL was also converted into an online module, making it accessible to additional students and grade eleven pupils (age 17).

The average medical student needs to master around 15,000 new terms of which 94 per cent are derived from Greek and Latin. In South Africa, we have a unique profile of students who enter studies in the medical field. The students originate from a variety of backgrounds; the clear majority have had little or no exposure to Latin and Greek. Considering the diversity of languages in the country, it should be stated that many of the students often study a third language, taught to them by means of a second language, during school hours. The 'medical language' that students need to acquire at university usually has a specialized vocabulary and an international character that increases the complexity of their linguistic understanding. The textbook called *Medical Terminology for Students of the Health Professions* currently studied by MTL students at UP was written by J. P. Bosman, J. P. K. Kritizinger, J. H. Meiring, C. J. Schumann, P. H. Abrahams and L. M. Greyling (Bosman et al. 2006). It is published in Pretoria by Van Schaik who assisted in developing an online programme for anyone interested in the course but was unable to attend lectures at the UP campus. Fortunately, Van Schaik was eager and able to develop the programme into a suitable online version and acted generously in sharing it with the Academia Latina for the centre's use. The reason for their enthusiasm was to promote the textbook, including both the hard copy and the e-book, sold at their multiple stores. All assessments and examinations related to the textbook are completed online.

Following a request by Grade 11 (seventeen-year-old) pupils, the Academia Latina offered the full academic course of MTL, for the past ten years, to an ever-increasing number of pupils interested in future medical or medically related fields at UP. Classes were taught by lecturers employed by the Classics department to both pupils and students. Pupils who successfully completed the course, while simultaneously attending school, received exemption from the MTL course offered within their formal studies in the medical field. However, only once they were registered students at UP.

The success of the Medical Terminology course added an additional 1,500 students to the dwindling student body of the Department of Classics, thereby ensuring the survival of the department in the past. It also served as a financial resource to the Academia Latina for many consecutive years, because it was extremely challenging to obtain sponsors elsewhere. The MTL online course is no longer available to Grade 11 school pupils.

Pro Medica *lectures*

Ten *Pro Medica* lectures (2001–2010) were hosted by the Academia Latina, in conjunction with experts in law, medicine and the Classics. Guest speakers presented lectures on relevant topics to the 'Friends of the Classics' and the students of Medical Terminology. Professor Pieter Carstens from the Department of Public Law at UP addressed the tenth consecutive annual *Pro Medica* on the topic 'medicus caveat'. On the day, Professor Carsten's audience consisted of 1,000 students and 400 honoured guests intrigued by medical negligence. Law students were also invited to attend his lecture to boost their curiosity in Latin.

Classics in the broader community of South Africa

The Academia Latina engaged in social community projects where the richness of Latin was made available to people suffering from disabilities. For example, a friend of Mr Tony Katchew, a patient with motor neuron disease, read the modules on classical culture, mythology and history of the Schola Scripta course to him in the last weeks of his life. This was an unfulfilled ambition of Mr Katchew and the Academia Latina presented him with the opportunity to fulfil his wish. UP is committed to community development and community service projects in South Africa; for this reason the university sponsored the Academia Latina to teach Schola Scripta courses to selected groups in the vicinity. This sponsorship and an unexpected grant from the vice-principal of UP empowered Schola Latina to teach the Schola Scripta course at the Pretoria Prison. Certificates of acknowledgement were issued to the seven prisoners who completed the Schola Scripta course. The head of the penitentiary selected several students, who he felt had the potential to benefit from the course. The prize-giving ceremony was conducted in the spirit of Horace's motto: *Carpe diem* ('Seize the day'), emphasizing the belief that even a prisoner can still have an opportunity to gain new and enriching knowledge. The head of Pretoria Prison thanked the Academia Latina for adding value to the prisoners' lives. Before ending the visit to the prison, the Academia Latina lecturers decided on the spur of the moment to teach the 200 prisoners the song, *Dona nobis pacem*. The result was moving and the lecturers hoped that the prisoners they left behind found some peace and inspiration in that moment.

The latest community project was a text-to-speech programme which enabled blind people to listen to the entries on mythology, classical culture and history contained in the SCHOLA SCRIPTA course content. This programme was available in the form of a CD; regrettably, there was never an opportunity to transform it into an online course. Unfortunately, this programme is no longer available in any form.

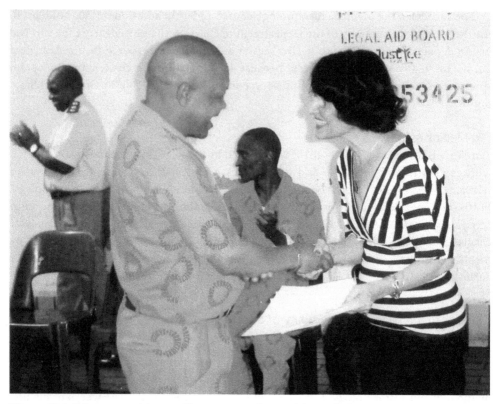

Figure 12.4 Prisoners receiving certificates on completion of their Schola Scripta course.

Conclusion

The Academia Latina served as a unique contribution to the educational system of the country, especially in the times of transformation that South Africa underwent and is still experiencing at present. The courses offered by the Academia Latina provided enrichment opportunities to South Africans from communities who for many years have enjoyed the privilege of a well-developed and highly refined education system, founded on modern Western educational principles and to communities in poverty-stricken areas. In this way, the Academia Latina contributed to a very important educational need in South Africa, bridging the gap between the privileged and the underprivileged, also including the distinctions between the African and European traditions. Throughout the years, the Academia Latina managed to keep its doors open by relying on funding from various sponsors, namely the Istituto Italiano di Cultura (IIC), the Classical Association of South Africa (CASA), Dr H. W. Snyman, PPS Insurance, Faction Media and others. The income derived from various courses that the centre offered, such as the Schola Scripta, SSLAW and MTL modules, also contributed greatly.

Regrettably, the Academia Latina had to close its doors at the beginning of 2017 due to financial constraints and restructuring within the Faculty of Humanities at UP. The Department of Classics now forms part of the Department of Modern Languages, African Languages,

Afrikaans, English and Ancient Languages. Schumann retired as head of the Academia Latina at the end of July 2017. The module in Medical Terminology will continue to be offered by the Latin department at UP. Latin for Law (SSLAW) will be offered at a private university as part of their law degree and Schola Scripta will be offered as an online course by the private institution.

Perhaps the project would have survived tumultuous times if it had been instilled in the rural areas within South Africa. This would have made Latin studies more accessible to a larger part of the country's population encouraging a greater interest in Latin studies. The lack of this can be attributed to an absence in sufficient resources. Moreover, the Latin department has also been fighting for its survival and has neither the time nor the manpower to assist in this regard. South Africa's currency was and still is under pressure; unfortunately, this only complicates sponsorships or the promotion of the Classics.

A renewed interest in the study of the Classics would require adjustments in the National Policies for Education in South Africa; nevertheless, staff members of the centre are hopeful that the Classics will gain popularity again one day. Perhaps the survival of the Classics lies, ironically, within modern technology. It may be a daunting task to implement, because sponsorships will be required to fund the expenses incurred in the process of transitioning the Classics to appropriate technological platforms. Nowadays, almost everybody has a mobile phone that can be used to access courses electronically. Young people are almost addicted to their mobiles and specific applications created for smartphones. It therefore will be sensible to create eye-catching mobile applications created for Schola Scripta, MTL and SSLAW, enabling students to study Latin according to their own schedule. In this case, entertaining lectures may be uploaded to the relevant applications, in the hope of developing a similar learning structure to that which students will eventually experience at university. This, in turn, may avoid significant overhead costs, creating an opportunity to charge students an affordable amount for the purchase of such applications, concurrently excluding the difficult process of searching for sponsors in the challenging economic state that South Africa is in. Advertisements in community newspapers, school newspapers, university radio stations and so forth may be used to promote these applications and at the same time encourage curiosity in the Classics.

Young working individuals in South Africa subscribe to educational platforms, such as Coursera and EdX for career development or enrichment. Perhaps, collaborating with educational companies and offering Latin courses on these platforms will enable working individuals to broaden their knowledge and even foster a foundation for the study of other courses available on these websites, for example a course in one of the Romance languages. The Classics will then be easily accessible to any person with a computer/mobile phone and it will surely raise awareness. Conducting business in South Africa and with other countries in Africa may require speaking Portuguese (a Romance language), since it is listed as an official language in Angola, Cape Verde, Guinea-Bissau, Mozambique and so forth. For this reason, it will be appropriate to suggest Latin courses to students intending to study a business degree or perhaps to postgraduates in the corporate environment to learn the foundational principles that Portuguese is based on. South Africa also trades with Europe, and therefore Spanish, French and many other European languages will also be applicable for the same reason.

Developing a campaign for secondary school learners in South Africa, stipulating the relevance of Latin at university, particularly in the medical and legal context, may establish a desire among pupils to learn more about the Latin language and help them realize that Latin is not a redundant subject, but a wealth of knowledge to succour the difficulties students are faced with in tertiary education.

Some students in South Africa wish to take a gap year before attending university, perhaps to understand the world and its history or to explore a dream destination, just like Virgil longed for Rome. Students in South Africa, considering the poverty headcount measured at 55.5 per cent in 2015, may lack the financial capability to do so (Statistics South Africa 2017). For this reason, a nonprofit organization or an outreach programme, focused on the idea of travelling through a medium of literature, could be established to give students the opportunity to experience the ruins of Rome through Roman literature. This idea was captured perfectly by an English teacher, Sally Law, who wrote 'through literature, we can visit cultures impossible for us to experience ourselves' (Law 2012).

On another note, publishing books on Roman literature, analyzed and explained in the eleven official languages of South Africa, especially isiZulu, may encourage interest among the youth of South Africa. It may also be beneficial to create links between the myths and stories in Latin literature and life as we know it today. The Holy Bible for the Christian faith has been translated into almost every language imaginable. Readers can therefore connect to the written text through their home language. In this way, a larger portion of the country's population will have access to Roman literature and culture. Creating aesthetically appealing and attention-grabbing book covers for the translated versions, applicable to the South African population, could unleash a new, yet favourite hobby for many (Huff 2013). Hopefully, when a student enters a public university or school library, they may reach for Latin books instead of the latest fiction novel. Latin education in the present multicultural South Africa should be given an African flavour by demonstrating the influence that the ancient world had on northern and eastern African cultures and vice versa. Collaboration is required with experts from other institutions who have embarked on similar projects, with the aim of enabling professionals to exchange skills and knowledge with one another. This may serve as an extension to Schumann and Lana Theron's visit to Oxford University in November 2013.

In conclusion, the quest for the survival of Latin is best described by the motto of UP, 'AD DESTINATUM PERSEQUOR', and from the *Novum Testamentum*: Ad Philippenses 111: XI V,

QUAS DEDERIS, SOLAS SEMPER HABEBIS OPES.
Only the riches you have given away, will always be yours.

References

Academia Latina (1989), 'The Memoranda of the Academia Latina Centre', Pretoria: Academia Latina. 1994.

Bosman, J., Kritzinger, J., Meiring, J., Schumann, C., Abrahams, P. and Greyling, L. (2006), *Medical Terminology for Students of the Health Professions*, Pretoria: Van Schaik Publishers.

Brohy, C., Du Plessis, T., Turi, J. and Woehrling, J. (2012), *Law, Language and the Multilingual State. Proceedings of the 12th International Conference of the International Academy of Linguistic Law*, Bloemfontein: SUN MeDIA.

Department of Basic Education (2012), *Annual Schools Surveys: Report for Ordinary Schools 2010 and 2011*, Survey, Pretoria: Department of Basic Education.

Department of Basic Education (2015), 'Government Gazette Republic of South Africa', *Draft Language Policy*, Pretoria: Republic of South Africa, 7 April.

General Council of the Bar of South Africa (1994), *Admission of Advocates Act [No.55]*, Sandton: General Council of the Bar of South Africa.

Huff, M. (2013), *Reviving Student Interest in Classic Literature: A Field-Experimental Study of New Edition and Shelf Display as Promoting Strategies*, Master's Thesis, San Jose: San Jose State University.

Law, S. (2012), *Teaching Classic Literature School*, 11 December. Available online: https://www.theguardian.com/teacher-network/teacher-blog/2012/dec/11/teaching-classic-literature-schools. (Accessed 12 September 2017).

Lundquist, J. (1989), *English from the Roots Up: Help for Reading, Writing, Spelling and S.A.T. Scores Vol I*, Medina: Literacy Unlimited.

Proctor, D. and Young-Adams, A. (2011), *Kinn's The Medical Assistant: An Applied Learning Approach*, 11th edn, St. Louis: Saunders, an imprint of Elsevier Inc.

Statistics South Africa (2012), 'Census 2011 Census in Brief', *Statistics South Africa*. Available online: http://www.statssa.gov.za/census/census_2011/census_products/Census_2011_Census_in_brief.pdf. (Accessed 10 September 2017).

Statistics South Africa (2017), *Poverty on the Rise in South Africa*, 22 August. Available online: http://www.statssa.gov.za/?p=10334. (Accessed 13 September 2017).

UNICEF (n.d.), 'SAF Resources Facts Children'. *UNICEF*. Available online: https://www.unicef.org/southafrica/SAF_resources_factschildrens22.pdf. (Accessed 10 September 2017).

Veriava, F., Thom, A. and Hodgson, T. (2017), *Basic Education Rights Handbook. Education Rights in South Africa*, Johannesburg: SECTION 27.

CHAPTER 13
TAKING CLASSICS INTO COMMUNITIES
Patrick Ryan, Francesca Richards and Evelien Bracke

A long way to Tipperary ... bringing classical drama to the community in Ireland

Patrick J. Ryan

The Limerick Classical Initiative began in 2009, as the result of a conversation with a retired Latin teacher who was then secretary of the Limerick Branch of the Classical Association of Ireland. The motivation was to explore how we might revive interest in classical languages and culture among the wider community, given the sharp decline in classical studies in Ireland from the 1960s (Coolahan 1981). Prior to that era, some 80 per cent of secondary schools offered Latin and some 25 per cent offered Greek; today the numbers taking the languages at School Leaving Certificate level are minimal (approximately 100–110 for Latin and 15 for Greek in the entire Republic of Ireland). Having discussed the potential for an adult language class in the city, we approached Limerick Education Centre, which serves the active and retired primary and secondary teachers in the area. The then director was highly supportive of our idea and provided facilities for the initiative. We opened in September 2009 with twelve beginners for Latin, and in subsequent years introduced intermediate and advanced classes, together with a beginners' Greek group from 2012, which later developed into an advanced reading group. Since the establishment of the initiative, we have brought one or both languages to around fifty people who might otherwise have had no opportunity to engage with Classics.

The events

The profile of participants may be of interest to readers. A significant majority are or were teachers of modern languages, but many others have joined for widely varying reasons. Some had studied Latin at school, often many years earlier, and wanted to connect with it again. The Greek class attracted several participants from the medical and veterinary professions, who had studied the languages as part of their training. A retired veterinary surgeon, who has since proceeded to the advanced group, told us his last contact with Classical Greek was in 1960, and that on joining our group after fifty-three years, he found immense gratification in resuming where he had left off. He also mentioned that his professor in veterinary college had strongly recommended Xenophon's *peri hippikes* and *hipparchicus* as reading material for aspiring horse vets, since Xenophon's precepts about the care and management of horses were still perfectly valid! The course also attracted a gentleman aged eighty-one, who had left school at 13 and worked in the motor trade all his life, and who was immensely pleased to finally achieve his ambition to read even a sentence in Greek. The following summer, he visited Greece for the first time and was delighted to be able to make sense of signs and directions. Cases like these make it all worthwhile. In response to a discussion in class, we added an introduction to Modern Greek for those who were inspired to follow his example, and as a result about half the group have travelled in Greece in recent years. We have even begun to read some Modern

Greek poetry, notably Cavafy's *Ithaka*. In the past year, we read George Seferis' *King of Asini* (truly a poem for archaeologists, 'the king of Asini, whom we've been trying to find for two years now, unknown, forgotten by all, even by Homer, only one word in the *Iliad* and that uncertain') and Yiannis Ritsos' *Charioteer of Delphi*, particularly interesting to us, since much of Ritsos' work has been translated by the Irish poet Desmond Egan, who was president of the Classical Association of Ireland (CAI) in 2004.

It has long been a tradition of the Classical Association of Ireland to include a play-reading as part of our annual conference each year, and since Conference 2009 took place in Limerick, we invited the language course participants to join us. This has since developed into an independent annual occasion, bringing together a wider group of archaeologists, historians and classical students, now known as the Orchard Yard Players, on a Saturday in June, when the education centre is on summer recess. The assistance of our local Newport Historical Society is much appreciated in this regard; they help out with catering and logistics arrangements on site and provide a valuable service for community cohesion. Of course, Irish weather is never guaranteed; we say in Tipperary 'If it's not raining at the moment, it will be very soon'. During our *Philoctetes* in 2012, Zeus took exception to some aspect of our interpretation, or possibly our *hubris* after previous successes, and unleashed his thunderbolts upon our heads. A strategic retreat under cover ensued, and the play concluded to the sound of driving rain outside. Happily, ongoing works at the premises ensure that a fully covered area will be available for future meetings. The other branches of the association have also responded: CAI has branches in Dublin, Cork, Galway, Waterford, Sligo and Belfast (also part of the Classical Association in Northern Ireland) in addition to ours, and most have sent representatives over time, making the event an important social, as well as educational, occasion for members.

Since its inception, the Orchard Yard Players have performed the following:

2009 : Plautus' *Casina*
2010 : Shakespeare's *Julius Caesar*
2011 : Aeschylus' *Prometheus Bound*
2012 : Sophocles' *Philoctetes*
2013 : Plautus' *Mostellaria*
2014 : Aeschylus' *Persians*
2015 : Sophocles' *Hekabe*
2016 : Aristophanes' *Knights*

Our productions take place at the Orchard Yard, a late-eighteenth-century farmyard in rural County Tipperary, formerly owned by the Ross Rose family (motto: *nulla rosa sine spina*). The yard still has its cobblestone paving and sandstone curtain walls intact, providing an atmospheric setting for classical drama. Its layout is such that a setting can be chosen suitable to each production – a rocky shore for *Philoctetes*, or a large stone barn for the senate-house in *Caesar*, whose double doors also serve as the *parodoi* for our Greek theatre. Donkeys and goats are readily available as extras, and sound effects are usually enhanced by the nearby lowing of cows and barking of dogs! The Players have adopted, by unanimous acclamation, a magnificent actor and escape artist named Meg the Goat as mascot of the Orchard Yard. She excelled in the *Knights* (2016), representing, in her animal form, the physical space of the *agora*, the Athenian marketplace (see Fig. 13.1).

Figure 13.1 The Orchard Players: Aristophanes' *Knights*, with Meg the Goat.

The first plays were read entirely in translation, but as our classes progressed, we introduced some lines and latterly sections in the original languages. The *Julius Caesar* went further; one of our Greek class members is a German national now teaching in Ireland, who added a whole new dimension to the language mix by reading the part of Calpurnia in German! For *Prometheus Bound*, we used the translation by George Derwent Thomson, published by Cambridge University Press in 1932. Thomson, a Londoner with no Irish family connections, became a fluent speaker and promoter of the Irish language, and indeed was known here by the Irish name Seoirse Mac Thomais. In recognition of his Gaelic side, Hermes, who arrived as a bicycle messenger in a postman's uniform, gave his part entirely in Irish. Our people are not short on imagination!

The lines or sections in Latin or Greek form part of the respective class in the weeks before the play-reading, and further study of the original text is undertaken when classes resume in the autumn. Participants report this method as one of the most instructive and enjoyable parts of the whole experience.

The *Julius Caesar* in 2010, while not strictly part of the classical canon, was deemed allowable by reason of its close derivation from the ancient world, and also because at this time we introduced our costume department, managed by a member of the Cork branch who wished to demonstrate her proficiency in the production of *togae*, and in subsequent years proved an excellent manufacturer of the Greek himation as well. Caesar's mantle with its twenty-three gory stab wounds drew pity from the audience when it was displayed as his body was carried on a stretcher provided by the local fire brigade, and Mark Antony intoned:

> You all do know this mantle: I remember
> The first time ever Caesar put it on;
> 'Twas on a summer's evening, in his tent,
> That day he overcame the Nervii:
> Look, in this place ran Cassius' dagger through:
> See what a rent the envious Casca made:
> Through this the well-beloved Brutus stabb'd;
> And as he pluck'd his cursed steel away,
> Mark how the blood of Caesar follow'd it,
> As rushing out of doors, to be resolved
> If Brutus so unkindly knock'd, or no;

The costume department provided more scope for the imagination in later plays; the cloak and headdress of Queen Hekabe (2015) were quite spectacular, while the Ghost of Polydorus was of such frightful appearance that we thought it best to banish all children from the scene; even Meg the Goat was somewhat taken aback. As we mention age, and lest it be thought that our group acts as a retirement activity for pensioners recalling their schooldays, our youngest participant to date was a lad of eleven, a son of our Waterford Branch chairman, who had seen his parents reading the play in the previous week and insisted on taking part. To his great credit, he gave a fine rendition as Misargyrides the moneylender in the Plautine comedy *Mostellaria* (2013).

To overcome any purist objection to *Caesar*, we interspersed the Shakespeare text with readings from the source material – Plutarch's and Suetonius' *Lives*, which we afterwards read in the original in our advanced language groups.

For *Philoctetes* (2012), we were fortunate to secure the services of a theatrical propsman, who among many other adventures acted in The Abbey, Ireland's National Theatre, and appears among the credits as properties manager in Channel 4's *Father Ted*. The Great Bow of Heracles defeated us until this gentleman came to the rescue with a fully authentic and working longbow (see Fig. 13.2). Naturally, our members tested it out in the field behind the yard, finding that it easily sent an arrow the entire width of the field – some 400–500 feet. We did, I hasten to add, first check carefully that there were no cows in the vicinity; the premature death of neighbouring farmer's cattle would undoubtedly bring about the equally premature end of the Orchard Yard Players! (see Fig. 13.3).

From 2016 we have added a sound effects operation, run by a teacher friend who is adept at such arts. The entry of the Knights was accompanied by the German march *Der Koniggratzer* while she also managed to include as diverse a range as Dad's Army, Status Quo, Dylan Thomas and the Soggy Bottom Boys with *In the Jailhouse Now*.

It will be clear from all of the above that our proceedings in Ireland have been occasions of great fun as well as of learning. The enthusiasm of participants is outstanding; the fact that many of them are parents and grandparents bodes well for the future of classical studies in the area, since undoubtedly they will try to pass on some of that enthusiasm to the younger generation. That in itself is a matter of great importance to our branch, since many of the founder generation have now passed on, and we have experienced difficulty in recruiting new and younger people to the cause, especially in a city such as Limerick, which has a university but no department of Classics. Therefore, long live the Orchard Yard Players, and we extend our invitation to all readers to come and join with us in a future production.

Figure 13.2 The Orchard Players: Philoctetes and the Great Bow of Heracles.

Figure 13.3 The Orchard Players: Staging Sophocles' *Philoctetes*.

The Spennymoor *Odyssey*

Francesca Richards

The UK's Research Excellence Framework (REF) impact agenda has put the question of how specific academic research shapes the wider world into the spotlight. The often time-limited funding of research projects means that creating long-term impact can appear to be a difficult prospect. However, in 2013, the Living Poets project – led by Professor Barbara Graziosi at the University of Durham and funded by the European Research Council – began public engagement work in the local County Durham community. In 2016 the project moved towards creating sustainable impact, as well as providing valuable research insights. The academic aims of the Living Poets project can be summarized as follows:

> From antiquity to the present, people have produced a vast range of narrative and visual representations of the ancient poets, drawing from three main sources: their understanding of classical poetry, other representations, and their own personal, lived experience. The main contention of this project is that representations of the ancient poets tell us something crucial – not about the actual poets of Greece and Rome, but about their readers. Classical poetry has been transmitted for over two millennia: this project focuses on the people who recognized its value, ensured its survival, and reconfigured its relevance for their particular contexts. These people often had a powerful sense of the poets' presence: they saw the ancient poets in dreams, had imaginary conversations with them, made fun of them, wrote biographies and anecdotes, produced portraits, and visited the places where they were supposed to have lived and died. An analysis of how readers imagined the Greek and Roman poets offers a powerful means of investigating the shifting social and cultural value of classical poetry from antiquity to the present.[1]

Accessibility was a key motivation for the Living Poets project: at its core was the creation of an open-access online database of biographical and visual representations of the poets, with guides to the relevant sources (http://livingpoets.dur.ac.uk). It was also clear from the research premise that we had a natural way into some public engagement – by hearing about how the public perceive ancient poets and their works, we could not only engage new audiences with the classical past, but gain insights into how contemporary audiences approach ancient poetry. There were two areas of concern before our engagement projects started: first, as academics, how could we create not just singular events, but a meaningful response to opportunities for classical engagement from within communities where there is limited engagement with universities as a whole? And, second, how could we make sure we reach a multi-generational audience from diverse walks of life?

Spennymoor

From the beginning, a decision was made to look beyond our immediate locality, the city of Durham: there are high-performing local schools and cultural organizations which would have been keen to participate, perhaps because they already had established relationships through their proximity to the university. However, the Living Poets team wanted specifically to try to reach people who would never put themselves forward to engage with us. It was clear that neither the department nor the wider university was going to be the place to do this; this is not to suggest that there is a lack of interest in academic ideas outside of the city – but rather little sense of entitlement to a dialogue on ideas with the university and its staff. We recognized that we needed assistance in facilitating a local dialogue from scratch: to change dynamics, we needed to do something unexpected. We collaborated with Changeling Productions, an experienced local theatre company, and with their local knowledge the town of Spennymoor became a focused base for our activities. Spennymoor is one of the many economically deprived former mining towns surrounding Durham; the closure of the Tudhoe Park colliery on the northern outskirts of the town in 1969 marked the decline of the mining industry in the area. Despite a brief successful switch towards manufacturing as the new local economy, the online Indices of Deprivation 2015 tool created by the UK government's Department for Communities and Local Government puts Spennymoor as among the top 20 per cent most deprived areas nationally for multiple indices of deprivation.[2] For deprivation affecting children, the same tool ranks it in the top 20 per cent worst affected areas nationally; for income deprivation, employment deprivation, health deprivation and income deprivation affecting the elderly, it ranks in the top 10 per cent most deprived in the UK. Though only seven miles in distance, Spennymoor is removed from both the city of Durham and the university, with limited public centres and exposure to the arts.

Given the challenge of testing a new kind of project in this community, we also had to decide how we wanted to qualify success. For us, there were two key markers: first, that participants thought differently about ancient poets as a result of our activities, learnt something new and enjoyed an activity that they might not normally have participated in. The second was the cultivation of interest in the long term, through possible ongoing future collaborations. The easiest and most obvious path was to approach local primary schools: the English national curriculum for pupils ages seven to eleven (key stage 2) includes the study of Greeks and Romans in the history component; but there was also scope to simultaneously cover the component of the English language curriculum which says that pupils should have familiarity with myths and legends from other cultures, including the oral retelling of some of these stories.[3] In this sense, primary schools provided a ready audience (and a certain safety in achieving something positive), and we could have accepted all schools that were willing to participate. However, to make the greatest possible difference to the lives of pupils and teachers by expanding their knowledge and appreciation of the classical world, it was important for us to approach only state primary schools who had little or no previous contact with the university, given the acute socio-economic pressures and disparities in the region. We started out initially at eight local primary schools in the Spennymoor area, including one special educational needs (SEN) school.

Into the classroom

Our school-based activities were adapted as needed for different classes: we had booked visits with pupils mostly in Years 4–6 (ages 8–11), but the different organizational structures between schools meant that a single class could contain a mixture of these year groups. Another key factor was time – some schools were happy for us to take over the classroom for the whole day, as in the summer, some of their peers were out on school trips; other year groups could only spare a couple of hours, or an afternoon. Practically, we needed to be adaptable for the variety of ages, and for time, but also for a range of academic ability within these classes: we wanted all children in the room to be able to engage creatively without the internal pressure of the need to imagine something in the 'right' way. Not only would an approach based on the pupils' own imaginings spark creativity but also encourage them to ignore any negative preconceptions of what classical studies might be 'about' or who it might be 'for' by making the task focused on their own, present imaginings. Importantly for us as researchers, it helped us to be aware of our own guidance to pupils – given that the project was about the multitude of ways in which ancient poets have been imagined, it also would have been disingenuous to try to steer the pupils' interpretations in the direction of our own. We also needed to be able to make a link between the poet and their work which the pupils could use to reflect on where their own impressions had come from.

Bearing all of this in mind, we decided to focus on Homer's *Odyssey*, for its imaginative appeal. Leading with a storytelling-based approach, all of the sessions had one central underpinning idea: to invite pupils to think about who the poet of the *Odyssey* might be, first through a basic introduction to the narrative of the poem, and then afterwards through their own imagined suggestions as to the identity of its author. This approach gave us the flexibility to respond in the moment to the engagement of the pupils in the class – adding greater specificity and more advanced vocabulary as appropriate (*e.g.* for older year groups we might include less well-known episodes from the *Odyssey* – perhaps mentioning Odysseus' raid on the Cicones from *Odyssey* book 9, or the cattle of Helios from *Odyssey* book 12). Working with our theatre partners, we set up the bare bones of the story of the *Odyssey*, asking pupils to fill in details – inventing a name for the hero and predicting plot developments. It turned out that aspects of the narrative would be familiar even to our youngest pupils: at points when we asked pupils what they thought might happen next in the narrative, some were obviously making use of their familiarity with archetypal characters (e.g. the alluring Sirens, the trickster) and of narrative arcs (i.e. that the hero will achieve his quest) from their other reading to fill in the gaps. However, there were also pupils who appeared to be influenced by other media sources – one pupil mentioning that he knew what a Cyclops was from a computer game and others name-checking the *Percy Jackson* book film series. As the story developed, we selected pupils to take on the roles of characters, and in some workshops this was supported by mask-making, drawings of specific sites in the poem and writing exercises designed to draw out personal reactions, which would develop their imaginary impressions of the poet. Later in the day, we asked them to imagine the author of the story they had created and give us (depending on the year group) visual and written descriptions. The diversity of authorial representations was striking – we had blonde teenage girl Homers who were in fact called Katie who wrote stories in her diary, and Homers who composed in bed, wearing pyjamas. Most interestingly, as well as the traditional portraits of a bearded, older man in a draped white garment with a wreath we also had local Homers: family members who were known for a good story, or grandfather-type figures. We could see already how the pupils were viewing the poet in a highly personal fashion. At the end of the day, we would unveil that the story we had based our activities on was the ancient *Odyssey*, drawing parallels between the story created by the pupils and the Homeric poem, and revealing to the pupils a little about ancient speculations about the figure of Homer. In subsequent years, we repeated similar sessions at some of these schools, offering training to deliver these workshops to graduate students from the Department of Classics and Ancient History. We collated feedback via e-testimonials in which teachers found these workshops 'fantastic' and 'inspiring'. We expanded our reach into the Durham City area as well as maintaining these links with Spennymoor. When the final round of workshops was completed in April 2016, we had reached sixteen schools in total with new schools joining us at every new round of activity, and with a committed interest in maintaining these relationships.

The empty shop

From the beginning of this project, we wanted to engage all ages, which was much more of a risk, but would pay real dividends at the end, both in terms of the process of learning about engaging our local communities and in terms of the creative insights that the community would offer. In addition to local primary schools and SEN schools, two other locations were the focus for our activities: the town library and an 'empty shop' on the high street. The first of these seemed promising as an already-established cultural centre in the town – and the library workshops (along the lines of the school activities, but tailored for all ages) were advertised through the local paper, in shop windows and through word of mouth. The latter may have seemed like a rather *laissez-faire* approach, but it was important for how smaller communities operate and organize themselves. Unfortunately, we did not have any takers for the library workshops as it soon became clear that residents were not going to come out to the library, even if they were curious. This was likely to be as a result of numerous factors – including a simple lack of appeal, but also related perhaps to the cultural patterns of residents, and where they were likely to choose to spend free time. However, our failed experiments were just as valuable as our successful ones in terms of understanding how to make a connection with communities like Spennymoor, and for self-evaluation.

The second location, the 'empty shop' opposite the local supermarket, was in many ways the most productive location. The shop has been used on an ongoing basis by various community groups for art and crafts: we took this space over for seven weeks each Saturday, so we could build a presence in the town, but like most small high streets, the footfall can be quite low. The local knowledge of Changeling Productions proved critical here, as they were able to advertice the shop activities informally among the community on a personal level: as a result, curiosity began to build. An artist from the team created Greek-style masks with animal faces and ancient faces, providing a visual signifier on the high street, designed to lead people to the shop on workshop days, where we could stop them to engage them: first to introduce the narrative of the *Odyssey*, then about its poet. Changeling's composer even built a replica *kithara* – the traditional instrument of the rhapsode. We asked visitors – who were of all ages – to imagine the poem within Spennymoor – where particular places in the poem might be relocated and how the figure of Homer would fit into this landscape. These encounters generated a fascinating collection of verbatim material – testimonies to creative engagements specific to this community, both physical and emotional: Calypso's island became the pub where there were lock-ins, the Cyclops' lair lay in the swampy bit of land outside of town, or the one-eyed clock-tower and the local job centre became the land of the Lotus-Eaters – the land where Odysseus' companions lose all sense of themselves. Homer himself became a figure with 'glasses and a flat cap', or 'with a long beard, sitting outside Kwiksave, observing people' or a 'homeless man', perhaps someone from the armed forces – County Durham has a long history of military recruitment, being home to the Durham Light Infantry that in 2007 was integrated into the Rifles (the largest infantry regiment of the British army). In this vein, the reunion of

Odysseus and Penelope seemed to strike a particular chord with families, and the reimagining of Helen of Troy as a familiar person proved popular.

Insights and next steps

One individual proved particularly interesting and illustrated how we need public engagement to interact with those already engaged and not just those who have not encountered the classical past. Visiting multiple times over three or four weeks, this man knew more about the epic cycle than many undergraduates would; he reeled off the relationship between the Homeric poems to the rest of the epic cycle, talked extensively about Gilgamesh and near-Eastern epic and offered his views on how the Homeric poems could be used to explain natural phenomena. One week, he brought along his Loeb edition of Quintus Smyrnaeus' *Posthomerica* for discussion. He had never studied Classics formally: he was an unemployed labourer who had picked up the *Iliad* years ago and then had delved into reading the rest of the epic cycle simply because he wanted to know how these stories fit together. In making multiple stops by our shop, he was able to have a unique kind of conversation – one that there just had not been the opportunity to have before. The slow burn of word-of-mouth was effective enough that after we had finished the project, word got back to us that interest had been piqued, but the project had ended before people could attend.

The element of surprise or unexpectedness continued to be effective in later sessions. What we achieved in 2013 was a small foundation for future projects, and subsequent applications were made for internal university impact funding. In June 2014, an event called 'Who Was Homer?' featuring children's author Gillian Cross and Changeling Productions brought similar activities into Durham City itself, drawing visitors from as far afield as Newcastle and York – and crucially, from Spennymoor. One local woman, who attended the event with her two children, and who had never been to a university-related event before, took the time to e-mail us afterwards:

> Just wanted to say how much we enjoyed Saturday's event. We were visiting Durham for an entirely different reason and just happened to be in the square watching the fashion show when we received the leaflet advertising your event. A case of serendipity you could say. Anyway, from a family who was unaware of the event, the book and the story, we felt it was a totally unique family orientated event which was very pleasurable. It was a delight to here [*sic*] Gillian read excerpts from the book and personally, I found it encouraging that so many children came to specifically listen to the passages of the book and who were, obviously, interested in the story.

This was exactly the kind of response that we had hoped for, and were delighted that the lady had taken the time to tell us exactly how she felt about the event. However, there will have been others who did not enjoy the event in the same way, and it was difficult to evaluate the event properly when running the day with a fairly small team. It would have been even more beneficial to hear what might have been more appealing to those who were not that enthused by what they had experienced. Indeed, evaluation was something that needed improvement: often working on a shoestring budget for short spurts of time, alongside the time constraints of work, meant that thorough evaluation slipped down the list of priorities. Apportioned funding for evaluation as part of awards, beyond the writing of a standard report, may have given us time to reflect on each round of activities in a more rounded way.

Following our work in Spennymoor, the next stage was to develop the premise of these workshops using support from both Durham University and the Arts and Humanities Research Council (AHRC) Cultural Engagement Fund, taking the experience to turn it into a touring primary school theatre piece that spread the project further into County Durham. This performance saw one actor enter the classroom claiming to be Homer, performing the *Odyssey* – grandiose in speech, with a cloak and walking stick, and another an interjecting workman, dressed in a hard hat and fluorescent jacket, who would offer his own opinion on 'Homer's' words with reference to the local area. In a final twist, this workman revealed himself to be the poet of the *Iliad* – leaving the question of the identity of Homer, and his representation in different sources across the ages to be explored in a classroom session that followed on directly from the performance. The research content of classroom sessions was developed with greater specificity, using key arguments and pictorial sources directly from a research paper (Graziosi 2015, pp. 25–47). These sessions have formed the basis of a successful application to Classics for All, and materials created for the AHRC project will be incorporated into these plans – with some schools who had participated in our earliest 'Spennymoor *Odyssey*' projects showing interest in developing projects in the long term.

Reflections

How far had we come in meeting the goals we set ourselves before the work in Spennymoor began? And what did we learn from the experience? Qualitatively, we certainly had some pieces of evidence that suggested that those we had met in Spennymoor had thought about ancient poets and their work differently as a result of our project – behavioural changes (repeat visits), written feedback (from visitors and schools) and the written and drawn accounts from school pupils. Though we had been initially uncertain, there was indeed a desire for unexpected, creative classical encounters within the community – the spontaneous and diverse range of engagements from the town centre proved to us that it was worth going out beyond formal organizations. The question of how to develop long-term projects in the community beyond institutions still remains open, but our project showed a community interest and willingness to engage that lacks long-term resourcing. Moreover, by testing a wide range of creative approaches, we were able to quickly identify what methods particular audiences responded to, but also had a range of approaches in our cache which we could call upon when needed – often spontaneously. It was also hugely important that we were working closely with an organization that knew the area and its people well – practically, and personally, in terms of making connections with local people. Finally, it taught us that we should never expect resistance to, or a disinterest in, classical ideas, and that members of communities like Spennymoor can provide stimulating insights into our own research.

How we quantified success was less certain – partly because the project was a learning curve for all involved, but also because the project had developed in relation to funding opportunities from multiple sources. From the outset, we had designed a resilient and flexible project that has allowed for adjustments to content, focus and scheduling: this made writing funding applications easier as we could make adjustments in focus and content in order to match funding requirements (*e.g.* the AHRC funding required an external cultural partner) and to be able to benefit from multiple funding opportunities. However, being dependent on relatively limited amounts of money, and on the availability of key individuals, meant that long-term planning could not be at the forefront of our minds, even if we had longer-term aspirations.

Our project taught us that academics need to be taking real risks – experimenting, devising new ways of communicating and being prepared for failure: it is these methods which are going to achieve the most effective and dynamic results in communities like Spennymoor.

Latin in the Park: Catullus and conjugations in the sunshine

Evelien Bracke

The Latin in the Park initiative was set up by the Iris Project in 2008, to increase access to Classics in the Oxford area in an informal, outdoor setting. At a cost of £1 per class, anyone from the local area had the opportunity to engage with the Latin language and ideas from the classical world (Middleton 2008). Classes ran for three summers in Oxford and London, after which the programme was discontinued as the Iris Project expanded its Literacy through Latin project and moved on to other initiatives, such as the establishment of the Iris Classics Centre at Cheney (formerly the East Oxford Classics Centre). In 2012, Swansea University took up the concept of Latin in the Park. This section discusses the Swansea programme, its aims, challenges and outcomes.

Aims and challenges

While access to Classics in the UK is steadily improving, there are major discrepancies between the constituent parts: Wales particularly lags behind England and Scotland, with only approximately 11 per cent of secondary schools offering Latin and even fewer offering Classical Civilisation (Bracke 2015, p. 11). This marginalization of Classics is a symptom of a larger ideology which focuses on Welsh while provision of other languages tends to be sidelined. In 2012, the Department of Classics, Ancient History and Egyptology at Swansea University therefore piloted the Iris Project's Literacy through Classics project with sixty-five primary school pupils in one local school (see www.literacythroughclassics.weebly.com). This project not only increases access to Classics in schools in South Wales but also allows university students to develop their employability skills in an increasingly competitive market. In order to complement this curricular provision for pupils, the department decided also to run a programme called *Latin in the Park* during the summer, targeting entire communities, in collaboration with the Department of Adult Continuing Education (DACE). The aim in doing so was threefold. First, we wanted to target families in an informal, playful atmosphere outside the curriculum. Secondly, by using student teachers rather than relying on academic staff to give up their time, we aimed to develop student employability further (Bracke 2013); indeed, the positive influence of student teachers on pupils in learning Classics is attested (Bracke 2016). Lastly, by creating a new opportunity for people in South Wales to engage with Classics, we wanted to raise the profile of Classics in Wales, which is hitherto still viewed largely negatively by virtue of being connected with an upper-class education.

When more than fifty people took part in the first lesson, we realized the thirst for Classics was greater than anticipated. After a successful pilot course, during which four undergraduate and master's-level students taught Latin for an hour on nine Saturdays in June and July at a cost of £3 per class – the profits of which help fund the Literacy through Classics project – the search for an ideal format began. Teaching during the summer is challenging. Participants going on holiday means class attendance is irregular and progression through the course material is –

while not impossible – difficult to predict. The Welsh weather is equally unpredictable, and so alternative arrangements always had to be made to teach indoors when wet. Works to nearby buildings and the summer ball provided noise-related challenges. For future years, we therefore settled on only five sessions, but ninety minutes rather than one-hour long, so participants still had the same amount of language instruction. In the two following years, we changed the title to Ancient Languages in the Park and also offered beginners' Greek, intermediate Latin (for people with some experience, who read a number of authors, such as Catullus and Tacitus), an introduction to ancient Egypt (including some hieroglyphs) and children's Latin (see Fig. 13.4). These courses tended to be less populated than the beginners' Latin class, but we were keen to support different aspects of antiquity and always had sufficient participants to run courses. After each lesson, we organized a talk by an academic on a subject related to antiquity, which complemented participants' more structured learning. The course was also brought to Neath, a nearby town with even less access to Classics. Interest there among both adults and children was also high in both 2013 and 2014.

In 2015, we did not run Latin in the Park as the new Swansea Summer School in Ancient Languages took up too much preparation time, which meant the continuity was broken. In 2016, we decided to run the course again, but changed the format and only offered children's classes. As these were undersubscribed, the courses did not run. The error made was no doubt related to the reason for setting up the children's course in the first place, namely to give parents an opportunity to study Latin at their pace while children were able to learn simultaneously at theirs. A format is currently being explored for 2018.

Figure 13.4 Participants at Ancient Languages in the Park.

Figures and outcomes

Approximately one hundred and sixty people took part in the courses between 2012 and 2014. They ranged from age 4 – 70, with professional adults and retired people as the majority, though many secondary school students also took part. Questionnaires were handed out at the end of the final lesson each year. The return rate for the questionnaires was quite low (21 per cent) and so it is not possible to draw firm conclusions. The returned questionnaires do, however, offer insight into participants' views of the course. First, the student teachers were rated as excellent by 94.4 per cent of the surveyed participants, which confirms the positive role of student-teachers also acknowledged by analysis of the data of the Literacy through Classics project (Bracke 2016). Secondly, the learning process itself was rated as excellent by 98 per cent, and a further 2 per cent rated it very good. Classics was thus taught at an appropriate level and with an appropriate methodology. Asked about the most inspiring or challenging aspects of the courses, the most mentioned aspect was that it was 'fun', 'friendly', 'accessible' and 'unintimidating'. In its aims of widening access to Classics, the project was thus successful. Several people mentioned that they 'never had the opportunity' to study Classics before and were grateful as it is 'not offered much in schools'. Participants did also mention they thought grammar or texts were 'challenging'. While a minority of participants thought the pace was slightly too fast, most connected its challenging nature with a sense of achievement, as these quotes demonstrate:

> An excellent and interesting introduction to Latin. It stimulated an interest. A lot was learned in a short time – some difficulty in retaining all the knowledge acquired, but encouraged to keep at it!

> The fact of feeling able to translate from Latin to English from the very beginning – more challenging each week. Thank you for providing the course.

Students teaching the courses also benefited from the experience, and many of them have since gone on to do a teaching qualification, such as the PGCE or TEFL (Teaching English as a Foreign Language), museum work or postgraduate study. As part of the broader Classics widening participation agenda at Swansea University, which includes both schools and community based short-term and sustainable interventions, this has led to a greater and more positive awareness of Classics in Wales, as the 2015 Western Mail article 'Could Latin be set for a comeback in Welsh classrooms?', for example, reveals (Turner 2015). The article acknowledges the various projects set up by Swansea University to provide access to Latin: 'Now more children in Wales are to be given the chance to learn Latin, once taught in classrooms all around the UK, but now more widely associated with independent rather than state schools'. In its three aims of widening access to Classics, increasing student employability and raising the profile of Classics in Wales, the project can be judged to have been successful.

The most innovative part of the initiative was the children's Latin classes, as these were aimed at four- to ten-year-olds, some of whom did not have proficient reading skills. I taught this course in order to gauge how Latin can be taught to younger children without a textbook, only with games and songs (see Fig. 13.5). You can find the lesson plans, resources and blogs on the project website at http://literacythroughclassics.weebly.com/latin-key-stage-1.html. In 2013, six pupils took part; in 2014, it was oversubscribed with fourteen children. It was challenging to teach

Figure 13.5 Children (age 4–10 years) learning Latin.

this course as learning outcomes for each class invariably had to be adapted. The 2013 group became preoccupied with the *Lupus Malus* story and wanted to narrate and act it *ad infinitum*, and the second group preferred more tactile games such as the play parachute, under which they ran towards each other to communicate in Latin, and water-pistol tag. Pupils were given homework after each lesson which was duly returned, and oral feedback was encouraging. Interestingly, the distraction level from other visitors and events in the park was much lower than I anticipated, possibly on account of the dynamic nature of the activities which they associated with play rather than learning. One and a half hour classes – the same length as the adult classes, so both parents and children could take part in the project – passed quickly, and pupils were reluctant to finish at the end. Pupils' continued attention to the classes in spite of their length demonstrates the success of the playful approach.

Conclusion

The provision of outdoor ancient language classes targeted at wider communities is a worthwhile, if time consuming, initiative. Its time-consuming nature derives from the need to be flexible, in preparation, in teaching and in dependence on the weather. Two key elements indeed need to be present for such a project to succeed. First, teaching must be done at an appropriate level with an appropriate methodology. For adult beginners, a gentle reading approach with focus on etymology and some games – such as *Pictionary*, hangman and ball games – is used. For children, creative play is required to maintain pupils' attention. Secondly, if the number of participants exceeds ten, it is helpful to have one person present who does not teach but is in charge of managing logistics and unexpected changes (from rain to splinters and financial issues). If these conditions are met, feedback suggests that participants appreciate the stress-free environment while learning a challenging subject. For children particularly, the park, associated with play rather than learning, provides a constructive learning environment. As a community-widening access activity, it is thus a successful format. As a complementary activity to the semester-based Literacy through Classics project, it helps to raise aspirations in pupils and boosts student employability.

Notes

1   See http://livingpoets.dur.ac.uk. (Accessed 12 February 2017).

2   See http://dclgapps.communities.gov.uk/imd/idmap.html – search for 'Spennymoor'. (Accessed 12 February 2017).

3   See www.gov.uk/education/primary-curriculum-key-stage-2. (Accessed 4 August 2017).

References

Bracke, E. (2013), 'Literacy through Latin! Employability and outreach go hand in hand', *SALT Conference Presentation*, 2 July 2013. Available online: https://saltconference2013.wordpress.com/programme/presentations/a5-evelien-bracke/. (Accessed 23 August 2016).

Bracke, E. (2015), 'Learning Latin in Wales: Report on research and practice', *Cymru Wales Classics Hub*, 30 November 2015. Available online: http://cymruwalesclassicshub.weebly.com/documents.html. (Accessed 23 August 2016).

Bracke, E. (2016), 'The Role of University Student Teachers in Increasing Widening Participation to Classics', *Journal of Widening Participation and Lifelong Learning*, 18 (2): 111–129.

Coolahan, J. (1981), *Irish Education. History and Structure*, Unknown: Institute of Public Administration.

Department for Communities and Local Government (2015), *Indices of Deprivation online tool.* Available online: http://dclgapps.communities.gov.uk/imd/idmap.html. (Accessed 12 February 2017).

Graziosi, B. (2015), 'On Seeing the Poet: Arabic, Italian and Byzantine portraits of Homer', *Scandinavian Journal of Byzantine and Modern Greek Studies*, 1: 25–47.

Middleton, C. (2008), 'A triumph of the ego', *The Telegraph*, 24 May 2008. Available online: www.telegraph.co.uk/education/3356293/A-triumph-of-the-ego.html. (Accessed 23 August 2016).

Turner, R. (2015), 'Could Latin be set for a comeback in Welsh classrooms?', *WalesOnline*, 26 November. Available online: www.walesonline.co.uk/news/wales-news/could-latin-set-comeback-welsh-10508958. (Accessed 23 August 2016).

CHAPTER 14

THE APPEAL OF NON-LINGUISTIC CLASSICAL STUDIES AMONG SIXTH-FORM STUDENTS

Aisha Khan-Evans

This chapter aims to explore some of the reasons for students (aged 17–19) choosing to study AS or A level Classical Civilisation in a post-compulsory setting. It begins with a brief introduction on the context of A levels, the popularity of Classical Civilisation and some elements involved in subject choice. The following sections outline factors which might influence students in their choice of Classical Civilisation as an AS or A level. These sections draw on literature on subject choice and on data collected during a research project conducted in two sixth-form colleges in the south of England, one in which Classical Civilisation was already an established subject and the other where it was a relatively new option choice. The chapter concludes with some thoughts on the challenges facing Classical Civilisation, in the light of examination changes, and on the benefits of an education in Classical Civilisation.

For the research project, questionnaires, from seventy-one A level (A2) students in total, formed the initial method of data collection, to give an overview of the students, including information on their education up to this point, whether they had any prior knowledge of classical subjects and an indication of their plans after leaving college. The questionnaires were followed up with a small number of interviews, nineteen students in total, which allowed for a freer discussion of subject choice and sought to explore whether there was any such thing as a 'typical' student of Classical Civilisation.

Context for A levels

Advanced level qualifications (A levels) were introduced in England in the early 1950s, when the official school leaving age was fifteen, primarily as the stepping stone to university admission, and the examinations were taken by a small minority of students. In the intervening years, however, the proportion of students remaining in school up to the age of eighteen, and those entering higher education institutions, has gradually increased. Nonetheless, England's education system has been seen by some as 'medium participation and medium achievement' (Hodgson and Spours 2008, p. 4). The government of the late 1990s set out its proposals to reform post-sixteen education in England, Wales and Northern Ireland, proposals which would become known as *Curriculum 2000*. The proposed changes were designed in part to increase access to A levels and broaden the curriculum (Hodgson and Spours 2008, p. 27) and, according to Rodeiro and Sutch (2013), over eighty different subjects have been offered at A level in England in recent years. The reforms divided the examination into two parts, each consisting of three modules; the Advanced Subsidiary qualification would provide the first half of the two-year course as well as acting as a stand-alone qualification and, since the introduction of *Curriculum 2000*, most students have taken four AS level subjects in their first year and have generally continued with three full A levels in their second year.

Rise in popularity of Classical Civilisation

As noted, one of the aims of the reforms was to increase access to A levels and the introduction of modular AS and A levels has seen the number of students taking AS examinations at the end of one year of study rise overall, with a significant increase for Classical Civilisation. While some increase in interest was noted before the first AS examinations in 2001 (Tristram 2003, p. 18), AQA and OCR entries for AS Classical Civilisation have increased by nearly 40 per cent since their introduction, from 3,369 in 2001 to 5,592 in 2015 (AQA 2015; OCR 2015). French and German, to give two other examples, have each decreased in popularity by nearly 14 per cent and around 23 per cent, respectively, in that time. What, then, attracts students to Classical Civilisation?

Factors influencing subject choice

Research on choice in educational settings suggests that influences might include previous attainment, socio-economic background, schools previously attended and other life experiences such as holidays (Stables and Stables 1995; Francis et al. 2003; Bell et al. 2005). In motivational theory, the co-regulation model of identity, among others, suggests the importance of social and psychological experiences (La Guardia 2009; Renninger 2009), which would include interactions with teachers and others at school and outside. Put simply, experiences and people have an effect on choices. Students often select Classical Civilisation as an AS without any formal experience of the subject and in settings, such as sixth-form colleges, where they are unfamiliar with the teachers as well as the subject. This, alongside the number of students intending to drop it after the AS year who revise their plans and then continue to the second year, adds to the interest in possible reasons for choosing Classical Civilisation.

What can Classical Civilisation offer learners?

Classical Civilisation teachers and lecturers often comment on the broad lens on the world offered by the subject as an important tool in the twenty-first century; students explore the nature of other cultures and the classical world provides the framework for doing so in a sensitive and neutral way. While much of the material presents issues relevant to the modern world, such as the role of women in society and politics and multiculturalism, the temporal distance and the presentation of a culture seemingly far removed from their own allows students to consider such issues from a more objective, less highly charged viewpoint. The study of Classical Civilisation facilitates enhanced cultural literacy, which can be seen as 'a form of cultural capital that enables us to act sensitively and effectively in a world of differences' (Wood et al. 2006, p. 20). Classical Civilisation exposes students to a rich variety of elements, encompassing history, literature of different genres, poetry and prose, drama, art and architecture, as well as philosophy. Classical subjects embody the notion of cross-curricular breadth and balance (Wilkinson 2003, p. 109) and perhaps it is not surprising that Classical Civilisation appeals to a wide range of students, in terms of both learners' prior experiences and previous attainment.

Who chooses to study Classical Civilisation?

As already noted, modular exams were intended to broaden A level choice. Nonetheless, Bell et al., in their 2005 study carried out a few years after their introduction, suggested that more than 20 per cent of students were specialists in terms of their choices: for example they tended to focus on science subjects rather than mixing disciplines. This specialization seems to remain the norm some years on, with various science subjects providing the seven most popular A level combinations for university applicants in 2014 and the top twenty combinations characterized as 'traditional' choices (Rodeiro and Sutch 2013, p. 36). Classical Civilisation students, on the other hand, often study a great variety of other subjects, including Art, Computing, Environmental Science, Film Studies, Politics and Music, with nearly as many subject combinations as individuals, confirming the wide-ranging appeal of the subject. Future plans are often equally varied; in the data collected from the two sixth-form colleges, they ranged from continuing with a classical subject at university to taking courses in TV and Film Production, Sports Science or Equine Studies. Perhaps this is unsurprising given the varied nature of students' prior experiences and the fact that they have often had no experience of classical subjects, nor do they necessarily know anyone else who has. Students are perhaps much less likely to be familiar with Classical Civilisation than they might have been thirty or so years ago; fewer schools offer classical subjects and, where they do, may be less likely to offer a key stage 3 Classical Studies course than might have been the case before the introduction of the National Curriculum in 1988.

As mentioned above, students of Classical Civilisation are not commonly 'specialists' in their selection of AS and A level subjects and thus it may be difficult to highlight one specific reason for their choice unlike, for example, a student who has enjoyed Geography at GCSE and chooses to continue with the subject at AS and A levels. In regard to subject-specific experience, learners will most likely have encountered some aspects of the ancient world in their primary education and it has been suggested that the introduction of *Curriculum 2000* 'increased the opportunity for classics to be taught within the programmes for English and History at all key stages' (Gay 2003, p. 24). Research suggests that 'many of the influences on choice [are] identifiable even amongst primary age children' (Foskett et al. 2003, p. 2). In practice, however, young people in the post-sixteen sector may have little explicit memory of their primary experiences and have not studied related subjects at secondary school. While students do occasionally recall primary school experiences of the ancient world, those memories often centre around the creativity of the activity recalled (such as dressing up, a jigsaw activity resulting in the construction of a Greek vase or making theatre masks) rather than the topic itself. Those who do recall something of the subject matter in their positive earlier experiences often comment on the appeal of 'stories' and 'adventure', as well as indicating an awareness of the ancient world as 'different' or even 'exotic', suggesting an intrinsic appeal of the subject.

Intrinsic interest

While intrinsic interest is not easy to dissociate from other influences such as prior experience, students of Classical Civilisation, as already mentioned, often comment on the stories of the ancient world, whether mythological or historical, and may sometimes recall books on mythology from their childhood. Journalists have also noted a more general interest in the classical world in recent years, such as that engendered by 'sword and sandals' cinema epics: 'nowhere has the resurgence of the classics been quite so visible as on screen' (Leith 2010). One might agree with *The Times* journalist who noted that 'Ridley Scott really started something [with *Gladiator*]' (Owen 2003). But it should be noted that *Gladiator* came out in 2000, after the initial increase in A level uptake quoted by Tristram (2003). As with recollections from primary school, learners' memories of Classics-related film or television are often equally vague, which might suggest they were not particularly influential. It is, as already noted, difficult to isolate individual influences, since 'choice itself ... is not based on a full rational analysis of influencing factors, but is a response to information received through various filters ... and then subjected to a range of psychological mechanisms' (Foskett et al. 2003, p. 2). In short, it is difficult to identify discrete reasons for the appeal of Classical Civilisation – its appeal is multifaceted and, to some extent, personal to the individual learner.

Classical Civilisation, as discussed earlier, is a multifaceted subject and could be seen as the ultimate humanities subject, attracting students with a wide range of interests. It presents us with stories of characters, history, politics and how cultures develop; these are stories about life. One former AS student summed up its intrinsic interest in her motivation to 'know more about the people who made the myths and came up with the ideas'.

Promotional material

Intrinsic interest, though, may also be accompanied by a serendipitous set of circumstances. Course descriptions seem to be, perhaps surprisingly, relatively important at the level of post-sixteen choice and learners with little or no prior experience of Classical Civilisation are most likely to rely on promotional material such as a prospectus. Former students have mentioned coming across the subject description by chance, simply stating, for example, 'I chose it purely from the prospectus ... I read through it and thought, that sounds good'. One university colleague also noticed Classical Civilisation by chance in a leaflet while at school and changed schools on the strength of it. In another case, a potential student stumbled into the Classical Civilisation room at an open evening in error and made his choice there and then, commenting that it seemed to be 'a fun subject'. Open evenings or other visits have been noted as particularly important for learners aged sixteen to nineteen (Whittaker et al. 2004, p. 19). This fact has important implications for teachers in the Further Education sector. The importance of subject advocacy and promotion must not be underestimated.

Complementarity

It may not be surprising, given the diversity of students of Classical Civilisation, that the breadth of the subject is appealing. Learners have sometimes chosen it to 'tie-in' with their other subjects, such as Art, English Literature, History and Politics, commenting on the complementarity of Classical Civilisation as an influence on their choices. One student, for example, described Classical Civilisation as a combination of his other subjects (Politics, English Literature and History) 'but a lot older', later returning to his enjoyment of the links between all his subjects. On the other hand, I have known a student who was struggling to choose between Art, English and

History and realized that Classical Civilisation provided the solution. One current university student describes Classical Civilisation as 'one of the broadest arts subjects offered at A level'. Others have selected their subject combinations, as already mentioned, to provide them with a broad range of subjects, with one describing Classical Civilisation as a 'refreshing change … welcome and very interesting'. In some ways, Classical Civilisation can be seen as a 'luxury' at the start of the course, with some learners describing it initially as 'a spare' but many of those who have taught the subject will have examples of this 'spare' becoming central to subsequent choices; students often intend to drop the AS during their second year, only to revise their plans during the course and ultimately continuing to the full A level. A former student of mine intended just this as she was going to study Maths at university. By the end of her AS year she had decided to continue and went on to take a degree in Classics.

Influence of family, peers and 'fashion'

The potential influence of peers has been documented in research literature (Stables 1996; Foskett et al. 2003) as has the influence of parents or other family members (Taylor 1992). Choice inevitably occurs in a social context, that is 'the broad social and cultural environment of the individual and their family' (Foskett et al. 2003, p. 6) although 'not based on a full rational analysis of influencing factors' (Foskett et al. 2003, p. 2) and it is therefore difficult to isolate specific influences which may be subconsciously absorbed. Classical Civilisation students who have discussed parental pressure or preferences, for example, have generally claimed to disregard them, with examples being parental preference for languages or other 'traditional' or better-known subjects. It might well be the case, of course, that sixteen- and seventeen-year-olds would be reluctant to highlight the influence of family or friends in making their choices.

Foskett et al.'s (2003) discussion of fashion and peer influence indicates that although what is fashionable can soon change, 'once fashionable choice patterns become established within particular social groupings, positive feedback processes may lead to substantial reinforcement of those patterns' (Foskett et al. 2003, p. 6). As already observed, students may not know anyone else who has studied Classical Civilisation at A level but where they have mentioned knowing someone, they generally say they would have picked the subject in any case. It is, of course, difficult to know whether or not the student would have done so but the responses suggest that such personal contact served mainly to confirm their choice and that it was the subject interest which came first. It might be that students choosing a less well-known subject display a higher degree of independence. This level of independence is more common for A level students: ' … matching choices … to the choices of friends and peers protects group identity and bolsters self-esteem' (Foskett et al. 2003, p. 6) and is likely to be more influential for students making choices pre-sixteen. Foskett et al. (2003) found some evidence that young men are more influenced by peer pressure in post-sixteen choice than young women. In the context of independence, it is worth mentioning that there are usually twice as many female students as male taking AS and A level Classical Civilisation, although Davies et al. (2008, p. 238) report survey data findings that there is now a decreasing effect of gender on subject choice (Davies et al. 2008, p. 238). Stables also notes that gender stereotypes are less noticeable at the age of sixteen compared with fourteen (Stables 1997, p. 199; also Francis et al. 2003) and Davies et al. (2008, p. 238) also found a decreasing gender gap in subject choice over the years.

While the possibility of 'fashionability' might be a factor, it would not explain why courses may have *become* fashionable. Suggestions might include greater media interest in classical subjects, for example in *The Times* quotation noted above, in relation to the release of *Gladiator*, which credits Ridley Scott with reviving the 'sword and sandals' epic (Owen 2003). When *The Observer* suggested the end of the trend, ahead of the release of *300* (Smith 2007), instead of killing off the classical epic, the film spawned a spoof version, *Meet the Spartans* (2008), surely the ultimate accolade for the genre, which seems to have maintained its popularity since then. It is not only on screen, however, that the ancient world is popular. More recently, 'There has been a small wave of popular books about the classical world. In high politics, there's Obama's ostentatiously Ciceronian oratory; in low culture, the video game *God of War* has introduced the PlayStation generation to classical mythology – if only for the purposes of disembowelling the odd centaur' (Leith 2010). Although students generally assert their independence in the choice process, and rarely cite such influences, it may be that films, books and computer games nevertheless have an effect.

Novelty/unfamiliarity

While potential students of Classical Civilisation may be aware of the ancient world in the context of films and computer games, there is also a novelty factor involved in choosing to study the subject. The attraction of complementarity across subject choices has been noted but in some cases it is linked with wanting to try something new alongside subjects with which they were already familiar. One student posed the question, 'Why learn something I'd been learning for ages?' and another wanted to 'learn about new things and work in different ways'. Many other former students have specifically identified a desire to study new, more 'exotic' subjects as influential in their choices, noting that Classical Civilisation was 'something new and interesting', 'something completely different' and other descriptions along similar lines. One AS student changed to Classical Civilisation after a few weeks of another subject 'because I thought it would be something *different*, something interesting to do'.

In making educational choices, the balance between the level of challenge and the level of threat is important. There are overlaps with, for example, Bandura's self-efficacy theory, where individuals are motivated by the belief in their ability to succeed (Lent et al. 1994), which again relates to previous experience and interactions. Perhaps *because* students are often attracted by the newness of Classical Civilisation, its perceived difficulty or otherwise may be less of a factor in choice than for other more familiar subjects. Students of Classical Civilisation in non-selective settings generally have a wide range of prior attainment levels and high-attaining students may be motivated by the level of challenge involved in taking up a new subject. Lower-attaining students may be more concerned with the perceived difficulty of a subject and Francis et al. (2003) note, perhaps unsurprisingly, that the perception of subjects as easy or difficult is an important factor in subject choice. Learners who have generally had lower levels of attainment in their earlier school career will obviously be reluctant to take a subject which they have already studied and found difficult. Similarly, Adey and Biddulph (2001, p. 441) note the 'possible link between "liking" and "being good" at a subject, which might be difficult to separate'. For many learners selecting Classical Civilisation at AS or A level, the 'clean slate' and balance of challenge and threat provided by taking up a new subject may be appealing.

Future challenges

The first wave of new AS and A level examinations were introduced (for first teaching) in England in September 2015 and the new Classical Civilisation specification has been active since September 2017. The reformed examinations 'decouple' AS and A levels, positioning AS level as stand-alone qualifications, normally taken after a year. All A level examinations will now be taken at the end of the course, that is, after two years of study. Thus, should a student change his or her mind after a year, their AS would not count towards an A level. This change poses a potential threat to the teaching of AS and A level Classical Civilisation in schools and colleges, as well as to other 'minority' subjects and/or those not included in the Russell Group's 'facilitating subjects' list. Students will need to be very confident of their plans at the start of their courses; a student opting for AS Classical Civilisation who then wishes to continue with the subject (assuming their school provision allows for this) would have to sit all papers at the end of two years, regardless of their grades in the elements taken at the end of their AS year. An added concern is that many schools may decide not to offer AS levels at all and students will need more certainty at the start of their courses than previously. For a subject such as Classical Civilisation, where students often have little or no experience earlier in their education, this change may well be nothing short of disastrous for the survival of the subject.

One overriding feature within my research data is that students enjoy Classical Civilisation and a quick search of the internet seems to confirm this to be the case more widely. A glance at the Studentroom (2013) website shows the popularity of Classical Civilisation AS/A level: 'I loved this A Level'; 'before my A Levels I thought I'd be a primary teacher but now I've switched to wanting to be a Classics teacher'; 'I really would recommend it … everyone in our class loves it, even those that weren't really that into it at the beginning'. A student quoted on the Classics for All website[1] comments, 'I love the variety of subjects that you get to study within classics: history, anthropology, literature … It's such a timeless subject with relevance to modern-day life.' The classical world has relationships and intrigue, politics and war. It encourages students to appreciate other cultures and to think about the lives of the people who inhabited them. For Socrates, the unexamined life is not worth living and Classical Civilisation enhances our critical thinking and our cultural appreciation, which help us to reflect on our own lives. To conclude with some wise words from Professor Edith Hall (2015), 'The failure to include Classical Civilisation among the subjects taught in every secondary school deprives us and our future citizens of access to educational treasures which can not only enthral, but fulfil what Jefferson argued in *Notes on the State of Virginia* (1782) was the main goal of education in a democracy: to enable us to defend our liberty.' Why would anyone not want to study Classical Civilisation?

Note

1   http://classicsforall.org.uk/about/why-classics-for-all/.

References

Adey, K. and Biddulph, M. (2001), 'The Influence of Pupil Perception on Subject Choice at 14+ in History and Geography', *Educational Studies*, 27 (4): 439–450.

AQA (2015), *Exam results statistics*. Available online: http://filestore.aqa.org.uk/over/stat_pdf/AQA-AS-STATS-JUNE-2015.PDF. (Accessed 3 August 2017).

Bell, F., Malacova, E. and Shannon, M. (2005), 'The Changing Pattern of A Level/AS Uptake in England', *Curriculum Journal*, 16 (3): 391–400.

Davies, P., Telhaj, S., Hutton, D., Adnett, N. and Coe, R. (2008), 'Socioeconomic Background, Gender and Subject Choice in Secondary Schooling', *Educational Research*, 50 (3): 235–248.

Foskett, N., Lumby, J. and Maringe, F. (2003), 'Pathways and progression at 16+ "fashion", peer influence and college choice', paper presented to the *Annual Conference of the British Educational Research Association*, Heriot-Watt University, September 2003.

Francis, B., Hutchings, M., Archer, L. and Melling, L. (2003), 'Subject Choice and Occupational Aspirations among Pupils at Girls' Schools', *Pedagogy, Culture and Society*, 11 (3): 425–442.

Gay, B. (2003), 'Classics Teaching and the National Curriculum', in J. Morwood (ed.), *The Teaching of Classics*, 73–84, Cambridge: Cambridge University Press.

Hall, E. (2015), 'Classics for the people – why we should all learn from the ancient Greeks', *The Guardian*, 20 June. Available online: https://www.theguardian.com/books/2015/jun/20/classics-for-the-people-ancient-greeks. (Accessed 1 July 2016).

Hodgson, A. and Spours, K. (2008), *Education and Training 14–19*, London: SAGE.

La Guardia, J. (2009), 'Developing Who I Am: A Self-Determination Theory Approach to the Establishment of Healthy Identities', *Educational Psychologist*, 44 (2): 90–104.

Leith, S. (2010), 'The return of swords "n" sandals movies', *The Financial Times*, 14 May. Available online: http://www.ft.com/cms/s/2/b9161614-5ecb-11df-af86-00144feab49a.html. (Accessed 20 August 2016).

Lent, R., Brown, S. and Hackett, G. (1994), 'Toward a Unifying Social Cognitive Theory of Career and Academic Interest, Choice and Performance', *Journal of Vocational Behavior*, 45: 79–122.

OCR (2015), *Exam results statistics*. Available online: http://www.ocr.org.uk/Images/247533-provisional-exam-statistics-june-2015-now-includes-gcse.pdf. (Accessed 3 August 2017).

Owen, R. (2003), 'My big fat Greek killing', *The Times*, 27 February. Available online: http://entertainment.timesonline.co.uk/tol/arts_and_entertainment/film/article1113354.ece. (Accessed 31 July 2016).

Renninger, K. (2009), 'Interest and Identity Development in Instruction: An Inductive Model', *Educational Psychologist*, 44 (2): 105–118.

Rodeiro, C. and Sutch, T. (2013), 'Popularity of A level subjects among UK university students', *Statistical Report Series no. 52*, Cambridge: Cambridge Assessment. Available online: http://www.cambridgeassessment.org.uk/Images/140668-popularity-of-a-level-subjects-among-uk-university-students.pdf. (Accessed 2 August 2016).

Smith, D. (2007), 'Spartan epic is last hope for sword and sandal movies', *The Observer*, 28 January. Available online: https://www.theguardian.com/uk/2007/jan/28/film.filmnews. (Accessed 16 July 2016).

Stables, A. (1996), *Subjects of Choice: The Process and Management of Pupil and Student Choice*, London: Cassell.

Stables, A. (1997), 'Perspectives on Subject Choice: The Case for a Humane Liberalism in Curriculum Planning', *Journal of Curriculum Studies*, 29 (2): 197–208.

Stables, A. and Stables, S. (1995), 'Gender Differences in Students' Approaches to A-level Subject Choices and Perceptions of A-level Subjects: A Study of First-year A-level Students in a Tertiary College', *Educational Research*, 37 (1): 39–51.

Taylor, M. (1992), 'Post-16 Options: Young People's Awareness, Attitudes, Intentions and Influences on Their Choice', *Research Papers in Education*, 7 (3): 301–335.

The Student Room (2013), '*A Levels: Classical Civilisation vs Ancient History*'. Available online: http://www.thestudentroom.co.uk/showthread.php?t=2513100. (Accessed 16 July 2016).

Tristram, D. (2003), 'Classics in the Curriculum from the 1960s to the 1990s', in J. Morwood (ed.), *The Teaching of Classics*, 6–19, Cambridge: Cambridge University Press.

Whittaker, S., Gallacher, J. and Crossan, B. (2004), *Learner Perceptions of Information, Advice and Guidance: A Review of Research*, Glasgow: Centre for Research in Lifelong Learning.

Wilkinson, J. (2003), 'Working at the Chalk Face', in J. Morwood (ed.), *The Teaching of Classics*, 106–116, Cambridge: Cambridge University Press.

Wood, P., Landry, C. and Bloomfield, J. (2006), *Cultural Diversity in Britain. A Toolkit for Cross-Cultural Cooperation*, York: Joseph Rowntree Foundation.

PART III
CLASSICS IN THE FUTURE

CHAPTER 15

CLASSICS ONLINE AT THE OPEN UNIVERSITY: TEACHING AND LEARNING WITH INTERACTIVE RESOURCES

James Robson and Emma-Jayne Graham

The Open University: On air and online

As a distance learning institution, the Open University (OU) has a long and proud tradition of using technology to support student learning. Not that the OU's enthusiastic use of modern media has always earnt it admirers: in the early days, this 'University of the Air' (as Harold Wilson put it during a speech given in Glasgow on 8 September 1963) was commonly mocked as an institution whose students gained degrees by watching television. But while the late-night broadcasts of OU lectures by the BBC may be a thing of the past, the university continues to find innovative ways to reach and teach not just its own students but the public at large. Alongside traditional broadcast media, such as BBC television and radio, the university now uses channels such as YouTube and iTunesU as well as new ways of engaging learners, such as MOOCs (Massive Open Online Courses) and BOCs (Badged Open Courses). Particularly notable for its scope and reach is OpenLearn, the OU's online learning portal, which contains over 12,000 hours of free courses (including plenty of Classics content) and attracts over 5 million unique visitors a year. Further free learning materials to be found on OU websites include interactive, open-access resources designed both to provide informal learning opportunities to the general public and to prepare would-be students for academic study.

Classicists at the Open University have eagerly embraced opportunities to use new media and develop free online content, from vodcasts on *Latin Graffiti at Pompeii* and *Troy Story: Homer's Iliad and Odyssey*, a condensed narrative animation, to an iTunesU course on *The Birth of Comedy*, and interactive OpenLearn courses on topics as diverse as *The Ancient Olympics* and *Herodotus 'The Histories'*. In this chapter, the focus will be on just two sets of online resources, however. First, the suite of open-access websites which support the study of ancient languages at the OU, especially those designed for students taking their first steps in Latin. And secondly, two very different online resources developed in conjunction with an honours-level module on *The Roman Empire*: an interactive map intended to support the acquisition of geographical knowledge while providing scope for independent exploration of the empire and an introductory game called *Hadrian: The Roamin' Emperor*. The discussion that follows is partly 'show and tell': an overview of the functionality and usefulness of these resources to students. But we will also explore the important topics of the design and underpinning pedagogy of these interactive offerings as well as considering student reactions, both positive and negative, and some of the potential benefits and pitfalls of using new technology in teaching.

Introducing Classical Latin

The launch of a new beginners' Latin module in 2015, *Classical Latin: The Language of Ancient Rome*, provided the opportunity to develop a whole array of interactive resources for students. A number of these are tied closely to the module's content: a vocabulary tester, interactive quizzes and a 'principal parts' tester (relating to the identification of Latin verbs in their different tenses, voices and moods), as well as a 'Story Explorer' which provides an interactive way for students to read the simplified Latin texts which form the spine of the course (key here is the 'click and look up' feature, providing students with instant help on vocabulary and grammar). These resources support student learning in what are fairly tried and tested ways (indeed, the Story Explorer uses the same technology as the Cambridge School Classics Project 'Explorer' tool and Latin vocabulary and drill testers have a particularly long pedigree). But as well as facilitating learning and consolidation throughout the module, the OU Latin team was also determined to make strides in the ways in which students are supported in the early stages of their language learning, even before their formal studies begin.

The main focus of these aspirations was a free-standing, open-access resource called *Introducing Classical Latin*.[1] This site is intended to allow students to encounter some of the basics of Latin in as fun and unthreatening a way as possible, all underpinned by an uncluttered and user-friendly design.

Introducing Classical Latin is structured in the following way. In the 'Sounds' section, students learn to pronounce Latin with the aid of an alphabetic list of clickable words (Figure 15.1). In

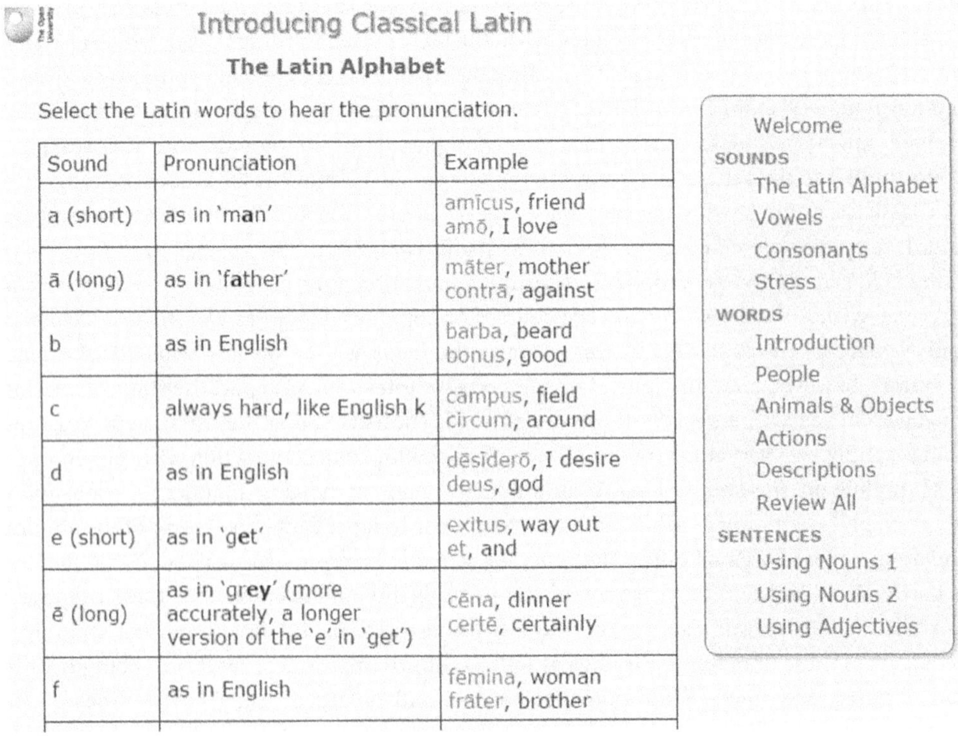

Introducing Classical Latin

The Latin Alphabet

Select the Latin words to hear the pronunciation.

Sound	Pronunciation	Example
a (short)	as in 'man'	amīcus, friend amō, I love
ā (long)	as in 'father'	māter, mother contrā, against
b	as in English	barba, beard bonus, good
c	always hard, like English k	campus, field circum, around
d	as in English	dēsīderō, I desire deus, god
e (short)	as in 'get'	exitus, way out et, and
ē (long)	as in 'grey' (more accurately, a longer version of the 'e' in 'get')	cēna, dinner certē, certainly
f	as in English	fēmina, woman frāter, brother

Welcome

SOUNDS
The Latin Alphabet
Vowels
Consonants
Stress

WORDS
Introduction
People
Animals & Objects
Actions
Descriptions
Review All

SENTENCES
Using Nouns 1
Using Nouns 2
Using Adjectives

Figure 15.1 The 'Sounds' section of *Introducing Classical Latin*.

the 'Words' section, students get to master a total of twenty-four vocabulary items, broken down into four sections covering nouns ('people', 'animals'), verbs ('actions') and adjectives ('descriptions'). The 'Sentences' section draws on this vocabulary to introduce the basic concepts both of inflection (through simple sentences comprising subject-object-verb) and of the agreement of nouns and adjectives on the basis of gender. At each stage there are short, interactive exercises which allow students to practise their understanding. The 'Words' section is also enlivened by cartoon flashcards (Figure 15.2), while the 'Sentences' section includes both images and animation (the pedagogical justification here coming from Piagetian principles of allowing learners to experience concepts in a concrete form before moving on to the abstract, thus mirroring, too, the use of visuals in modern Latin school textbooks [Gay 2003, p. 83]).

Aims and objectives: Outreach, recruitment, retention

In the spirit of outreach and serving the wider Classics community, *Introducing Classical Latin* is designed to be of use to anyone starting out in Latin. The vocabulary items encountered are common words, for example, that will appear in most Latin courses that a student might go on to study. In terms of OU students, however, *Introducing Classical Latin* is intended to fulfil a number of different purposes. Open University Greek and Latin modules recruit less well than their non-language-testing equivalents, so recruitment is one function. More pressing, however, is retention. Historically, drop-out rates on language modules at the OU are high

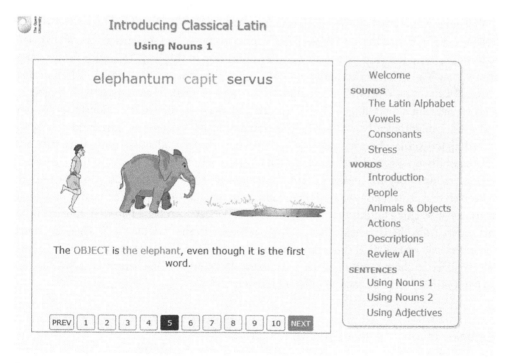

Figure 15.2 The 'Using Nouns' section of *Introducing Classical Latin* (featuring the very popular elephant).

and this resource was designed to play an important part in the battle to reverse that trend. And so, the vocabulary and grammar learning that students undertake while working through *Introducing Classical Latin* gives a useful taster of what learning the language involves and can help students to decide whether Latin is for them. Moreover, for those who are keen to study further, the site provides a firm foundation to help students better negotiate the crucial early stages of language acquisition during the first weeks of the module itself. In its first year, an impressive 96 per cent of students submitted the first assignment of *Classical Latin: The Language of Ancient Rome*, the vast majority of whom had worked through the *Introducing Classical Latin* site (instructively, this represents a 15 per cent improvement on the beginners' Latin module it replaced). The pass rate for the module as a whole was also extremely healthy at 97 per cent.

Design and pedagogy

It is worth taking a moment to reflect on the design principles that underpin this and many of the other language websites developed at the OU. *Introducing Classical Latin* is designed as a site with clear objectives and simple tasks, which is straightforward to navigate and which aims to provide feedback that is easy for students to digest. Important to the way we construct interactive language resources, too, is the 'one thing at a time' principle: that is, sites are structured in such a way as to focus on one key skill per section (*e.g.* 'Sounds', 'Words' and 'Sentences') or per resource (*e.g.* vocabulary learning in the case of our *Latin Vocabulary Tester*; grammatical forms in the case of our *Latin Grammar Tester*).

Of course, while a website that aspires to have limited text, repeatable activities and simple feedback supports well the kind of 'surface learning' so important for early stages of language acquisition, 'deep learning' is arguably harder to achieve in this way. This said, the teaching of topics such as inflection and grammatical gender in the 'Sentences' section of *Introducing Classical Latin* does represent an attempt on our part to make users engage with linguistic *concepts* and not simply linguistic data (indeed, to draw on the work of Cousin, inflection and gender might even be considered as belonging to the category of 'threshold concepts': according to Cousin, these are potentially transformative for student learning, since they are capable of disrupting students' previous assumptions about a topic, that is in this case their understanding as English speakers about how language works [Cousin 2006, p. 4]). The desire to keep textual explanations to a minimum also prompted us to adopt an 'inductive' approach to grammar teaching on this site, with grammatical concepts explained upfront. Interestingly, this differs from the largely 'deductive' approach used in the module itself, where students encounter new grammatical concepts when reading synthetic Latin texts before these concepts are explained to them in detail in the accompanying grammar. One benefit of this variation, perhaps, is that it helps to cater to different learning styles.

Engaging students with interactive resources

Introducing Classical Latin and its sister site, *Introducing Ancient Greek*, are just two of the open-access sites hosted by the Open University. Various other resources support student study of the JACT textbook *Reading Greek*,[2] while OpenLearn courses providing opportunities for complete beginners to engage more deeply with Latin and Greek exist in the form of *Getting Started on Classical Latin* and *Discovering Ancient Greek and Latin* (whose more involved, explanation-rich approach aims to facilitate 'deep learning' about linguistic concepts).[3]

How can these sites improve or change student learning? One important advantage that they have over a classroom environment is that students can take as much time as they need to cover the material, repeating exercises or forging ahead as appropriate. And moving learning activities online can also facilitate a 'flipped classroom' approach, where tutorials are largely given over to practicing new skills and dealing with students' questions, rather than 'chalk and talk' explanations of new grammar or going over homework (this is particularly valuable in an OU context, where instructors enjoy only limited contact time with their students). Another role that 'testing' or 'drilling' sites can provide is assessment practice: our *Principal Parts Tester*, for example, is set up to mirror a similar question on the examination paper. This 'constructive alignment' of the interactive resource with the assessment question is designed both to increase student use of this website and to strengthen student performance on a challenging area of language acquisition (on 'constructive alignment', see Biggs 2003, pp. 25–31).

Student feedback: The good, the bad and the surprising

Feedback on the interactive Latin resources has been largely positive. 89 per cent of the 36 students surveyed in 2016 rated *Introducing Classical Latin* as either 'very helpful' or 'quite helpful' with 46 per cent claiming to have spent at least three hours using the site and another 33 per cent one to two hours. Responses to the site from Latin instructors have also been upbeat ('I **LOVE** the elephant', 'Excellent!', 'A very good resource to point those who are just wanting a taste'). 50 per cent of students also reported using the *Latin Vocabulary Tester* at least once a week and a pleasing 61 per cent of students were either 'extremely satisfied' or 'very satisfied' with the interactive resources on the module as a whole. In terms of where we might have made improvements, perhaps the starkest lesson we learnt was in respect of the *Latin Vocabulary Tester*. A handful of glitches here led to some students losing their confidence – or worse their patience ('I have used it a few times and found it hugely frustrating').

Negative feedback is always disappointing, but an interesting development here was that a handful of students went on to develop interactive learning resources of their own in response to the *Latin Vocabulary Tester*'s perceived shortcomings, for example, and especially using freeware such as Quizlet. The professional way in which they went about this certainly gives pause for thought. Students co-operatively producing and tailoring resources to their own needs does present issues, of course (*e.g.* student workload, possible absence of underpinning pedagogy and lack of technical support), but this is an inspiring model nonetheless and, importantly, gives students ownership of their own learning. Does producing high-quality interactive resources run the risk of encouraging too much of a spoon-feeding approach? Perhaps one question for the OU to consider in the future is whether the positive elements of this kind of self-sufficiency can be better harnessed, for example, by providing students with appropriate tools to create their own resources.

The Roman Empire interactive map

Designing an entirely new 60-credit third-level module to introduce OU Classical Studies students to the Roman empire presented a number of different challenges. When would we begin and end? Would we cover all the territory associated with imperial Roman rule? Should we adopt a chronological, geographical or thematic approach? Opting for the latter, how could we help students to contextualize the individuals, communities, places, artefacts and texts that they are learning about and, significantly, understand why it is important to do so? Selecting a textbook with a chronological overview to accompany the bespoke module materials solved the issue of historical context, but geography was more problematic. Although the module provides an introduction to the Roman empire (a subject not otherwise covered by existing OU modules at Levels 1 and 2) students would still be expected to work at a level appropriate for Level 3 (honours level). This involves achieving learning outcomes associated with the independent identification, selection, critical evaluation and application of material from a diverse range of ancient sources and contexts to address defined issues, as well as understanding the contested nature of current knowledge concerning the empire. Students would therefore be required to think for themselves about where evidence comes from and why that matters. One option was to pair the chronologically oriented set text with a traditional printed atlas, but concerns were raised about this hampering full engagement with the empire as a dynamic and complex entity and implicitly endorsing passive learning. Importantly, the module was to be underpinned by a strategy which fosters deep active learning, requiring students to 'do meaningful learning activities and think about what they are doing' (Prince 2004, p. 223) in a manner which takes account of the fact that 'discovery-oriented and student-active teaching methods ensure higher student motivation, more learning at higher cognitive levels, and longer retention of the knowledge' (Cherney 2008, p. 154). Consequently, the decision was made to develop a digital interactive map which could act in a dual capacity, hosting supported learning activities and providing a resource for independent discovery.

Mapping the empire

The interactive map was produced by combining freely available geospatial data for ancient sites and monuments (*e.g.* theatres), boundary polygons for provinces and shapefiles for road networks and rivers. It drew especially on data available via the *Digital Atlas of the Roman Empire* and the Pleiades project, as well as map tiles sourced from the Ancient World Mapping Center.[4] These were enhanced with 'info boxes' featuring customized text, images, audio recordings and films to meet the needs of specific learning activities.

Technical limitations were imposed on the map: it had to be hosted within the digital storage constraints of the OU Virtual Learning Environment (VLE) and remain compatible with ordinary computing and download capacities. Ultimately, this led to the development of a series of maps with the same design and functionality, presented to students as snapshots or versions of '*the* interactive map'. In total, ten versions of the map were produced, each designed to support specific directed and independent learning activities:

- *General view*: all sites within the empire grouped into 'heat clusters' at lower zoom levels (Figure 15.3)

- *Searchable map*: search for any province/location (by ancient or modern name) (Figure 15.4)
- *Province map*: the location and status of all provinces, with sliding timeline allowing learners to explore the chronology of imperial territorial control
- *Hadrian's Wall*: sites on the wall, supporting a discovery-led activity (Figure 15.5)
- *Rome*: multiple period-specific on/off layers displaying key public buildings
- *Volubilis*: city plan populated with 'info boxes' to support a discovery-led urbanization activity
- *Baths, cemeteries, theaters and amphitheaters, Barbarian incursions* – four empire-wide maps populated with a restricted number of bespoke 'info boxes'.

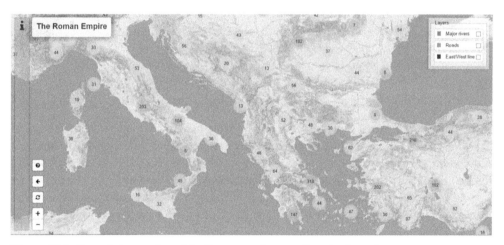

Figure 15.3 General view version of the Roman empire map, featuring heat clusters.

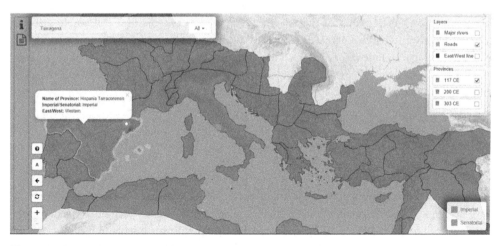

Figure 15.4 Searchable version of the Roman empire map, showing the results of a search, as well as the application of the roads and province layers.

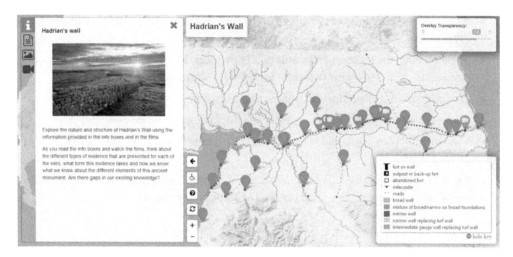

Figure 15.5 Hadrian's Wall version of the Roman empire map, showing clickable sites along the wall (after Jones and Mattingly 1990) and the 'info box' containing the instructions for the accompanying activity and links to multimedia resources.

In addition to a search function, each empire-wide map offers the learner the option of switching additional layers on/off: rivers, roads, an East/West line (to provide basic contextual information at a glance) and three period-specific provincial configurations (117 CE, 200 CE, 303 CE). These enable the learner to engage actively with the data and to manipulate it in order to address questions or develop independent enquiries, thereby promoting 'experiential learning, [and] learning by doing' in which students 'process content themselves' (Carr et al. 2015, p. 174).

Specific activities introduce the map early in the module as part of the general chronological and geographical scene-setting, urging students to explore its capabilities through a series of basic information gathering and navigation activities. For all compulsory activities, links are provided to 'sub-versions' of the relevant map, where students find collapsible sidebars containing full instructions and a link back to a follow-up discussion.[5] Each version is also available as a stand-alone resource which students are encouraged to make use of to 'find out more' (i.e. during their independent study time) and when they encounter unknown places in the course of their reading.

Exploring the wall

Hadrian's Wall features early in the module and provides a good example of how the map facilitates an active enquiry-based learning experience. As advocates of this style of learning have articulated, active learning 'calls forth images of active, student-centered, participatory learning' (O'Loughlin 1992, p. 792), and importantly it requires students to 'process content themselves in order to learn' (Carr et al. 2015, p. 174). In line with this approach, our students are required to explore Hadrian's Wall using the information provided within the map, thinking especially about the strengths and limitations of the available evidence. This begins the process of thinking critically about how the nature of sources impact upon our knowledge. Students are directed to watch a series of short bespoke films embedded within the map at appropriate locations (*e.g.* milecastle, turret, fort, the ditch and bank system known as the *vallum*) before exploring an extensive series of 'info boxes' associated with other features. These contain text, images and links to external websites, including the online *Roman Inscriptions of Britain* (*RIB*) database.[6] Embedding the films, images and written information within the map reinforces the importance of examining evidence within its appropriate geographical and topographical context. It is suggested to students that they watch the films in a recommended order but they are free to explore the various resources in a way that enables them to think for themselves about how to address the questions they have been asked to consider: they become 'the authors of their own learning' (Cherney 2008, p. 155).

Early feedback and ongoing challenges

The map was frequently singled out when students were asked what aspects of the teaching materials, learning activities or assessment they found particularly helpful to their learning, noting that it was an engaging and useful resource (*e.g.* 'I enjoyed using the interactive map because I found it very helpful in understanding locations'; 'I thought it was really innovative and helpful'; and 'The interactive map series was particularly helpful for getting things in perspective generally, and for detailed study in the films and individual notes'). The most encouraging comments suggest that it successfully achieves its primary objective: 'it gave a geographical perspective, and it pinpointed places in relation to each other. This brought to life much of the development of the empire through time and placed provinces and cities in relation to each other'. Indeed, some students evidently wanted it to do more than it was designed to do, noting that it 'was useful but could have been better … [it] should have allowed for multiple searches in one go so that you can seen [*sic*] places relative to each other,' and 'It is such a useful resource that it would be brilliant to see it developed further'. Although these comments were sometimes expressed as frustration with its limitations, they can also be interpreted as evidence that this type of multipurpose interactive resource has genuine potential for supporting deep active learning and independent discovery, reinforcing the observations above about the power of student self-sufficiency and creativity. Some of the requested modifications have already been implemented, including more detailed scale information and the ability to hold a number of sites in a search history as well as pinned to the map itself.

Not all students were so enamoured, citing slow loading times, an inability to download it to portable media storage and a general sense of irritation about having to switch back and forth between online activities and printed books. As a result, the map neatly spotlights current tensions within blended forms of distance learning which combine print and online resources (although such experiential and practical issues tend to be overlooked by scholarship focused on the challenges of technology within distance education; see, *e.g.*, Conole 2014). These issues will undoubtedly become more acute as open-access digital resources and publications increasingly represent the conventional products of academic research, creating both exciting opportunities and new difficulties. For example, in order to provide students with an expansive resource which they can manipulate, the sheer scale of the data embedded within the map prevents the creation of the downloadable, portable resource that some students would might have appreciated. On the other hand, continuing to host the map on the OU server does allow for ongoing development, more responsive updates and greater connectivity with new external websites. Future iterations of the model, currently being adapted for other OU Arts and Humanities modules, should enable greater compression and a smoother user experience (*e.g.* a version incorporating information about the Greek Mediterranean will feature in a new module available from October 2018: A229 *Exploring the Classical World*; the model has also been adopted and adapted by Art History and History modules). There are nevertheless other challenges too. In accordance with standard OU practice, accessibility issues were addressed in the course of development, including the use of screen-readable text-transcripts and compatibility with adaptation software used, for instance, by learners with visual impairments. Unfortunately, however, the online nature of the map renders it inaccessible to the OU's community of Students in Secure Environments (formerly known as Offender Learners or Learners in Prison). For these accessibility-related reasons, students are encouraged to use the interactive map to support their assignment preparation but no compulsory elements of assessment are directly dependent on accessing the map.

Hadrian: The *Roamin'* Emperor

At the other end of the spectrum, but still with an intention to develop understandings of the relationship between history, geography and primary sources, *Hadrian: The Roamin' Emperor* is a stand-alone educational game developed for OpenLearn, in conjunction with the OU's Open Media Unit and Make Sense Design.[7] Again, learning is presented as explorative, but this time in a light-hearted manner appropriate for the informal to formal learning process promoted by OpenLearn (see Fig. 15.6).

Players build Hadrian's passport (discovering certain facets of his character) before accompanying him on his travels around the empire, doing some myth-busting along the way. They answer questions designed to introduce bigger issues surrounding what it meant to be emperor and how the empire was secured and maintained. At the end of each 'scene' the player who has answered at least one question correctly can choose a 'souvenir' from a selection of real artefacts, texts or monuments to take back to Tivoli, requiring them to think carefully about which item will provide the best evidence for what they have learned. The game is designed to be entertaining, hence the tongue-in-cheek animations, but by the end the user will understand something about the nature of imperial rule and Hadrian himself.

Since it went live in August 2014, *Roamin' Hadrian* has attracted over 22,000 unique users (as of 31 July 2017), each of whom spends around twice as long engaging with the site as the average visitor to other OpenLearn resources (8.63 minutes compared with a site average of 4.40 minutes). The success of the game as a means for potentially converting informal learning into formal learning is indicated by the fact that 14 per cent of users subsequently click through from *Roamin' Hadrian* to a course site on the main OU webpage, compared with a current OpenLearn site average of 8.58 per cent. Users also click through to additional Classical Studies resources available through OpenLearn.

Figure 15.6 A screenshot from *Hadrian: The Roamin' Emperor*, showing Hadrian and Antinous in Egypt By Helen Forte.

Informal learning with Hadrian

Game-based learning such as this offers immersive learning in context and the 'development of soft skills' appropriate to an informal learning context (Conole 2014, p. 223; see also Gros 2010). *Roamin' Hadrian* is designed not only to allow learners with little or no prior knowledge to find out about Hadrian, but to *understand* something about the Roman world and its study. Students studying *The Roman Empire* are encouraged to play the game at the start of the module as a way of engaging with some of the issues surrounding their study of the empire. Although designed primarily as an adult-oriented educational resource, the interactive nature of the game, cheerful graphics, low-stakes questions and gradual discovery of historical information means that it also has relevance for school groups. Additionally, it has attracted and challenged those with an existing interest in the subject (comments received from established academics suggest that they have also enjoyed playing, often finding it a genuine challenge to achieve a score close to 100 per cent!). The appearance of *Roamin' Hadrian* is radically different from the more sober interactive map of the Roman empire, but the underpinning pedagogical principles are the same: that explorative, discovery-led learning where 'facts are learned in the context of meaning' (Nicholls 2002, p. 31) contributes to the development of a deeper understanding of a subject and promotes an attitude towards learning which emphasizes understanding over memorization.

Interactive online resources: Looking ahead

As the Open University and other higher education institutions increasingly seek to make use of digital learning materials, including, for example, the opportunities offered by augmented and virtual reality (*e.g.* a beating heart model used in an OU Level 1 Science module on *Hominid Developments*),[8] it is crucial that Classics continues to assert its place within this emerging use of interactive technology for pedagogic purposes. Indeed, as shown by the growth and success of research based within the Digital Humanities more broadly, Classics-based interactive resources such as *Pelagios Commons* continue to lead the way in the development of open data methodologies and tools designed to support research projects, fundamentally changing the ways in which we are able to approach the study of the ancient world.[9] If these digital advancements, new methodologies and ways of questioning classical texts, objects and voices are to continue to shape the future of the discipline it is imperative that they also become embedded in the ways in which students learn about – and, more significantly, *learn how to learn* about – the ancient world. Incorporating online interactive resources into the teaching of Classics is a first step towards this, building on tried and tested forms of teaching as well as existing pedagogical methods and theory to enhance what we already offer and to reach a wider range of students, and potential students, with varying learning needs and styles. Indeed, the examples cited in this chapter suggest that interactive resources not only serve the more traditional ends of Classics teaching within higher education – that is, to enable students to find out about the Greek and Roman worlds and acquire a set of discipline-specific skills – but also open new doors to those students in terms of the ways in which they learn, as well as the more widely applicable skills that they develop and put into practice. Interactive resources such as the map of the Roman empire encourage the formal learner to actively explore and question the knowledge and information available to them, while *Roamin' Hadrian* provides a reminder to the informal student, and those who might never have considered studying Classics, that learning about the past is something that is both accessible to everyone and can be (perhaps should always be) an enjoyable experience. Moreover, as the case of Latin students creating their own vocabulary testing resources demonstrates, online interactive tools might even offer opportunities for students with a range of existing skills to get creative themselves and to find ways to work innovatively and collaboratively to support their fellow learners. Most excitingly, open-access online platforms such as OpenLearn mean that these opportunities can be opened up to a community beyond the formal student, reaching the informal learner, even the merely curious.

Notes

1   *Introducing Classical Latin* can be found at www.open.ac.uk/Arts/introducing-classical-latin/. (Accessed 1 April 2018).

2   These resources are usefully collected together at www.open.ac.uk/Arts/reading-classical-greek/. (Accessed 1 April 2018).

3   See the many resources available at www.open.edu/openlearn/. (Accessed 1 April 2018).

4   These resources are available at http://imperium.ahlfeldt.se, http://pleiades.stoa.org and http://awmc.unc.edu/wordpress/. (Accessed 1 April 2018).

5   For a fully interactive demo of the map of Hadrianic Rome, see the section of a free short course available at http://students.open.ac.uk/arts/openlearn/rome.html?activity_id=activity_3. (Accessed 1 April 2018).

6   Available at http://romaninscriptionsofbritain.org/. (Accessed 1 April 2018).

7   *Hadrian: The Roamin' Emperor* can be found at http://www.open.edu/openlearn/history-the-arts/history/classical-studies/hadrian-the-roamin-emperor. See also the Make Sense Design website at http://makesensedesign.com/hadrian. (Accessed 1 April 2018).

8   More details, including a video demo and a link to download the relevant human heart app, can be found at https://arvr.kmi.open.ac.uk/. (Accessed 1 April 2018).

9   Pelagios Commons is available at http://commons.pelagios.org/. See also the *Hestia Project* http://hestia.open.ac.uk/ and *Google Ancient Places* (GAP) http://gap.alexandriaarchive.org/gapvis/index.html#index. (Accessed 1 April 2018).

References

Biggs, J. (2003), *Teaching for Quality Learning at University*, 2nd edn, Buckingham: Society for Research into Higher Education/Open University Press.

Carr, R., Palmer, S. and Hagel, P. (2015), 'Active Learning: The Importance of Developing a Comprehensive Measure', *Active Learning in Higher Education*, 16 (3): 173–186.

Cherney, I. (2008), 'The Effects of Active Learning on Students' Memories for Course Content', *Active Learning in Higher Education*, 9 (2): 152–171.

Conole, G. (2014), 'The Use of Technology in Distance Education', in O. Zawacki-Richter and T. Anderson (eds.), *Online Distance Education: Towards a Research Agenda*, 219–236, Athabasca: Athabasca University Press.

Cousin, G. (2006), 'An Introduction to Threshold Concepts', *Planet*, 17: 4–5.

Gay, B. (2003), 'The Theoretical Underpinning of the Main Latin Courses', in J. Morwood (ed.), *The Teaching of Classics*, 73–84, Cambridge: Cambridge University Press.

Gros, B. (2010), 'Game-Based Learning: A Strategy to Integrate Digital Games in Schools', in J. Yamamoto, J. C. Kush, R. Lombard and C. J. Hertzog (eds.), *Technology Implementation and Teacher Education: Reflective Models*, 365–379, Hershey, PA: Information Science Reference.

Jones, B. and Mattingly, D. (1990), *An Atlas of Roman Britain*, Oxford: Oxbow Books.

Nicholls, G. (2002), *Developing Teaching and Learning in Higher Education*, London: Routledge.

O'Loughlin, M. (1992), 'Rethinking Science Education: Beyond Piagetian Constructivism toward a Sociocultural Model of Teaching and Learning', *Journal of Research in Science Teaching*, 29 (8): 791–820.

Prince, M. (2004), 'Does Active Learning Work? A Review of the Research', *Journal of Engineering Education*, 93 (3): 223–231.

CHAPTER 16
CLASSICS AND TWENTY-FIRST-CENTURY SKILLS
Arlene Holmes-Henderson and Kathryn Tempest

In *The Watchmaker of Filigree Street*, when Natasha Pulley makes Grace Callow dismiss her room-mate Bertha's studies of the Classics as 'the most pointless subject in the university … poring over the linguistic cleverness of men who had been dead for two thousand years', she expresses a train of thought as equally at home in the nineteenth-century world of her characters as the twenty-first-century publication date of the novel. Indeed, it is a perception of the subject which lurks behind the question we have probably all been asked at some point in our academic lives: what do students do after studying Classics?

There are numerous ways of approaching this time-old question. One might be to point to the plethora of talented and successful graduates and highlight the vast range of careers entered into by classicists. As one British Academy report found when it researched the contribution of the Arts and Humanities to the nation's wealth, 'graduates with a non-occupation specific degree are suitable for a wide variety of employment and are less pressurised to find work that exactly fits their training because they have skills that are applicable to a large number of different sectors' (British Academy 2004, p. 64). The study of Classics offers a particularly strong advantage here owing to the diversity of skills mastered by the average student – from language learning through to literary criticism, art appreciation and historical research.

However, we are currently operating in a climate where schools and universities need to make skills development more explicit – one in which we are also encouraged to provide opportunities for increasing employability. As in the case of humanities subjects more widely, there is a potential conflict here between the academic training in Classics and the demands of preparing students for employment or entrepreneurship. We need to make sure we integrate the development and awareness of the skills students are acquiring without compromising on academic rigour. Ways in which we might do that will form the basis for this chapter – a reflective essay on Classics and twenty-first-century skills in both schools and universities. The aim is not to suggest that a focus on employment should drive course and assessment design – far from it. More simply, we would like to share examples of how we can help students understand and enhance the skills with which the study of Classics already provides them (Section I), as well as how we might update these for the unpredictable demands of the future job market (Section II).

Section I: Classics and the cultivation of twenty-first-century skills

Despite the increasing focus and attention, there is still no single or widely accepted definition of twenty-first-century skills. This is the result of multifarious agendas held by diversely positioned stakeholders in schools, universities, government departments and British businesses (for a detailed literature review, see Cambridge Assessment 2013). However, twenty-first-century skills can be broadly conceived as the core competencies which young people need to cultivate at school in order to succeed in life, learning and work. In 2003, four government departments in England (the Department for Education, the Treasury, the Department for Trade and Industry and the Department for Work and Pensions) joined forces and produced a twenty-first-century skills strategy which sought to 'transform the economy and society' (Department for Education 2003, p. 9) by refocusing the school curriculum on skill development. Since then, twenty-first-century skills have been afforded increasing importance in educational policy and curriculum design. In Figure 16.1, we give a summary of the skills which regularly appear in the list of priorities for global school curricula.

What does the study of Classics contribute?

As we shall see in Section II, there are a number of ways in which the study of Classics at university can help cultivate collaboration, initiative, productivity and leadership; indeed, the very experience of going to university has long been recognized as providing 'life skills' (especially social skills and flexibility) which graduates need to succeed in the world of work. However, as we discuss in this section, there are also ways in which the study of Classics in secondary schools can develop learning and thinking skills such as critical thinking and communicating, as well as making a significant and positive impact on learners' literacy skills.

Critical thinking

To thrive in the twenty-first century, learners need to develop higher-order thinking skills: the ability to analyse and solve problems, and to think logically, creatively and critically. Evidence suggests that learning a second language not only improves grammatical skills in one's first language but also enhances one's overall thinking skills and abilities (Holliday 2012; Sullivan et al. 2014). Language learning increases the ability to conceptualize and think more abstractly, and it improves mental flexibility and the ability to explore multiple solutions to a problem, and thereby the ability to think about the use of language. Inflected languages such as Latin and Greek offer special opportunities for the cultivation of critical thinking skills since judgements

Learning and Thinking Skills	• Critical Thinking • Creative Thinking • Collaborating • Communicating
Literacy Skills	• Functional Literacy • Information Literacy • Media Literacy • Digital Literacy
Life Skills	• Flexibility • Initiative • Social Skills • Productivity • Leadership

Figure 16.1 Skills for the twenty-first century.

need to be made about the role of individual words within a clause. For example, students must analyse noun and adjective endings to determine number/case/gender, and must apply their knowledge of verbs to evaluate tense/person/voice/mood. The application of critical- and creative thinking skills, together with problem-solving skills, is at the core of learning Latin and Greek. Through detailed linguistic analysis, learners are able to think critically about comparisons between their own linguistic and cultural systems, and those of ancient languages.

But the benefits of Classics in developing twenty-first-century skills are not limited to classical *languages*. The study of the classical world in translation also offers learners a range of opportunities to develop critical thinking skills. Classical Civilisation and Ancient History are subjects which present the social/religious/political/military dimensions of life in the ancient world and learners have to cope with incomplete historical sources. They learn how to appreciate and evaluate authorial bias, and to question the relationship of texts and contexts. When reading classical literature in translation, school pupils have to think critically and, again, make judgements (based on the evidence available to them) about life in ancient times. To do so, they must extrapolate key information to enable them to make accurate comparisons and perceptive contrasts to the contemporary world. The study of the classical world engages students in conversations about citizenship, identity, gender, diversity and religion – all topics which remain relevant today (Parker 2008). To be able to consider such complex issues sensitively is a valuable skill in itself.

Literacy

When they read classical literature in translation, students practise both functional and information literacy as they decode extended passages of prose or verse in an effort to establish meaning. The same is true, of course, when reading texts in other humanities subjects. However, by reading and engaging with texts from the *ancient world*, students develop an appreciation of the interconnectedness of ancient and modern societies and the rich cultural legacy of the classical world. Reading classical literature in translation goes beyond functional literacy because it requires the sort of personal and critical engagement which creates the potential for transformational learning. Studying the political systems of the Greeks and Romans in translation promotes cultural exploration for personal growth and can contribute positively to active participation in contemporary society. For example, students read texts which address ancient political systems or dramatic tragedies which have, at their core, issues concerning the human condition, and they learn to critically analyse and evaluate the meaning of those texts as they relate to issues of equity, power and social justice. Moving from functional literacy to critical literacy, learners explore the impact of these ancient ideas on their own contemporary world view, which boosts learners' awareness of political literacy and can lead to informed, critical and responsible citizenship (Holmes-Henderson 2016).

The study of classical languages also has a direct impact on functional literacy since learners acquire new vocabulary and are able to trace derivations from Latin and Greek in other languages. The structured nature of Latin and Greek provides the opportunity to learn important linguistic foundations which underpin the mechanics of language use. By studying classical languages, learners are introduced in a formal way to morphology, accidence and syntax – equipping them with the knowledge and skills they need to apply this information to their learning in other curriculum subjects (*e.g.* English, Modern Languages, Science and Geography). It also builds their linguistic competence for further study and prepares them well for the world of work.

Communicating

In the UK, Latin and Greek are not traditionally taught as 'living languages'. This approach is gaining popularity in the United States (Patrick 2011; Asher 2012) and some British teachers are beginning to adopt elements of the communicative approach (Clark 2013). The emphasis of teaching in the UK, however, remains on reading (and sometimes writing) in Latin and Greek, rather than on speaking and listening. Nevertheless, the study of classical languages can improve the accuracy of learners' speech in English and other modern languages, since they have been exposed to a range of new vocabulary and have studied language structures and use. For students who have had the opportunity to study political orations (either in a classical language or in translation), classical rhetorical theory offers unique contributions to the development of communication skills as it provides a neat framework around which students can learn to construct arguments, deconstruct arguments and practise speaking and listening skills. By studying the rhetorical method, rhetorical techniques and tropes, as well as ancient tips concerning non-verbal communication (such as the use of body language), students may begin to understand the role of persuasion in contemporary communication and learn to 'read between the lines' (Holmes-Henderson 2013) of the content they hear from politicians, advertisers and broadcasters. The opportunity to apply this knowledge and develop communication skills in class helps learners to model and practise the construction and deconstruction of argumentation. The rhetorical method gives them a tried-and-tested template which they can use to express their ideas and opinions effectively, which in turn equips them well to participate orally in society as confident and articulate citizens.

What is particularly important, though, is that teachers make explicit the communication, learning and thinking skills which are being developed through the study of Classics. For students to maximize the transferability of metacognitive skills they must be equipped with the terminology to identify and describe the learning process in and beyond Classics. In so doing, teachers are contributing to the cultivation of skills which will open up possibilities for pursuing a range of university and college programmes and lead to opportunities in the world of work.

Section II: Skills and employability

Insofar as the study of Classics helps develop skills in critical thinking, communication and literacy, it enables learners to develop lifelong attributes that will undoubtedly prepare them for future study or employment. But in recent years – and especially following the so-called 'marketization' of higher education – the focus on graduate employability requires that we do more to make students aware of and able to articulate the skills they have acquired. How, then, can education providers help students achieve the potential to be employable? To a large degree, extra support staff can offer help with regard to career advice, CV building and interview practice. Yet there are a number of ways in which we can embed employability and skills awareness into our course design without negatively affecting the academic rigour of our modules. In particular, as this section will aim to demonstrate, we can encourage students to reflect on their acquisition of skills and hence communicate and understand how their studies have contributed to both their personal and professional development.

To begin with, it might serve us well to pause and reflect on what we mean by 'employability' – for the definition of the term is a complex and frequently contested one. On the one hand, we might imagine a checklist of attributes that can be achieved through the study of any subject, such as those discussed below. On the other, we might argue that employability is not just skills-based: according to the annual education and skills survey conducted by the Confederation of British Industry in 2015, for example, by far the most important factors looked for by employers are the right attitudes and aptitudes. Dacre Pool and Sewell (2007) suggest broadening the concept. In compiling a framework to help students develop their employability, they have taken the following broad definition as a starting point: 'Employability is having a set of skills, knowledge, understanding and personal attributes that make a person more likely to choose and secure occupations in which they can be satisfied and successful.' In addition to subject knowledge and generic skills, they hence add the need for experience and emotional intelligence. And yet, it is perhaps better not to view these two approaches as competing models. For, as we demonstrate in this section, each can contribute to an evolving and ongoing commitment to developing employability across a three-year programme.

Skills, modules and employability frameworks

At the most basic level, simple frameworks can be embedded to help familiarize students with the 'language' of employability. For even if the simple acquisition of skills is not in itself sufficient to produce an all-round, employable candidate, still the act of getting students to understand and communicate the skills they have acquired is a worthwhile enterprise. An example of such a framework has been developed by Day (2006–2009) and it has accompanying notes on how it might be utilized by teachers and learners. By this model, students are taught the language of employability and they are prompted to reflect on how these skills have been developed. According to this study, key areas which contribute to a student's employability are personal development (PD), work experience (WE), subject skills (SS), research skills (RS), team work (TW), career development (CD), reflection (R), project planning and evaluation (PP), innovation (IV), communication skills (CS), problem-solving (PS), business skills (B), sector skills (SE) and examples of social & cultural awareness (SCA). Not every module a student studies at university can impart all of these skills at once; rather the result has to be cumulative. However, without the least amount of change being made to the traditional essay and exam format of a module, Figure 16.2 demonstrates how the learning outcomes for a course on Vergil have been repackaged for students in employable language using Day's approach.

Assessment	Employability Skills

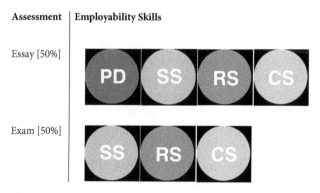

Essay [50%] PD SS RS CS

Exam [50%] SS RS CS

Figure 16.2 Learning outcomes for Vergil course.

However, while the theoretical literature and models make convincing and stimulating reading, the problem of engaging students with skills development exercises remains a real practical challenge. After all, a primary motivator for students entering higher education is the desire to study a specific discipline in-depth and for humanities students in particular, enjoyment of the subject area largely outweighs considerations of employability when choosing a degree subject (Allan 2006, p. 24). As the Classical Civilisation team at Roehampton have already reflected in an earlier paper on employability, students have typically proven resistant to personal development-style portfolios (Behr et al. 2009). Therefore, in order to help students recognize and unlock their potential, it is important to implement measures that are first and foremost linked to their academic studies.

The role of non-traditional teaching, learning and assessment in the acquisition of new skills

Going beyond the essay-exam mode of assessment, it is not uncommon to find innovative forms of teaching and learning in many UK Classics departments. Oral presentations, online discussion forums, student surveys, posters and academic debates – all examples of so-called 'non-traditional' methods of teaching, learning and assessment – have intrinsic pedagogical value for increasing academic performance; when used alongside traditional assessment activities, they are also useful tools for training students in skills that are relevant in the workplace (see Barrow et al. 2010).

The use of electronic resources deserves particular comment here, because it has become a basic requirement for successful academic studies, as well as an essential requirement for most jobs: as was identified in Figure 16.1, *digital literacy* is classed among the top skills in the twenty-first century. The concept of literacy has expanded to mean far more than the ability to read and write; the processing and presentation of data (*information and media literacy*) are also required of the twenty-first-century student. To be sure, by the time they start university, we can largely expect students to be more technically advanced than their counterparts just ten or twenty years ago. And, at the very least, they are generally more confident at experimenting with new technologies. However, by utilizing electronic resources in teaching and assessment, and by providing students with further technical training, we can still encourage students to discuss and reflect on their uses of the internet more critically.

That electronic resources can help encourage deep learning by students is not a new observation. With appropriate academic guidelines, blogs, websites, wikis and other media offer a far more flexible platform on which students can present their ideas and engage in debates. Far from using the internet passively as a source of information, by introducing students to effective online research tools, and by equipping them with the skills to present their considered opinions, a creative use of the internet enables students to take ownership of their learning process (Race 2005; Barrow et al. 2010). One case study is the compulsory first-year skills module at the University of Roehampton – *An Introduction to Classical Civilisation* – which makes extensive use of e-learning. The assessment for this module requires students to develop an independent project on a topic of their choice; the only limitation is that they are not allowed to choose a topic they have studied in any depth before. As in the process of supervising a dissertation or any research essay, the role of the tutor is simply to guide students through the individual stages of the process. The module as a whole is divided into three main components: (1) Research, in which – following the obligatory library tour at the start of the course – students learn how to retrieve relevant academic information, especially using resources, such as Jstor, e-books, Oxford Reference and Loeb Digital Library, among others; (2) Reasoning, in which students present ideas and engage in debates to help develop their ability to weigh up and evaluate different points of view (for this part of the module, students are divided into small groups according to their research interests); and (3) Rhetoric, in which students study communication skills and apply them to the development of their final project – a portfolio and an oral presentation of their findings.

The portfolio tasks are clearly linked to the stages of research: (1) a completed and correctly formatted bibliography; (2) an article review on an individually chosen piece of secondary literature; and (3) a commentary on a primary source relevant for understanding the individual project. The final component is a reflective diary on the research process and the completion of the project, including an analysis of the skills each student thinks he or she has acquired using the employability framework discussed above. In sum: although the tasks are guided and developed in accordance with the skills deemed important for new students to develop at university level, the fact that they are attached to an independent project engages the students more fully in the learning experience. Module evaluations consistently point to the positive nature of a student-led rather than a lecturer-enforced method of skills acquisition: hand-written comments by students have reinforced the value of taking ownership of the project, and the freedom to choose their own topic is the feature students particularly enjoyed. The module thus meets the academic learning outcomes for a first-year skills module, as well as targets for student satisfaction.

What is more, university-generated feedback (see Figure 16.3) demonstrates how one cohort of 35 students rated the acquisition of specific skills. With 28 responses to the survey, 96.4 per cent of students saw an improvement in their communication skills; 92.9 per cent in self-management; 71.4 per cent in creativity and 64.3 per cent in information technology. One challenge, which might account for the comparatively low scoring for information technology,

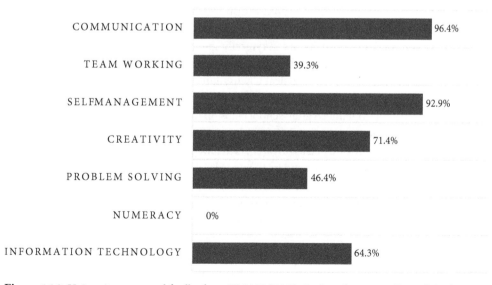

Figure 16.3 University-generated feedback on CLA020C135S: *An Introduction to Classical Civilisation.*

has been that the university formerly required for portfolios to be created within Mahara: an interoperating learning system with Moodle which students have found inadequate and unnecessarily difficult to use, despite the training provided by our e-learning team at the start of term. Building on this feedback, the university has committed to purchasing a WordPress licence, which will significantly enhance this aspect of the course design, since it will offer students a clearer potential to develop information technology skills which can be transferred more easily between education and workplace environments.

One final comment is perhaps worth making here. The fact that the academic content of their projects was individual to each student resulted in an impressive array of topics such as gender and sexuality; conquests and crises; politics, society and identity; literature and drama. Working in groups, and by sharing their own topics in weekly presentations to the rest of the class, students got a far fuller introduction to the classical world than a traditional survey module could have covered in twelve weeks.

Putting skills into practice: The value of work placements

So far all the activities we have described are aimed at making the acquisition of skills relevant to the workplace more explicit to students. However, we have also noted that employers also look for other attitudes and competencies such as self-confidence, independence and adaptability. Education providers can help develop these attributes but it is becoming increasingly expected that students obtain some work experience before they leave university. To take another case study from Roehampton, one module that students can take either in their second or third year is specifically geared towards employment and work: the work placement module. When we first introduced this module in 2001 we were the first classical programme in the UK that offered the option of work experience as an integral part of the BA programme. Meanwhile, more and more BA programmes in the Humanities are providing opportunities for work placements and report encouraging and interesting results that counter the common misgiving that practical work during the BA programme distracts from a student's academic studies. We would even suggest that they enhance it.

To begin with, students at Roehampton typically spend a minimum of thirty-five hours on placement, which roughly corresponds to the contact hours for a taught module. Placements have to be closely related to their Classical Civilisation degree to ensure students experience how their academic studies are relevant in the work situation. For example, students have taught Latin in schools, organized after-school clubs on topics from the ancient world, worked in museums with ancient artefacts, participated in archaeological excavations in the UK and abroad, acted as tour guides, helped as researchers in film production and so on. In addition, the assessment of the work placement requires the same level of academic input as the preparation for traditional lecture and seminar courses. The largest part of the assessment (75 per cent) is an academic essay in some way connected to or developing an interest founded in the work placement. The topic might be related to an object or an artefact, the institutional sector of the experience or another such line of enquiry. Since these studies often require students delving into entirely unfamiliar topics – such as issues of pedagogy, challenges facing the museum sector, cultures of display and archaeological techniques – they present new opportunities for research and broaden students' understanding of the classical world, its heritage and preservation.

Furthermore, a 25 per cent portfolio component enables students to reflect on their experiences and their employability. Assessed tasks include initial background research into their chosen placement which is intended to train students in a fundamental aspect of any job application: to understand their host institution, its history and ethos, and how they might contribute to it. Students are further asked to upload a CV from both before and after their placement to show how their experience has contributed to their skills acquisition and potential employability; a future development of this model might have students building a LinkedIn profile. As an optional extra, they are advised to obtain and upload a reference from their employer. The largest portfolio task is a reflective diary on the challenges they faced and how they overcame any problems they encountered. Scheduled workshops throughout the term support students in the completion of all these tasks: how to find and apply for volunteering and placement opportunities; writing a CV; and presenting themselves in interviews. They are also encouraged to seek help from the university careers' services.

Instead of distracting students from their academic studies, work placements may in fact enhance them. At the same time they provide students with important work-related skills. Students who completed an evaluation of the module commented on the range of skills they had acquired: personal development (especially confidence and understanding the value of their own ideas); work experience; subject and research skills; team work; career development; reflection; project planning and evaluation; innovation; communication and sector-specific skills as well as problem solving were all identified. Social and cultural awareness was further required as students needed to operate and work within different teams and environments. Looked at from the perspective of the twenty-first-century skills with which this chapter opened, students gained important life-skills: they collaborated with others, used their initiative, saw enhanced productivity and experienced leadership. In short, the work placement module ticks the essential criteria of basic frameworks but also contributes to the candidate's overall employability in developing their competencies and supplying proof of these to future employers (Dench 2008).

And yet, having commented on the way the work placement had provided opportunities to exercise each of the above skills, the final question students were asked in a recent module questionnaire was: 'Which of the above skills were *unique* to the work placement module (i.e. skills that you would not otherwise have developed on your degree programme)?' The answers pinpointed only three: work experience, sector-specific skills and (for one student) social and cultural awareness. But one comment deserves repeating: 'I feel Classics is a far reaching degree, covering many skill sets which are relevant to "real world" industries.' This student evidently did not see the study of Classics as something that was disconnected from his/her future development after graduation. In short: the inclusion of a work placement module is an added bonus to an already rich curriculum; it might not even be one that some students desire to take. It certainly helps students reflect on their career development and amass skills relevant to the sector in which they work. But it is just one of the many ways in which we might enhance or help students understand the skills with which the study of Classics already provides them.

Conclusion

This chapter has aimed to present a number of ways in which the study of classical subjects can equip students with twenty-first-century skills and prepare them for the workplace. Studying the ancient languages requires critical skills when students are faced with the challenge of dissecting inflected forms; a similar engagement is required of students who study the texts in translation and have to cope with questions of historical veracity, genre and contexts, as well as sensitive issues which span the gap from antiquity to today. Reading classical literature is one way in which the subject develops a high level of literacy; for students who study the ancient languages functional literacy is enhanced further by the need to understand morphology and syntax, acquire vocabulary and to trace the routes by which Latin and Greek came into English. We have also pointed to the importance of studying rhetoric as a fundamental skill for making an empowered and informed contribution to citizenry.

The study of classical subjects in schools is part of a longer process by which students acquire skills which prepare them either for further study or for the workplace; at university level, we have shown how we can build upon and develop them further. 'Poring over the linguistic cleverness of men who have been dead for two thousand years', as Grace Callow put it in the quotation which opened this chapter, will necessarily form and remain a central staple of the study of Classics; the close and critical reading of texts is probably, after all, the prime motivating factor for most who study or teach the subject. And it is great fun. But we have shown how even a traditional module on one of those men, Vergil, can be repackaged in a way that emphasizes the skills it imparts.

We can go further still. There is an increasing demand on university teachers to highlight and discuss the skills being developed. But, from the perspective of the instructor, this discourse needs to be initiated in a manner which enhances, instead of compromises, academic rigour; we also need to engage the students' own interest in reflecting on the variety of ways they have progressed through their learning of Classics. As we hope to have shown, a skills module which gives students intellectual freedom and independence has proven largely successful in imparting information, media and digital literacies. Even though most modules at the university now require students to use electronic resources – both for research purposes and for submitting and receiving feedback on essays through virtual learning environments – a dedicated module which prompts a reflective approach enables them to identify the acquisition of skills which are transferable from university to the world of work. At the same time, a module which awards academic credit for undertaking work experience can provide students with life skills such as productivity, leadership, initiative and collaboration. In providing these case studies, we hope this chapter will provide fresh incentive for course instructors who also want to consider the benefits of embedding and communicating employability into their course design. At the very least we hope to have shown that the drive on skills and employability is not a threat to our subject area. In fact, it may provide new opportunities for us to demonstrate the relevance and value of studying Classics for learners of all types in twenty-first century.

References

Allan, R. (2006), *A Wider Perspective: Investigating the Longer Term Employability of Humanities Graduates*, York: Higher Education Academy.

Asher, J. (2012), *Learning Another Language Through Actions*, Los Gatos: Sky Oak Productions.

Barrow, R., Behr, C., Deacy, S., McHardy, F. and Tempest, K. (2010), 'Embedding Employability into a Classics Curriculum', *Arts and Humanities in Higher Education*, 9 (3): 339–352.

Behr, C., Barrow, R., Deacy, S., McHardy, F. and Tempest, K. (2009), *Teaching the language of employability to Classical Civilisation students*. Available online: http://www.llas.ac.uk/events/archive/3226. (Accessed 8 July 2016).

British Academy (2004), *The Full Complement of Riches: The Contribution of the Arts, Humanities and Social Sciences to the Nation's Wealth*, London: British Academy.

Cambridge Assessment (2013), *21st Century Skills: Ancient, Ubiquitous, Enigmatic?*, Cambridge: Cambridge Assessment. Available online: http://www.cambridgeassessment.org.uk/images/130437-21st-century-skills-ancient-ubiquitous-enigmatic-.pdf. (Accessed 16 November 2016).

Clark, E. (2013), 'An Assessment of the Effectiveness of TRPS as a Means of Teaching Latin Vocabulary and Grammar', *Journal of Classics Teaching*, 28: 34–42.

Confederation of British Industry (2015), *Pearson Education and Skills Survey*. London: Confederation of British Industry.

Dacre Pool, L. and Sewell, P. (2007), 'The Key to Employability: Developing a Practical Model of Graduate Employability', *Education & Training*, 49 (4): 277–289.

Day, H. (2006–2009), *Ceth Employability Framework*. Available online: http://escalate.ac.uk/downloads/6465.pdf. (Accessed 8 July 2016).

Dench, D. (2008), 'The Work Placement Module at Roehampton', *CUCD Bulletin*, 37: 8–9.

Department for Education (2003), *21st Century Skills: Realising Our Potential*, London: Crown copyright. Available online: https://www.gov.uk/government/uploads/system/uploads/attachment_data/file/336816/21st_Century_Skills_Realising_Our_Potential.pdf. (Accessed 10 October 2016).

Holliday, L. (2012), 'The Benefits of Latin', *Educational Research Quarterly*, 36 (1): 3–12.

Holmes-Henderson, A. (2013), *A Defence of Classical Rhetoric in Scotland's Curriculum for Excellence*, Doctoral thesis. Available online: http://theses.gla.ac.uk/4705/1/2013holmeshendersonedd_Redacted.pdf. (Accessed 10 October 2016).

Holmes-Henderson, A. (2016), 'Responsible Citizenship and Critical Skills in Scotland's Curriculum for Excellence: The Contribution of Classical Rhetoric to Democratic Deliberation', in P. Carr, P. Thomas, B. Porfillo and J. Gorlewski (eds.), *Democracy and Decency: What Does Education Have to Do with It?*, 213–228, Charlotte: Information Age Publishers.

Parker, J. (2008), 'Can We Account for Classics' Complex Skills?', *CUCD Bulletin*, 37: 9–14.

Patrick, R. (2011), 'TPRS and Latin in the Classroom: Experiences of a US Latin Teacher', *Journal of Classics Teaching*, 22: 10–11.

Race, P. (2005), *Making Learning Happen: A Guide for Post-Compulsory Education*, London: SAGE Publications Ltd.

Sullivan, M., Janus, M., Moreno, S., Astheimer, L. and Bialystok, E. (2014), 'Early Stage Second-Language Learning Improves Executive Control: Evidence from ERP', *Brain and Language*, 139: 84–98.

CHAPTER 17
CLASSICS IN OUR ANCESTORS' COMMUNITIES
Edith Hall

The study of the ancient Greeks and Romans is in Britain facing a moment of historical change. Although there are significant initiatives working to reverse the tide, the number of children and teenagers given access to the Latin and Greek languages in our state-funded schools and sixth-form colleges has long been in decline (Hunt 2016). Meanwhile, qualifications in Classical Civilisation and Ancient History, wide-ranging courses taught through ancient sources studied in English translation, are becoming more popular (Fleiner 2014); the first recognition of their importance, at any rate at the level of national research subsidy, came in 2017 with the Arts and Humanities Research Council (AHRC) funding of the project *Studying Classical Civilisation in Britain: Recording the Past and Fostering the Future*, or 'Advocating Classics Education' (ACE), led by Dr Arlene Holmes-Henderson and myself from the Classics department at Kings' College London (KCL).[1]

Our project, which aims to affect future policy as well as record the history since the Second World War of secondary-level qualifications in classical subjects taught in translation, grew out of a previous AHRC-funded project at KCL, *Classics and Class in Britain 1789–1939*. For that slightly earlier project, the research was conducted by Dr Henry Stead and myself between 2013 and 2016. *Classics and Class* examined the history of the consumption of classical antiquity from a class-conscious perspective. It tested the widespread assumptions that Classics has always been an elite subject and that access to it was long confined to males in families rich enough to fund their children's undertaking of several years of training in the Latin and Greek languages. Since even rudimentary education for children aged five to ten years did not become compulsory until the Elementary Education Act 1880, the opportunities for studying ancient languages were inevitably limited to households above a certain level of income.

Yet *Classics and Class* uncovered substantial evidence for working-class Britons' knowledge and enjoyment of the ancient Greek and Roman civilizations. This called into question the elite monopoly on this high-status intellectual property. The material unearthed will be presented in detail in our forthcoming volume *A People's History of Classics*, to be published by Routledge Taylor & Francis in 2019, simultaneously as a printed book and on an open-access platform. A sample of the evidence is already publicly available via the project's website.[2] I here give a preview of some revealing case studies. The aim is to provide some historical background to the diverse current enterprises discussed in *Forward with Classics*, enterprises which seek to democratize the study of the ancient Greeks and Romans and bring it to as wide a public as possible. 'People's Classics', it turns out, has just as long a history as the Classics establishment conventionally identified with the language-based tuition of the privileged in our ancient universities.

Alongside the learned divines whose portraits hang in Oxbridge college dining halls and libraries, there is a fascinating lineage of ancestors who read, taught, learned and talked about 'Classics' in factories, mechanics' institutes, workers' libraries, pubs, theaters, fairgrounds, shops and workplaces. There were women among them, including a handful of female classical scholars of extraordinary dedication, despite facing institutional exclusion and intellectual derision, whom I have recently excavated in another volume co-edited with Dr Rosie Wyles (Wyles and Hall 2016). One inspirational figure is Constantia Grierson (1706–1733), the self-taught Roman Catholic daughter of illiterate Co. Kilkenny peasants. She married the King's Printer and herself produced three important editions of Latin authors Ballard (1752, pp. 461–464). Further afield, there were also many people of colour who succeeded, against tremendous odds, in reading classical authors and ancient history, even before the abolition of slavery in the British colonies in 1833 and throughout the United States in 1865 (see Ronnick 2004; Hall et al. 2011). But most non-elite classicists were simply very poor indeed.

Perhaps the most poignant individual whose history we have excavated was the Welsh autodidact 'Dic of Aberdaron', alias Richard Robert Jones or 'Dirty Dic' (1780–1843) (see Fig. 17.1). Dic was the son of an impoverished boatswain from Aberdaron, a coastal village in North Wales, whose small cargo boat shuttled between Wales and Liverpool. In childhood Dic taught himself Hebrew and Greek, which he could write beautifully as well as read. His father used to flog him regularly for reading on the boat instead of watching the tiller, but nothing could diminish the dreamy child's passion for Classics. He wrote a Greek-Latin lexicon and a Hebrew Grammar. He understood Arabic and Persian and was completely fluent in Latin, French and Italian. He once visited Bangor School, where he was 'tested' on his Greek, passed with flying colours and given some classical books which he accepted with delight and gratitude. Dic, sadly, spent much of his life as a homeless beggar in Liverpool, where he was a well-known and celebrated character. His life improved slightly when the radical Merseyside poet William Roscoe gave him a small regular stipend. But Dic remained eccentric. Although his favourite author by far was Homer, he liked to sing the psalms in Hebrew, accompanying himself on a Welsh harp and turned up at an *eisteddfod* with an ancient Greek essay on types of stringed instrument. Dic died as he had lived, a wandering bard and intellectual – or 'a perfect child of nature', as one obituary called him. He was buried in the churchyard of St Asaph's Cathedral in Denbighshire (Humphreys 1866).

Dic both read sources on ancient religious music in English and learned ancient languages. But the radical conceptual chasm between studying Latin and Greek sources through translation and in the original tongues had already begun to yawn in the early years of the eighteenth century, when 'Classics' became identifiable as a discrete and dominant constituent of the curriculum. It was then that new meanings of both terms, 'Classics' and 'class', emerged. The lexicological culprit here is the literary miscellany *Attic Nights*, written in the second century CE by the Latin grammarian Aulus Gellius. He is quoting Fronto, a previous expert on rhetorical style, on what verbs should be used in the plural and what in the singular, such as whether it is correct to say 'sands' or 'sand'. He recommends consultation of some respected author as a way to discover the best usage (19.8.15), '… provided he be one of the early orators or poets, that is to say, a writer of class and substance, not one of the proletarian writers' (… *illa dumtaxat antiquiore vel oratorum aliquis vel poetarum, id est classicus adsiduusque aliquis scriptor, non proletarius*). Aulus Gellius metaphorically transfers the idea of different social classes to distinguish between authors of different aesthetic quality. 'Classical' authors are superior in literary terms to 'proletarian' authors. The metaphors are even more specific than that: *classicus adsiduusque*, which I here translate 'of class and substance' could equally well be translated 'of the taxpaying class', one specific meaning of the term *adsiduus*.

Figure 17.1 Early nineteenth-century caricature of Richard Robert Jones.

When the Romans heard their Latin noun *classis*, it contained a resonance that we do not hear when we say 'class': deriving from the same root as the verb *clamare* ('call out'), a *classis* consisted of a group of people 'called out' or 'summoned' together. It could be the men in a meeting, or in an army, or the ships in a fleet. The word has always been associated with Servius Tullius, the sixth of the legendary kings of early Rome, who was said by Dionysius of Halicarnasssus (book 4) and Livy (book 1) to have held the first census in order to find out, for the purposes of military planning, what assets his people possessed. He had them summoned and divided, for the purposes of calculating tax bands, into five different classes, of which the lowest, the proletarian, was not required to pay tax. It is this procedure that explains the ancient association of the term 'class' with an audible call to arms (see Hall 2008).

The *Attic Nights* was a favourite Renaissance and Early Modern text, first printed in 1469. By 1602, it resulted in the occasional use of the word 'classique' in English, as it is still used today, to describe a canonical text of any era: William Perkins says in a theological work written in 1602, 'Besides, neither *Plinie* (who writ after Paul) nor any other ancient classique author, doth make mention of *Phrigia Pacaciana*' (Perkins 1604, p. 657). He needs to distinguish between 'ancient' classic authors and more recent ones, and he also includes St Paul's epistles among 'classical' works. By 1645, with the increasing familiarity in European literary circles of the Greek treatise attributed to 'Longinus', *On the Sublime* (the first English translation, by John Hall of Consett, was published in 1652), Sir Dudley North fuses the idea of a top literary class derived from Aulus Gellius with the new interest in 'sublimity': 'Farre more sublime and better Authours have discovered as little order, and as much repetition; witnesse the Collections of Marcus Aurelius, St. Augustines Confessions, and some of a higher Classe' (North 1645, p. 181). By 1694, the former Archbishop of Canterbury, William Sancroft, can be praised posthumously by another learned divine for having acquired great learning at Emanuel College:

> His Accomplishments in Human Literature were very surprising, and within a very little while after his being there, he became Master of the whole Circle of it: Which upon all Occasions in Public as well as in Private, shewed itself very remarkably. In this he had a peculiar Talent, being an admirable Critic in all the Antient and Classic Knowledge, both among the Greeks and Romans .... He made it subservient to the carrying on his unwearied Labours in *Theology*.[3]

Here, one religious man is concerned to stress that another Christian he is praising did not allow his love of non-Christian ancient authors to come between him and his theological priorities. For the first documented time in the English language, this writer uses 'Classic' adjectivally, albeit clarified by the word 'Antient', to designate the same, pagan Greek and Roman field of knowledge which we designate as belonging to the field of 'Classics' today.

But it is only in 1712 that 'Classic', without any qualification at all, has become associated specifically with the authors of ancient Greece and Rome in the context of an educational curriculum. Richard Steele publishes an article in the *Spectator* containing what he claims are letters he has recently received from two schoolboys. One of them, a fourteen-year-old, complains that his father, although very wealthy, does not think that training in ancient authors will do his son any good, and will not buy him the (expensive) books he needs to further his studies of Latin authors: our teenager laments, 'All the Boys in the School, but I, have the Classick Authors in usum Delphini, gilt and letter'd on the Back.'[4] By 1712, acquisition of the famous and elegantly bound French 'Delphin Classics' series had become indispensable to what was beginning to be called 'a Classical Education'. The twenty-five volumes of Latin texts, with Latin commentary by thirty-nine scholars, were commissioned in the 1670s for Louis, le Grand Dauphin, but they went on to transform educational practice and intellectual life across Europe. Crucially, one of the authors published in the series had been Aulus Gellius himself (Proust 1681).[5]

Increasingly, the term 'the Classics' came to designate specifically and often exclusively the pagan authors studied by privileged British youths – not only those of Rome but of ancient Greece as well. This is the sense in which Henry Felton used the term in his *A Dissertation on Reading the Classics, and Forming a Just Style*, written in 1709 and first published in 1713 (Felton 1713). It was addressed to his aristocratic pupil, John, Lord Roos, who later became the 3rd Duke of Rutland. Felton takes a dim view of translations of 'the Classics', the assumption being that his genteel reader would have total command of the ancient languages, and despises almost all the English-language translations available: he expostulates (his word) against 'every idle, half-witted, half-learned *Noddle*' who imagines himself to be 'well enough qualified for a *Translator*'. Felton describes his own aim: 'to rescue the Classics out of the Hands of every ignorant Pretender, that they may not be mangled and abused in their *Transmigration* from one Language to another'. Translation turns magnificent ancient authors into something paltry: 'the Spirit of a Lion seems *Translated* into the Spirit of an Ass' (Felton 1713, p. 134).

Yet studying the ancient world through translations already had equally staunch defenders. Those of us thinking about maximizing the diversity of avenues of access to Classics today would do well to consider their sensible words. The anonymous translator of a selection of Lucian's dialogues published in 1700 prefaced them with a newly composed dialogue on the merits of reading 'Classick' authors in one's mother tongue. The speaker who attacks translation is named 'Eumenes'. This choice may deliberately display the anonymous author's erudition, since this was the name of the Attalid ruler Eumenes II (97–159 BCE), who admired intellectual culture and massively expanded the Library of Pergamon. One of Eumenes' main objections to translation is that it will put the great authors of antiquity within reach of anybody who can read, even the 'ordinary Mechanick':

> You say Every Man may now read Plutarch and Tully, and the rest in his own Language, and is not this the way to make Learning common, cheap, and contemptible, when every ordinary Mechanick shall be as well acquainted with these Authors as he that has spent 10 or 12 Years in the Universities? … Those rich Treasures of Knowledge and Learning are now unlock'd indeed, and scattered abroad among the Rabble. (Anon. 1700, p. 10)

But this elitist position has a robust rebuttal in a speech by Eumenes' interlocutor, Philenor (whose name carries the sense of 'philanthropic', or 'kindly to men'): 'Those rich Treasures of Knowledge & Learning among the Antients are no longer now lock'd up in unintelligible Words … Translating "has to our Country brought/All that they writ, and all they thought …."' Men may now familiarly Converse with the Wits of Greece and Rome … ' (Anon. 1700, p. 7). Philenor here quotes a poem by Edmund Waller, originally printed as part of the prefatory materials to John Evelyn's famous English verse translation of Lucretius (1656):

> For here *Lucretius* whole we finde,
> His Words, his Musick, and his mind:
> Thy Art has to our Countrey brought
> All that he writ, and all he thought (Evelyn 1656, p. 4)

Philenor adds that there are plenty of people who would never encounter classical authors at all if they could not do so by translation: 'I have known Some who wou'd never have taken the pains to read and understand some Greek Authors, if they had not been first charm'd with the Translation, and at the same time entertain'd a Belief that they must needs be much more Agreeable and Taking in the Original' (Anon. 1700, p. 14).

The language of pleasure here – 'charm'd', 'agreeable' – reminds us that it was the enjoyable aspects of the stories told in ancient authors which helped them prove consistently attractive across the class spectrum, regularly reaching even illiterate Britons through the medium of leisure-time pursuits. Episodes from classical myth and history abounded in the hippodramas performed at Astley's circus, in the variety of 'spectacles', 'panoramas' and 'dioramas' beloved of Victorian Londoners, in the extraordinary genre of classical burlesque, in the shows of strongmen and gymnasts and in early cinema (see Saxon 1968; Altick 1978; Hall and Macintosh 2005). Even at the time when the terms 'Classics' and 'class' were acquiring their co-dependent modern meanings, in the first decades of the eighteenth century, quite as important a medium for the story of the siege of Troy as Dryden's Virgil or Pope's Homer was Elkanah Settle's spectacular fairground droll *The Siege of Troy*. This was a huge hit at both the Southwark and Bartholomew Fairs in London, revived repeatedly from 1707 until the 1730s (Hall 2018).

In the same period as Settle's droll, puppet shows on classical themes drew crowds to Covent Garden, for example the hundred classical gods and heroes impersonated by puppets which William Penkethman displayed in his 'automaton show', about which we know from advertisements in the *Spectator*:

> Mr. Penkethman's Wonderful Invention call'd the Pantheon: or, the Temple of the Heathen Gods. The Work of several Years, and great Expense, is now perfected; being a most surprising and magnificent Machine, consisting of 5 several curious Pictures, the Painting and contrivance whereof is beyond Expression Admirable. The Figures, which are above 100, and move their Heads, Legs, Arms, and Fingers, so exactly to what they perform, and setting one Foot before another, like living Creatures, that it justly deserves to be esteem'd the greatest Wonder of the Age. To be seen from 10 in the Morning till 10 at Night, in the Little Piazza, Covent Garden ...[6]

Another medium which made ancient civilization available to all but the most indigent social strata included the sometimes semi-pornographic shows called *tableaux vivantes* or *poses plastiques*, associated in the public imagination with the thoroughly working-class and (in her youth) uneducated Liverpudlian Emma Hamilton (née Lyon). Hamilton herself became a considerable expert on ancient myth, history, art and statuary in the course of researching her many different classical 'attitudes'.[7] Victorian London offered many such shows, but they were available in provincial cities, too. The Royal Parthenon Assembly Rooms in Great Charlotte Street, central Liverpool, on 20 May 1850 advertised the week's programme of tableaux and songs, 'a truly CLASSIC exhibition, with "a SUCCESSION OF NOVELTIES of a superior character"'. The scenes ranged over ancient history and myth, and were accompanied by vocal soloists. 'Brutus Ordering the Execution of his Son' was followed by a tableau 'Diana Preparing for the Chase', designed by A. Cooper, R.A., and another entitled 'A Bacchanalian Procession, from the Borghese Vase.' Later in the programme the audience was promised three further classical tableaux, under the headings 'Greeks Surprised by the Enemy', '"the Amazons" Triumph', and 'the Grecian's Daughter' (Broadbent

1908, pp. 347–349). The doors opened at half-past six, and the performance commenced at seven. Entrance to the Parthenon was free; any profits were raised by selling food and drinks.

The intelligent pseudo-Lucianic dialogue published in 1700 shows that despite the amount of time required to learn the ancient languages, by the dawn of the twenty-first century there had already been three centuries of unfortunate and wholly unnecessary conflict between advocates of exclusive original-language study and those who look kindly on access through translation. Moreover, the conflict, from its inception, was perceived and felt in terms which had to do with social class. In the second half of this chapter, I therefore flesh out the picture of this struggle for ownership of the ancient texts by introducing into the discussion some of the individuals in our ancestral communities across Great Britain who were either inspired by reading Classics in translation or progressed from non-elite points of access, against many odds, to learn the ancient languages themselves.

On the cusp between 'entertainment' and 'self-education' is the phenomenon of the recital or public performance of an elevated ancient text in a *declassé* environment. Ancient authors kept the most unlikely audiences enthralled in the most unlikely places. You could hear the entire works of Homer recited in late-eighteenth-century Jedburgh. Esther Easton, a flower arranger, was also an exemplary autodidact. She would have been lost to history had she not been visited by the poet Robert Burns, on his travels through the Scottish borders, on 9 May 1787. He was taken to meet this prodigious wife of the gardener on the Lindsay Estate, and she astonished him. He recorded that she was 'a very remarkable woman for reciting poetry of all kinds, and sometimes making Scotch doggerel herself – she can repeat by heart almost everything she has ever read, particularly Pope's "Homer" from end to end; has studied Euclid by herself; and, in short, is a woman of very extraordinary abilities' (Currie 1838, p. 127).

Thirty-six miles west across the borders, it was not Homer but Josephus who was enjoyed in English-language performance. A man named Tam Fleck kept the townsfolk of early nineteenth-century Peebles entranced with tales of the fall of Jerusalem. In the biography of the noted Victorian publisher Robert Chambers written by his brother William, we are introduced to Tam in the description of Robert's childhood in Peebles before the family moved to Edinburgh in 1813. Chambers records how he and his brother, sons of a cotton manufacturer, used to visit the house of an elderly relative in the poor part of town, where they would be 'delighted listeners' at Tam's recitals. Tam, the owner of a copy of Roger l'Estrange's eighteenth-century compressed translation of Josephus' *The Wars of the Jews* (L'Estrange 1720),[8] would tour the households of Peebles reading that narrative 'as the current news'. He would intersperse his readings with commentary, and never read more than two to three pages of text. Wherever possible he ended on a cliffhanger, taking care to break off in the same place at every house, so that all his listeners would be left in the same suspense. As Alistair McCleery points out, this had the effect of turning Josephus into a sort of soap opera (McCleery 2005).[9] In this way, he would take about a year to get through the whole Jewish War, at which point he would simply start again. Despite this, according to Chambers, 'the novelty somehow never seemed to wear off':

'Weel, Tam, what's the news the nicht?' would old Geordie Murray say, as Tam entered with his 'Josephus' under his arm, and seated himself at the family fireside.

'Bad news, bad news', replied Tam. 'Titus has begun to besiege Jerusalem & it's gaun to be a terrible business.' and then he opened his budget of intelligence, to which all paid the most reverential attention. (Chambers 1872, pp. 25–26)

This account suggests a strong degree of emotional investment in the narrative on the part of Tam's audience. The famine that fell upon the besieged citizens of Jerusalem (described in a number of memorably horrific passages in Josephus, principally *Jewish War* 6.199–216), 'kept several families in a state of agony for a week', while the final fall of the city (6.230–442) elicited 'a perfect paroxysm of horror' (Chambers 1872, p. 26).

British social history affords a handful of examples of working-class individuals whose combined intelligence and good luck resulted in their aptitude for Classics being identified, fostered and eventually rewarded with remuneration and/or employment (although not always happiness). The most conspicuous example is Richard Porson (1759–1808), a weaver's son from rural Norfolk. His mother, a cobbler's daughter, was clever and literate and ensured he attended the village school regularly, followed at the age of nine by the free school in the village of Happisborough, until a local nobleman, impressed by the boy's classical prowess, paid for his education to be continued at Eton (Clarke 1937, pp. 1–2, 6–7). Several other patrons financed Porson's studies at Trinity College, Cambridge, where he was elected a Fellow. However, in 1792, when it was decided that fellowships were no longer open to laymen, Porson declined to take holy orders and so lost his stipend. Unwillingness to take orders in fact took a great deal of courage, since no great level of piety was required of the academic clergy at that time, and there was small chance of earning an adequate living outside of schools or universities, but Porson was proud and principled (Clarke 1937, pp. 31–33). He was politically fairly radical, supporting the French Revolution in its early days, advocating parliamentary reform and adamantly opposing Pitt's government.

He was subsequently supported by an annuity raised from friends' subscriptions. He is remembered for Porson's Law, applied to Greek tragic metrics, alongside the Porson Greek typeface based on his own handwriting, as well as his acclaimed textual work on Greek drama. Yet his lack of social niceties, foul mouth and capacity for alcohol were notorious. He regularly passed out in company and fell asleep under the table (Barker 1852, p. 14). His antics shocked even Lord Byron, who in a letter of 1818 likened his behaviour to that of Silenus: 'Of all the disgusting brutes, sulky, abusive, and intolerable, Porson was the most bestial'; when he thought people were ignorant, he insulted them 'with the most vulgar terms of reprobation'. Byron elaborates this unlovely picture: 'He used to recite, or rather vomit, pages of all languages, and could hiccup Greek like a helot' (Byron 1839, p. 374).[10] Since Byron did not usually object to drunkenness, the language here – 'vulgar', 'helot' – implies snobbery based on social class. Porson probably had what we would now call a photographic memory, which, while useful, was also apparently a source of misery to him as 'he could never forget anything, even that he wished not to remember' (Page 1960, pp. 13–14). Such memories no doubt included those of his own, lowly upbringing. His dislocation from his class roots may have contributed to his alcoholism, which killed him in 1808.

Porson once wrote a fractious letter complaining about some criticisms of his edition of *Hecuba* (1797) which had been published in a review by a much more contented lower-class Greek prodigy. Andrew Dalzel (1742–1806)[11] was a carpenter's son who rose to be a leading Edinburgh intellectual. He was born on the Newliston estate in Linlithgowshire; after his father died, his talent for languages was spotted at parochial school. After school he went to Edinburgh University and by 1779 he succeeded to the Chair of Greek, which he held for over thirty years. In 1785 he received the additional appointment of university librarian. Dalzel turned round Greek Studies at the university, which had dwindled to almost nothing under his predecessor. He soon had over a hundred students enrolled. He was proud of the standards of learning his students achieved and compared them positively with those at Oxford and

Cambridge, where 'dissipation, idleness, drinking, and gambling' predominated. 'The English Universities are huge masses of magnificence and form, but ill calculated to promote the cause of science or of liberal inquiry' (Dalzel 1862, p. 14).

Dalzel remained conscious of his background and correspondingly free from snobbery. When Robert Burns arrived in Edinburgh, he wrote enthusiastically, 'We have got a poet in town just now, whom everybody is taking notice of – a ploughman from Ayrshire – a man of unquestionable genius.' (Dalzel 1862, p. 71). He was also an exceptionally hardworking pedagogue, teaching two classes daily of two hours each. The first focused on the Greek language through engagement with Lucian, Homer, Xenophon, Anacreon and the New Testament. The second class, which was itself divided into groups depending on level of linguistic attainment, focused on Thucydides, Herodotus and Demosthenes, supplemented by more Homer, some tragedy and Theocritus. Dalzel also gave two lectures a week focusing on Classical Civilisation, or, as he described it, 'the history, government, manners, the poetry and eloquence' of the ancient Greeks. His student Lord Henry Cockburn recalled him as:

a general exciter of boys' minds … Mild, affectionate, simple, an absolute enthusiast about learning particularly classical, and especially Greek; with an innocence of soul and of manner which imparted an air of honest kindliness to whatever he said or did, and a slow, soft formal voice, he was a great favourite with all boys, and all good men. Never was a voyager, out in quest of new islands, more delighted in finding one, than he was in discovering any good quality in any humble youth. (Cockburn 1856, pp. 26–27)

Nobody was surprised when Dalzel hired as his assistant a poverty-stricken humble youth named George Dunbar (1774–1851), a gardener, who eventually succeeded him in the chair.

Porson and Dalzel were 'discovered' when still children by philanthropic patrons. For young people with little or no elementary education, the only choice was autodidacticism unless classes run by charitable, non-conformist or workers' organizations happened to be locally available. The problems facing a worker who decided to teach himself were legion, but the worst were lack of time, physical exhaustion and the expense of the necessary books. Ben Tillett was a prominent Trade Union leader who struggled desperately to self-educate himself in Classics while working full time as a docker. A native of Bristol, he was labouring in a brickyard by the age of eight, followed by work as a fisherman, cobbler and sailor. He moved to London and in 1887 formed the Tea Operatives and General Labourers Union, later renamed the Dock, Wharf, Riverside and General Labourers' Union, while working at Tilbury docks. He became famous as a union leader in the London Dock Strike of 1889, and as a co-founder in 1910 of the National Transport Workers' Federation, later the Transport and General Workers Union.

Tillett became aware of the need to get some education when the harshness of life in the East End persuaded him to become an agitator and (as he put it himself) a 'fanatical evangelist of Labour'. But he felt ill equipped. As he recalled in his *Memories and Reflections* (1931), 'Before I could enter upon that stage of my career there were arrears of education to make up. I had much to learn, as well as something to forget.' He began reading systematically and soon discovered his own talent as a wordsmith: he could have been a professional writer, he wrote, if he had been born 'under a luckier star, with fuller opportunities than I enjoyed in the way of leisure, and a more intensive cultivation of my native qualities'. But one paragraph of his memoirs stands out for its stark presentation of the sheer exhaustion induced by dock work.

As a docker I had tried to save money, and starved to buy books. I was struggling to learn Latin, and was even trying to study Greek, lending my head and aching body to the task after my day's work on the dock-side, or in the tea warehouse where I was employed – work which meant carrying tons on my back up and down flights of stairs.

And he returns to the theme of his missing education much later in the volume: 'If I have one grouch against the world rather than another, the lack of opportunity for acquiring education in my earlier days is that one big grouch' (Tillett 1931, pp. 76–77, 81, 94, 271).[12]

What Tillett needed was a night school and emotional support in his project of self-education. The miracles which can be worked by supportive teachers within the context of adult education is no better illustrated than by the life of Joseph Wright, the workhouse boy who became Professor of Comparative Philology at Oxford (see Fig. 17.2). Perhaps the most prodigious of all nineteenth-century autodidacts, Wright worked from the age of six as a donkey driver at a stone quarry near his home in Bradford. Illiterate at the age of fifteen, in 1870, he became a wool sorter and taught himself to read. But, unlike Tillett, he then joined a Wesleyan night school where he studied French, German and Latin, and discovered his huge gift for languages. He also immersed himself in the fortnightly *Cassell's Popular Educator*, one of several inexpensive publications which made aspects of ancient Greek and Roman culture widely available. Wright supplemented his income by opening his own night school, became a schoolmaster, taught himself Greek and managed to fund a PhD at Heidelberg by teaching incessantly. His thesis, passed 6 June 1885, was entitled 'The qualitative and quantitative changes in the Indo-Germanic vowel system in Greek' (Wright 1932, pp. 85–86). He was appointed lecturer to the Association for the Higher Education of Women in 1888, teaching German, Historical Greek Grammar, Historical Latin Grammar and Greek Dialects at Oxford University. But his background led him to specialize eventually in Germanic and Old English dialects.

According to his wife Elizabeth Mary Wright's biography, *The Life of Joseph Wright (1932)*, Wright insisted that 'it was owing to his plebeian ancestry that he brought with him to the field of science and letters that prodigious vitality of brain which enabled him to accomplish the intellectual feats which marked his progress' (Wright 1932, vol. I, p. 37). He remained proud of his origins all his life, and especially of his Primitive Methodist mother, who, when shown the grand buildings of All Souls College at Oxford, retorted, 'Eh! but it wod mak a grand Co-op!' (Wright 1932, p. 5). His wife was young woman from a much more privileged background whom he met when she was studying at Lady Margaret Hall. She also recalled a rare occasion on which he had rebuked her. She had facetiously complained that doing philology, and consulting big dictionaries, required excessive 'manual labour'. Wright quietly pointed out that 'manual labour' meant *working*, for example with a wheelbarrow (Wright 1932, pp. 131, 189).

Wright's route to self-fulfilment lay at Wesleyan night school. The biographies of many other non-elite classicists similarly reveal the importance of Non-Conformism; classical authors had often held a major place in the curriculum of the so-called Dissenting Academies (see Wilson forthcoming). Numerous working-class people were brought into contact with Classics because John Wesley himself believed that Methodist preaching could be improved by training in classical rhetoric. At Oxford, Wesley, who himself read the classical languages fluently, had studied Ciceronian oratory and its presentation in neoclassical handbooks. But he was convinced that his preachers, many of whom had hardly any previous education, would benefit from hands-on training, often in the open air, in the principles of classical rhetoric, and enthusiastically

Figure 17.2 Photograph of Saltaire wool sorters with Joseph Wright, age 19, standing on the right.

supervised them himself; he encouraged them to learn Greek and Hebrew, the languages of the bible, as he did the miners' and preachers' sons educated at Kingswood, the school he founded near Bristol.[13] But he also insisted that the preachers learn, from an English version of the Dutch scholar and theologian Gerard Vossius' introduction to Aristotelian rhetoric, the fundamental classical oratorical precepts of deportment, appropriateness, sublimity, force, relevance, simplicity and brevity (Vossius 1606).

This systematic approach was expertly accommodated to the non-university education of most of Wesley's preachers, and thus had important implications for the challenge to class hierarchies that Methodism presented. The preachers developed brilliantly honed techniques in public speaking, through oral, practical training, but applied them in the simple language of working-class people. This fusion of classical method and contemporary verbal medium goes a long way towards explaining the staggering success of the first Methodist preachers, who were instrumental in the rise of Trade Union oratory a few decades later. The Duchess of Buckingham was appalled, writing to the Methodist Countess of Huntingdon in 1742 to complain about these politically 'levelling' preachers, 'Their doctrines are most repulsive and strongly tinctured with impertinence and disrespect towards their Superiors, in perpetually endeavouring to level all ranks and do away with all distinction. It is monstrous to be told you have a heart as sinful as the common wretches that crawl on the earth.'[14]

The perceived alliance between classical education, Non-Conformism and self-emancipation from social oppression is no better instantiated than by the lifelong efforts made by the Reverend John Relly Beard to bring classical education to all working people. A passionate Unitarian minister, he opened a school in Salford and later an important college for training Unitarian preachers. He was a crucial force behind the movement for popular education in Lancashire. His father was a Portsmouth small tradesman, with nine children, who were therefore brought up in a degree of poverty.[15] At a time when other Unitarians feared that training ministers from the lowest classes would harm their cause, Beard never wavered in his zeal for universal education to the highest level. He wrote *Latin Made Easy* (1848), the sections on Latin, Greek and English Literature for *Cassell's Popular Educator*, and many accessible works on biblical subjects. He demonstrated the true extent of his political radicalism by publishing a biography of the leader of the Haiti slave rebellion Toussaint L'Ouverture (Beard 1853. See further Hall 2011, pp. 3, 7, 34). In his *Cassell's Lessons in Greek … Intended Especially for Those who are Desirous of Learning Greek without the Assistance of a Master* (1856) (see Fig. 17.3), he is explicit about the readership he assumes: 'The wants of such, the want of what may roughly be termed *the uneducated*, will be carefully borne in mind by me, while I prepare these lessons. Little more than some general acquaintance with grammar, and some general knowledge, shall I take for granted as possessed by my students.' What Beard intends

> is to simplify the study of Greek so as to throw open to all who are earnest in the great work of self-culture. Nor need any industrious person of ordinary capacity despair of acquiring skill to read the New Testament; and if he pleases, and will persevere, he may go on to an intimate acquaintance with Xenophon, Demosthenes, Thucydides, Homer, and the other Greek classics. (Beard 1856, p. 3)

The primary motive for learning Classical Greek may be to do with developing as a Christian, but the wonderful treasures of pagan literature will simultaneously become available to any diligent autodidact.

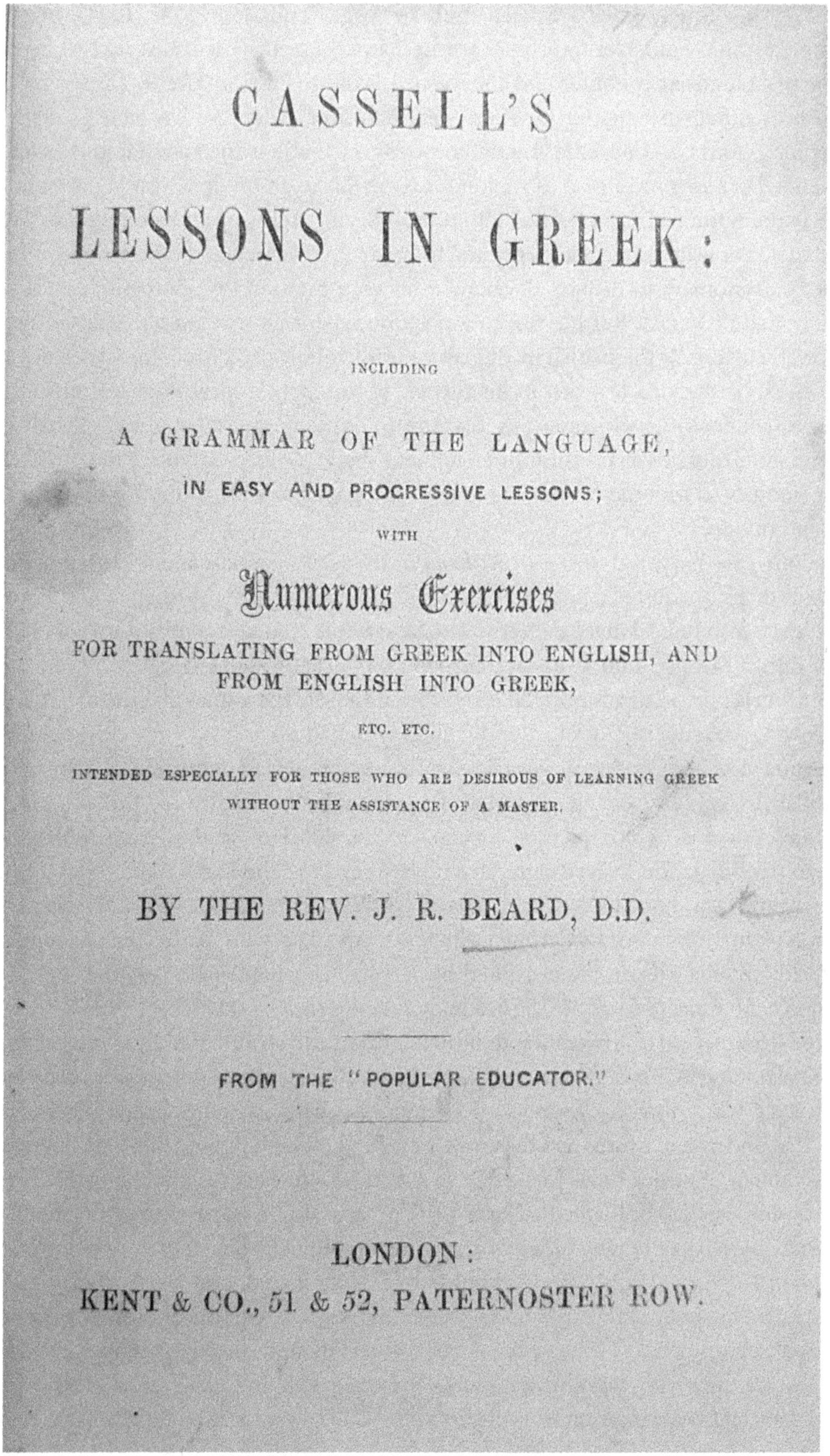

CASSELL'S

LESSONS IN GREEK:

INCLUDING

A GRAMMAR OF THE LANGUAGE,

IN EASY AND PROGRESSIVE LESSONS;

WITH

𝕹umerous 𝕰xercises

FOR TRANSLATING FROM GREEK INTO ENGLISH, AND
FROM ENGLISH INTO GREEK,

ETC. ETC.

INTENDED ESPECIALLY FOR THOSE WHO ARE DESIROUS OF LEARNING GREEK
WITHOUT THE ASSISTANCE OF A MASTER.

BY THE REV. J. R. BEARD, D.D.

FROM THE "POPULAR EDUCATOR."

LONDON:
KENT & CO., 51 & 52, PATERNOSTER ROW.

Figure 17.3 John Relly Beard's Victorian 'Teach Yourself Greek'.

Beard's primer may well have been used by Roger Langdon (1825–1894), originally a wholly uneducated Somerset farmhand whose natural curiosity led him first to become an excellent self-taught astronomer and thence to learning Classical Greek. He took a railway job as a switchman in Durston Junction, near Taunton, where he was able to stare at the stars for long hours and become deeply knowledgeable about the celestial bodies and their movements. On being promoted to stationmaster at Silverton on the Great Western line from London Paddington to Penzance, he built himself his first telescope. Over the following years he constructed another three telescopes and his own observatory, and became one of the most respected astronomers in Britain, developing his own method for photographing the moon and the transit of Venus. But his rise to a position where he was academically respected in the highest echelons of the British intelligentsia was supported by his competence at Classical Greek, which he decided to learn in his forties. Fortunately, a local Baptist minister named John Jackson offered Greek classes in Taunton to workers, for a fee of only a halfpenny a week. Langdon took great pleasure in Greek and made rapid progress. It must have helped him enormously to find the confidence to deliver a paper in 1871 to the Royal Astronomical Society in London.[16]

Langdon's case is typical of the experience of the late Georgian and Victorian autodidact not only in that he acquired access to training in ancient languages through a non-conformist mentor. It was also typical that his interest in Classics was related to another area of intellectual interest, rather being confined to the narrowly philological: no astronomer, even those far more amateurish than Langdon, could avoid coming across the names of Aristotle, Aristarchus or Ptolemy of Alexandria. Countless individuals who had no access to any classical education knew a good deal about particular aspects of the ancient world because they were experts in a particular field of interest and enquiries of a general nature introduced them to the ancient Greeks and Romans. A conspicuous example is the sport of boxing. Tom Molineaux, the American freedman and heavyweight boxer, was billed as 'The Black Ajax' (even though the Greek hero Ajax was not a boxer but a wrestler – in *Iliad* 23 he draws with his rival Odysseus). Born on a plantation in South Carolina, the Black Ajax had won his freedom in a prize fight and after many victories in America had been invited to England by another ex-slave, Bill Richmond, who ran a famous boxing academy in London.

On 18 December 1810, on what was dubbed the 'Campus Martius' near East Grinstead, in front of a cross-class audience laying enormous bets, Molineaux was finally defeated in a racist umpire's decision by a white British opponent. Contemporary Irish journalist Pierce Egan, however, insisted that underhand means and the crowd's bias had robbed him of a glorious victory: 'It will not be forgotten, if justice holds the scales, that it was Molineaux's colour alone that prevented him becoming the hero of that fight' (Egan 1812, p. 461). And it was Egan's writing that brought the classical ancestry of boxing to an enormous readership. His *Boxiana; or, Sketches of Ancient and Modern Pugilism* (1812) is now acknowledged as the foundation text of sports journalism and won Egan the soubriquet 'the Plutarch of the ring'. It opens with the praise of the divine boxer Pollux, Spartan brother of Castor, who won his seat on Olympus through his pugilist skills. Egan quotes Horace, supplying but also translating the Latin, mindful of his cross-class readership. His list of ancient boxers continues with Eryx the Sicilian vanquished by Hercules, Dares and Enetellus, and Amycus visited by the Argonauts. Egan contrasts ancient boxing in weighted gloves with modern bare-knuckle fighting, discusses the Greek and Latin boxing vocabulary and compares contemporary prize fighters with Hercules, Ulysses, Coriolanus and Mars.

Professional interests could turn people into classicists, too, as a fascinating strand in the history of Aberdonian Classicism reveals. Born in 1794, Alexander MacDonald was the son of a poor Perthshire crofter, and only educated at elementary level. His father could not even afford to pay him a wage to help on the farm, so the young Alexander took up an apprenticeship as a stonemason, which he completed in 1820 and moved to Aberdeen. There was a good supply of beautiful local stone in the form of granite, which could be made into matte-surfaced mantelpieces, paving stones and funeral monuments. But Alexander was frustrated because neither he nor anyone else could work out how to give the gritty local stone a sheen and polish equivalent to that which could be given to marble. The breakthrough came when in 1829 he read about an exhibition at the British Museum of ancient sculptures from Egypt, some of them from the Hellenistic period. They had been brought to Britain by the colourful adventurer Giovanni Belzoni, a fairground strongman-entertainer and explorer. MacDonald travelled all the way to London to visit the exhibition and was astonished to see that the statues made of granite – even those with rounded surfaces – were highly polished. The Egyptians and Ptolemies, mysteriously, had known how to do what no stonemason had done ever since. MacDonald set about trying to reproduce the lost art, but polishing by hand was just far too laborious and time-consuming to be remotely practicable. He did manage to crack the problem of the rounded surfaces by using a wheel turned by two workers. But since everything had to be done by manual labour, it was far too slow to be viable except for tiny pieces, and even they took days.

The second breakthrough came when his neighbour John Stewart, who ran a comb-making factory, let him use power from his newly installed steam engine. With the aid of steam power, which drove the cutting and polishing machinery, monumental polished granite artefacts became feasible again for the first time since the Ptolemies. The granite industry of Aberdeen was now unstoppable. Polished, shiny granite gravestones became the rage, and ever bigger monuments and edifices were built, constructed out of granite exported from Aberdeen and exported all over the British Empire. In London alone, think of Waterloo Bridge, the terraces of the Houses of Parliament or the reddish granite of the fountains in Trafalgar Square.

The ancient inspiration behind MacDonald's granite was reflected in Alexander MacDonald's son and heir, also named Alexander, who inherited his father's classical interests and became obsessed with the Greek-themed paintings of George Watts, Frederic Leighton and Lawrence Alma-Tadema. Alexander Junior spent some of the granite profits on his fine art collection, which he eventually bequeathed to Aberdeen Art Gallery, including Alma-Tadema's lively tambourine-bashing brunette in *A Garden Altar* (1879). The tradition lived on: the gallery actually contains some of the most famous Victorian and Edwardian painted images of ancient Greek stories, including John Waterhouse's *Danaides* (1906) and *Penelope and the Suitors* (1912).

Classics then re-encountered the issue of social class in the same gallery through another important Scottish philanthropist who, like Alexander MacDonald Senior, transcended his impoverished birth-rank and lack of formal education. George Reid was born poor and received little formal education. But he grew up to become a famous painter, mostly of portraits but also of scenes of working life – fishermen and farm labourers. When the more prosperous citizens of Aberdeen decided to add to their Museum and Art Gallery a great new hall to display casts of ancient Greek statues, Reid's own benefaction was a magnificent reproduction of the entire Parthenon frieze, similar to those on display at the Fitzwilliam Museum in Cambridge and in

Manchester Museum. It runs around the entire interior of what was then the 'new' sculpture court. He was an intellectual leveller and wanted to make the beautiful artworks of the ancient Greeks available to everyone in Aberdeen. The new gallery was opened at a splendid reception in April 1905. A specially commissioned train arrived from Euston containing sixty-two distinguished passengers. Among them was the novelist and poet Thomas Hardy, the poor boy from Dorset who had been apprenticed to a stonemason in his early teens, but had managed to learn some Greek and classical mythology in the evenings. He was thrilled on this occasion to be awarded, at last, a degree, conferred on him as an honour by Aberdeen University. The story of Aberdeen granite and its classical connections has run full circle, since Hardy was himself once a stone-mason and had made that the trade of the protagonist of his *Jude the Obscure* (1895), the working-class classical autodidact, forever excluded from the groves of academia in Christminster (i.e. Oxford), where he becomes so desperate to study.

Earlier we saw that it was around the beginning of the eighteenth century that in Britain the ideological battle-lines were first drawn up between advocates of studying classical authors in the original languages and advocates of a broader education encompassing the wide reading of ancient authors in English translation. One voice which can be added fruitfully here is that of one further stonemason, Hugh Miller of Cromarty (1802–1856). His enquiring intelligence, work with unhewn rocks and intimate knowledge of the Highland landscapes in which he was raised combined to turn him into a pioneering, world-renowned and much-published geologist, inspired by the stories of renowned explorers, including Odysseus. He read all of Homer in Pope's translations and wrote with passion about the impact the epic poems had made on his young mind. But as an adult he also gave considerable thought to the issue of education. He had attended the local dame school, and the parish schoolmaster decided he was clever enough to be given a classical education alongside the more high-class boys. Miller's memories are instructive. He came from a family of practical skilled tradesmen, and simply could not be persuaded that Latin grammar had anything to offer him that he had not yet already learned from his continuous and wide reading of books in English:

> I laboured with tolerable diligence for a day or two; but there was no one to tell me what the rules meant, or whether they really meant anything; and when I got as far as penna, a pen, and saw how the changes were rung on one poor word, that did not seem to be of more importance in the old language than in the modern one, I began miserably to flag, and to long for my English reading, with its nice amusing stories, and its picture-like descriptions. The 'Rudiments' was by far the dullest book I had ever seen. It embodied no thought that I could perceive – it certainly contained no narrative. (Miller 1993 [1854], p. 46)

The dullest book Miller had ever seen was the work of another Scotsman of working-class background, Thomas Ruddiman's *The Rudiments of the Latin Tongue; or, A Plain and Easy Introduction to Latin Grammar*, first published in 1714. Ruddiman was the quick-witted son of a poor tenant farmer in Aberdeenshire who ran away from home at sixteen to compete (successfully) for a prize bursary at King's College, Aberdeen. He embarked on a publishing career, and his *Rudiments* was a financial success, repeatedly revised and reprinted throughout his life and until as late as 1886. It helped generations of schoolchildren, adult learners and autodidacts take their first steps in Latin, since crucially it was bilingual in English and Latin throughout. But Miller was unimpressed. He worked out instead how to pass himself off as proficient in Latin, while secretly sneaking in copies of Virgil in Dryden's translation, and Ovid in English, to read in entirety during class. He used to learn chunks of the translations off by heart and repeat them back parrot-fashion (Miller 1993 [1854], p. 46). For someone like Miller, with huge intelligence and potential, studying languages was perceived as *impeding* his ability to read as many books, on as many subjects, as he could, before starting up his adult life's work as an earth scientist.

Miller's views on what the classical curriculum on offer to his peers had to offer them still hold some lessons for today. He kept in touch with some of those school friends, who unlike him continued their classical studies at university: 'I sometimes could not avoid comparing them in my mind with working men of … the same original calibre. I did not always find the general superiority on the side of the scholar which the scholar himself usually took for granted.' The scholars who had mastered Greek and Latin were, he admits, excellent at their specialism and well trained in framing analytical arguments. But the really cultured men in his view, 'the men most extensively acquainted with English literature – were not the men who had received the classical education' – they were working men with enquiring minds, like his own two uncles, modest mechanics, who read every book they could lay their hands on (Miller 1993 [1854], p. 351).

That Miller has the good grace to acknowledge that the classical graduates were not only good at the languages they had studied, but superior at framing arguments, reveals an impressive objectivity. But he is also clear that there is a tension between the amount of time required to learn Latin and Classical Greek and the breadth of the reading required to equip an individual for a broad understanding not only of ancient literature but of the world in which we find ourselves and of other intellectual interests. Surely the future of Classics can be best guaranteed by looking for a compromise between these two approaches. As we move forward with Classics today, the battle-lines drawn up in the early 1700s, which made language acquisition and reading in translation mutual enemies rather than allies and best friends, antithetical rather than intersecting and mutually complementary, need to vanish from our horizons altogether.

Notes

1   See http://aceclassics.org.uk/.

2   See http://www.classicsandclass.info/.

3   Remark of writer calling himself 'M.M.' in Sancroft (1694, pp. xiii–xiv).

4   *The Spectator,* no. 330 (19 March 1712), reproduced in Addison and Steele (1841, p. 67).

5   The text became a 'classic' of pedagogy, running into five editions and reprinted all the way until 1791.

6   The first issue of the *Spectator* in which the advertisement appeared was no. 46 (23 April 1711).

7   The best biography, which includes extensive discussion of Emma's lowly origins and considerable knowledge of Classical Civilisation, remains Fraser (1986).

8   I am grateful to Jonathan Davies for drawing Tam Fleck to my attention.

9   Based on a lecture originally delivered at the Museum of Edinburgh, Huntly House.

10   I am grateful to Jo Balmer for pointing out this text to me.

11   Letter of 3 September 1803, in Luard (1867, pp. 85–92).

12 *Memories and Reflections*. Published by J. Long. Unknown location.

13 See Graham (1990), who notes that the girls, unlike the boys, were not taught classical languages (p. 12).

14 Quoted in Whiteley (1938, p. 238).

15 On his life, see further Beard (1907).

16 Langdon (1909, pp. 70, 73–77, and especially 74, n. 1), which reports that the paper, on the markings visible on the surface of the planet Venus, was quoted by several distinguished contemporary scientists.

References

Addison, J. and Steele, R. (1841), *The Spectator: A New Edition, with Biographical Notes*, London: J. J. Chidley.

Altick, R. (1978), *The Shows of London: A Panoramic History of Exhibitions, 1600–1862*, Cambridge, MA: Harvard University Press.

Anon. (1700), *Lucian's Charon: Or, A Survey of the Follies of Mankind: Translated from the Greek. With Notes, and a Prefatory Dialogue in Vindication of Translations*, London: Loudon Farrow.

Ballard, G. (1752), *Memoirs of Several Ladies of Great Britain, Who Have Been Celebrated for Their Writings or Skill in the Learned Languages Arts and Sciences*, Oxford: W. Jackson.

Barker, E. (1852), *Literary Anecdotes and Contemporary Reminiscences of Professor Porson and Others*, vol. 2, London: J. R. Smith.

Beard, J. (1853), *The Life of Toussaint L'Ouverture*, London: Ingram, Cooke and Co.

Beard, J. (1856), *Cassell's Lessons in Greek*, London: Kent and Co.

Beard, J. (1907), *John Relly Beard, D.D.* (unpublished typescript, British Library).

Broadbent, R. (1908), *Annals of the Liverpool Stage from the Earliest Period to the Present Time*, Liverpool: Edward Howell.

Byron, Lord G. (1839), *Life, Letters and Journals of Lord Byron, with Notes*, T. Moore (ed.), London: John Murray.

Chambers, W. (1872), *Memoir of Robert Chambers*, Edinburgh and London: William and Robert Chambers.

Clarke, M. (1937), *Richard Porson: A Biographical Essay*, Cambridge: Cambridge University Press.

Cockburn, H. (1856), *Memorials of His Time*, Edinburgh: Adam and Charles Black.

Currie, J (1838), *The Life of Robert Burns: With a Criticism on His Writings*, Edinburgh: William and Robert Chambers.

Dalzel, A. (1862), *History of the University of Edinburgh from Its Foundation, with a Memoir of the Author*, vol. 1, Edinburgh: Edmonston and Douglas.

Egan, P. (1812), *Boxiana; or Sketches of Ancient and Modern Pugilism*, London: G. Smeeton.

Evelyn, J. (1656), *An Essay on the First Book of T. Lucretius Carus De rerum natura. Interpreted and Made English Verse*, London: Gabriel Bedle and Thomas Collins.

Felton, H. (1713), *A Dissertation on Reading the Classics, and Forming a Just Style*, London: Jonah Bowyer.

Fleiner, C. (2014), 'The New Integrated Masters Degree in Classical Studies at the University of Winchester', *CUCD Bulletin*, 43: 1–10.

Fraser, F. (1986), *Beloved Emma: The Life of Emma Lady Hamilton*, London: Weidenfeld and Nicolson.

Graham, W. (1990), *Wesley's Early Experiments in Education*, Ilkeston, Derbyshire: Moorley's Print and Publishing.

Hall, E. (2008), 'Putting the Class into Classical Reception', in L. Hardwick and C. Stray (eds.), *Blackwell Companion to Classical Reception*, 386–397, Oxford: Blackwell.

Hall, E. (2011), 'Introduction: An Invaluable Lesson', in E. Hall, R. Alston and J. McConnell (eds.), *Ancient Slavery and Abolition: From Hobbes to Hollywood*, 1–40, Oxford: Oxford University Press.

Hall, E. (2018), 'Classical Epic and the London Fairs, 1687–1734', in F. Macintosh, J. McConnell, S. Harrison and C. Kenward (eds.), *Epic Performances*. Oxford: Oxford University Press. Forthcoming.

Hall, E. and Macintosh, F. (2005), *Greek Tragedy and the British Theatre 1660–1914*, Oxford: Oxford University Press.

Hall, E., Alston, R. and McConnell, J. (eds.) (2011), *Ancient Slavery and Abolition*, Oxford: Oxford University Press.

Humphreys, H. (1866), *The Celebrated Cambrian Linguist, or the History of Dick Aberdaron*, Carnarvon: H. Humphreys.

Hunt, S. (2016), *Starting to Teach Latin*, London: Bloomsbury.

Langdon, E. (1909), *The Life of Roger Langdon*, London: Elliot Stock.

L'Estrange, R. (1720), *The Wars of the Jews in Two Books*, 2nd edn, Glasgow: Thomas Crawford.

Luard, H. (ed.) (1867), *The Correspondence of Richard Porson, M.A*, Cambridge: C.J. Clay.

McCleery, A. (2005), 'Defining Characters', *Textualities*. Available online: http://textualities.net/author/alistair-mccleery. (Accessed 24 March 2018).

Miller, H. (1993 [1856]), *My Schools and Schoolmasters*, ed. James Robertson, Edinburgh: B & W Publishing.

North, D. (1645), *A Forest of Varieties*, London: Richard Cotes.

Page, D. (1960), *Richard Porson*, London: Oxford University Press.

Perkins, W. (1604), *A Commentarie or Exposition, vpon the fiue first chapters of the Epistle to the Galatians*, Cambridge: John Legat.

Proust, J. (ed.) (1681), *Auli Noctes Atticae*, Paris: Simon Benard.

Ronnick, M. (2004), 'Twelve Black Classicists', *Arion*, 11: 85–102.

Ruddiman, T. (1714), *The Rudiments of the Latin tongue; or, A Plain and Easy Introduction to Latin Grammar,* Edinburgh: Edinburgh University Press.

Sancroft, W. (1694), 'Occasional Sermons preached by … William Sancroft, late Lord Arch-Bishop of Canterbury. With Some Remarks of His Life and Conversation', in a *Letter to a Friend,* London: Thomas Bassett.

Saxon, A. (1968), *Enter Foot and Horse: A History of Hippodrama in England and France*, New Haven, CT: Yale University Press.

Steele, R. (1712), 'Letter from a schoolboy', *The Spectator,* 2 March 1712, London.

Tillett, B. (1931), *Memories and Reflections*, Unknown: J. Long.

The Spectator (1712), London.

Vossius, G. (1606), *Oratoriarum institutionum libri sex*, Leiden: Andreas Cloucquius.

Whiteley, J. (1938), *Wesley's England: A Survey of 18th Century Social and Cultural Conditions*, London: Epworth Press.

Wilson, P. (forthcoming), 'Classics in Dissenting Academies', in I. Rivers and M. Burden (eds.), *A History of the Dissenting Academies in the British* Isles, *1660–1860*, Cambridge: Cambridge University Press.

Wright, E. (1932), *The Life of Joseph Wright*, Volume 1, London: Oxford University Press.

Wyles, R. and Hall, E. (eds.) (2016), *Women Classical Scholars*, Oxford: Oxford University Press.

CONCLUSION: ACHIEVEMENTS OF THE CLASSICS IN COMMUNITIES PROJECT

Arlene Holmes-Henderson, Steven Hunt and Mai Musié

Lessons learned

This book has shown some of the exciting projects and achievements of individuals and groups in bringing classical subjects to students in schools and universities, and the public at large in theaters, factories and even prisons across the UK and beyond. What, then, have we learnt from these experiences?

Perhaps the biggest lesson we can learn is that once schools and institutions have lost Classics, it is very difficult to get it back. Evidence from the UK is clear on this point: according to Jones (quoted in Tristram 2003, p. 8) in 1968 there were around 46,000 students who took the O level Latin examination and around 6,500 for the A level. By 1979 the totals were around 33,000 and around 3,000 respectively. At the time of the 1988 National Curriculum numbers stood at around 16,000 and around 2,000 (Lister 2007). The aftermath of that educational reform was catastrophic for Classics: numbers swiftly dropped even further and the present totals have hovered around the 10,000 and 1,500 ever since (Joint Curriculum and Qualifications Agency 2016). Efforts to reverse this trend have so far met with failure – at least in terms of examination entries. But examination entries are not the whole picture. Despite these apparently discouraging figures, ordinary teachers and academics have made it almost their life's work to try to staunch the flow and change its direction. What seem sometimes to be the most adverse situations often bring out the best in people: they become energized by the challenges that face them and they take on the opportunities with which they are presented. The stories within this book suggest that indeed the tide might be turning at last.

In the UK we see this with numerous initiatives, both small and larger in scale, in classrooms, theaters, lecture halls, boardrooms, the corridors of Whitehall, muddy fields and factories. The two Classics in Communities conferences held in Oxford in 2013 and in Cambridge in 2015 showcased many of them. The conferences brought together teachers from primary and secondary schools, university academics, artists, charity representatives, educationalists and policy makers and put them in front of an international audience. Papers were delivered on a range of topics: widening access to classical languages, emerging practices in Classics pedagogies, improving community cohesion through Classics, the cross-curricular value of classical languages and the appeal and merits of non-linguistic Classics. The organizers of the conferences celebrated the successes in bringing Classics into communities which had not traditionally benefited, and explored some of the challenges which existed in promoting Classics even further. The outcome of the conferences was not just this book: it was also about bringing together otherwise disparate groups to learn directly from each other about, and from, their experiences and to foster dialogue about what learning about Classics is or could be. This dialogue continues.

Forward with Classics

There have been many new developments since those conferences and we are pleased to provide an overview of these here.

Collaboration between academics and teachers

In the UK there has been increasing synergy between universities and schools. The universities have developed more coherent and sustainable access and outreach policies. Some of this may have been driven by the need to demonstrate research impact in the wider community under the Research Excellence Framework (REF), a system for assessing the quality of research in UK higher education institutions, or it may have been driven by the need for universities to demonstrate their commitment to widening participation by reaching out to members of communities that have been previously neglected. Classics faculties across the UK have shown this commitment on a wide scale. The long-standing scheme of sending visiting speakers into schools and colleges continues. But it has been supplemented by many different kinds of activities which show a real engagement with schools that did not happen ten years ago. The University of Oxford has developed the OXLAT scheme (2017) whereby students from local state schools can come to learn Latin at weekends in the Classics Faculty building. The Faculty provides a venue for continuing professional development for teachers and events for students, such as study days and lectures. The University of Warwick, in collaboration with the Ashmolean Museum, put on a series of training events for teachers in the use of material culture in the classroom, culminating in a re-enactment of a Roman funeral procession through the museum galleries for the public (Masséglia 2016). It has also instituted an annual Greek play performance, in English, to compete, perhaps, with those long put on by Oxford, Cambridge, KCL and University College London, along with lecture series and talks. The Faculty of Classics at the University of Cambridge too has not been idle, putting on study days for students and continuing professional development courses for their teachers at GCSE and A level, with some funding from the charity Classics for All. The Faculty has developed an engaging website with video-clips about the courses it offers, some insight into life in the University and incentives to participate in competitions, such as the video-production of a classical myth (University of Cambridge 2017). Linking in with academia, the charity Classics for All has made a significant difference in establishing Classics in schools across the UK, especially in areas without good provision. It has also been developing Classics hubs with consortia of schools and universities working together to promote classical subjects in their wider communities and extend provision in schools (Hodgson and Murray-Pollock 2016). Among others, the Universities of Birmingham, Leeds and Exeter have begun to develop closer links with nearby schools in areas where little Classics provision is apparent. In the University of Manchester, the Classics hub provides teaching for local students, lectures and talks for the public and has links with Liverpool College in providing a centre for the teaching of Classical Greek. In the University of Bristol, great strides are being made in creating a network for Classics teachers in a city where until recently, there was no provision for Classics teaching outside the independent sector (University of Bristol 2017).

Academics at the University of Swansea have developed a Classics hub of its own to meet the particular needs of Classics being taught in Welsh-medium schools. They have also been instrumental in building links with the Ministry for Education in Wales to support teacher training in Classics for the Welsh curriculum which is currently under development (University of Swansea 2017).

In Scotland, academics at the Universities of Glasgow, Edinburgh and St Andrews are collaborating in an effort to widen access to the study of Classics in Scottish state schools. With the help of Dr Holmes-Henderson, they are liaising with the national regulatory body the General Teaching Council of Scotland (GTCS) and the Scottish Council of Independent Schools to explore ways in which teachers qualified in an allied subject (for example History) might attain GTCS registration to teach Classical Studies. Scotland's adoption of the European 1+2 languages initiative (where all primary pupils learn English or Gaelic as the medium of instruction plus two additional languages) represents a golden opportunity to introduce the learning and teaching of Latin as the third language (L3) in such a system. To make this a reality, Classics for All has established a hub in Scotland and the charity will provide training for Scottish primary teachers. Dr Holmes-Henderson has advised on the creation of Latin resources which fulfil the aims and outcomes of Scotland's Curriculum for Excellence and she is working closely with SCILT, Scotland's national centre for Languages, and with the Scottish Association for Language Teaching. There is a great deal of goodwill in Scotland, from academics, teachers and local authority education officers to boost the learning and teaching of classical subjects. This will only be possible through continued dialogue and collaboration.

Academics in the Classics faculties of UK universities are showing increasing interest in pedagogy and teachers' experiences of the issues faced in state schools today. Although there are no formal mechanisms by which academics can meet with policy makers at the government level after the A level Consultation Board was disbanded in 2014, nevertheless some academics keep in contact a little less formally through other subject meetings: the OCR examination board's *fora*, the Classical Association's Teaching Board and the Classics Development Group. The Classical Association has recently become more proactive in encouraging teachers to present papers at its Annual Conference and academics to attend them. The making of connections between universities and schools such as this can only be beneficial to both parties.

New ways for schools to offer classical subjects

There is some anecdotal evidence that the number of schools which have chosen to start classical subjects has continued to increase. Research carried out by the Cambridge School Classics Project (CSCP) in 2009 suggested that around 25 per cent of state schools in the UK offered some form of Latin, although this was not reflected in entries to national examinations and provision of Latin outside London and the South East was patchy and often very poor (Cambridge School Classics Project 2009). Since then CSCP has been in the forefront of encouraging some 400 state secondary schools to offer Latin and other classical subjects with training and teacher support. This was given added impetus with the award of a substantial grant (£250,000) from the Department for Education via the University of Oxford. CSCP continues to offer training events throughout the year using its in-house experts. The charity Classics for All has also made a huge contribution to setting up classical subjects in schools across the country, raising over £700,000 to help 500 schools in both the primary and secondary sectors (Classics for All 2017).

One of the success stories of UK government educational policy seems to have been the requirement for students in primary schools to learn an ancient or modern language at key stage 2. The number of schools nationally which have taken the opportunity to teach Latin is, not surprisingly, tiny – and that of Classical Greek even smaller. However, those which have chosen to do so, have done so enthusiastically. Recently, forty-eight teachers have been trained in the use of Barbara Bell's primary school Latin course *Minimus*. The first training event took place in an area of deprivation: a coastal town suffering from years of underinvestment and the decline in its fishing industry. For them, the principal's idea of having Latin as the key stage 2 language seemed at odds with the realities of daily life. The second training event took place in what seemed to be a more natural habitat for a school which offered Latin: neat hedgerows, views across fields and country cottages – an idyllic location. But the special needs register showed that 25 per cent of the students struggled with literacy. In both events the teachers knew little or no Latin at all. Anxiety was initially high. But soon, they cast off their worries and started to look not so much at the Latin (which is, it is fair to say, quite minimal in *Minimus*) but instead to look for the learning opportunities that there were there for their students. At the end their pronunciation was not quite right; their knowledge of Latin was fairly small. But they relished the chance to build interesting lessons which linked to other curricular areas in the school and which delivered learning on so many levels: cultural and historical awareness, linguistic understanding, development of confidence in discussions, improvements in English literacy through reading, speaking and writing, opportunities for drama, music and the creative arts.

Something of that richness of Classics teaching at the primary level seems, unfortunately, to be being driven out of the secondary curriculum. Teachers who ignore the three Gs – Gove, Gibb and GCSEs – do so at their peril. The focus on examination results and the accountability measures derived from them are a relentless pressure for conformity. Meanwhile cuts in funding for schools make all minority subjects vulnerable to closure. In 2016 the effects of the financial squeeze led to Classical Greek being threatened at a number of selective state schools. Nationally, numbers of students entering examinations for Classical Greek is very small, with 1,270 at GCSE and 239 at A level in 2015. Of those, 153 and 28 respectively were from state schools (Joint Curriculum and Qualifications Agency 2016). Is Classical Greek to disappear from the state sector entirely in the next few years? To try to prevent this from happening the charity Classics for All took charge of some £150,000 from the Polonsky and A. G. Leventis Foundations to support and develop the teaching of Classical Greek and Greek history in state schools through its Electra Project (Classics for All 2017). Other resources to teach Classical Greek have recently been developed, including Gorilla Greek (Wright 2016) for primary school students and an online Greek project for beginners (Griffiths 2017). Batrackhos, a course book, is also under development.

For non-linguistic Classical studies there have been some significant developments. For the new reformed courses at GCSE and A level in Classical Civilisation and Ancient History, a set of accompanying textbooks have been published by the publisher Bloomsbury Academic in conjunction with OCR. Written by teachers for teachers and students the books are filled with advice about how to study the set materials and how to begin to answer exam-style questions. While some might decry the close alignment of the OCR examination and an OCR-endorsed textbook, it has to be remembered that such resources have never before been available for teachers or students in classical subjects. This new venture might well support teachers who are new to teaching Classical Civilisation and Ancient History and who are not trained classicists and, in turn, lead to growth in the provision of Classics in UK schools.

Classical Civilisation is the 'Cinderella subject' of the four classical subjects offered in UK schools. It attracted 4,237 students at GCSE in 2015, equally balanced between state and independent sectors (Joint Curriculum and Qualifications Agency 2016). At A level more than three times as many students study it at than all of the other three subjects combined, with 4,466 entries in 2015, and twice as many state school entries as independent (Joint Curriculum and Qualifications Agency 2016). Classical Civilisation is the original egalitarian classical subject and facilitates entry for many students to the Classics departments in the research intensive universities beloved by the government in its drive to improve social mobility. Yet Classical Civilisation is not included in the English Baccalaureate measure (Department for Education 2017) and some headteachers are reluctant to provide it for their students for that reason. Arguments in an open letter published in *The Times* newspaper to the government to improve this situation had fallen on deaf ears (Liveley and Liddel 2014). A new initiative, led by Professor Edith Hall of King's College London, is attempting to reverse the political decision not to include Classical Civilisation in the measure and make headteachers, students and parents understand the value of the subject. The 'Advocating Classics Education' project engages directly with subject associations, teachers, schools and the public in a series of public events in fifteen regional centres across Scotland, Wales, Northern Ireland and England, designed to maximize dialogue that feeds into their research and public impact (Hall and Holmes-Henderson 2017). The AHRC-funded research project will include the publication of a history of the teaching of Classical Civilisation and the dissemination of resources and materials.

Latin continues to be the most popular classical subject on offer at key stages 3 and 4 in schools. Outside those schools which have traditionally offered it, one of the biggest growth areas could be in sponsored academies. These are formerly local-authority maintained state schools that have been transformed to academy status as part of a government intervention strategy because of the students' low attainment in national examinations. Many of them are in small academy trusts of two or three schools linked together or in large, multiple academy trusts (MATs) of some dozen upwards in the same region. Many of these schools have requested Latin training for their staff, in East Anglia, the South Coast and South London: in each case the academies' principals' rationales for introducing Latin have been to raise aspirations among the students and to signal to parents and the surrounding community that the academy concerned has changed direction. Readers might throw up their hands in horror at what seems to be so elitist a stance – a perception of Latin that Classics teachers have been fighting for fifty years – until they look closer: in virtually every academy Latin is not being offered to one or two 'top sets', but is being offered to *every one* of the sometimes 200 students in each year group. And getting Latin into one academy which is part of a MAT opens the door to the others more easily. Are we going to see an upswing in student numbers in areas at last where Latin has not been offered since the demise of selective education in most parts of the UK?

But state schools which wish to include the subject on their timetables face a challenge: they are often unable to provide a full-time position for a fully trained Classics teacher while the subject is still at the development stage in the school but, at the same time, teachers of other subjects already in post lack the expertise to commence teaching it. Some of the innovative approaches to teacher development and training are described below.

New approaches to teacher development in the UK

Sussex University has developed an innovative PGCE in Classics and History. Under the leadership of Rowlie Darby (see Chapter 9) the university took the opportunity offered by the relaxation of Department for Education restrictions on training numbers to expand its teacher training provision to around twelve per year. These trainees receive instruction in teaching methods for both History and Classics and many have found positions in local state schools along the South Coast where provision for Classics had been previously restricted to schools in the independent sector.

In London, the Harris Federation is a MAT of forty-four primary and secondary schools in the Greater London area. After a meeting with the charity Classics for All in 2015, the Federation decided that it wanted to introduce Classics into some of its secondary academies. In the two academies which were chosen, there was no history of teaching Classics and the Harris Federation Teaching School had no experience of training Classics teachers. Steven Hunt provided training for the two with a bespoke Initial Teacher Education (ITE) course. It was a challenge for both of the teachers who were starting from scratch in schools with no department or specialist mentor. A great deal was learnt about the process in this initial phase: the teacher mentors – not subject specialists themselves – who would be supervising the trainees were given training in what to look for in basic Latin pedagogy; the trainees were selected for the course for their secure subject knowledge and robustness (both had taught before for a year as unqualified teachers elsewhere); there was frequent contact between the head of ITE, supervisors and the trainer. After graduation, a full-time post has been developed for one teacher which is shared over three neighbouring local Harris Academies in East London. This teacher has recently added key stage 2 Latin to his portfolio in the primary academy which is the feeder academy to his own. A number of advantages have accrued from this set-up: the teacher has a position with sufficient Classics across neighbouring academies to justify his retention in service; as the number of classes expands it creates more opportunities for the employment of further Classics teachers to be deployed in several academies further afield; the feeder primary academy supplies students ready to learn Classics at key stage 3 and has the potential to 'lock in' students to the curriculum. In the academic year 2017–2018 Harris Federation Teaching School is training six new teachers of Classics for its academies in other locations in London. Training sessions are now offered in collaboration with the Classics teacher in post, now newly qualified, with the intention of preparing him for a larger mentoring role in the following year.

Liverpool Hope University also pledged to offer a PGCE in Classics, with support from Classics for All and from Liverpool College, a local state-maintained academy with a very strong tradition in Classics teaching. Although there is a fairly large cluster of state and private schools in and around the City of Liverpool, the area has lacked provision for teacher training in Classics for a long time. Four new teacher trainees started the new course with a commitment to wanting to work in schools locally. Two more started their PGCE training at Bishop Grosseteste University in Lincoln at the same time, to add to the two at the long-standing school-based course at King Edward's Consortium in Birmingham. Thus, adding in the eighteen at each of the traditional PGCE courses at Cambridge and KCL, the number of training places for state-school teachers (sixty-two in total) is probably the highest it has been for over ten years – and better distributed across the UK.

Innovation in Classics pedagogies in the United States

Other countries too have their own challenges with teacher supply and teacher training. The United States is no exception. However, what is of particular interest about developments in Classics education in the United States is the debate about classroom practice. US teachers have always had more autonomy in defining their own curricula, designing resources and creating their own assessments. It has been teachers – not politicians – who were the developers of the Standards for Classical Languages for the American Council on the Teaching of Foreign Languages. The standards present a holistic view of education in the Classics – what Latin does for the student rather than what can the student do 'for Latin'. Assessment is based around levels of proficiency in language use rather than around mastery of specific grammatical concepts. Teachers have developed the National Latin Examination and its ancillaries. Teachers run conferences for each other to share ideas and resources and to recognize their own achievements and reward members for their students' successes. Meanwhile interest in communicative approaches to teaching Latin is gaining powerful momentum. Truly innovative, by comparison with what has gone before, the communicative Latin movement aims no less than to improve learning for every student in the classroom. But we think that this movement is also representative of the teachers' determination to reassert their own professionalism in the face of threats to diminish it. When teachers choose to reject traditional teaching approaches, course books and assessments, and make life (let's be realistic here) hard for themselves, they are not showing a wilful disregard for their students' performance. Instead they are showing a belief in doing what they think is absolutely right for their students by using the knowledge gained through proper training, classroom experience and their own professional judgement – not in subservience to the rules and regulations devised by school boards, state officials or politicians divorced from daily classroom reality. Digital technology has played a huge part in this. Ten years ago, interest in it focused on digitized course books, interactive whiteboards and computers in the classroom. Few foresaw the role that smartphones and social media might play in developing and maintaining teacher communities. Members of the communicative Latin movement can be sharing their ideas on an almost daily basis through social media in posts of all kinds: discussion threads, pleas for help, images, links to websites and recordings of class activities are all easily possible. Long gone is the time when the teacher closed their classroom door on the outside world and none knew what went on behind it. The movement promises to have a genuine and positive impact on established classroom practice in the United States. Teachers across the world are observing with interest.

Moving beyond Greek and Latin in 'Traditional' national curricula

The provision of Classics in other countries varies immensely. In most countries where it is offered Latin and/or Greek are the only subjects. In many countries it retains its secure position in school curricula because of tradition, the nature of the school or a requirement for university entry. Pedagogy in many of these places tends to the traditional, often to the detriment of the students' engagement and success. The success of the Ancient History course in Australia deserves a closer look by everyone for lessons to be learnt about how to develop an interesting and engaging curriculum for everyone with no linguistic element required. Meanwhile, outside schools and universities 'public Classics' seems to thrive everywhere. Performances of classical drama, cinematic representations of classical stories, documentaries, exhibitions and books attest to the enduring attractions of the classical world. Classical references and allusions have appeared in quite unlikely situations: at the Grayson Perry exhibition at the Serpentine gallery in London an enormous painting depicting the artist himself referenced the Venus in a seashell wall painting in the House of the Marine Venus in Pompeii (Serpentine Galleries 2017); a conference held at Senate House London on comics with a classical subject matter (University of London 2017); Facebook has a group which specializes in Cambridge Latin Course memes (Cambridge Latin Course Memes 2017); Bromans (a television competition with a Roman theme) aired on ITV2 – not quite to critical acclaim (ITV2 2017).

Final thoughts

> So I wrote my name; and I stood like that until those ahead of me produced their work, and I paid attention to the pronunciations of the teacher and of my fellow student. For it is from this that we progress, from paying attention to others, if they are advised of something.

The above quotation comes from the collection of bilingual Greek and Latin texts known as the *Colloquia Stephani*, in the book *Learning Latin the Ancient Way* by Eleanor Dickey (2016, pp. 18–19). They were probably originally written in the first century BC for schoolchildren as *exempla* for good conduct in class. This one seemed somehow appropriate when we were writing this conclusion: a school pupil stands obediently in the line before the teacher, listening to all that his peers say before him. He learns from what the others have said and what the teacher has said to them. We hope the reader has learnt a little from all the contributors to this book and we hope that the ideas and thoughts described within help the promotion of Classics into the future.

References

Cambridge Latin Course Memes (2017), *Cambridge Latin Course Memes*. Facebook. Available online: www.facebook.com/LatinMemes. (Accessed 1 April 2018).

Cambridge School Classics Project (2009), *A Statistical Report on Latin in UK Secondary Schools*, Cambridge: Cambridge School Classics Project.

Classics for All (2017), *The Electra Programme*. Classics for All. Available online: classicsforall.org.uk/get-involved/schools/grants-and-support-for-schools/the-electra-programme. (Accessed 1 April 2018).

Department for Education (2017), *English Baccalaureate (EBacc)*. Department for Education. Available online: www.gov.uk/government/publications/english-baccalaureate-ebacc.

Dickey, E. (2016), *Learning Latin the Ancient Way. Latin Textbooks from the Ancient World*, Cambridge: Cambridge University Press.

Griffiths, W. (2017), Hands-Up Education. Available online: https://hands-up-education.org/ancientgreek.html. (Accessed 4 April 2018).

Hall, E. and Holmes-Henderson, A. (2017), 'Advocating Classics Education – A New National Project', *Journal of Classics Teaching*, 36: 40–42.

Hodgson, H. and Murray-Pollock, X. (2016), 'Classics for All: Establishing the Classics Hub', *Journal of Classics Teaching*, 33: 48–49.

ITV2 (2017), *The Bromans* [Television series], London: ITV2.

Joint Curriculum and Qualifications Agency (2016), *JCQA Inter-Awarding Body Statistics*, London: JCQA.

Lister, B. (2007), *Changing Classics in Schools*, Cambridge: Cambridge University Press.

Liveley, G. and Liddel, P. (2014), 'Championing Classical Civilization and Ancient History. An Open Letter to the DfE and Ofqual', *Journal of Classics Teaching*, 29: 11–14.

Masséglia, J. (2016), 'Rome's Walking Dead: Resurrecting a Roman Funeral at the Ashmolean Museum', *Journal of Classics Teaching*, 33: 31–34.

OXLAT Latin Teaching Scheme (2017), Classics at Oxford. Available online: www.classics.ox.ac.uk/OXLAT-latin-teaching-scheme.html. (Accessed 1 April 2018).

Serpentine Galleries (2017), *Grayson Perry: The Most Popular Exhibition Ever!* Serpentine Galleries. Available online: www.serpentinegalleries.org/exhibitions-events/grayson-perry-most-popular-art-exhibition-ever. (Accessed 1 April 2018).

Tristram, D. (2003), 'Classics in the Curriculum from the 1960s to the 1990s', in J. Morwood (ed.), *The Teaching of Classics*, 6–19, Cambridge: Cambridge University Press.

University of Bristol (2017), *University of Bristol Classics Hub*. University of Bristol. Available online: www.bristol.ac.uk/classics/hub/. (Accessed 1 April 2018).

University of Cambridge (2017), *The Greeks, The Romans & Us*. University of Cambridge. Available online: www.greeksromansus.classics.cam.ac.uk. (Accessed 1 April 2018).

University of London (2017), *Drawing on the Past: The Pre-Modern World in Comics*. Available online: https://drawingonthepast.wordpress.com/. (Accessed 1 April 2018).

University of Swansea (2017), *Literacy through Classics*. University of Swansea. Available online: http://literacythroughclassics.weebly.com/. (Accessed 1 April 2018).

Wright, A. (2016), 'Running a Greek Club: The Hereford Cathedral School Experience', *Journal of Classics Teaching*, 32: 21–24.

GLOSSARY

ACARA. The Australian Curriculum, Assessment and Reporting Authority. ACARA's functions include the development of the Australian national curriculum, administration of national assessments and associated reporting on schooling in Australia.

A Level. The Advanced Level is a subject-based qualification conferred as part of the General Certificate of Education at a higher level than the GCSE and the O Level. It is an examination taken by students aged seventeen to eighteen in secondary education in England, Wales and Northern Ireland. A levels are usually treated as a measure of attainment suitable for university entry.

AS level. The AS level is a subject-based qualification taken at the midpoint of the two-year course of study which the A level comprises. Students may complete their studies at the end of the AS level or use it to complete their qualification at the higher A level standard.

AQA. The Assessment and Qualifications Alliance examinations board.

BME. Black and Minority Ethnic (used to refer to members of non-white communities in the UK).

CfA. Classics for All, a British charity which seeks to support the expansion of classical subjects in non-fee-paying schools.

CLC. Cambridge Latin Course.

CPD. Continuing Professional Development.

CSCP. Cambridge School Classics Project.

CUCD. Council of University Classics Departments.

Department for Education (2010–present).The Department for Education is a department of the UK government responsible for issues affecting people in England up to the age of nineteen, including child protection and education. It has previously been known as the Department of Education and Science (1964–1992), the Department for Education (1992–1995), the Department for Education and Employment (1995–2001), the Department for Education and Skills (2001–2007) and the Department for Children, Schools and Families (2007–2010).

EAL. English as an Additional Language.

Eduqas. Eduqas is an examination board that is part of WJEC. It operates under this name in England, Northern Ireland, the Isle of Man and the Channel Islands.

English Baccalaureate. The English Baccalaureate (EBacc) is a school performance indicator linked to the General Certificate of Secondary Education (GCSE). It measures the percentage of students in a school who achieve 5+A*–C grades in traditionally academic GCSE subjects.

GCSE. The General Certificate of Secondary Education is an academic qualification awarded in a specified subject to students aged fourteen to sixteen in secondary education in England, Wales and Northern Ireland.

GTCS: General Teaching Council for Scotland.

HE. Higher Education.

HEI. Higher education institutions are universities, colleges and other institutions offering and delivering higher education.

HEFCE. Higher Education Funding Council for England.

JACT. Joint Association of Classical Teachers.

Key Stages. Key stages are the legal terms for the periods of schooling in maintained schools in England and Wales. Key stage 2 refers to the period of four years comprising Years 3–6, when students are aged seven to eleven; Key stage 3 refers to the period of three years comprising Years 7–9, when students are aged twelve to fourteen; Key stage 4 refers to the period of two years comprising Years 10–11, when students are aged fifteen to sixteen. Key stage 5, referring to the period of two years comprising Years 12–13, is colloquially referred to as the *sixth form*.

LSEF. The London Schools Excellence Fund is part of the Mayor of London's Education Programme. £20 million in funding came from the Department for Education; the Mayor of London provided an additional £4.25 million. A further £1.5 million has been awarded from the European Integration Fund.

MAT. Multi-Academy Trust.

MFL. Modern Foreign Language.

OCR. The Oxford and Cambridge and RSA examinations board.

Ofsted. The Office for Standards in Education, Children's Services and Skills is a non-ministerial department of the UK government. The services Ofsted inspects or regulates include state schools, independent schools and teacher-training providers, colleges, and learning and skills providers in England.

O level. The O level was a subject-based qualification taken by UK school students at the age of 16. It was superseded by the GCSE.

PGCE. The Postgraduate Certificate in Education is a one-year higher education course in England, Wales and Northern Ireland, which provides training in order to allow graduates to become teachers.

SCITT. School-Centred Initial Teacher Training.

SD. School Direct.

SEND. Special Educational Needs and Disability.

WJEC. The Welsh Joint Education Committee examinations board.

INDEX